FORGET NOT
THE SPARROWS

AN AFRICAN STORY:
*Unfinished Conversations
with my Grandmother*

Yene Assegid, PhD

ISBN-13: 978-0615509419
ISBN-10: 061550941X
Library of Congress Control Number: 2011938291

Shola Stories
P.O. Box 424832
San Francisco, CA 94142-4832
www.sholastories.com

DEDICATION

To Almazesha

And even to this day, your love remains with us.

And while nothing can ever fill the void you left,

What comforts me is the "we" we've been

and always will be.

— Yene July 26, 2011 —

ACKNOWLEDGEMENT

Writing our stories and speaking about my relationship with my Grandmother, Almazesha, has been a healing process—a process of coming to terms with the landscape of my life and letting go of so much I had carried with me through the years. It has been a chance to revisit the past and draw from it the wisdom, compassion, and love to understand that ours is the duty to live our best lives here and now, in the present moment: Waking up in the morning is not to be taken for granted, and each day we have is a most sacred gift.

My gratitude to Will Moyer, Casey Hynes, Terry Ann Hayes, and Leslie Peters Designs for working with me in terms of the cover design, book layout, and interior detail as well as website development.

My editor, Anna M. Fitzpatrick, has been as always such a partner throughout the entire course. To Anna, thank you so much for all your patience, for your understanding of the spirit of the story, and for your inspiring encouragement along the way. One factor that made it easy for me to jump into writing this book is knowing that we could work together again. Thank you so very much.

This book and the stories within would not have existed without my family whom I love dearly and am grateful for. I would like to thank my parents, Assegid Tessema and Sally Makonnen; all my aunts and uncles and especially my aunt Elene Makonnen who has been both a mother and a mentor for me; my parents-in-law Werner Reusing and Rose-Marie Reusing; and my sisters, brother, and cousins for their support, love, and friendship. A special thank you and gratitude go to my sister Fofi and to Rahel Azmi, who have both been such encouraging and inspiring angels in my life. Finally, to my daughters Rosi and Leoni I must give the greatest appreciation and acknowledgement. They have been with me each step of the way, giving me time to work when I needed it, asking me inspiring questions when I needed it, and always being so enthusiastic about all the stories I had to tell them about the old days when I was a little girl. To my husband Matthias, I must present my deepest gratitude for encouraging me to write this book and tell the stories. For all the long evenings and weekends you spent reading, commenting, and editing many drafts of the manuscript—I can only say thank you so very much and I could not have done it without you.

Last but not least, my infinite gratitude and expression of love to my grandmother, Almazesha, and my grandfather, Ababi. How fortunate we are to have had to chance to grow up and learn of life through them.

CONTENTS

My child, never forget that this too shall pass; there is nothing permanent in life. Our lives on this earth might be an illusion. We think we are in control, yet the truth is that we are to be transported by waves of events, circumstances, and conditions that come and go. And as the events come and go, you will see that your life changes in so many ways—at times to your advantage, at times otherwise. Throughout it all, as much as we should not let success intoxicate our sobriety, so in the same way, we should not allow hard times to kill our spirit. Remember always that it all passes, my child. It all passes. And only when you realize this impermanence will you be free of attachment—therefore free to live fully without being caught up in the constrictions and illusions you might be facing.

–Lady Almaz Haile Mariam
(Almazesha, my grandmother)

I remember Almazesha saying this to me again and again, and through the years my interpretation of her message changed along with my own evolving level of consciousness and understanding of life. Through the pages to come, I hope to share the stories and wisdom I have inherited from her throughout my life. As much as this book is about sharing the story of my relationship with my grandmother, it is also a personal process to reflect on my life, and to reflect on the events that have shaped our lives as a family, both in the sense of a community and also in our own individuality. This story is about generations, changing times, and holding to culture and tradition despite the impact of immigration, despite the challenges of trying to adapt to change in its many forms, and despite the pull of modernity, globalization, and the subsequent fragmentation of the family. This is the story of the constant negotiations between the way it used to be and the way life has come to be.

PREFACE

Like anyone, I am who I am because of those around me, those who have loved me and continue to love me. For all of us, and perhaps especially for me, it is our mothers and sisters, our brothers and fathers and uncles, our cousins and relatives, our spouses and children, and the entire community that surrounds us who award us with the textures and colors we bear in our being and hopefully use to shine our lights.

Yet often it is these same individuals we call "family" and "community" who also teach us the hardest lessons of life. Is there even a single person in this world who doesn't complain about their family? If so, that is certainly a rare person. My Aunty Etetila always told us to be as gentle with our family members as we are with others outside our family. It's funny how the ones we love the most are often the ones we end up, at best, not attending to or, at worst, hurting.

My grandmother, Lady Almaz Haile Mariam, whom we all call Almazesha or Emaye for short, has shown many of us—in my family and beyond—the best examples. She is one who was known to be courageous, wise, compassionate, and kind, as she was equally known to be strict and one for discipline. Discipline does not exclude love, of course; in fact, it is when there is enough love that one can think of discipline as a way for molding, shaping, and polishing the gem within each of us.

This book tells the story of my life and that of my grandmother. We had a very special relationship, one that is perhaps beyond words. I have meant to write this book for years, yet years passed before I could find the discipline to sit down each day and write. Unfortunately, this book came to fruition several months after I lost my grandmother. How happy I would have been to have written it when she was still around—I would have loved to take a copy to her just to see her smile.

Almazesha did not talk much. Her face and expression were the equivalent of hours of lectures. Her signature smile is what kept us going. No man or woman, whether a child or a soldier, could disregard the power of her eyes. It was all in there and kept us all in check. For me, Almazesha was more than "just" a grandmother: She was and always will be my soul mate. I miss her each day. Not a moment goes by that I don't think of her, whether through dreams or through my untamed thoughts running through the hills like wild horses. I have written this book as a process of paying my respects to her, a process of mourning and healing, and a process of embracing the unknown. I have lived all my life under her tutelage, and it is odd for me to wake up without this mast at the center of my ship. Through the writing of the stories in this book, I have healed, I have reflected, and I have learned anew the lessons that she always tried to teach all of us. When I say "all of us," I mean my entire family, the entire community that lived around her, and the countless lives she touched.

These stories are at times quite personal, but I cannot talk about our truth without talking of the personal. The stories are mainly speaking of the relationship between my grandmother and me, at times touching upon my immediate family and close friends. I have chosen not to mention people by name when it was not necessary; it is easier to write that way, and more anonymous.

Being the grandchild of Almazesha came a sense of responsibility to live up to her expectations, those she had for us and that others had for us as her children. She was a very exceptional woman, a brilliant mind, with a heart that could fit the entire planet and possibly more. There was no limit to what Almazesha could plan or conceptualize—I think she was ahead of her time, and I was lucky enough to be close to her from the time I was born. Almazesha did not believe in telling children silly children's stories: She told us true stories, and in these stories she embedded principles of life in a way that we could understand. I never really thought of her as an older person or as an adult, because she made me feel like a full-fledged person even when I was just two or three years old. She would listen to me and give me her time as she did for any other adult around her.

Our grandfather, on the other hand, was a very practical man, very loving but very organized and regimented. I believe his last job was working in the accounting department of the Ministry of Foreign Affairs of Ethiopia, and after he retired, Almazesha set up a small-scale industry within the house to keep him busy and to provide the family and the

Yene Assegid

community around our compound with the means to survive.

Ababi, as we called my Grandfather, took every job very seriously. Every day, he woke up at 6:00 sharp, no matter what. Every day, by 6:00AM, he was usually in the bathroom washing up, brushing his teeth, making a lot of noises, and sneezing loudly enough to wake the entire neighborhood. Every day as he sneezed so loudly, my grandmother shook her head and sighed, saying, "This man will never change." And he never changed throughout his life.

Today, he is no longer with us physically, but in spirit he is always around and I miss his loud sneezing in the morning. When he finally came out of the bathroom in his robe, completely fresh, washed up with his cologne done and hair combed out, he dressed in a very religious, almost meditative way, through all the different layers of clothes from an undershirt, a t-shirt, a shirt, a sleeveless sweater, a jacket, and then something else on top. He just looked perfectly fine—he was a handsome man, very charming and polite. After his usual breakfast, he would go to his car, the grey Volkswagen Beetle. Ababi bought her in the early 1960s and drove her all his life. For many years, he was the only one allowed to drive her, and she is still around today at Laïbet. This car was not just any car—it was a "she" and she had a name, *Volssouwa* (the Volkwagens' nickname expressed in the feminine gender). But as time went by, she lost this nickname and received another name: we called her "*ye Ababi Makina* [Ababi's car]." He always checked the odometer to see if anyone had taken her out and around town. He knew this car inside and out and loved her passionately. Even today, when you sit inside Volssouwa, the scent of Ababi's one and only cologne takes you hostage. Ababi hardly ever changed his cologne (he always wore the French cologne, Caron) and this was his space—his car and his little working area.

After he retired, Almazesha set up a small office for him located at the top of the compound of Laïbet, right next to the main gate. From his little working area, he had a great vantage point to see who was coming and going. His job was to look after the coffee that was being sold and make sure that the drivers were delivering the coffee to the proper destinations.

This is the place where I grew up, the house where I spent my first few years of life—*Laïbet* or "the upper house." It is the upper house because, of course, there is a lower house; the upper house is the house that Almazesha built maybe ten years before I was born. She decided to build it so she could have a place for her children, a place to entertain, and a place that was presentable.

Before that, she lived in the lower house, a very modest dwelling where she raised all eight of her children. Even though it was small and modest, she told me that it was one of the cleanest houses around. She did not really have much help and certainly did not have much money, so she used to make clothes for her daughters and her sons herself. She was very brave. She wanted her children to have everything that everybody else had in terms of basic clothing and education.

Ababi, on the other side, was committed to his children's education and spent most of his modest salary to pay for his children's school fees. My mother and my aunt tell me that he used to take them to school on his motorcycle, the kind with a little seat attached to it like in old World War I or II movies. All three sisters used to sit in that little sidecar, and he would take them to school; the fourth sister Koky, was too small to go to school. Growing up we were told stories of how, when Ababi was called to school because his children were ill or not feeling well, he would pick them up in this same motorcycle, buy them some sweets or ice cream on the way home, and then drop them off at home to be nursed and taken care of. He was a father who truly loved his children. He wanted a quiet home and a modest home, but the irony is that he married a woman who might be quiet and very poised in her heart but who had many great ambitions of building, of constructing, of inventing, of bringing innovation.

Almazesha had so many different friends from all walks of life, and when we sat at the dining table (that fit 8-10 people), Ababi's seat was fixed and so was hers, but all the others were open. For Ababi, it was almost always a surprise as to who was present at that table; for Almazesha, she was just enjoying entertaining her family and friends. Seats would fill with her colleagues, her partners, those who were going to dream along with her and who were coming to share a meal. Ababi, I think, did not really agree much with that—he wanted just a peaceful meal, but this difference of character comes from their individual backgrounds. Almazesha came from one of the oldest aristocratic families, of educated intellectuals, and Ababi came from a very modest family dedicated to the church, from the Wollo region. His family was known as learned in theology and religion; the pizzazz and grandeur that Almazesha brought was far from his demure being.

I was always very close to Ababi and Almazesha mainly because I just tagged along wherever they went and I loved their stories. At the Laïbet compound that defined my life, on a daily basis at a hundred people came and went. The gatekeeper never had time to be bored and traffic flowed non-stop, people, cars, donkeys coming to deliver goods from up country, and even cattle sometimes sent for upcoming events. I do not know if anything in Laïbet was locked. Everyone was welcome.

Almazesha and Ababi were always dedicated Christians, and they could not turn their backs on anyone. When I came to eat at Laïbet as an adult, I sometimes went to the little living room behind the big dining room, very tiny and intimate, and sometimes there were guests. I never asked who the guests were. I just sat looking at my feet, waiting until somebody came from the kitchen asking me if I wanted to eat something, very discreetly.

In this home I learned from Almazesha to always be welcoming and generous, as much as I can, to give and to serve, and to do it all with utter discretion. To put myself in the other person's shoes, to try to understand the circumstances that might be pressuring the other or the constraints that other person might be living through, and to be a point of comfort for others. This is Laïbet.

I am proud of my grandmother, this beautiful and incredible lady, and it is with much heartfelt pride that I share our story with you. I am certain there are legions of grandmothers and grandfathers who have left imprints on our lives, and it is also to them that I bow in the name of all of us.

BACKGROUND

Often right before sundown, between 17.30 and 18.30, many of us—children, grandchildren, and family—would come to Laïbet to sit with Almazesha either in her room or on the veranda, the famous veranda that makes the passage from the living room to the bedroom wing of the house. If this veranda could talk, it would have a million stories to tell. It has seen family, friends, guests, famous visitors, and visiting relatives from the countryside step in and out of Laïbet through the years. This veranda has witnessed the feudal days of the Emperor Haile Selassie, his brutal overthrow, the early days of the Derg[1] terror, and the coming of the new TPLF[2] government,

---

[1] The Derg was the communist military junta that took power in Ethiopia after the overthrow of the monarchy. Comrade Mengistu Haile Mariam led the DERG for seventeen years.

[2] The Tigrayan People's Liberation Front (TPLF) is the political party that took over the Ethiopian Government after overthrowing the Derg and the Mengistu Regime in 1991. The TPLF is one of a number of ethnic political parties that make up the ruling government coalition called the EPRDF (Ethiopian People's Revolutionary Democratic

intertwined with weddings, funerals, parties, disputes, reconciliations, and even boring Sundays. The best, however, are the weddings.

On this veranda brides have been celebrated and our family ceremoniously pushed back the entourage of the groom and his men, spraying them with perfume and singing joyfully the songs of marriage: "*Amora be smay siyash wale.*"[3] There is always at least one person with a strong voice who leads the others, who sings first so the others can repeat the refrain: "*siyash wale.*" My favorite part is that if the followers don't add energy and rhythm to the refrain, they get scolded, and so it is with fun and a bit of fear of being scolded that everyone sings for the bride and groom. There are songs that are mostly sung by men, like "*Eehhm Newu*"; the "*Elilta,*" on the other hand, is monopolized by women. Once women get started with the "*Elita,*" the entire house gets drenched with their voices expressing joy and the energy soars to the heavens. All the singing settles down when the groom and his convoy of friends reach the living room to find the bride sitting quietly, all veiled and made up with the best of the best from head to toe. Lights are on, cameras flashing like shooting stars gone mad, and the bride sits in a field of peace while the commotion

---

Front). The leaders of the TPLF, once a liberation front and later a political party with a potent army, now rule Ethiopia (http://abbaymedia.com/Facts_About_TPLF.htm)
[3] "The Eagle has been staring at you from the sky." I suppose this insinuates that the bride is so beautiful the eagle can't help staring, or it can also be interpreted that the groom is the eagle who has been staring and finally he dives down to scoop the bride off and fly away with her, as eagles swoop down to scoop up their prey. This is one of many traditional wedding songs sung with heart and fervor by family and friends as their daughters leave the home to enter the life of marriage.

around her is a mixture of chaos, emotions, celebrations, and anticipation for the day. The commotion is also outside where cars are prepared to move out in a convoy—there are people standing everywhere, and the festive mood is increasingly intense and contagious.

We have also mourned and cried on this very veranda for the many who have passed on. For funerals, it is customary to listen to the professional criers and follow them in singing songs of mourning to bid farewell to the one from whom we have parted. At times, the weeping reaches unimaginable depths of sorrow and sadness as new mourning voices permeate the compound—new people, be they friends or family, arriving for the first time since the passing of that person. Each time new people arrive, they enter the compound expressing their grief in song, in loud weeping or just screaming out their pain. The arrival of new people can take days, as word of the funeral spreads. Some of the hardest moments are when we hear the strongest and toughest members of our community break down and cry, grieving publicly. At such moments, the entire mourning process reaches another crescendo, reaching depths of mourning that words cannot describe. Of course, no professional crier can ever express sorrow in their songs like the new members of the community coming into the compound do—there is a difference between a scripted mourning song and one that just emerges out of a bleeding heart. When we hear the bleeding heart's howl, we all enter a collective state of trance. Crying together allows us to grieve well, to share, and to be with the bereaved; it almost takes the bite out of the loss and allows us all to gently say goodbye. New bonds are established, and a new configuration of the "us" takes place. In a way, it is through the collective mourning process that we birth a new way to continue living without the departed.

And when there are no weddings, funerals, or political upheavals, this veranda is a place of the sweetest conversations. There are a maximum of only four chairs: two or three facing out to the mountains, perpendicular to the entrance to the living room, and one facing the entrance of the living room positioned against the wall next to the door leading to the bedroom wing. There is a little room in the passage from the veranda to the bedroom wing, a tiny room that has served many purposes. At times it was a study for children to do homework; it has also served as Ababi's private office or as just an extra closet area. At times of social unrest, the glass walls of this same little room have heard hushed conversations about strategies and means to overcome the situation. When someone is not well, this is the room where the visiting doctor often gives directions to the caretakers.

On the veranda, we repeat the same stories each time, but each time the story gets better, and each time we listen attentively to the storyteller. Even though we all know each and every turn of the stories, we still listen to the stories again and again, each time as if it is the very first time. Each time we laugh again as hard as we laughed the first time.

The best storyteller was Almazesha. She spoke of history, politics, and activism, yet she always managed to wrap it all in a personal story—that's why we all always listened savoring each word and wishing that the time would stop and allow us to soak in the moment forever. For me, I loved to sit there with her, and whenever I could have a moment alone with her,

I was in heaven. If we were on the veranda, I would always try to sit next to her so we could hold hands and look out in the same direction. If we were in her bedroom, I usually sat right by the famous window of her bedroom that gives view to the entire compound. I sat at the foot of her bed and from there continued the everlasting conversation we had for a lifetime, the one that continues in this book. I told her what I did during the day, what projects I might have in mind, and asked her a gazillion questions about everything. When I was a child, she prompted me with questions that triggered a fountain of a conversation. We would laugh so much together. There is something special about laughing with someone you love—to laugh while looking in their eyes is like sharing a special moment in eternity.

I equally loved to sit on the veranda with Ababi, my grandfather. There is a particular panoramic view from the veranda: we could see the mountain range on the horizon, and closer in front of us the rooftops of the houses of the neighborhood cluttered together told the stories of the families that lived within them. The better roofs meant a well-to-do family, and the more modest roofs with rusted, corrugated iron sheets spoke of the modest means of the family within. The interesting thing is that earlier on, I never noticed the differences. It was all just roofs, some of which I recognized whose house it was. It is only later that I noticed the quality of the roofs and made a link to the social and economic status the roofs indicated.

At the beginning, before the communist revolution of 1974, Almazesha's rose garden faced the veranda. But later, right after the revolution, Almazesha built a warehouse on the space to house her small cottage industry. She started a salt refinery to generate enough revenue to sustain her household. This cottage industry was established just shortly after Ababi retired from his lifelong position of accountant at the Ministry of Foreign Affairs. She loved her roses—even though the larger rose garden had to make space for the warehouse, Almazesha moved some rose bushes alongside the warehouse and near the veranda. Despite all the changes in the compound, somehow Almazesha managed to keep it green: Laïbet was always full of plants, flowers, and bushes. Almazesha knew each plant and regularly bought new pots or new seeds to maintain her plants.

What never changed in Laïbet, no matter what, remains the electricity main power line that stretches from one electric pole to the other, parallel to the horizon and facing the main veranda. On this electricity line, the sparrows used to come and sit all the way along the line, mostly facing the same direction, and wait for their daily rations. They would wait there each day for the grains that Almazesha and Ababi would put out for them. Ababi would call, "*lejoch, bakachehun, esti, le wofochu ehel amtu* [children, please bring some grain for the little birds]."

Whoever was passing by at that moment would either run to get grain or call out to someone else to get the grain from the miniature silos in the back of the "*yetachiganw wot bet* [the lower kitchen]." Ababi would wait, standing around with his hands crossed behind his back, pacing back and forth on the veranda, at times going down the steps into the compound to look and see whether someone was coming with the grains. Then, as soon as the grains were thrown and the sparrows flocked to peck, a veil of satisfaction would cover his face. The same with Almazesha—she would look at times from the veranda and at times from her bedroom window. Often she would mutter to herself with a deep sigh that seemed to have started its journey at the dawn of time, "*yezger miskinotch* [God's meek beings[4]]."

As she muttered these words, Almazesha's day would continue: make phone calls, pass orders to this or that person to do this or that thing, prepare food to be taken for someone in prison or someone in the hospital, write up a new project or plan the next wedding process or see how she might mediate this or that conflict. Her life was nonstop. And in the middle of it all, she found time to sit with her visiting relatives, guests, children, grandchildren, or host members of the Church, or counsel this or that person on some life challenges or marital difficulties they encountered, or give them business coaching to either start something new or increase the production of an existing entity. Her energy was phenomenal and her generosity unsurpassed. She always gave everyone whatever they needed, unconditionally and with the utmost discretion.

I don't know how she could pack all that into a day and have all the names and affiliations in her mind without ever needing a notebook as a memory back-up. If someone unexpected passed by, she would immediately recognize them and then—of course—ask about their family, their parents, or their spouses (by name) and share an intimate story making that person feel absolutely connected. In all of this, it goes without mention that she always checked the quality

---

[4] These few words convey the feeling, "If mankind could have the spirit of sparrows and the faith that tomorrow is not ours to worry about, life would be so different."

of the food being prepared, and the cooks would regularly send up to her room or to the living room a small sampling of the latest *Wot* [stew] simmering in the giant pots. She was rarely satisfied because often the cooks would put too much salt or make the Wot too hot (spicy) or would not cook the legumes or meat in a way that was ideal. The trouble was that Almazesha was a great cook herself, so there was no way the cooks could get by with doing something less than excellent. But even in her dissatisfaction, she never told a cook to change things in a way that would harm that cook's morale. She was always very gentle, and when she could still walk around easily, she would walk down to the *Yetachegna Wot Bet* [the lower kitchen] and take the time to show the cooks herself how to work with the ingredients, the level of the fire, and the way of stirring to get it right. Just as a wine expert could tell about the wine just from the scent, she could tell the quality of the Wots just through the scent. She just had the touch, the inner talent to make the best Wots.

We sat there on this veranda and watched the sparrows peck on the grains. We watched as random guests would come to visit or people walked from the front gate straight down toward the main cooking quarters, and as they passed in front of the veranda there would be a series of bowing and greetings that Almazesha would reciprocate. Ababi would often just nod or mumble some greetings. We used to hold hands as we sat together. Ababi had beautiful, strong, muscular hands with very gentle and soft olive-colored skin. He was a Wolloye, and many in that part of the country have skin that is very fair. My sisters, cousins, uncles, and aunts would also trickle in and join in the conversations on this veranda—this was the best time. Often, Almazesha's uncles like

Ababa Bistate would also visit. Ababa Bistate was a French speaker. He was very sharp and sophisticated, with a sensitive sense of humor. He would visit on his daily stroll from his house that was about 400 meters away. This is the time that the best jokes came out, the best stories were re-told again, and the fellowship soared. This short hour or so as we watched the sunset holds such memories for me: memories of love and laughter, of times long gone, and of stories passed on from generation to generation.

As I write this story, it is now exactly nine years since Ababi passed on, and it seems like yesterday that we were all together on this magical veranda. Although I am now grown with a family of my own, living in Sierra Leone, the little girl in me who sat with her grandparents, listening to their stories, witnessing the dynamics of their world, and watching the sparrows peck away the grains—she is still inside me somewhere. It's a part of me that fills me with emotions and keeps me company when I am lonely. It is these living memories that sustain me each day and allow me to handle the cards life deals me with faith and perspective. It is as if these memories keep anointing me with love and compassion, keeping me solidly anchored in my lineage. It is as though these memories maintain the sense of protection and cozy nest my grandparents offered not only to me, but to the entire family and the greater community.

This story does not follow in order, in a neat line of time from one moment to the next, like soldiers on parade. Memories and stories bubble up, each a distinct moment yet all part of the same stew. I share these stories the way they come to me, each iridescent moment full of color, feeling, and sound. They overlap and interweave—this is the tapestry of my life, the weaving Almazesha left me.

The day I call "eternal"

There are some days in our lives that so mark us, it almost doesn't matter what date they have—days where the incidents and events so change our lives forever that life is sliced into post- and pre-. Although there may have been many memorable days in my life, the one day that has marked and divided my life is the day I heard she had left us. My life before this day compares in no way to my life after this day. It's a day that marks a loss of an era, the end of a story—a beautiful story. And as we all sat wishing that the story continued, we were all confronted with the fact that from here on it would be our responsibility to live up to the compassion, standards, morality, and ethics that Almazesha's stories dictated.

On this day, Saturday October 3, 2009, my flight landed in Addis Ababa at the crack of dawn. How many times had I landed at Bole Airport in my life as a child, as a teenager or young adult? For twenty years, landing at Bole airport had carried a sense of comfort for me because I knew that I would see Almazesha or drive straight to Laïbet. On this day things were different. There was a void. There was a feeling of insecurity of the unknown and at the same time a sense of crossing through a virtual gate whereby my first steps on the ground of this country I call mine would be challenged because my anchor was no longer there. My entire body was shaking internally from the moment the aircraft started to descend, and as we landed, the inner shaking I felt intensified. I wanted to fly out of the plane and run home. I wanted to run to Almazesha. I wanted to fly to her and call her name gently in front of her bedroom, as I had always done. I felt held back, bound, human, weak, and yet I knew that through this new vulnerability I was entering another phase of my life. I was to learn of something essential to humanity: the lesson of what it is to have loved and lost. Isn't it strange, these lessons that life signs us up for, that we didn't really want to go through? I know I didn't want to learn such a lesson.

If I didn't run, my heart would burst, I was certain of it. As the plane taxied on the tarmac, I told the flight attendant that I was not waiting for everyone to disembark. "It's an emergency!" I told her, "I have to go." A few minutes before the descent I had gone to change from my normal clothes to the ceremonial black expected on such days, and this had brought attention from the flight attendants and other passengers. I put on my sunglasses and tried to just keep breathing until they let me out. The flight attendant could see that I was in great distress and she did let me out first with the business class passengers. I only had a carry-on and so I rushed through the airport to passport control.

Funny how this time around I didn't care about the entirely overbearing security that hovers around Bole Airport. Me, I wanted to run home, and if these security people had an issue, they would have to run faster than me to stop me. Usually arriving at Bole is stressful. People can stare you down and not even nod hello or acknowledge you with eye contact. As far as security is concerned, you have those who are in uniform, those in civil attire, and those who pretend to be cleaners—all "security" to me. I appreciate it in a way, because security is important for our safety, but when you come home it would be nice to feel a sense of being welcome. How do we come home when we are so scrutinized? It's not even about real security issues, but just about being watched and not knowing why we are being watched—not a good feeling.

On this day, however, things were different. As I said, it was the crack of dawn, when the air outside was still cool and wet from the night. People were not fully awake yet, and many would be swathed in *gabis* and netelas.[5] I knew this time well. It's the time of day when, back at Laïbet, Gashe Tilahun wakes up and breaks the silence of the night that had fallen on the compound with his deep, coarse voice. It is the time that some of us head to church on Sundays, or lay in bed listening to the chanting from neighboring churches or minarets. It is the time when the drivers come into Laïbet to start up the cars. It's the time when the day starts a minute at a time. Yes, I was very familiar with this time, which in a way made it all the more difficult to go through the motions of exiting the airport.

My heart ached, literally. For the first time in my life, I literally felt that my heart was about to jump off my chest and onto the floor, gibbering. My hands, well, my hands were not on duty on this day. All they did was shake as if some kind of mechanical glitch had taken place inside. My knees followed my hands, and although I stood tall and straight as Almazesha had

---

[5] The Ethiopian *gabi* and *netela* are handwoven 100% cotton. The gabi is more like a blanket and the netela is more like a thinner scarf version of the blanket. It is not far from the truth to say that all Ethiopians have not one but several gabis and netelas. While the gabi is worn by both men and women, the netela is mostly for women only. Both gabis and netelas are usually white and only vary by their hand-embroidered colorful borders.

always taught me, I could sense that my knees were about to give in. Only regular, deep breathing steadied me and took me through the motions. Each step I was making was difficult. My eyes were constantly filling up with tears, making it hard to see. "Wouldn't it be great if God had given us windshield wipers?" I thought. I felt dizzy. Wiping my eyes, sniffling my watery nose, I tried to walk out of the airport as fast as possible and keep myself together.

It was the first time I wore black from the heart; other times it's been more for protocol. The color swallowed me. It suffocated me. I could not breathe. I had never felt the distress that comes with wearing it.

I was already feeling empty and lightheaded when I had packed these black clothes back in my bedroom before leaving Freetown, Sierra Leone. But for the sake of remaining "together," I did everything on autopilot. That's what helped me not to break down before reaching home, before reaching Laïbet.

My younger sister, Fofi, and my father (whom we call Boubiye) were waiting for me at the arrival lounge. I wasn't sure how I would react upon seeing them. It was my knees I couldn't control. They felt wobbly. I could not stand properly and kept losing my balance. We didn't say anything and just got in the car. Ato Solomon, who has been working for my parents for as long as I can remember, was the one driving. He never changes, never gets old, and I just don't understand where he gets his energy. He was already retired when he started working for my parents, so I know that by now he must be well past his seventies, but he is still very sharp.

We drove down Bole Road, deserted because it was so early, and it all appeared in slow motion. We passed Stephanos Church and the Hilton, drove up through Arat Kilo, crossed through to the Menelik roundabout, and up we drove on Mesfin Harar Road. At this point, my heart started pounding—I thought it was going to burst. What to do when the one thing that you have always dreaded comes without warning? It's so difficult, but there is no other choice than just going through it.

When we neared Laïbet, we found the same kind of buzzing commotion as when something happens to a queen bee. There were people all over the place starting a few blocks before Laïbet, near Ababa Bitsate's home, people and cars. No one was talking loudly—even Gashe Tilahun who is always so loud was quiet today. The car stopped on top of the hill in front of the Shoa Bakery, next to Afro's Fruit Shop. There was no way to drive into the compound that was located just down the steep side road between the bakery and Afro's shop. We had to walk down the hill to reach Laïbet. I was afraid to get out of the car. I didn't want to. I thought that if I got out, I would have to accept what just happened. I tried to delay with this or that excuse, but eventually I had to step out of the car and start walking.

As I walked down, the crowd that was filling the small path leading to Laïbet opened up. I could see them looking and staring, both with empathy and some curiosity as to how I would react. I tried to keep myself together. It was hard. I knew most of them; we grew up together. We were children then, and now we are all sort of adults with some traces of who we used to be as children. My tears, of course, kept on filling up my eyes and my nose joined in, and between my uncooperative eyes and nose, I was obliged to sniffle and wipe my eyes with the back of my hands like a small child that just fell. I felt gutted. Empty. I felt dizzy. I wanted to shout out the pain I felt, but not a single sound left my mouth. I found that I was completely mute. I just stared blankly into emptiness.

Just as I was heading down the path to Laïbet, I saw my cousin Timmy, my aunt Koky's son. I remember when he was born, and now he was taller than me. I literally fell into his arms. "*Ayzosh, ayzosh,*[6] Mimiye,[7]" he repeated. I begged him to take me through the back door and take me to her. "Please take me to her and I don't want to see anyone until I see her." He comforted me and rushed me through the crowd. I had never experienced this feeling of extreme vulnerability and surrender.

The gates of Laïbet were wide open. Although the compound was full of people, the open gates felt to me like the open doors of a house where a family has just moved out. There was a sense of abandonment. A sense of "it's over now." A sense of knowing that the one who had kept us together for so long had now left.

I was grateful I knew ahead of time that Almazesha was no longer with us. Usually, and traditionally,

---

[6] *Ayzosh* is a word of comfort along the lines of "don't worry," "hang in there," "find comfort," or "find strength within you"—it's difficult to translate verbatim. In this case, the word is conjugated to the third-person singular feminine.

[7] Although my nickname is Mimi at home, the ¬*ye* ending adds a sense of endearment or closeness and love to the name.

family members are never told in advance until they reach home. The usual message to indicate a loss to faraway family members is to tell them that the person is not well: "*be tena tamewal* [he/she is very ill]." When reaching the home of the bereaved, people wail and weep as they enter the gate. I could not wail or weep. My tears were flowing but there wasn't a sound I could make. My voice was mute. Nothing came out. I tried to vocalize, but—the same way as it happens in nightmares—nothing came out. I only heard the thumping of my own heart, beating faster and faster each minute.

I recognized many faces, but it was also all a blur. I was mixing people up. I could not recall names, and all the faces came up as flashes—flashes of when I might have seen them last and contrasting those moments with seeing them again now that Laïbet had become a space of memories. "Memories of what?" I wondered. Did we really have the time we had, the laughter, the drama, the life that defined who I was and who I am? Do I still have an identity? Can a branch survive without the trunk and the roots of the tree? So much of who I am is defined by Laïbet and my relationship with Almazesha that my mind was short-circuited, brain freeze. I couldn't think anymore, and at the same time a million thoughts ran through my mind with fury.

I saw everyone sitting in the tent erected in the compound, a normal response to such an event, but unusually, the tent was white. I was surprised but later learned that this was Almazesha's wish: She did not like dark colors and had asked that when she went, the tent be white. We always put tents out for the mourner because the houses cannot handle the amounts of people who show up. I saw my aunts, my uncles, cousins, and family friends. Everyone was there, even people I had not seen in ages. It was like a mega-reunion. But I only glanced at them. I did not want to make eye contact with anyone; I was afraid that such eye contact would throw me into an abyss of never-ending sorrow and grief.

Timmy sneaked me through the back of the tent and down the little path leading to the living room, but when we tried to open the door, it was locked. The priests were still praying and chanting and had locked the door so as not to be disturbed. I had never faced this door locked, keeping me out. I felt as though my time in Laïbet was finished—"the door is locked, I am left out," I thought. Things were spinning. My heart rate has never been so fast, and my thoughts were racing in all sorts of directions. Timmy led me away from the door and back down the little path to go through the *yelagnaw wot bet*, the main house kitchen and dining room.

We crossed paths with Dr. Seyid Abdulai, my Aunt Zene's husband. He is usually able to keep his composure, but on this day when I met him on the little path that leads to the kitchen, he seemed as shaken up as me. Who was to comfort whom? He held both my hands and looked me in the eyes for what seemed an eternity. "I did not know you were here," he said softly. "I just arrived," I blurted out. We did not speak more but stayed there for a second looking into each others' eyes—unable to speak, unable to admit to each other the reason that had brought us all together. It was the unspeakable. So we just stood there, stoic.

Timmy tugged at my sleeve and I followed him on to the kitchen, this kitchen that I had entered so many times with dozens of stories to tell Almazesha. There were so many people standing, sitting, just staring out, some weeping and others sighing heavily in disbelief.

The kitchen leads to a small sitting area, *Tinishu Salon* [the little living room], the room where we had had the best conversations and where we had laughed until we cried or made crazy plans to change the world. Again, it was full of people. Then I entered the dining room, where I would usually see Almazesha sitting on her sofa in the living room. This was where she usually smiled to me and we exchanged smiles of complicity. Instead, the room was full of the scent of Frankincense, often used in Ethiopia for the last blessings and prayers for the departed. In special cases the monks, deacons, and priests come and chant all through the night—that's what they had done for Ababi, and now they were doing the same for Almazesha. They had been chanting all night long. At the end of the chanting and prayers, about 9:00 am, we would traditionally head out to our family burial place, at a monastery about two hours from Addis Ababa.

I could not believe that I was in Laïbet but instead of finding her in her room or in the living room, waiting for me with a smile and embracing me with her signature kisses (where she holds my face in both her hands and looks at me up close, then kisses me many times over), I was finding her asleep in a coffin. The coffin was closed. I wanted to reach out to her but couldn't, so I just slipped into the middle of the circle of priests moving in cadence around the coffin to the gentle sound of the massive drums they had brought in and to the sound of the *click-clacks* of the swinging brass censer from which burning frankincense infused the room with the scent of the Church. There were many priests and deacons chanting ancient songs of worship dating back to hundreds if not thousands of years; these chants have been sung from the dawn of time in Ethiopia. I sat on a chair right next to the coffin. I was not sure if that was permitted or not, but I did it anyway. Orthodox ceremonies are not very flexible and it was very possible that the priests would ask me to wait away from their circle of prayers. I knew that, but still did not care. After all, it was our mother they were praying for, so I just went right into the circle and found a chair to sit on. I sat there next to the coffin wishing I had come earlier to see her one last time, when she was still alive. Not even a few weeks ago, on the phone, she had asked me whether I was planning to visit—how foolish of me to explain that Sierra Leone is so far, the girls had just started school, and I was caught up in work, and this or that...

I was not making excuses; my explanation was genuine. The constraints of life preventing me from seeing her were painful yet nonetheless a reality I had to accept. Despite all the excuses I gave Almazesha for not coming when she gently asked if I would come soon, I cannot believe that not even three weeks later, I flew home. I did just get on a plane now, didn't I? What if I had listened to her gentle and subtle request and come to see her when she asked me to? It's often like that. We don't do things when our loved ones are still around, and then we are eaten with regret or with "I wish I had..." sentences.

My thoughts were still spinning. I was hoping that all this was a nightmare. How strange it was to be filled with thoughts and at the same time not be able to think of anything at all. I don't remember what I was thinking—just a million things. I was grateful to still be able to say goodbye to her one last time, even if she had already gone to sleep. It was Boubiye who insisted I fly home for the funeral. I didn't want to come, in fact. I thought that if I did not attend the ceremony, she would remain alive for me. How foolish. Now I was sitting next to her, staring at the coffin where she lay. Despite the hollowness gutting my spirit, I was glad I came home. I was glad I could pay her a last tribute. With the depth of sadness and sorrow that words cannot describe, I sat there in silence with images of our lives racing through my mind. I was at peace in one way, and in another way completely disoriented and broken. The wrenching pain of separation left me in a daze, present but also absent—not there, watching from afar, witnessing from a place far, far away.

In the past, each time I had come to visit her from wherever I lived, as much as I rejoiced in the moment I kissed her hands when I arrived, I dreaded saying goodbye to her until I could come back again. I always dodged the farewell moment. I was always afraid that it would be the last time I saw her. Each time I had to kiss her goodbye, I avoided it and tried to do it as fast as possible and dash out of her sight. Until now, I had been lucky with the chance to come back and always find her. But this time—this time was the last time. From now on, as I told my daughters Rosi and Leoni, she has become an angel, and while she will always remain with us in spirit it will not be possible to see her in person. Only through our memories and thoughts can we find time to be together again.

The priests and monks were chanting as they moved in a circle around her, shaking their Frankincense in the shiny brass censor. They looked meek, making me think of the verse in the Bible "Blessed are the meek." They moved with such synchronicity, it was hypnotic. I could not understand their chanting; it was in the Ge'ez[8] language. They had giant drums, about 1.5-meters tall with a drumskin close to a meter wide. The sound of drums set the cadence of the slow-motion, almost spellbinding circular movement to accompany the heavy rhythm of the chanting. Their voices were eternal, coming from a time afar. Once in a while, the movement would sway to the opposite direction, always circular. As they moved in circles, their bodies would also gently swing from left to right, and right to left, as if the movement of their bodies carved virtual grooves on the borders of the circle. They looked up to the sky as if in a conversation with God or angels. It looked like they were praying and pleading with God. It seemed that they were accompanying her soul, escorting her to the heavens. And then they would look to the coffin as if they could see through it, and with their heads tilted to one side or the other, they would re-engage their chanting with added passion in synchrony to the verses of the chants.

They all had peculiar faces. They had big eyes, at times eyes that seemed tired from reading in the dark. They had sunburnt skin with wrinkles all over.

---

[8] The Ge'ez language (or Ethiopic Language) is an ancient South Semitic language developed from the Sabaen/Minean script in the northern region of Ethiopia. The earliest recorded inscriptions in the Ge'ez script date to the 5th century BC. The language became the official language of the Kingdom of Aksum and Ethiopian imperial court. Today, the language is still used by the Ethiopian Orthodox Tewahedo Church, the Eritrean Orthodox Tewahedo Church, the Ethiopian Catholic Church, and the Beta Israel Jewish Community (http://www.omniglot.com/writing/ethiopic.htm).

The wrinkles were gentle, almost like the contours of old rice fields descending to the flat grounds. With turbans of white and cream-colored cloth wrapped around their heads or the usual round and flat-topped priest hat, dressed in their *gabi* with a special *Tilet* (embroidery with the code of arms of the Medhane Alem Church), these holy men continued to chant tirelessly. It was amazing to me because they had been standing and chanting since midnight, and now it was past 8:00 am. The ceremony and prayer session they held for her is not common—it is a rare and special process that very few have the opportunity to have, an honor of the highest order.

I could see that there were also younger monks getting direction from the older ones. I suppose they were in the process of learning and receiving the way of chanting. "There you go—on the job training takes place even in the church," I thought to myself. Aleka Makonnen was there orchestrating the whole thing. He was Almazesha's "*nefs Abbat*,"[9] the guardian of her soul. Aleka Ma is a kind man. I found solace when I recognized him, and I wanted to cry when I saw him. So many times during his visits to Almazesha, he would sit on the sofa, the one next to the chimney and facing the chair Almazesha usually sits in. From her chair, with just a glance, Almazesha orchestrated the hosting ritual. She just looked at any one of us who was there and nodded to us indicating that we should bring a beverage, tea or coffee. She would nod to have the table set and the food served. All the

---

[9] Literally "soul father," a *Nefs Abbat* is a priest who engages in a special relationship with respective members of his parish as spiritual father or mentor, and in most cases, he is also the one known to lead the funerals and burial ceremonies for each person he mentors (assuming he outlives them).

while, she would continue her conversation with him and anyone else who might also be visiting at that time. The moment I saw him chanting together with all the other priests, I was engulfed with tears. I found myself staring at him, lost, reliving the times when he used to visit when she was still with us. My heart started pounding. I could not breathe well. I could not speak, but in my heart I wanted to ask him: "Now that the day has come when she has walked out, what will become of us now?" Once more, the question stayed in my throat. My voice was still mute.

Aleka Makonnen and Almazesha shared long, philosophical conversations. They spoke of current affairs in the country and in the world; their discussion of the Bible reached depths beyond my understanding. They both knew the Holy Book inside and out, and their conversations on the interpretation and application of the Bible to our lives translated the complexity of the messages into such simple language that we all learned a lot from them. Their conversations were now part of another time, long gone now and tucked away in our hearts. Now, she lay there in the midst of the chanting voices, heading to her eternal home—and he was there, the guardian of her soul, her Nefs Abat, still loyal to their friendship and sacred relationship in the same living room where they had talked for hours on end.

Although the chanting and the drumming were well audible, it was calm inside this space. The chanting was soothing. I was in a zone, maybe in some kind of spell. Tears were flowing out, but I was not crying; they were just flowing both out of sadness and out of celebration of the beautiful life that Almazesha had. It was tears of gratefulness mixed with deep sorrow for my own self. I guess we cry for ourselves, when it comes down to it. We cry for how the situation is affecting us. For me, my tears flowed because I felt naked. I felt vulnerable, and in some strange sense I felt as though I had lost my country. From here on, there might never be a place that I could truly call home. Here were my roots, and the tree that spread those roots just came down. I felt exposed. I wanted to hide, or better yet, I wanted to run.

I couldn't really explain it well, but I knew I was crying for myself. I knew that Almazesha passed on like a saint, without pain, without suffering, and while she was still able to take care of herself independently. She was such an independent person that I don't think she would have liked to be dependent on others for her basic needs. But now, in the same way that she lived her life with dignity, humility, and autonomy, so she passed on. Yes, I cried for my own sake; but for her, I was grateful for the life, grateful for all her blessings, and grateful that she left in the way that she had always wished.

About an hour after I arrived, it was time to move the convoy to Debre Libanos Monastery, to the family mausoleum. The chanting was finished. The priest started coordinating the transfer of the coffin from the house to the hearse. More people started coming into the living room and standing by the main door of the living room, this door through which she had received so many guests, through which many brides and grooms walked with her blessings on their wedding day, through which we came in and out so many times...now, it was through this very door that she would bid us farewell. I envisioned her as a half-dove, half-human being, a being so light that she would float. I saw her leaving the compound of Laïbet. She was young again. She was light. She was floating out—I don't think she looked back. I think she wanted to head back to her ancestors, her uncles and aunts, her father whom she loved so much, Ababi who would be waiting on that side, and many more of her relative and friends. Even though I was so deeply broken, inside I knew that this departure was no accident. I am sure she wanted to go.

Before I even departed Freetown, I had asked for the chance to see her one last time. Now that the chanting was over, I thought this was my chance, and I asked my aunts and cousins to please open the coffin for me. My cousin Kidist, whom I also remember as a baby, was now grown and a young medical student. She was the one who opened the coffin for me. She is my Uncle Pastor Daniel's daughter. I remember when she was about two and was summoned to Almazesha's room for disciplinary issues because she would refuse to get dressed in the morning to go to Kindergarten. Gashe Gemeda is the one who carried her, just like a Frenchman would carry his bread—he had her hanging on his hip and was holding her little body with just one arm curled around her. Baby Kidist had no idea where she was headed and as she passed us, she waved to us with a big smile. She thought it was all a game. Then Almazesha got ahold of her, and as usual, she got dunked in a cold bath. As much as Almazesha may have spanked and strictly disciplined her children, when it came to the grandchildren, she didn't have the heart, so she usually just stuck us in a cold bath. Anyway, it was now this same baby Kidist, all grown now, who opened the coffin for me and showed Almazesha laying there.

Almazesha looked peaceful. She just seemed to sleep and was at rest. She looked beautiful. She was just radiating peace. I wanted to cry but couldn't. I gently caressed her left cheek with the back of my right hand. Her skin was so soft, as usual. I had so many things still to tell her. I think we all had so many things to still tell her. I wish I could have been alone with her, but it was not possible. For that to happen, I should have been there several days earlier, and that was not possible. So for now, I was just appreciating the chance to see her one final time and say goodbye for now. I was sunken in a silent conversation with her amidst the commotion going on, and then someone gently tugged me back. "It's time to go, we have to seal the coffin"—the words sliced through my heart. "One more minute," I pleaded as I held her hand and squeezed it. *One more minute.* Time had slipped away. I remained there for what seemed to me a lifetime, just holding her hand as if I could keep her a little longer. "We have to go now," the voice insisted, and I surrendered. I stepped back. Part of me stayed with her and part of her stayed with me. It's over now. Life for me and for all of us is fundamentally changed forever. It was all so strange— I felt that a part of me had been chunked off and taken away, and I had no way of bringing it back. I felt hollow inside.

The hearse that would drive her to Debre Libanos arrived and parked out in the courtyard. The funeral company men came in uniform, though I noticed that some of their armbands were not finished properly and were hanging down. They encircled the coffin, counting in order to synchronize the lifting. My Uncle Solomon carried a beautiful framed portrait of Almazesha and walked in front of the coffin. How can I ever find the words to describe the emotions of seeing her depart from Laïbet? They carried her out. She left as she had lived, celebrated and loved.

When the men in uniform and my Uncle Solomon emerged onto the veranda in full view of all, the wailing took on a new level of intensity. Women were beating their chests; others were chanting the mourning songs and jumping on the spot as they beat their chests with closed fists or open hands as if they were drumming their hearts. Men were equally weeping, howling, and tearing their shirts. It was tough. The hardest scenes for me were to see those whom I knew and grew up with weeping with such pain and sorrow. A new fear haunted me—through her loss, would we also lose this central place where we had always met? Would losing the connector who brought us together result in our dispersing in all sorts of directions? I feared that we would be scattered as the leaves of great trees are scattered in the Fall by the blowing wind. I felt lonely. I felt isolated and unable to communicate with anyone. I couldn't really cry as much as I wanted to. My tears flowed continuously, but so much more sorrow was bottled up inside. I envied those who managed to cry out, sing out the mourning songs, or shout out their grief.

The gates of Laïbet remained open, just as wide as when I arrived. Now, hundreds of people were moving out of the compound, slowly boarding the buses prepared to drive us all to the monastery. Some took their own cars, but most people boarded the buses. My cousin Andy had arranged for special buses, about ten long-distance coaches, for the immediate family, friends, and relatives. There were 25-30 other buses rented to carry all the mourners who had gathered from all parts of the country. Being together in the bus was nice and took the sting of the loss away.

We drove for close to two hours. As we passed the town where Almazesha was born, Gurene, a group of horsemen showed up in their warrior gear. They wanted to chant and mourn the loss of a warrior—they counted her as their leader in spirit. The last time I saw them was when Ababi's convoy passed by there, and I remember that Almazesha got out and chanted with them the song of mourning. They sang in Afan-Oromo, one of Ethiopia's main languages. It's a language that the rest of us don't speak, but Almazesha spoke it fluently so she could sing with them when we came by for Ababi's funeral ceremony. She could mourn with the warriors and descendents of the warriors who had fought the wars side by side with her uncles, her father, and many of her relatives.

Now as the warriors chanted, wept, and mourned her in songs, we all came out of the buses and stood in a big circle around the horses, who were also dressed in traditional warrior's decorative equestrian costumes. But we could not understand their songs; I don't think any of us spoke enough Afan-Oromo. So we just stood there to receive their blessings and share the expression of our common grief and sorrow. None of us could chant along with them. In the circle around the warriors, we all stood in silence. It was as if, through their songs, we each traveled through time to when these men and their forefathers fought valiant wars against invaders.

I don't think we have warriors anymore. We have soldiers; it's all institutionalized. There is something special about warriors, something rebellious and resilient—as Almazesha had always been throughout her life. On that day they wept and bestowed upon her the titles of Warrior of Change (*Ye Lewut Arbegna*) and Warrior of Peace (*Ye Selam Arbegna*).

Debre Libanos is a holy place and the site of an ancient monastery founded by Abune Teklehaimanot, a 13th-century Ethiopian saint. It is believed that he meditated in a cave for 29 years and was led to establish this monastery in the high canyon of the Rift Valley. In this monastery, my family has buried our departed loved ones for generations; now we were once more returning to Debre Libanos to lay to rest our mother. For me, for all of us in fact, the journey to the heart of the mountains was hard. We all tried to be strong, hang in there, and pretend that it didn't happen, but inside, our world was shattered and we each wept silently—not only for the loss but also (and perhaps mainly) for the lonely future ahead. What is one supposed to do when she who held it all together leaves? What happens when the Queen bee goes?

Once we reached Debre Libanos, the coffin was taken out of the car and carried to a special small chapel next to the monastery. There, the priests and monks of the monastery carried out an entire new ceremony for Almazesha, with chanting and prayer, in a way handing her over to the divine creator. It might have been a private mass, or it might have been a welcome mass—I chose to think of it as a welcome mass. It took about an hour, with the same kind of prayers, chanting, circular motions, and blessings with Frankincense. By the time the mass was complete, the courtyard of the monastery had filled up with mourners. It's hard to estimate the number of people. All I know is that the courtyard was full to the brim.

The call

Freetown, Sierra Leone—Sunday, September 27, 2009. "Call me back urgent" was what the SMS read. It was Fofi. I knew she was traveling from

Washington DC to Philadelphia with Noela and Quentin. I feared the worst. She never sends me such messages. Did they have an accident? Then I thought maybe it was Lily, my baby sister—did she have an accident? What was so urgent? A dozen more questions flooded my mind as I flipped through the myriad of numbers saved on my cell and finally dialed Fofi back.

"Are you okay?"
"We're fine," she said.
"Is Lily okay?"
"Yes," she said.
"What is it then?" I asked.

This was the call I always dreaded—it was happening this morning. It's *Meskal*[10] in Ethiopia, but the SMS was not to wish me Happy Meskal.

"*C'est* Almazesha," she said.
"*Elle n'est plus des notre?* [Is she no longer part of us?]" I asked.
"*Oui, appelle* Enaniye[11] [Yes, call Enaniye]."

---

[10] Meskal is an annual religious holiday in Ethiopia, as per the Ethiopian Orthodox Church. It falls on September 27th in the Gregorian Calendar or on the 28th for leap years. This holiday marks and is based on the belief that in the 4th century, Queen Eleni (aka Queen Helena) had a revelation in a dream. She was told to make a bonfire and that the smoke would indicate where the True Cross was buried. So she ordered the people of Jerusalem to bring wood and make a huge pile. After adding frankincense to it, the bonfire was lit and the smoke rose high up to the sky and returned to the ground, exactly to the spot where the Cross had been buried. Meskal is also referred to as Demera.
[11] Enaniye is our mother's nickname; Her full name is Selamawit Makonnen.

In Ethiopia, the tradition is that when someone passes, relatives inform one another not by literally saying that the person has passed, but by saying that the person is "in the process of getting tired: "*Dekmoyl/Dekmewal.*"

> But "Did she pass?" I asked bluntly. I needed to know.
> "I spoke to Enaniye, and her voice is muffled— she's been crying. I only called to wish her a good trip back to Brussels, but now she has canceled her return. You better call her and talk to her. Call me back afterwards."
> With that, Fofi hung up.

That's how our call ended. That was the beginning of the rest of my life, a life without my guide and mentor. Almazesha was my Grandmother officially, but in truth she was the best friend I ever had. I was glad that Fofi told me the truth. It allowed me think straight, at least until I could get myself to Addis for the funeral.

I dialed the new cell number Fofi gave me to reach Enaniye in Ethiopia. She had traveled from Brussels to Addis about three weeks earlier to spend time with Almazesha—because of life constraints, years had gone by without the two of them spending time together. Enaniye had also come to Addis to witness the Protestant Church's celebration to honor and recognize the 40 years of service of Pastor Daniel Makonnen, her younger brother. In this ceremony, Pastor Daniel received the appellation of Apostle, an honor of the highest order and one that is rarely awarded. The celebration had taken place about a week before on a Saturday, in the stadium. After the stadium event, Almazesha had organized a late lunch at Laïbet for just over 300 guests. The lunch was set in the courtyard under a massive white tent, and the mood at Laïbet was very festive that day.

The past three weeks had been weeks of celebration in Laïbet. For the first time since the passing of Ababi, Almazesha was surrounded by all eight of her children. They had all come to be with her. There was joy and happiness filling every corner of the house. For the rest of us who did not make it to Addis due to this or that engagement, we had to satisfy ourselves with calling in as much as possible and sharing in the joy through the phone and through stories.

In fact, not even five days ago, I had called in to tell Almazesha that Rosi had just celebrated her tenth birthday. As I called the phone in Almazesha's room, there was no answer; I tried the other number and there was still no answer. I tried her cell phone and there was no answer. (Almazesha received so many calls that she has several lines. I usually called on her cell phone because lately the land lines had not been as reliable.) Finally, I tried Aunty Etetila's phone and got an answer: "Are you looking for Almazesha?" asked Etetila with a bubbly voice, "well, she is right here next to me." She passed the phone. By the time I was through with this call, I had spoken to so many aunts and uncles and cousins, mainly repeating the same greetings and the same questions and getting or sharing the same updates. I knew from the number of people I talked to that the living room must have been full, as it is often full in times of great celebrations like weddings and religious holidays. These are the good times, I thought to myself, and I was regretting that I was not there in person. But there was no way I could have been there—Rosi and Leoni had just started the school year, traveling from

Freetown to Addis was nothing short of an odyssey, and the cost of traveling was always extremely high. I was just too far and not in a financial situation to quickly go home and come back. Yet I so wished to be home at that time, just to soak in the same stories I had heard over and over again through my life.

After close to 30 minutes on the phone that day, being passed from one aunt, cousin, or uncle to the next, I finally came back to Etetila. In the meantime, more guests had arrived and it was not possible to talk to Almazesha. Etetila asked me to call in a few days when it would be less busy. I hung up the phone with regret that I did not get my little conversation with Almazesha. I didn't know this would be the last time I could have talked to her. I did not know.

As the phone rang in my ear, as I called Enaniye to confirm this news I did not want to hear, my heart was hijacked by thoughts from all directions. It couldn't make sense that all these good times, especially in the last three weeks, had taken an unexpected turn and I was calling in to confirm news that ripped my heart out and dislodged my soul from its seat. I heard the ringing, but no one picked up. My heart was thumping. finally, I heard Enaniye's voice and it was muffled, as Fofi had said. She spoke as if her nose was congested, but it was from crying. Enaniye could not speak to me clearly—she spoke in spurts of words and strange sentences.

> *"Bitmetchi yishalal* [It's better ... if ... you come back]," she said, laboring to get the words out. "It's better if you come back...It's better if you come back," she kept on repeating.

I interrupted and asked her, "Did she pass or is

she still there?"

"She's left us," Enaniye said, straining to make the words come out of her throat that seemed to have a knot the size of a tennis ball.

We did not stay long on the phone; I hung up. I sat on the floor. I could not cry. I was shocked. It was only about 1:00pm in Freetown, and Matthias was preparing lunch as he always does on Sundays. Rosi and Leoni were playing somewhere in the house. My head was spinning. I did not want to believe what I heard, but somewhere inside I knew it was true.

I called again within minutes, but this time there was no answer from Enaniye. I called Etetila's number and she was sobbing: "Mimiye, are you coming? Are you coming? Have you heard that she left us? She left us! She's left us..." I think I called maybe moments after it had happened, because Etetila was in utter shock.

Etetila passed the phone to Koky, who was sobbing too. I could hear others howling and crying with the sounds of agony, the agony of knowing that the last of the giants had gone. We were now left alone, without such giants to stand there for us, offering us shade from the possible hardship of life, offering us a place to come to, a place where we could bring our hard-earned bounties. It seemed all that was over now, and we were all collectively broken to pieces like shards of a giant crystal vase that has shattered in a million pieces.

We were not crying for her. We are crying for our own selves and the fate that awaited us without her in our lives.

My mind was racing about how to possibly organize the voyage back to Addis. What route to take, when to leave, how to leave. I wondered how Matthias would handle the children without me, as he was swamped with work. Now was not a good time for him to leave work early to shuttle the girls to and from school. But is there ever a good time? Just about two weeks ago, Almazesha had asked me when I planned to come back, and I had told her "I am so far, I just can't come so easily." It's true, Freetown, Sierra Leone is a lifetime away from Addis Ababa, Ethiopia, mainly due to the fact that the flight connections in West Africa seem not to care about the convenience they could offer to passengers. It takes me literally two or three days to travel back, with an overnight stay in Accra, Ghana. Sometimes it's easier to fly to Brussels and then fly back to Addis from there. Almazesha didn't make me feel guilty for telling her that I could not come. She did not insist— she never did. She had a way of understanding the constraints of others. Instead of speaking about my coming home or not, she spoke to me about my dissertation, asking when I thought I might finish.

Just the last night before this tragic Sunday, a good friend of ours had imported mussels from Brussels and invited some twenty of us for an amazingly sinful culinary dinner, together with a handful of friends. I knew everyone at the dinner. It was a small party, so it was possible to have deeper conversations. For some reason, right after dinner as we sipped coffee, I had a long conversation about funerals, death, and the mourning process in Ethiopia. I was telling my friend how such events take place and what our culture offers to comfort the bereaved. In Ethiopia, we mourn for 40 days and then hold memorial services several more times during that same year of loss, as well as annually for the years that follow. I told him that in my family, we have been taking our departed to a mausoleum built in a very old monastery tucked away in the rocky mountains of the Rift Valley. We spoke at length about burial, about dealing with grief, etc. Nothing heralded this conversation—it just happened.

Once more thoughts were flooding me from all directions. I stood in my bedroom not knowing what to think, not knowing what to do next. "Wasn't it strange," I thought, "that just last night I was talking about funerals and mausoleums and now this happens."

I decided not inform the girls about Almazesha until I came back from Addis. I didn't want them to mourn in my absence. I wanted to be there to hold them in my arms, to tell them stories long gone, and I wanted to cry together with them. We have shared so much joy together as a family, and this moment of sorrow was also a part of the life Rosi and Leoni had to learn. I wanted to be there as they learned and experienced their first meeting with separation through death. I knew that there is no way to prepare for hearing of the death of someone we love—it's always shocking. So, there is nothing to learn about it per se. All I could do, as a mother, would be to be present and accompany my children as they learned this thing called death.

It is so hard to get to Addis from Freetown, Sierra Leone. It is an odyssey on its own, starting with having to cross the peninsula by helicopter, ferry, or speedboat. It's just not easy to jump on a plane and go—it's a lot more complicated. And then to make matters worse, there are no daily flights. Kenyan

Airways (KQ) comes about three times a week, and is the only airline servicing Freetown and connecting to East Africa. KQ meant transiting in Nairobi, Kenya to reach Addis. I did not want to go to Nairobi. If I am in East Africa, then I want to directly land at home. This meant that I would have to take Ethiopian Airlines (ET), which flies to Accra; going through Accra meant spending an extra day in Ghana because the flights leaving Freetown to reach Accra and the ones going from Accra to Addis were not synced in terms of timing and schedules. It felt good to consider flying with ET. Strangely enough, I wanted to be on our "own" Ethiopian airlines this time. I wanted to be with *my* people for some reason; "Isn't that strange, I thought." Maybe subconsciously I was hoping to find some consolation, or maybe I thought that just being on the flight was like being home, in a way.

My thinking was not very clear. Everything was happening so fast and my heart was making somersaults in all directions. For the first time in my life, I felt my entire body tremble with a sort of electric buzz that I couldn't really understand. I felt present physically without being there in spirit. I was absent, and in order not to alarm my children, I consciously assumed a presence through my conversation with Rosi and Leoni, through making the table as usual and serving lunch as if all were still normal. But it was all mechanical. I had to remain mechanical, and I spoke mechanically to pretend a fading stability in my state of mind. I was detached and I remained detached. It was better. I could not allow myself to even start absorbing the truth about what just happened. If I did that, I would not be able to stand on my feet. My knees, my legs, and my spine would all turn to Jell-O.

The best I could do was to call Matthias to our bedroom. I asked him to sit. "Honey, I have a bit of sad news," I told him. He nodded; I could see that his heart jumped. So I held both his hands and looked in his eyes and said: "Almazesha" very slowly. I did not need to say that she had passed. He knew from the way I said it that I meant to tell him that she had left us. He took me in his arms and squeezed me very tight. We stayed like that for a while. We could not speak; we could only sit there in silence, and this silence was as comforting as it was overwhelming. My mind kept racing in all sorts of directions. The French say "*déboussolé*,"[12] and that is what we were. It was like our compass lost its ability to point north.

Matthias agreed with me that it would be best not to tell the children. It was in the process of telling Matthias that I started to cry for the first time since I heard the news. Now, telling the news to Matthias, actually speaking the words referring to her passing, I suddenly felt my heart cracking. This was the very first and small step of internalizing what had happened. Still, I was far from truly realizing the grief that Almazesha's loss would cause in my life. Is it easier to cry when another is there to witness our grief? Is it easier to cry when we are in the presence of someone who can relate to our loss? Maybe so.

The rest of the day was spent planning my return to Addis. I had a short assignment scheduled somewhere up-country in the coming week, and I knew that if I did not do the assignment before heading for Ethiopia, I would be in no shape to complete it when

---

[12] *Boussole* means "compass" and *déboussolé* is an expression to say "losing one's direction, losing one's mind, or being panicked or confused."

I returned. So, we opted that I would fly at the end of the week and I would make it for Saturday, the day of the ceremony. Enaniye had insisted that I arrive before 8:00 am because the convoy to Debre Libanos would leave Laïbet at about 9:00 am.

During lunch, I could not help but pray for God to carry me through these coming days. I looked at Rosi and Leoni—they were both always so proud to tell everyone stories about their Great-Grandmother. They were very proud of her. I dreaded the moment when I would have to tell them what happened. I watched them. Both were going on with lunch, chewing their little bites, grating cheese, and telling us stories about the latest events at school. Almazesha always told us that we should speak with children with as much respect and truth as we would with grown-ups. She had so much respect and love for children. I know that I had to tell Rosi and Leoni the truth in a way they could understand and yet not be traumatized.

Prepare to say goodbye

Tuesday September 29, 2009—Bo, Sierra Leone. I found it odd that I was in Bo today. For all the time I had lived in Sierra Leone, it was the first time I had come upcountry. As I said earlier, I had made a prior engagement to perform an organizational assessment for three humanitarian organizations located in Bo. I could not cancel, even though I was scheduled to travel to Addis on Thursday.

Yes, I finally got the call I have dreaded all my life. I know I am repeating myself and that I have said this before, but I still could not believe what seemed to have just happened. Fofi called me on Sunday the

27th. I saw her missed call on my cell phone and thought she called to wish me happy Meskal. She usually would just call back, but this time she didn't. I only received her text message: "Call me back, it's urgent!" I called back. I knew it would not be good. She spoke of Ethiopia. Her throat was tight. "It's Almazesha." "She's not well"... "We've lost her"... "Call home." She spoke like a telegraph. I remained calm, or tried to, at least. I called home to the new cell phone number Fofi gave me to reach Enanaye. When Enanaye said, "She's left us, we've lost her," I could only swallow my breath and tell her that I would call her back. No matter how much you think you're ready to hear breaking news of the death of a dear one, each time it happens it's like a whole new thing.

I just told Rosi and Leoni that Almazesha was very ill and not well at all. I was perpetuating the same tradition that I despised—telling that someone is not well, when in fact that person is gone. I just wanted to be quiet.

I did not tell Yéshiyé (who helped me raise the girls) either, at least not on Sunday. I would tell her on Monday when the girls were at school. Yéshiyé and I grew up together, and Almazesha is just as much of a reference to her as she is to all of us. The youngest sister of Atila, who raised me until I was about three years old, Yéshiyé raised many of my cousins, as did her sister, Konjit. Yéshiyé also took care of most of our elders in their last days, so she was a special person I was happy to have with me in Freetown and a beloved member of our family though not by blood.

As the days passed, I came to realize I had lost my mother in losing Almazesha. She was gone. If there was anyone in my family who accepted me the way that I am, it was her. If there was any place in the world that I could go to and feel the utmost peace, it was her bedroom, sitting on her bed. Talking to her and being with her gave me so much peace. Now this space would only be available for me in meditation and virtual realities. Almazesha's bedroom never changed in all of my forty-some years of life. It was always the same. The furniture was the same and the scent of cologne was the same. The light was the same, and the setup of the furniture as well as the feel of the room was the same. It was a constant in all of our lives, a place that steadied us as a family. No matter what happened, we could always go there and sleep, and know that everything would be all right. It was my sanctuary, and the sanctuary of everyone in our family.

Throughout my life, I had often been haunted by the thought of the day I would not be able to go back to Laïbet or be with Almazesha. Being aware that one day in the future, the time would come when I could not be with her, made me all the more conscious of our time together. Now that time has come, and I sit to write our stories. I had been meaning to for years, but for years I had failed to have the discipline to sit and actually dedicate time to put our stories on paper. Why does it always take great shake-ups in our lives to actually get going with the things that we have always wanted to do? Why don't we do what we want without needing to be pushed by the events in our lives? For me, I only wrote now once she was no longer with me.

A few years ago, Etetila had asked me to find someone to record Almazesha's life. I was ready to do that myself, but never found the time to just be in

Ethiopia. Looking back now, I regret not having made the time. We can always find time—it all depends on how much of a priority we make the task at hand. Hoping that it is never too late and instead of remaining with the feeling of regret, I started to tell this story of ours. This is why I have started this journey of writing and telling the stories that should have been told a long time ago.

The stories in this book are the stories of our lives in Laïbet, through the lens of my personal life. I write to celebrate the life of Almazesha, and to celebrate her legacy. This book is about what I have learned from her and how my relationship with her has shaped and molded me. The stories begin with the early years of living in Laïbet and continue with the tragic turn of events when a communist government took over the nation, leading many Ethiopian families to flee the country. This book speaks about the pain of migration due to conflict, war, and social injustice; it talks about what it means to be an immigrant without a name. It is all based on my own personal life and the special friendship I shared with my Grandmother. I include letters I wrote to her, to find a way to have the conversations we never had a chance to finish while she was with me. I am certain that she hears my letters. I am sure.

I write to heal my soul. I hope that through the process of writing I can overcome the emptiness I feel inside. I wish to write not necessarily the story, but the conversations as I would have had them with her, on the veranda or in her bedroom.

As I write these words, it is hardly three days since she left us. But I don't think she left us. She is here in spirit with us; I can feel her around all of us. She is here being with us through our dreams, through our thoughts, and even in random and ordinary events in our lives. Last night as I prepared to go to sleep in this hotel room in Bo, all the lights suddenly went out—the generator had broken down. The room was pitch dark and I could not see a thing. Even at my age, I am always so scared of darkness, especially with my imagination going wild about the insects and creepy crawlies that could potentially run around all over. Last night, however, I sat on my bed with my eyes trying in vain to make out the shapes in the room, waiting for the hotel staff to put the generator on. And something changed: I was not afraid. I felt a sense of security and peace. It was completely dark, and any other time I would have jumped under my covers, but last night for a moment, I heard her voice. I felt her presence, maybe a presence that I invoked, but nonetheless a reassuring presence. I knew that in spirit she was there, and it gave me comfort. No matter our physical separation, our departed loved ones are always with us at heart—or so I believe.

Journey back

Accra—Ghana, October 1, 2009. A few days after that call, I was on a flight to Addis on Ethiopian Airlines. From Freetown, Sierra Leone, I had to fly to Accra, Ghana, spend the night, and catch the connecting flight that would bring me to Addis. The route is long: before reaching Addis, the plane makes stops in Abidjan, Ivory Coast and Lagos, Nigeria.

Standing at the boarding gate at the Kokota International Airport in Accra, I waited anxiously for the Ethiopian Airlines plane to arrive. I am usually happy to see an Ethiopian Airlines aircraft land, associating it with home. But this time, as I saw the aircraft descend on the runway and twirl around to come and park at the gate, my heart twirled with it. It was a strange feeling I could not describe, a feeling of extreme sadness coupled with a deep and clear realization of the impermanence of life.

Almazesha did not make it. As my thoughts bounced back and forth, I remembered that in 1996, exactly 13 years ago to the day, I returned to Addis to start living there for good. It was also Meskal the night I arrived. I was so happy then to finally have made the major move back to my country to try and build my life there, living close to her and all my aunts and uncles. It seemed a lifetime ago.

Now I was flying home for a completely different reason. My only concern was to make it in time for the convoy to Debra Libanos and get a chance to see her one last time before they laid her to rest. My flight was due to arrive at 6:00 am—technically there was no problem getting to Laïbet by 9:00 am, but knowing how delays can arise I was conscious that there was a slight chance I might not make it on time. I knew I was cutting it close. Somewhere in my heart, I was sure she would wait for me before she went to join her father and mother, and all her uncles, aunts, and family members who lay in the family mausoleum.

Starting at the airport in Accra, all through the flight, I did not know what to do with myself. I was conscious of witnessing the end of an era, the end of a generation, and the turning of a page. As this plane chugged along from West Africa to East, I sat by the window looking at the dark skies, remembering the times I had with my grandmother. "My grandmother, my grandmother, my grandmother," I kept repeating in my head. Almazesha had passed on, not even a week ago—it seemed unreal. I found comfort in denying it all; I kept saying to myself that I was sure she is in a coma for now, but that she would come back.

What is life without her? Who will I be calling to chat, to ask advice, or to just hear a loving voice on the other end? We, the family and community around her, have all been called home. In these past few days, every plane that landed in Addis must have had at least three or four members of my family, if not more. Almazesha was and will always remain our mast. She has been and is the main mast that keeps not only the immediate family together, but the immense community around her.

For now, beyond the good she did in this world, beyond the fact that she stood for justice, human rights, and compassion for all living beings on this Earth, I write as a grandchild. Apprehensive of the days to come, as a grandchild I now faced a major turning point in my life, as the one who mentored and guided me all my life had joined the world of Spirit. For all practical purposes, Almazesha is my mother. She has always been my best friend in many ways.

I started writing this book many months ago. At that time, it was just going to be a reflection on my own life. I was hoping to finish it and give her a copy. I was looking forward to the sparkles in her eyes and that smile that she always gave when there was some sort of complicity between us. I knew when I had done something good or something that made her proud because I saw a particular smile on her face—her signature loving and mischievous smile. And then she would not even mention the work or deed, but rather ask me if I have eaten, or tell me to come and sit by her side or rest on Ababi's bed. That is what she told all of us when she was proud of what we had done and wanted to acknowledge our efforts. Now these same stories I wanted to write are laced with her loss, and so take another turn.

All my life, she was the one friend who remained true and steady. She has been my ever-loyal partner in crime and my best advisor. She was the one I called first when I had accomplished something or when I was confronted with a wall or major challenge. I called her first when I heard a good joke because nothing made me happier than making her laugh.

From the moment I heard she had passed on to the other sphere of existence, I have been faced with the reality that it is now time to grow up and rise up to be the human being that she has raised me to be. Isn't it funny to talk of growing up when one is already past 40 years of age? Yet I realize that as long as we have parents, we can remain children; we almost don't have to truly assume adulthood in all its aspects because in some little way, there is still someone who calls us "my child." But when that person is gone, then that space is no longer there. I feel that I am now faced with the obligation to shed some more skin of childhood. It makes me feel old.

On the plane that day, it had been less than a week, but I could feel that I had mellowed. My heart had expanded. My tears were heavier, but at the same time my heart was thumping to a slightly different beat, one with so much more compassion and love. Could it be that whatever she had bestowed on me was now transforming from seed to plant?

There are so many ways to start a story. Today, I think it is best to start telling you my story with something that Almazesha always used to tell me.

As we sat on the balcony, she used to joke with me and say: "Many years from now, when you are a grandmother and I am no longer around, you will tell your children and grandchildren the story of one little lady that lived up the hill, in a house looking toward the mountains of Entoto." Then she held my hands and changed the subject to stories of the days when she used to care for me when I was still an infant and toddler. "You were such a naughty baby...look at you now, no one would know how spoiled you were back then." She would tell me how she told me the story of the Mouse being chased by the Cat, and when the Mouse got caught in the story, I would cry. "First your lower lip would curl down, and before long heavy tears would drop one by one," she would say as she mimicked how I looked when I started crying. "That's why I always change the story and tell you that the Mouse ran out of the mouth of the Cat and reached her house without being eaten. You would first make sure that the Mouse truly escaped and then start laughing and giggling with joy even though some tears were still dripping out."

She would laugh and tell me how easy I was to fool and how the next day, the same story would make me cry again. Then she smiled as if she could relive the scenes and the long-ago times that she talked about. It was her smile that got to me the most. It held such authenticity; her smile would expand and would extend into her eyes. With rosebud lips and straight white teeth, Almazesha's entire face was always ready to smile or entertain a good laugh—but let not her humor fool you. She was as sharp as one can be with a brilliant mind. There was nothing we children could be doing that she would not catch. In fact, as much as she was ready to laugh, she was also extremely disciplined and wanted that discipline to be observed by all of us. Her scolding was lethal—sparse, measured, with no wasted breath. The scolding was all in her big brown eyes: she would just look straight at us, and that gaze held the lecture. No words were needed. The stick would certainly have been an easier alternative than being subjected to her reprimanding gaze.

And so, in honor of my grandparents, Almazesha and Ababi, here is my little story of our lives in Laïbet. These stories lead into the greater scope of the memories I hold as a grandchild, the one who carries the memories that sustain me always. This story defines who I am and anchors me, each day, to a stable ground—no matter the ebb and flow of life.

Once upon a time: *Keletat Aned Ken*

Keletat aned Ken, aned azawont neberu iyalesh teretun tenegriachewalesh [One day you will tell the people the story and you tell them: once upon a time, there was an old sage...] Yes, the day has come for me to tell the story. As she once told, I now bring you this tale of the wonderful sage.

Once upon a time, in a land full of mountains, there was a tiny little lady with the biggest heart in the world. This tiny little lady lived in a house on the way to the Entoto Mountains. To go to her house, you go up the hill on Churchill Road, pass the municipality building, go around the roundabout with the statue of Emperor Menelik sitting on his bucking horse, facing the beautiful church of St. George. Go around the roundabout and keep going straight up the road as if heading for the mountains. You pass a few houses, some shops, and about 500 meters later, you reach on your right a bakery called Shoa Bakery and a little vegetable shop. The vegetable shop belongs to Afro and his family. Right between Afro's shop and the bakery, there a tiny narrow street goes down a steep hill. As you come down this tiny narrow street, you would smell the scent of fresh roasted coffee. There were only two compounds down this tiny street, so you couldn't get lost. Just follow the coffee, and before you knew it you would be at the bottom of the hill in front of a large gate on the left-hand side. This gate, which changed colors each time it was repainted, would open for you. Step in, please don't be shy—Gashe Tilahun will make sure the dogs are held back. As you stepped inside or drove in, you would know that you were welcome. You had just entered a special home. The home we call Laïbet.

As you entered this courtyard, you would see in front of you and to the left a beautiful house with a warm veranda, always painted in sunset colors. If you were lucky, you would then see Almazesha, the tiny little lady, sitting on this veranda looking out to the mountains, talking and greeting all the people going up and down the compound. You might also see Grandfather Ababi who usually sat in his office located near the main gate of Laïbet. He sat right by the window and regularly leaned out to see who was coming and going. He kept an eye on all the action in the courtyard.

Almazesha and Ababi lived in this house for almost a century, and through the years this house and compound we call Laïbet has seen history, witnessed celebrations and wars, and known good times and hard times. We have held numerous weddings there and many funerals as well; we have laughed and cried so many times over that the emotions have carved permanent grooves on our souls and on the tarmac of the compound. Laïbet is the foundation and center of many of our lives; it is the place where the community of Shola[13] found its source and inspiration.

Almazesha was tiny physically, yet inside this tiny body there was a heart that could embrace the whole world twice over. She had the heart of a lioness, with enough love for everyone. And when I say everyone, I mean *everyone*. Whether nice people or bad people, whether family members or not, whether saints or criminals, she had a way of finding in her the power to love everyone unconditionally. That is what made her incredible. In good times and in hard times, there were two attributes that never left her side: her sharp sense of humor and her amazing mathematical and strategic mind.

Almazesha had more courage than could seemingly fit in such a little lady. She had no fear but for God. And for the sake of justice, human rights, and compassion for all living beings, she had the inner strength to stand up to anyone and anything—she feared not for her life, but was more concerned for the welfare of others.

This was our mother, our grandmother, and our great-grandmother—my soul mate and my friend who shaped me into the person that I am today. But she

---

[13] Shola is the name of our neighborhood in Addis Ababa. There are two neighborhoods called Shola, so ours is also often referred to as Shola Medhanialem (Medhanialem is the name of the church in our neighborhood).

was not just "ours" per se in terms of her biological children and grandchildren; Almazesha was a mother for hundreds if not thousands who knew her. I don't even know how many children, women, and men look to her as a mother. To those who knew her and had the chance to live around her, she is and always will be the Alpha of all mothers, the ultimate heart that could embrace and love everyone who came her way.

No one knows how she managed in terms of finances and logistics—all we know is that in good times and in tough times, her hospitality never flinched. Somehow she held it all together without ever making us feel the times of financial hardship. She lived in abundance and shared unconditionally all that she had. No one coming to Laïbet would be allowed to leave without having a meal and something to drink, coffee or tea and anything else that was available. It would be unheard of to come to Laïbet and leave without having to sit down for a bit to chat or have a bite to eat. If one was visiting from upcountry, then for sure a bed would be made right away so the traveler could rest before continuing the journey. It's the only place I know where the house help worked in shifts, the day shift and the night shift—that's how much there was to do to maintain the tempo with the vibes of Laïbet. It is the only place I know where once someone was hired to work there to cook or help out with domestic chores, within a short time, the new person would be integrated into the family and become one with all of us there.

When Almazesha was with children, she could manage to be with them in her full presence and make them feel like grown-ups. She always said never to talk "silly" to children: "You will numb their brain and stunt their intellectual capacity," she used to say,

"Talk to them properly. They are full souls in little bodies." I remember that she used to tell us the best fairy tales there could ever be. Many of us had the chance to grow up right under her influence, and I can't express what a gift that was. In everything she did, every story she told, she bestowed on us the fairy dust of her wisdom, the wisdom passed on to her from generations before.

When you did something wrong, she had a way of sitting you down and explaining why it was wrong. You had best be open and face up to your mistake—otherwise, she could also talk in a way that was so straight to the point that sometimes you wished she would just beat you so you wouldn't have to listen to the stinging truth in her disciplinary speech. And if that was not getting through to you, then for sure she would not hesitate to take a switch to you or dunk you in an ice-cold bath to bring some sense into you and change your behavior.

To me, she was a combination of everything. She was my mother, even though I was her grandchild. She was my friend and my mentor. Almazesha was everything to me. In this book I tell her story and the story of my family through the lens of my life as a child, an adolescent, and the adult I have become.

She has been the center of my life, like the central pillar of my whole being and architecture. As much as I loved to spend time with Almazesha, the process of writing this book allows me to be with her in a different way. And I cherish this opportunity.

This book is for the sake of all the children who will come in the future and will not have a chance to listen to the stories from the elders. I write as a way of re-living the good times and also processing and healing from some of the hard times in our lives. I have incorporated parts of the writing I started about a year before Almazesha passed. I start by sharing the background of my life in the first part of the book. In the second part, I have put together the daily letters I have written to Almazesha since she left. These letters are at times the conversations I wish we had had, and at times a reflection of my life without her physically with us.

So here comes the story: *Keletat Ande Ken, aned azawont neberu...* [once upon a time there was an old sage...]

Almazesha, in honor of the life we have shared. In honor of all that you have bestowed on us—the love, the compassion, the resilience, and the humor—I stand up to applaud you and celebrate you. I bow to you, Emaye. I bow to you.

Here's to you, Emayiye and all that you stood for—justice, peace, change, and human rights. We all stand up to celebrate the life we used to have together at Laïbet. And as part of my process to commemorate the mosaics of our lives, I feel that the best way is to write to you and tell you some of the stories we may not have had the chance to talk about.

Yes, and so it is. This is where I start.

PART I: LAÏBET

More times than not, when I meet up with friends and people in general, it is not unusual that I talk of my family. Whether it is stories of childhood and whatever adventure we used to have, or lessons I learned from my parents or grandparents, I end up talking about my family, maybe because I keep my family in my heart. Wherever I go they are always with me, especially Almazesha—she never leaves my side.

I tell the stories about my early years growing up at Laïbet, with Almazesha, Ababi, my parents and my sisters, my aunts, my uncles, my cousins, and neighborhood friends—a whole community. I tell the stories, because in these stories I exist. And as I speak of our lives and tell our stories, I revive in a way. It's good to tell our stories. It keeps the culture alive. It keeps our traditions alive, and keeps our community's institutional memory refreshed. It maintains the way of life and allows generations to share the collective wisdom. As we tell our stories, I feel that we are keeping a sort of special, eternal and subtle space of existence alive.

Yet when I thought of putting my stories in writing, I didn't know where to start. There is so much to say. It's like having to bite into a plump apple and not knowing which side to bite first to get going with it— once the first bite is taken, then the rest flows with ease. But where to bite first? Isn't that the question?

It was very difficult to choose the story to start with. Where do I start? Where does one start to tell the story of one's life, the story of a community, the story of generations? In the end, I decided to tell the story as it comes to me and as I feel moved to tell it.

One thing that must be made clear is that the stories in this book are based on my perception at the different stages of my life. All the events and incidents are viewed through the lens of my life and my own particular situation, my specific state of mind and consciousness.

As much as this can be seen as the story of one person, it is far from being unique. This story also represents the stories of those of us who had to leave our homes and find a life in exile, those of us who had to recreate our lives in new environments, those of us who managed to return home after many years and find ways to reintegrate ourselves, and so on. It's the story of families, of change, and of challenges; it's the story of transformation; and it's the story of pain and tears and rapture. It is the story of immigration and exile, telling of societies broken by internal conflicts and war, of societal resilience as well the as the innate ability of the collective to remain solid through the cement of culture and tradition. But most of all, I am aware that the stories are the fibers of who we are; it's the stories that define the texture of our societies. And it is important to impart our stories to our community as well as to a larger audience to bring understanding, to leave marks and records of how life has been for some of us, and most of all, to sustain the way that life once was... and keep it all fresh in our memories.

Without these stories, I could not exist. I would not find my bearings. It would be like losing my compass and being unable to navigate back home. The stories are the places where I get comfort. These stories give me the place where I go to re-energize and the place I go to check in with myself, to know whether I am balanced or not, to know that I am still aligned with the principles my elders have taught me. In our current globalized world, where we are living all over the planet, where living and working close to our community and neighborhoods has become rare, where we can be in one country one day and in another the next day—these stories have been my anchor and the compass of my existence.

Yet as much as I was eager to sit and write, I confess to a certain anxiety that I felt about the whole exercise, a certain sense of fear about writing the tale. It's the kind of anxiety and fear that someone who has lived without a mirror (literally or in a figurative way) experiences suddenly when offered the opportunity to see his or her reflection in a lake or a river. When we are faced with the choice of looking at our reflection, of knowing what we really look like—be it from looking in a mirror or be it from suddenly finding our life written on in black and white—there is something almost fatalistic about it. Will I be wondering whether this is really how it was?

The whole process of writing is a path of discovery and exploration, with we "ourselves" being the terrain to be explored and discovered from another angle. I wondered if, at the end of the process, my world would crumble or if the stories would be even more alive. It is all in my heart—it is in my mind in a nebulous format where the boundary between reality and fantasy has faded. One blurs into the other, and many years later, it all morphs as part of the story: the same stories we always talk about.

When all the family gathered around Almazesha at Laïbet, we repeated the same old stories, and each time the story was re-told, it had another texture. We knew it from beginning to end, but each time we listened to the storyteller as if it was the very first time. It was amazing to me—even the comments after the stories were also often the same and very predictable. You knew when a new person was in the storytelling circle because their comments would be new, sometimes out of sync from the rest. It would take one or two rounds to bring them into harmony with the rest of the circle. And then there were certain stories that could only be told by certain people. Some stories don't sit well in just anybody's mouth; there is a particular mouth that has to tell it. Yes, it's like that.

And each time we repeat the stories of this uncle or that uncle, the stories of war, the stories of victories, the stories of invasion, and the stories of defeat, and we talk of the fun times and the funny anecdotes— again and again it's the same final line that comes up in the script. No one ever wrote the script—it's alive. It renews itself and rewrites itself as time passes. These stories just exist in the realm and the dimension of our collective fantasies about who we are, how we lived, and how we relate to each other and to our environment.

I am certain that while we all loved to exist collectively, we have each individually contemplated the time when our collective existence would be no longer. Such thought has always brought sadness to me. What will happen now that Laïbet can no longer be? What happens when the Queen Bee has gone and the bees are still in the hive? Almazesha was the one who kept us all together, and I feared the day she would leave us for good. She was the Queen of our hive; she was the sage, the oracle, and the mother of all. I was afraid of the day she would leave us, because along with her, our circle of stories might also go. I was afraid we would lose our fellowship because she was the only one with a heart big enough to hold our community, our family, our village, despite the usual family drama.

The only way we can keep this community alive is to put the stories in writing, hoping that in the writing we are able to pass on the stories in their fullness. I had to move past my reluctance and have faith that what would come out of this process of writing would be a representation of the way we used to be, the way we still are today and will hopefully remain.

Despite my doubt and anxiety, I knew that I wanted my stories written. It might not fully reflect what truly was: on one hand, I am conscious that I write from my particular perspective and bias, and on the other hand, each reader reads the words and sentences according to his or her perspective. We each read differently. Every word that I use may have a slightly different meaning for another. Nonetheless, I trust that the essence of the message I want to pass on will come through these pages.

At times we live in the dimension of the stories, in

our own collective reality—throughout the changes that have taken place in society over decades, throughout the fluctuation of cultures and politics, we have remained unchanged as a whole. There is a way of being that is accepted in Laïbet: Such behavior is defined as always being available to be of service, remaining humble and modest, working hard, and always being ready to help others. These are all traits we take from Almazesha and Ababi.

The first time I realized my attachment to my traditions and to my home, Laïbet, was after I left Ethiopia, many years after, when I had moved on with life. I must have been in my late 20s or early 30s when I came to the realization of this attachment. I had this urge to stop. I needed to look back, to try to understand the principles, the history and foundation that had made me the person I had become. I wanted to connect again to the lineage behind me, to know the stories and the texture of my community. Of course, my perception of Ethiopia remained framed in the picture I had of the concept of country as the small child I was when my family moved to Europe. My understanding of our societal norms, of what was right and wrong, also remained very much attached to what I had learned in Laïbet until the time we left.

Growing up at Laïbet

What Laïbet is
Laïbet is an institution. In Amharic, *Lai* means "up" or "upper" and *Bet* means "house." *Laïbet* means "upper house," and the whole compound of Almazesha and Ababi gained this name very naturally when Almazesha built the second and major part of the house. Initially, when she first started her life

with Ababi, they had only a little house with two bedrooms built right at the southern corner of the compound. It was a small house. All the children were born there. She always had it in her mind that she would build a bigger house further up in the compound, designed and adapted to accommodate her growing family and growing children. The right time to expand Laïbet and build the bigger house came when Ababi went on mission to Rome in 1963–1964.

Almazesha took the savings he had accumulated (all in cash) and safely kept hidden away in his nightstand drawer. She spent the entire savings to lay the foundation of this new part of the house. When Ababi returned back home, he was both surprised and upset by her actions. Almazesha always smiled when she spoke of this time. It made her laugh because Ababi was really not willing to build this house. He could not understand why it was necessary. But she had plans. Although she repaid him in full, he always thought of her as mischievous and unpredictable—in fact, he thought she was irresponsible with money. In return, she used to think he could not see opportunities at hand and was too risk-averse. We grew up listening to their loving arguments based on this axis. She was a risk-taker who could see opportunities miles ahead; he, on the other hand, was very risk-averse and preferred to go the conservative and moderate way.

In any case, Almazesha always said that once the construction was finished and they moved into the new part of the house, Ababi was the first one to show friends and family around. He was extremely happy and proud of the new place, which acquired the name Laïbet. The other part of house, the older part, then became *Tachbet* (*tach* meaning "lower").

There are different parts in the house called Laïbet, which became an institution over the years—not just for family, but for friends and the larger community. There is the main veranda where there are always two or three chairs, where Almazesha or Ababi or both often sat with us in the early morning or late afternoon. There is a beautiful view of the Entoto mountain range, and the veranda faces an incredible rose garden that Almazesha used to prune herself. I had the best conversations with her in that garden or in the other garden, the one that is closest to the main gate. Our conversations were slow, almost meditative. As we talked she would continue to check on her roses, pruning them, removing dead leaves or buds. The conversations flowed gently from one topic to the next. It was my time alone with her. Our conversations on the veranda were also great; sometimes we sat there holding hands, on the two chairs that faced the mountains. It did not matter what we talked about. It was always a pleasant conversation about future plans, or about how life used to be when she was a child, or sometimes about history or stories about her forefathers, the men and women who were among the warriors who protected Ethiopia from all possible foreign invasion.

Rules of Laïbet
From the outside, Laïbet appeared to be a functioning compound with a large family in it, but for those who knew, it had a whole other dimension. There were rules in Laïbet—unwritten, needless to say, but we just knew them by default. There was no one to make sure that the rules were followed, but we all knew there were consequences for breaking them.

One of the most foundational rules I remember is respect for hierarchy, but the values of the hierarchy were not based on whose child you were or whether you were a blood relative, but rather on merit. Parentage or kinship were unimportant—what mattered was that you had earned the respect of all. The way to earn respect was very simple: It had to do with the capacity to be of service, the willingness to work hard, courage in the face of trials, and concern for the greater good of the whole over individualistic thinking. Part of the respect also came from a genuine modesty and humility that we had to embody. Should one be found to be boastful, arrogant, or at all selfish, then that person would lose the collective respect.

This respect for the rules extended even to how I entered the house. Sometimes when I came to Laïbet, I came in through the kitchen. There is a small passage from the parking area to a passage that leads to a sitting area. The sitting area started out as a veranda, many years back when we were still little, but later the veranda was covered and the kitchen there was transformed into a sitting area. It became the *tinishu salon* [the small living room], and a new kitchen with an extra washroom was built in the space remaining outside.

As I came through this little passageway that leads to the *tinishu salon*, there was a way that we all entered that space. It was both with gratitude and reverence. As I might not know the persons sitting on the sofas on the veranda or in the *tinishu salon*, there was a way to come in that did not disturb them. It was about coming in as discreetly as possible. And as I made my way to the dining room inside, the one connected with the main living room, I bowed and greeted, and bowed and greeted, and bowed and greeted everyone I saw. Slowly, I made my way to the living room.

At times I found Almazesha sitting on her chair, strategically placed where she could see both the guests and family in front of her in the living room, as well as those coming from the kitchen area and the *tinishu salon*. Right by her chair, Almazesha could discreetly press on a button that caused a quiet ring in the kitchen area, telling the ladies in the kitchen area that she needed them, and you could see them rushing to her. The more activity there was on any particular day, the more you saw the traffic of ladies coming and going from where Almazesha was, each one taking some kind of order to either serve food, serve drinks, call a driver, deliver something, call someone, or do whatever was necessary. You could also see a wide range of slippers lined up right outside the living room—out of respect, the ladies took them off when they came into the house.

As soon as I saw Almazesha, no matter how many people there were or what was happening, she greeted me with her particular smile that never changed in all my life. It was a smile of unconditional love, coming straight from a source of abundance. "*Mimiye metash* [Mimiye, so here you are]," she would say to me, "*Ney kutch bei* [come and have a seat]." And then if there were guests that I had not met before, she would introduce me as "*Ye lej lejai nat* [she is my child's child]," and the conversation then continued from where it left off.

The only thing that may have changed through the years is that earlier on, I might have come running in to see her along with all the other children. Sometimes we ran in to see her, and sometimes we ran to hide behind her because we had been up to some mischief and there was someone chasing after us.

This rule of servitude and compassion is what we have all inherited from her, the heart for empathy she taught us all, and the respect for all living beings that she bestowed on us. I suppose she had all these traits in her partly from her lineage, partly from her studies and dedication to spirituality, and also partly from her life experiences. As the greatest healers may have been afflicted by substantial illness, in this same way, the challenges and circumstances of her life gave her the gift of understanding, the gift of tolerance, the gift of love, and the gifts of both courage and humor.

Almazesha

By any standard, it is amazing that Almazesha made her life what it was, especially when we know that her life abruptly changed at the age of nine when she was given in marriage and lost her mother shortly after. While she could have become a short-sighted, bitter person, she instead grew to become a visionary leader and pillar for the lives of thousands of men, women, and children.

Almazesha was the first daughter of Kegn Azmatch[14] Haile Mariam Gezmu and Lady Berhane Wodaje; the firstborn was her brother Mulugeta. As much as her father was a wealthy and well-to-do entrepreneur, Kegn Azmatch Haile Mariam was renowned for his immense intellectual capability. His profound knowledge of history, culture, and philosophy, combined with a pleasant savoir-faire about life,

---

[14] *Kegn Azmatch* is a title in the military that refers to his role and the position of his troops in times of war.

allowed him to share his life with all members of the community regardless of their social status. He was gifted with languages and excelled in several Ethiopian languages as well as European languages such as English, French, and Italian. He was truly a multilingual thinker with deep concern for humanity. If I had to describe him with a single phrase, I would choose "renaissance man ahead of his time." In his home library, it would not be uncommon to find the works of thinkers such as Dante, Voltaire, Rousseau, Goethe, etc. Of Dante's work, his favorite was *Inferno*. He very much enjoyed the poetry of Rousseau and often translated and published some of Rousseau's selected work in the main newspapers of Ethiopia. The Ethiopian book of the Glory of Kings, *Kebra Negest*, and the *Holy Bible* were part of his regular reading. Kegn Azmatch Haile Mariam was likewise known for the historic role he played as leader of a strategic military group within a resistance army led by renowned national hero Ras Abebe Aregay during the Italian invasion of Ethiopia.

Almazesha's mother, Lady Berhane Wodaje was the first daughter of Dejazmatch[15] Wodaje Wube and Lady Gessessetch Hagos, who herself was the first daughter of Lord Hagos Mercha, brother and strategic military partner of Emperor Yohannes IV, formerly called Ras[16] Kassa Mercha. The Wodaje family were known by the community for their kindness and generosity, reaching out to all people around them. Despite their royal lineage, the Wodaje family was best recognized as an old, pious, God-fearing Christian family, always demure and humble.

---

[15] *Dejazmatch* is a nobility title.
[16] *Ras* is a nobility title equivalent to Duke.

On Almazesha's paternal and maternal lines both, the shared commonality was the family's profound commitment to human dignity for all and devotion to the Christian faith. Both families were dedicated to the welfare of the community at large, especially the welfare of those community members who might have been underprivileged or destitute. Both families stood to uphold peace, justice, and human rights. These were among the nation-builders of their time.

So, Almazesha was a child born into a lineage of well established, very well-to-do, deeply faithful Christians and recognized resistance fighters. Until she was nine years of age, when she had to marry, Almazesha grew up under the tutelage of her paternal grandmother, Emahoye[17] Askale-Mariam. This matriarch had a natural and God-given inclination to provide emergency assistance and medical help in her day-to-day work as well as to the wounded during the Italian invasion war. Emahoye Askale-Mariam was a key supporter of the heroic resistance movement. Her home was one known by troops as a place to replenish food supplies, find shelter and medical help for the wounded, and get a change of horses. Through her role in the resistance, she embodied the role of women in nation-building in Africa. Together with her son, she helped train young officers in her son's troops in handling firearms and marksmanship (known as *Illama*[18]); she also trained women and other community members in various fields. The teachings she imparted were mostly in theology, history, and

---

[17] *Emahoye* means "Nun"—after her husband Kegn Azmatch Gezmu passed away, Emahoye Askale became a nun and dedicated her life to serving the church and the community.

[18] *Illama* means "marksmanship."

philosophy. She was also a famous midwife who helped several women deliver their babies and trained them in how to care for the newborn. In fact, Emahoye Askale-Mariam later helped Almazesha deliver her first baby, Enaniye.

From Emahoye Askale-Mariam, Almazesha received intensive education in theology, history, and philosophy at a very young age just as the rest of the community did. At the same time, her grandmother also taught her about war and strategies for resistance fighting, including the use of firearms. Emahoye Akale-Mariam trained Almazesha in handling firearms with ease and professionalism, and wanted Almazesha to be able to use firearms with confidence and without fear. Through her military training, Almazesha learned much of military discipline and decisiveness. At times, Emahoye Askale-Mariam would test Almazesha's acquisition of her lessons by blindfolding her and then asking her to load, unload, take apart, and put back together the various firearms. Emahoye Askale-Mariam was loving yet at the same time very strict. A well established fighter herself, she made it her commitment to teach her little granddaughter to shoot as well as any soldier, if not better. This military training did not by any means detract Emahoye Askale-Mariam from teaching her granddaughter the etiquette of the feminine; she taught Almazesha how to be a woman and a lady, graceful and elegant, while remaining strong and confident, gentle and tolerant, deeply compassionate and determined.

Growing up, Almazesha loved to ride her grandmother's horses. For recreation, she and her older brother, Mulugeta, used to gallop through the hills surrounding her grandmother's home in Gurene in the Shewa region. Because the saddles were too big for her and often reserved for the soldiers, Almazesha and Mulugeta rode the horses bareback. Once in a while, Mulugeta and Almazesha would sneak away and climb up the rocks to go adventure and play in the surrounding hillsides and caves. I remember stories Almazesha would tell us about what they would find in the caves. It was not uncommon for them to find what looked like a human body wrapped up in clothes, all dried up and stiff; I suspect these might have been mummies tucked away and left to rest in the hidden cave or possibly the bodies of hermits who used the caves as a place for retreat and prayer. Almazesha continued studying theology and philosophy as well as history even after she married. She also continued to practice her marksmanship; she remained a sharpshooter and hardly ever missed a target until late in her life.

All of the rules of Laïbet were a reflection of who she was for us, her community—a reflection of the character of her ancestral lineage and a reflection of her unshakeable faith in the Holy Trinity. In fact, the shortest way to express the rules of Laïbet is what she always used to say to us: *"Even if no one sees you, don't forget that Fetariachen [our Creator] sees all things—so behave and live accordingly."*

Ababi

There were also rules in Laïbet that reflected Ababi. While Almazesha was full of sparkles and lived life at full speed and full heart, Ababi was reserved and demure. He worked as an accountant most of his life, and he lived in the same way he held his accounts. He did not want any liabilities or unnecessary accounts payable. He didn't borrow money, nor did he lend any out. He had few friends, but those friendships were deep and for a lifetime. Ababi came from Wollo. Born to a highly respected spiritual leader, he traveled to Addis at a young age to continue his education and eventually find work. As much as Almazesha had the energy of a shooting star, he was more of a quiet breeze. He had a stable routine in his life. He wanted peace, and disliked commotion and unnecessary chatter. If he spoke, it was to say exactly what he had to say—nothing more, nothing less.

There was something about him that was very punctual in all things he did. Ababi woke up by 6:00am every day of his life, and then woke up the whole household by sneezing and coughing as he washed up and made himself ready for the day. He was in bed by 8:00pm at the latest and asleep shortly after he listened to the National Radio's evening news broadcast. He listened through his small pocket radio, which he held very close to his ear as he lay in bed, nicely wrapped up in his Gaby; he had a way of wrapping up his Gaby so that it also covered his head and shoulders. Everybody in Laïbet knew that Ababi was not very good at diplomacy: he said what he thought and thought what he said. He never ate spicy food and never missed his macchiato in the morning around 10:00 am. In the later parts of the day, he would also take a break and come and sit on the veranda.

From Ababi we learned dependability and the importance of punctuality in life. Unlike Almazesha, he was very reluctant about adventures. He preferred to have a calm life. Later on, I will tell you about the time that Almazesha was incarcerated because of the political party that she founded. When she, along with many people from the house, did not come home that particular day, it was not easy to break the news to Ababi and tell him that Almazesha had been arrested. When we finally told him, he sighed in surrender in a way that expressed both his worries and also how he just could not understand why she would get herself into such situations. In fact, in the early days of this political party that started right in the living room, I would sit with him on the veranda because he did not take part in the discussions. He would hold my hand and ask me, "Mamishet, who are all these people? Have you seen all these cars?" I always answered that they were people who had come to see Almazesha, and he would just sigh and look into the mountain range. He would sigh, shake his head, and mumble that he just did not understand why she got involved in so many things. He called her Almaz, and she always called him Ato Makonnen or Ababi.

Almazesha was militant, and nothing could make her budge from standing firm for her convictions. For justice, welfare, and human rights, she never hesitated to take whatever action was required. She executed her decisions radically, whatever they were, and she did so with compassion and thoughtfulness. This is what led her to start the political party I will talk about later on. She would always tell us, "*Make up your mind and be decisive about your stand, and leave the rest to God. He will show you the way.*"

My first relationships: My grandparents
When I think back to the first relationships I had in my life, I think of my grandparents, Ababi and Almazesha. All that I have fundamentally learned of life, I learned mostly from them.

As the years unfolded, some things never changed in the way we lived together, like the ritual sitting on the veranda. The times on the veranda has so marked me that even my dreams often take place on that veranda. About two weeks before Almazesha passed on, I had a dream that I drove to Laïbet with Gashe Mulugeta, the one who lived in Brussels. We met up with Almazesha. She was sitting on the veranda dressed in her housecoat with a *netela* on top of it, covering her head loosely; she also had the white knitted shawl she always wore covering her shoulders and wrapped gently around. Almazesha also had her glasses on, the ones she used to watch TV or put on when her eyes were a bit tired. She spoke kindly with Gashe Mulugeta, greeted him, and asked him about his health, and he did the same with her. I woke up feeling very good, as if I had been to Laïbet. But I did not realize right away that it was just a dream—it seemed all so real. Later in the day, I realized that it was a dream. I also remembered that Gashe Mulugeta had passed on years ago. It's funny how I really had felt his presence. I told Yeshiye about the dream. In our culture, we say that seeing someone who has passed on in a dream could indicate the forthcoming passing of another person. I remember telling Yeshiye that maybe something was about to happen with me or with Almazesha. She told me that was not possible, that it was just a *kijet* (random dream or nightmare). Sadly, I learned some days later that Almazesha had left this life. How could I have missed this message and failed to interpret the dream? How I wished I had called Almazesha to tell her about the dream, and let her tell me what she thought of it.

Much of my relationship with Almazesha was anchored in the conversations we used to have. We always spoke so candidly; there was not a single topic in this world that we couldn't talk about.

From the time I was a little girl, she used to tell me stories. Earlier on the stories were folktales, but as time went on she spoke to me about her childhood, about the things she used to do, and about how she saw the future. She would joke with me and tell me that many years from now when she would be very old, she would come to visit me and my children. Then she would imitate the walk of an old woman struggling to move on with a cane. It all seems like yesterday. Although Almazesha did not have many years where she could be described as old, the many surgeries that she had to have did take a toll on her overall physical energy in the last years of her life.

In our conversations, we also talked about dreams. She would listen to me as I told her my dreams. Whether by coincidence or not, often times my dreams turn out to be premonitions. When I was about 7 years old, I told her about a dream I had had about my godfather, that I had seen him being chased by people with spears and rifles. Very shortly after that, we learned that he had been part of the 60+ officials executed by the military regime that overthrew the emperor in the 1970s. On another occasion around the same period, I told her that I had seen my uncle Solomon[19] return home. She joked with me and said that I was so small when he left, I must be mistaken. "Do you even remember him?" she asked. Knowing me, I probably argued back that I knew him well and I had seen him in my dreams. Shortly after this conversation, he returned home from America where he had gone for college.

---

[19] Solomon is my uncle, the seventh child of Almazesha and Ababi, who studied in the United States.

From the time I was a small child, I have remained in conversation with Almazesha through and through. Over the years, these conversations have been the channel of my learning from her, my means of soaking in her teaching. But it was only the conversations we had in her rose garden that went uninterrupted. If we sat on the veranda, our conversation was put on pause for her to give greetings each time someone passed, either coming from the main gate and heading to *tachbet,* or going from *tachbet* to the main gate or the kitchen outside the *tinishu salon.*

Sometimes there would be farmers from far away with goods on their donkeys. She would speak to them in Afan Oromo, a language I never understood; I could only guess from their gestures what they talked about. Almazesha was a master multitasker. As she talked to such farmers, she would call out to someone to come to her side and then she would tell them to prepare food for the one who just came and also have water and some hay for the donkey. *"They too are creatures of God; they too get hungry, thirsty, and tired."* One of these farmers was Ababa Kebede, who always brought us *segatura* [wood shavings used to start cooking fires and make *Injera*, the Ethiopian Bread]. Eventually, years later, his daughter Gete came to live and work at Laïbet. Once, another farmer came and brought us honey. Back in those days, honey was kept in dried sheep hide or goat hide. Gete had just come from the countryside. Apparently she wanted to have a bit of the honey but in the process of sticking her fingers in the hide and licking them, she ended up with her tongue bitten by angry bees. Soon after, she was asked to call Gashe Tesfaye, who at the time was the gatekeeper. She shouted at the top of her lungs, "Gash Tebsay!"— mispronouncing his name because her tongue was swollen. He shouted back at her teasingly, saying, "*Yefsabish?* [May the devil fart on you]."[20] The entire compound busted out laughing at the back-and-forth between them. Almazesha laughed hard, too, saying as she laughed: "*Ende min nekachew!* [Have they lost their minds?!]"

Life in Laïbet
As I mentioned earlier, at Laïbet there was a hierarchy and a system that functioned, and for each of us, the ability to comply with this way of being and system allowed us to enjoy being there. Life in Laïbet was life in a community; for me as a child and even today, the life there represents my entire life and identity. It is my country, in a way. All that I relate to in terms of my identity as an Ethiopian emanates from Laïbet and the community around Laïbet. Sometimes I think that the thoughts I have about Ethiopia are completely biased because I am subconsciously associating the way we live in Laïbet with the way things are in Ethiopia. This has led to much disappointment in the past, especially in the days where I tried to return from living abroad back to Ethiopia with the intention to build my life there.

As children, we had the best time in Laïbet. There were many children: those who came from the neighborhood to play with us, the children of the ladies working at Laïbet, and the grandchildren. At the time, there weren't many grandchildren. It was mainly my sister Fofi and I, and later on my sister

---

[20] The name Tesfaye means "my hope," and when Gete called to him, she said Tebsay, which doesn't really mean anything. But he replied back saying Yefsabish—this sort of means "may he fart on you." 'He' likely refers to the Devil because he is the one we refer to in insults or curses.

Noela was born. Our cousin Samson, Etetila's son, came to live with us for about two years, but then returned to the United States to live with his parents. By the time my youngest sister Lily was born, my cousin Timmy (my Aunt Koky's son) was also just born. There were also cousins like Kassu, and at times another cousin of ours, Mame, used to come to play with us. Both Kassu and Mame were grandchildren of Ababi's brothers. In the same generation as Timmy and Lily, there were Debby, Kidist (aka Mamitoo), Elias, Zelalem, Haimanot, Alemnesh, and so many more. All in all, there would be about fifteen to twenty children on any one day.

We played games, but they were not games to us; we thought we were doing our things as the grownups did theirs. Our favorite game was to play house. We would want to cook meals, so we took the pots and pans I had received as birthday gifts and got a fire started to cook the base of the stew. We stole toilet paper, newspaper, matches, and benzene in order to make a serious fire. We often lit our fire in a hidden corner away from the main courtyard. The stew ingredients were grass, water, mud, whatever veggies we could steal from the kitchen, and the spices we could get our hands on. To thicken our stew, we just added more mud. At times, we even would set traps to catch a bird and then we would pretend the bird was our sheep. Kassu would be the one who killed the bird—it had to be him because we always heard that only men could slaughter a sheep. We thought it would be sacrilege if one of us girls did it, because that's what we heard the ladies in the kitchen say. We just watched as Kassu did his work, and then when he was done he would give us the parts that we mixed into the mud stew. We gave it time to simmer, as we had seen the cooks of Tachbet do. It would take us all day to cook. We used real fire, and copied exactly what we saw the ladies in the kitchen doing.

Once we felt the stew was ready, we then invited the guests. Our group would break up and re-form with some of us being the hosts and others being the guests. We followed the entire protocol of greeting and hospitality. Then at one point we served the stew with a lot of pride. And I must say, we sat there eating the little piece of bird stew cooked with mud and grass! I don't recall being sick; we were all too happy to have had a meal that we cooked ourselves.

There were other games we played. At times we would collect the cigarettes butts and play as if we were the big guests who sometime came to visit Almazesha. The collected cigarette butts were preciously kept in a tin box and hidden in the garden. As we played our cooking games, we would sit around holding the butts and pretend to smoke and speak like the grownups. We served drinks as well. It was our version of *Tela* (a home-brewed dark beer). To make our Tela, we just diluted water with a bit of mud and served it in small tea glasses that we also stole from the kitchen.

For every game, we did the best we could to have the necessary items. When we played hospital and doctors, we used our stash of syringes that we collected from the syringes and hypodermic needles that Gashe Tilahun, our medical person, left in the trash. Given the number of people living at Laïbet, he came regularly—someone was bound to be ill at any time. He often came to the house to give vaccinations or give someone a shot for whatever illness. Most of the syringes were disposed of in the trash can in Almazesha's bathroom, which was emptied daily into the large trash bin tucked under the bushes of climbing purple Bougainvillea to the right of the stairs leading to the veranda. Each time Gashe Tilahun came to Laïbet, we would be on the lookout to gather medical items. We would wait until the coast was clear and collect the syringes from the trash cans. We kept them under the bed in *tachbet*. Kassu was in charge of their safekeeping. We were not sure who we were going to treat, but we thought the opportunity would soon come.

In the midst of all this, around the time I was about 5-6 years of age, I was struck by what I thought was a brilliant idea. With all the children running around in Laïbet, it was very common that a number of us got harshly scolded or even physically punished for whatever we were caught doing. At times it was well deserved, but sometimes it was uncalled for. Some of the nannies or even just any adult person in the compound delivered painful pinching or spanking. So, my idea first started as creating some kind of retaliation, and then evolved to finding a way to make money with the retaliation.

A gang with a purpose: Security or revenge for sale
The purpose of our gang was very clear: to bring in revenue, in cash or chewing gum. The best commodities to sell were security against adults who abused their status, revenge against those who harmed us or wronged us in one way or another, and insurance for property such as toys, pets, or marbles. We also sold insurance that any marble games were conducted fairly, with fair wins and losses. This gang established Kassu and me as the ultimate rulers among our peers; this was true not only for the children of Laïbet but for the neighborhood as well. Most if not all of the children within the community

of Laïbet until about Noela's generation were part of this gang; the others were too small to play with us, so we left them out.

We spent our days going up and down that compound looking for trouble, after school or all day on weekends. There was always so much to do. As I grew up a bit and reached age six or so, there were a lot more children. I realized that a lot of the grownups would unfairly beat us at times. They would beat some more than others. I thought that it would be a good thing to organize a defense mechanism. So, I told the others that if they paid me 25 cents or a packet of chewing-gum a week, I could ensure revenge on whoever laid a hand on them; needless to say, the coins started rolling in. I put the coins in my piggy bank that was in the shape of the Ethiopian Commercial Bank. I don't remember how long this initiative lasted, but it was one of the most lucrative ones—I was able to build a wooden cabin with two rooms. I heard later that this cabin was rented out when we left the country.

This initiative was also the foundation of a sort of council that we had among the children. We would meet and sit together under a tree or in some corner in the garden and talk about the life around us. We talked about what we saw and what happened. In time, the complaints started coming in about grownups who were beating some of us. Nowadays we might have referred to our conversations as a brainstorming session, but back then we did not know. We just sat there talking about various approaches to implement revenge for maximum effect but also in a way that we would not get caught or get into more trouble. Because if they found out that those incidents were coming from us, then we would be in serious trouble with Almazesha.

Onions in the stew

Some of the revenge operations were very damaging. For example, Mama Berhane, one of the oldest cooks at Laïbet, used to give all of us regular *kurkums*[21] or *kuntitchas*[22] of the utmost caliber. In terms of the *kuntitchas*, she would first get a good hold of the skin right under our arms, about an inch before the armpit, where the skin is soft. Then, to deliver the *kuntitcha* she would twist the skin so tight that we would rise up on the tips of our toes with excruciating pain. It would not last long, but was very painful for the time it lasted. We didn't cry about it, though. We were too stubborn to cry and held our tears back. When she released us, we would just bounce back and go our way as if we didn't even care, shrugging like it didn't even hurt—even though at times our tears would just be on the verge of flowing out. She would be our first target for the retaliation. We decided we ought to do something to get proper revenge.

It took a lot of conversation to figure out what to do. Then one day, the best occasion presented itself—it was a God-send, we thought. We heard that in a few days, Almazesha would be hosting a dinner and that most of her uncles and other important people would be attending. Within days, the entire compound went into festive preparation mode: a lot of supplies were purchased and more cooks came in to help. I didn't know what the occasion was, but looking at the

---

[21] Making a fist and knocking that fist on someone else's head. To make a *kurkum* worse, the knuckles of the middle finger protrude for added spike.

[22] Pinching someone.

number of sheep and chicken brought in, I knew it would be a big event. The chickens were brought in for the famous Doro Wot (a spicy chicken stew prepared for special occasions).

This would be a good day for retaliation. We all had devilish grins of anticipation and satisfaction, knowing that very soon we would all be avenged for all the *Kuntitchas* that we had been subjected to.

The preparations were many, as they often were for important dinners. On the day of the dinner, the table inside the dining room was repositioned into a buffet format. More tables were added in order to make enough space to display the wide variety of dishes. We watched as some of the younger ladies of Laïbet dressed the long line of tables with special tablecloths and pinned a skirt around the tables to make them look uniform and attired for the event. Then the tables were decorated with flowers, fruits, and candles running down the length of the buffet. Almazesha finally came in to check the setting of the buffet and left instructions about which dish to put where on the buffet. Others were busy shining the silverware, glasses, and plates. Others were busy wrapping up the silverware in cloth napkins and piling it on the buffet in a pyramid shape. All glasses were shined one by one and lined up on a rolling bar. Drinks were brought from the storage where they were kept. A special meat rack was brought in for hanging and carving *Tire Siga* (Raw Beef) filets for the guests. Others were dusting and cleaning the chairs and sofas, and making sure that the living room area was re-set to handle the number of expected guests.

The height of the preparation was just a few hours before the guests arrived; at this time, the final touches are done, the stews are almost ready and expected to taste perfect, all the glasses are lined up, and there is a clash between the silence of the anticipation of the guests and the noise of the commotion of the last-minute preparation. About an hour before the guests arrived, Almazesha dismissed everyone who was expected to help so that they could have time to eat, drink, take a small break, and change into nice clothes. She always insisted that those who serve must eat before the festivities started. She didn't rest, however—she would walk around making sure that all was done, all was ready, and everyone was okay and well.

Finally, the courtyard started filling up with cars of all sorts, as the guests arrived one by one. Some drove themselves, others had drivers, some brought their children, and others just had their spouses. This was still in the days before the revolution, and many of Almazesha's uncles and relatives whom we lost during the revolution were alive and well. Almazesha loved to entertain, and as each guest came in, she greeted them with warmth. Entertaining was her way of sharing what she had and bringing people together.

Once all the guests had arrived and were well into their conversations with drinks and small snacks, Almazesha gave a sign for the dishes to be served. The table started filling up with various dishes served in special bowls and platters. Many women were running up and down the compound to bring the dishes from the lower kitchen to the upper kitchen, and then have the food served and brought to the table. When the table was finally full of a broad range of dishes, Almazesha came around the buffet to check whether it was all in order. She did that all the time— she would come and inspect things and make sure everything was proper. While she checked on the table, the guests were invited to wash their hands. In Ethiopia, we always wash our hands before we eat, because Ethiopian food is eaten by hand. When the guests are older or are guests of honor, someone comes with a brass bowl, an elegant brass pitcher full of warm water, and a towel hanging on their forearm to allow the guest to wash their hands right where they are sitting. By the time Almazesha finished checking on the food, most people had had a chance to finish washing their hands. Then she called her guests to the buffet. As they took up their plates, she insisted on serving them.

We, the usual suspects, were standing not too far away that day, just outside the back veranda at a place that allowed us to peek in. Our retaliation was about to take place. We had done everything right, and now all we had to do was to wait and see. Our hearts pounded in anticipation. As Almazesha plunged the serving spoon into the Doro Wot, everything went into slow motion in my head. She pulled out the spoon, but instead of coming up with the expected piece of chicken, the spoon came out loaded with raw onions. I can still see the expression of horror on Almazesha's face. I don't think any of the guests saw what happened because she plunged the spoon back in, calling on one of the helpers from the kitchen to remove the dish from the table. She continued serving everyone. Later on, she called Mama Berhane and said to her, "*Berhane, min alkush enate. Bilesh bilesh shinkurt eskene nebsu makreb jemersh?* [Berhane, what have I done to you, now you start putting raw onions in the stew?]." She said it all in a very gentle way. Almazesha never shouted. She never said anything that would diminish someone. Mama Berhane was shocked because she had not put the onions in the stew—we did. On that day, as children we felt such a sense of victory. But when I think of it today, I feel so bad about it. Thank God Mama Berhane just shook it off and went on with her work. We never told anyone what we did.

For me this was a great moment because now I had proven to the others that I could follow through on my promises. It gave me a lot more "street credit" in the compound, and the subsequent revenge incidents I orchestrated became a lot more daring. Money kept on coming in. Once in a while, the others would get caught trying to get 25 cents somewhere. If they were caught stealing, there was no getting out of being disciplined with the stick. But throughout the entire time we kept our operation completely underground.

Balambaras and the broken Berchuma

Balambaras[23] Demissie was Almazesha's uncle on her mother's side. He was a big, broad-shouldered man who always walked around wearing boots and suited up with his grey coat, his umbrella, and his hat. His hat was one of those beige hard hats often seen on colonials; he liked his hat very much. His umbrella never left his side, and the coat never really changed.

Each time Balambaras came to visit Almazesha, we had to go and greet him. His way of enforcing greetings was special. For one, we had to kiss his knee, not his cheeks. In fact, he was doing us a favor because the true greeting would have been to kiss his shoes out of recognition and respect for his status as an elder in the community. Kissing his knee would not have been so bad, if it weren't for the fact that he

---

[23] Balambaras is a nobility title.

would hold us by the skin under our chin and pull us down in a way that would guide us to both knees, one at a time. I hated it when he did that because not only did it hurt to have him pinch the skin under my chin, but each time I landed on his knees I would inadvertently crush the tip of my nose. My only solace now was that I knew that one day, he too would not escape from our silent retaliation. I just waited for the right time to see revenge happen.

One day, we saw Balambaras coming down from the main gate toward the house. He did not know that Almazesha was out. We knew she was not around, which quickly made me realize that this would have to be the day of our retaliation. As he got closer to the house, some of the ladies responsible for hosting guests started running up and down and creating some commotion to summon him to come into the living room and relax until Almazesha returned. He insisted on staying on the veranda, so we volunteered to bring him a *berchuma* [three-legged traditional wooden stool]. He even blessed us for it, but we were not intending to give him a proper one. There was one old *berchuma* that only had two good legs; the third leg was about to break off. We chose to bring that one and offered it to him. He did not notice the damaged third leg, but thanked us again and proceeded to sit. We stepped back and once more watched from afar with grins on our faces from the pleasure of witnessing our revenge. When he sat on the *berchuma*, everything seemed to go in slow motion: him trying to sit, us watching, him losing his balance, the *berchuma* failing, him rolling on his back, others running to help, his hat flying off, his umbrella falling to the side... A lot of people rushed to his aid, but we just stood there, pretending to help but not really raising a hand. We didn't need anyone to associate the incident with us. We knew who had done what, and that was enough for us.

I don't remember whether Balambaras continued to pinch us and force us to kiss his knee. It didn't really matter what he did, because we had managed to retaliate. Not to mention that my street credit kept on soaring, and the vengeance programs evolved to greater heights.

The scarf in the toilet

One of the meanest nannies we had was Letay; she was from Tigrae and had absolutely no tolerance for children. I wonder why she even bothered to be a nanny, but my mother hired her for some reason. Within days of her joining our home, she started showing her true colors. The lady was so mean we were in shock. She had a tendency to distribute *kurkums* for no reason at all. And if she had a reason to hit us, then she would dispense a mega-*kurkum*, with the middle finger's knuckles protruding, knocking our heads with this protruding knuckle right on the crown of the skull.

I did not have the usual smooth Ethiopian hair; instead, my hair was very nappy. In fact, I was often teased by everyone around that my hair might sometimes require police intervention[24] to be brought into order. One day I had just had my hair plated in cornrows in the Apollo style (inspired by the Apollo rocket) where the hair would be braided in the

---

[24] In Amharic *metasr* means both "to be tied" and also "to be arrested," so when people said that my hair needed police intervention, it was based on this dual meaning and implied that the hair was unruly and needed forceful intervention.

direction from the edge of the hairline up to the crown of the head and form a bun on top (the bun is subject to the person having enough hair to make a bun. In my case, there wasn't any hair, so the little tails of the braids just stood there like an abstract scuplture). That day, my hair was plaited so tightly that it changed the shape of my eyes to almost look Asian. I had not complained at all during the braiding, even though it hurt as the braider parted my hair and tried to get every single hair into the cornrow. After my hair was done, I went on the stairs at the back of our house. I had my little pots and pans. I made a mud stew.

As I played quietly, stirring this wonderful mud stew, Letay came from nowhere. She was wearing a brand new dress. It seemed that she was ready to go on an afternoon break. She stood over me and started shouting at me. I didn't respond. Then she shouted some more, and when I did not react she planted a mega-*kurkum* right on my head that was already so sore from the tight cornrows. It was the first time in my life I saw red from an anger that emerged from very deep inside me. I felt my head literally splitting in two and making some kind of hollow sound. All colors, all senses, all emotions got brighter. My anger was beyond what my little body could handle, and in a swift movement I looked up to her and defiantly threw my mud stew on her shiny new dress. I can still see her face, staring at me in shock and then looking down at her dress. I got up and jetted to Almazesha's before Letay had any time to think of her next move. I ran as fast as my legs could go. Once at Almazesha's, I just caught my breath in one swallow and sat there with Almazesha as if nothing happened. "Why are you out of breath?" Almazesha asked. I didn't reply; I just smiled and leaned on her. "What have you done?

Who's chasing you now?" she asked as she chuckled.

Almazesha knew that I would always get in trouble, but the beauty of it is that she always offered me refuge, no matter what. To this day, when I think of a refuge, she is the only one I can think of. That's why I am so heartbroken to know that she is no longer part of this physical world. I feel lonely without her.

Anyway, soon I jumped out of Almazesha's room and went looking for the gang. I wanted to sit with them and agree on a revenge operation against Letay. It was not easy to formulate vengeance against her because we did not know much about her. She kept to herself, and we were also slightly scared of her. But to me, it was important that retribution be done. After much thinking, we found a weak point: her favorite yellow scarf. The decision was made that this scarf would be the object of our retaliation. So, a few days later we found the scarf hanging on the clothesline. We sent Kassu, the tallest among us, to grab the scarf while the rest stood guard and covered for him. Once the scarf was in our hands, we went to the outhouse (the toilet used by the help in the house) and dropped the scarf in the hole. You could see the yellow color pumping its light out of this deep hole. The beauty of the reprisal was that the scarf was so deep, no one could reach it, yet it was close enough that anyone could see it.

Sure enough, within thirty minutes Letay came in looking for her scarf. All we did was to start to sing. We made up a song to answer her search, and it basically said: "Go look in the outhouse." As we hummed our song, we gently made it back out of our compound and ran to Almazesha. We reached Laïbet, and after a few minutes we could hear Letay's scream when she saw the yellow of the scarf deep in that dark hole. Poor Letay left our home days later. I think she felt she couldn't deal with us. We were pleased by her departure, and I was delighted that I had managed to set the score right.

Our adventures and determination to continue to stand for justice (according to our definition of justice) did not stop when we all entered school. In fact, it continued throughout time. With the advent of school, I think we got even better at planning our revenge operations.

The first time Kassu went to school, he had to attend the *kes temari bet* [priest school] right on top of the street from Laïbet—I could hear them reciting the alphabet. I would sit there and wait for him to return. I only went to school about a year after Kassu, to Peter Pan Kindergarten, and that would be a whole new level of adventure.

Life 101

Dealing with rejection: First day of school
In my first few days of kindergarten, I had my first experience ever of not being included. It felt very odd to be rejected, when I had always been an integral part of life at Laïbet. But I did not allow that to bother me.

Until that day, I had spent my days mainly in the compound of my grandparents' house. Until that day, as the first grandchild and the only baby around, I can say that I had more attention than I could handle. I just remember playing and playing and playing with everyone. Then, I was told I would go to school and I was prepared for it. My uncles and aunts taught me how to write my name, and taught me the alphabet. I was very proud to know all this and to be able to count.

On the first day of school I must have been escorted by no less than eight uncles, aunts, cousins, etc. Some of my uncles and aunts took me to my classroom while the others waited in the car. I didn't cry as most children do when their families leave them at school on the first day. I had no fear; I had been prepared in so many ways. Some of my aunts had taught me to write my name, others to count, and others to recite the alphabet. I wanted to go to school and was very excited about the whole idea of being in school. I was enthusiastic to see all the other children. During break time, I rushed out to play with the children. But, sadly, each little group that I went to play with told me, in one way or another, that they did not want to play with me and I should go away. One group of little girls told me that I could not play with them because I did not have pigtails (hair parted in two and tied with a ribbon). Well, I did not have pigtails because I did not have much hair—I had proper nappy hair with a hairline that was far, far, very far back.

I remember clearly a moment of choice: I knew I could either spend the rest of my days running after the other children to get them to play with me, or I could have my own way and play on own. I chose the latter. Soon, I had a flock of invisible friends with whom I played. I think the conviction with which I played struck the others. Eventually, a few days later, they came asking if they could play with "us" (me and my invisible friends). I told them they could, and that was the end of the story.

I had such a strong background at home that the school community did not mean much to me. School was just a place I spent time, and real life was always waiting for me at Laïbet. Each time the car drove back into the compound, it was like entering a magic kingdom. The strength of community and the sense of belonging I had with Laïbet, with Almazesha and Ababi and everyone else, gave me the power to deflect pressure from other kids.

This ability to repel external pressure that tried to affect me continued long after kindergarten. I just never really cared for belonging to groups or cliques. Of course, such a stance has often contributed to making me a social anomaly, but I enjoy the independence. I like to see this as a quality and a gift that I received from the loving upbringing I had. But in fact, it was a lot more than the upbringing—it also had to do with how we were groomed. When I say "we," I refer to all the children of Laïbet who grew up under Almazesha's tutelage. Weakness was not accepted. She taught us to be courageous and daring. She taught us to go our way and follow our convictions even if everyone else was heading in a different direction. Almazesha taught us to negotiate for what we want, and if need be, put up a proper fight for it.

The fighting part was always a bit difficult for me because I don't really like confrontations. I try to avoid fighting as much as possible; because I am not at ease with fighting, I think it's messy. But should there be no other way out, should all the negotiations fail, and should my patience run out, it is usually a pretty bad sign for my counterpart. In that circumstance, it's like I am not me anymore and I have both boldness and strength (I have no idea from where); by the time the fight is over, the other person is usually in bad shape. I have had about 3-4 physical fights in my entire life, and each time, after the fight when I regained my senses, I have been shocked at what happened. It is the anger that fuels my strength, so if I am not angry, I can't really fight at all. The best is just to avoid crossing paths with whoever I was fighting.

Later on in primary school, at the Lycée Français Gebre Mariam, I realized that there was a certain way to gain street credit in the schoolyard. One either had to have an older sibling or one had to be known for being tough. I did not have an older sibling, so the only option I had was to show that I was tough. In the same kind of strategic thinking that we had applied for the security/vengeance schemes in Laïbet, I was convinced that the best way to prove I was tough was to find the biggest kid in class, pick a fight with him, and kick his ass like there was no tomorrow. This was one of my first fights ever. In theory, the plan was brilliant. I knew that if I could manage to pull that off, I would ensure complete respect. The challenge was to actually implement the plan—I am far from being the fighting type.

One day, I took my courage with both hands and I just stared hard at the biggest boy in our class who was known to be a ruthless fighter. His name was Tilahun. Keep in mind that we were only about 6-7 years old, but it all seemed too real at the time.

I stared at him and made the "I cut your throat" sign by sliding my index finger very, very slowly across my throat while I was squinching my eyes to add muscle to my threat. Once the throat cutting was done, I then proceeded to show this boy four fingers (indicating 4:00pm, the time school let out). As he looked at me both with surprise and disbelief, because I was usually among the quietest students in class, I made sure he got my message. I made a fist with my left hand and then hit that fist into my other hand, to really make him understand that today, I was going to smash him. At this point he flipped and replied to my menace by squinting his eyes as well and nodding his head up and down very slowly, as if to tell me that I had just signed my death warrant.

I can't really say that I launched this duel consciously—it all just happened automatically, as if my body was making the motions and I was just following my body. I remember how the other children looked at me. I was known to be rather shy and quiet, so this behavior came as a complete surprise to everyone. For the rest of the afternoon, I just kept staring at the big clock on top of the blackboard. I was almost hypnotized by the ticking of the seconds hand. The closer the time got to 4:00pm, the faster my heart rate and the more my mind swirled to elaborate on this theory of mine to kick this big guy's ass. Maybe this wasn't such a great plan after all I thought, but it was too late to retreat. I had to muster whatever courage I had and get the strength to at least throw in a few honorable punches. I imagined the scene over and over in my mind. Yes, I thought, I could certainly kick his ass—I just have to make sure to get a head start. From there on, I would just emulate the boys around Laïbet and that should work out fine in making me a proper fighter.

Then, when the bell rang at four, it all went into slow motion. I played my part, even though inside I knew that this fight might mean the end of my life. I walked straight, without looking back, with a certain fatality in my steps. I had never had a physical fight in my life, ever. But like with everything in my life to this very day, moderation was not a word in my vocabulary, so instead of learning to fight a little at a time, I went straight on to this big guy. Maybe I saw my life passing before my eyes. I thought of Fofi. I had not told her that I was going to engage in this fight. I was worried that she might find me all bloodied, maybe even dead.

As I went down the steps to reach the courtyard, a flock of children were following me and another flock was following Tilahun. His face was scratched up from all the fights he had had, and he walked right up to me as he drew up the snot from his one nostril as if he had a vacuum cleaner tucked up in his nose. He threw his school bag in one movement that showed how casual he was about it. Me, I didn't throw my bag, I just moved very slowly with sure and definite steps to the wall and dropped my bag there, and then came back to the circle with just as much confidence. The circle formed around us, and before I knew it I was now face to face with this boy I had threatened. Why in the world did I threaten Tilahun for no apparent reason, other than my own hidden agenda of kicking his ass just to establish myself as a tough girl? It was too late now. There was no going back.

I saw him roll up his sleeves, so I did the same. I saw him move in a circular motion, so I did the same, and as he made a fist and headed to me, I said, "Stop. Rule number one: no pulling hair." That took the breath out of the entire circle of children. The same motions started again, and again I said, "Stop. Rule number two: no spitting." We spent the next ten minutes or so spent going in circles with me stalling the event each time to announce yet another rule.

Finally, the supervisor saw the commotion and headed toward us. Fights were forbidden on school grounds, so even better than kicking someone's ass would be to get some kind of school reprimand for fighting—that would make it all very official and would ensure that I got my street credit for life.

The supervisor was a kind man, so he did not give us any kind of reprimand. He just scolded us and told us to break it up. I stood there trying to look disappointed in a way that might be more common in Western movies. As I left the circle and headed to get my bag, I turned halfway and blurted out all the insults I had ever heard, ending it with "you lucky bastard," and walked out. I did not know what all the insults meant. I just repeated them as I had heard them when fights broke out outside Laïbet on the little path that leads up to the bakery.

This was it. I had initiated the fight. It almost took place and we almost got school reprimands, so I had done my job. Now I was safe from school bullies, plus my sisters would not be bothered by anyone, as they would have an older sister with serious street credit.

It was much later in my life that I actually learned how to handle conflict and then how to be good at conflict resolution. I stopped avoiding confrontations and instead I can say that I started welcoming confrontations, because with every confrontation we get a chance to bring a solution, to check ourselves and our stand while at the same time continuing to let go of the fear of confrontation.

More changes happening: Rejection at home
Just as I had learned to deal with the rejection in

kindergarten, one day I was surprised to find all of Laïbet in our house. Everyone was bustling around my parents' room and there were many hushed conversations taking place. As I entered the bedroom, one of the older Aunties, Etiye Tirfe, said to me: "We don't need *you* anymore—we have a brand new baby." Etiye Tirfe had been among the first members of Laïbet, coming with Almazesha when she left her parents home to set up her new life as a married woman, and so she had been a part of my mother's life (and that of my aunts and uncles). Etiye Tirfe seemed thrilled to see my puzzled face. It was her way of teasing me, but her news came to me like a shattering moment. As I looked at her again, all I could see was her smile, with lips that were curling in because she had lost most of her teeth and the few she still had were randomly spread about.

I looked up to my mother, and sure enough there was a crib next to her. No one had told me that there was a baby coming! It all just happened overnight in my book. I went to look at the baby, and as I peered in two things happened at once: I heard my mother's voice forbidding me to get close because I had not washed up yet, and at the same time, the baby, cooing and wriggling in the little crib, stuck its tongue out at me. I declared war instantly on this intruder.

For a few years, I tried in vain to get rid of the baby, the intruder who had come into my life and disrupted it in such a way. (Thank God, I never succeeded in my plans. Now, this one-time baby enemy is my soulmate and best friend, Fofi.) Once, when she was about three or four years old, I told her that in fact there was a great secret that the adults had not yet told her but that I had found out, a secret about the magic powers we may have, one of which is that we can fly. "Go ahead and get up on the windowsill. You will see how you can just jump and fly up to the sky," I said to her. Fofi, as most younger sisters, always believed me and treated me as if I had all the knowledge in the world. But on this day, when she heard the great secret that we could actually fly, she seemed so excited and happy. "Let me try off of the bed first," she said and stood up on the bed in preparation to jump off and fly. "Give a good push and just aim for the ceiling," I said to her. And with my encouragement, she jumped—and of course fell hard on the wooden floor. It made a lot of noise. She didn't cry. She just got up and said, "Maybe I am not yet ready for these powers." She seemed disappointed, but then with a smile she said to me, "Good thing I didn't jump out the window!" She was right. We were upstairs, and had she jumped, she might have seriously injured herself or possibly even lost her life.

In any case, at that moment after kindergarten, I was still staring at this baby the way warring opponents might gaze at each other. I marched out of the bedroom, out of my parents' house, and straight to Laïbet. I did not say anything, and continued my life there as if nothing had happened at home. In the process, I ended up expanding my territory in Laïbet, and by the time the baby was old enough to play with me and the other children, it was implied that access to Laïbet and the children's community there would be with my blessings only.

When I think of it now, I realize that at this time in my life, I deepened my relationship with Almazesha. It was already a very tight relationship, but now I found in her the maternal attention I was missing at home. At home, I moved from being just a child to being the "first child," a role as opposed to a state of being. I assumed my role as the first child in our home, while in Laïbet I maintained my identity as an individual and as the child of my grandmother. It was almost like having parallel lives. There was a part of me in our home, another part of me that was in school, and most of who I was remained in Laïbet in relationship with Ababi and Almazesha.

It's funny how such splits happen in one's life. And it's even more interesting to me how much I didn't really realize these early life events and their effect on me until Almazesha passed on. With her passing I suddenly realized that a part of me had gone with her, or maybe a part of her remained with me. I don't know which, but I do know for sure that my life changed significantly after she left. I had to re-confirm to myself my identity, to revisit the past with a slow-moving magnifying glass in order to re-understand the dynamics and re-establish what I considered to be my truth.

After Fofi's birth, things accelerated in my life. Suddenly (to me), school had become more serious— there was homework. Obligations emerged, such as combing my hair, getting it done, having to be disciplined with time, and respecting the schedules for bathing, meals, and sleeping. All of this encroached on the freedom I had had. I just did not like it.

Enaniye hired an older woman to come and braid our hair each week. As God would have it, my hair is especially tightly coiled and it became an issue. The woman who came to braid my hair was rather large. She would sit on a large stool and then have me come and sit facing in various directions for her to get all the hair divided, braided, and sorted. The worst was when she would make the "Apollo" style, where all the hair is braided up and set into a bun on top of the head. Well, each time she tried to braid the back of my head, she would have me sit facing her, with my small shoulders between her knees and my head kind of crammed on her lower tummy. It was hot in there, and I could not breathe. Each time I moved, she would just press my head down and keep me under. By the time she would finish braiding, I would be sweating from the heat, short of breath from lack of air, and filled with tears from the pulling on my hair. It was torture.

Fofi, on the other hand, had beautiful hair and never went through such ordeals. Once they took us to the hairdresser to get proper hairdos for a function we were to attend—I think it was for my aunt Koky's wedding. I remember that women would comment, comparing Fofi and me as they passed by. We were sitting on big salon chairs, suspended there with white nylon full-body aprons tied around our necks. The women would come and ask if we were from the same mother and same father. Then, when they heard we were true sisters they would "tsk tsk" away, feeling sorry for me. "Oh, this one really got the short end of the stick," they would say, referring to my hair. "But, she is lucky to be light, at least she can make out on that," another one would comment. "But the little one is as pretty as Mariam (referring to St. Mary)," they would add. Neither Fofi nor I said anything. We just sat there, taking in all the comments.

It was not easy. To make matters even more complicated, I had a hard time in school. We attended the Lycée Gebre Mariam primary school. I did not like the school nor did I appreciate the teachers. I just didn't really care too much for the whole environment.

Enaniye hired a tutor for me. He was an Italian/Ethiopian University student. All I remember is that Enaniye made it so that all the tutoring would happen in Laïbet, in the main dining room. She also bought a whip and gave it to him, telling him that if I did not work well, he would have her permission to use it on me. Of course, now I know for sure that she was kidding. But at that time, I believed it was true, and it only added to my terror and alienation from her. I became more and more distant from home and focused my entire life in Laïbet. I think I might even have just shut down the part of me that was meant to be Enaniye's child.

By now, my sister Noela was born and she was a very peaceful baby. Abaye also came into our lives at about this time. She first joined our family to care for my sister Lily when she was born; later on, when we left the country for Belgium, Abaye came along with us and my parents officially adopted her; she has always been an older sister to us. There were also many more children born in Laïbet: some were relatives, others were children of the people living and working in Laïbet, and others were just children from the neighborhood.

As the number of children increased, Kassu's and my power within that territory increased. We were inseparable, and commanded that compound with rules and regulations we invented each day and subjected other children to. I would jump up and run to Laïbet any time I had the chance. I did not want to study and only wanted to play. This did not agree with Enaniye, and our relationship became that of cat and mouse revolving around the homework issue.

Once I came home with a report card with straight Ds. I received a warning that if I did not improve in the coming month, I would not be advanced to the next grade. I was heavily chastised by Enaniye, and then when she was through, I ran to Laïbet to sit in the Tachbet with all the old cooks and children and bring forth my problems. "A, B, C, D," said one of the old cooks called "Boloke" (it means beans, and she got the nickname because she was very light-skinned and worked on Almazesha's bean farm. Others teased her, saying that she looked like the white beans she was farming—hence her nickname). Boloke counted with her thumb, doing the counting as her thumb touched each finger on her hand, starting with the pinky finger. In Ethiopa, we often count with the thumb. For each finger the thumb touched and counted, she said the letters of the alphabet (*yeferengi fidel*, or the foreigners' alphabet) which she sang out as best she could "Aaae, eBeee, eeeeC, eeeDeee." Finally, as she said "eeeeDeee" with her thumb resting on her index finger, she said to me with a smile: "Mimi, that means you are fourth among all your classmates—that's pretty good!" Well, that cheered me up for while.

But eventually, I had to go back home to our own house. I dragged my feet, but once I was home, Enaniye asked if I had done my homework. And of course I had not Done it—I hadn't even looked at it. So she said to my nanny that I could go ahead and change into my pajamas and she would come beat me later after she finished bathing. I waited for what seemed a century for her to come out of her bath and give me the beating I was promised. I did not cry or complain when she hit me. I was as stubborn as mule. It didn't even hurt, in fact. But in my heart, I felt very humiliated and shamed. I decided that I would never go back to this home nor to her; even if I lived there physically, I would never be there again.

Sadly for my relationship with my mother, even though I was about 6 years old, I stuck to my decision to detach myself from her. I never looked back—until now, some forty years later, after the loss of Almazesha, when I was put in a position to reconsider my life, my relationships, the meaning of family, and how I will continue to exist without Almazesha.

As I reflect now, I know that Enaniye was not a mean mother by any means. She was very hard working and she was trying to make sure that my sisters and I did not slip up in our education. When I look back now, I realize that she was just in her early twenties at this time; it might have needed a mature woman full of patience and wisdom to deal with my energy and approach to life. In Ethiopia, also, it is often said that if your first child is properly disciplined, all the others will follow. Children are like sheep they say: the one at the head is the one who will set the example for all, so make sure you have that one on a tight rein. So it is common that the eldest child gets a really hard time, and I think this is what was happening with me.

Another side of me emerged at this time—a side that was strong and did not care much about getting attention at home, a side that decided to float above all of it and create my own world.

Meeting the Devil
Around this time, I made a breakthrough in my little "business" at Laïbet. One day, I was going to Kassu's room in the *Tachbet* area, and as I walked through the

dark room that preceded his room, sliding my hand across the wall, something just bit me! I looked more closely and found that it was an open electrical outlet. Instead of reporting it right away, I instantly thought that this would be a great chance to make more money. I called in all the children and told them that I met the Devil. All their eyes bugged out, bewildered. "Yes, I have met him, and you can too!" I stated, like a good politician running for office. There was reticence among them—they were confused, scared, not sure what in the world I was talking about. But there was also peer pressure to agree to meet the Devil. "It's 25 cents per handshake," I announced. "I don't know how long he is staying, but if you want to meet him, go and get the money." All the children scrambled, running out in every direction. Some had some coins stashed away; others went to pickpocket their mom's purse or just ask for the money. In any case, within a short time I had a queue of Laïbet's children going down the hall in front of Kassu's room.

"Line up, line up, line up" I shouted. "You will be allowed to go in one by one," I continued to shout. Then, I told them that they had to sweep the wall as they walked in the dark room, and that at one point, the Devil would grab their hand to shake it. I know they were afraid. I kept a straight face. I made them pay first, and as the first one entered, all the others leaned out of the line to look, hear, run, or whatever had to be done. As soon as the first child got the electric shock, he screamed with such agony and despair, it made all the children also scream out of fear. I told them to be quiet because if we disturbed the Devil, he would leave. And so, in a state of terror they each handed me their coins, drenched in sweat, as their turns came and they walked in to get their handshake from the Devil. I made a lot of money that day. Combined with what I had already saved up, it amounted to almost 100 Ethiopian dollars (at that time, 1 US dollar was worth 2 Ethiopian dollars, so it was quite some money).

No one ever spoke of this day. I saved all the money and eventually built a small two-bedroom cabin that I used as a playhouse. Later on, after we left the country, this little cabin was rented out for someone to live in.

Abrupt ending: The revolution

I had just turned nine when my family left Ethiopia. We left because of the communist revolution that overthrew Emperor Haile Selassie. As the revolution unfolded, and this took about 2-3 months, although I was not old enough to understand fully what was going on, I remember feeling that something was wrong in the neighborhood and among the different families who visited us at Laïbet. Almazesha was also different—she was not laughing with us as she used to. I was too young to really understand why things had gone wrong. There are three things I remember vividly, though, just before the revolution—the fireworks for what would be the Emperor's last birthday, going to Harar, and the signs of change in the general atmosphere of our lives.

The year the revolution happened, there were fireworks one night in August, still during the rainy season. We had been out of school for two or three months, and were all at Laïbet that night. We could not see the fireworks; we just heard the loud thumping noise they made. My uncle Solomon was there with me, and I remember watching the sky in vain, hoping to see some of the fireworks with him from the back veranda of Laïbet, the one that is just outside the kitchen and facing the garden. "Today is Janehoy's[25] birthday," he said to me. "Do you know how old he is?" I didn't answer verbally, but nodded my head right and left to say I didn't know how old the Emperor was. I was listening to intently to my uncle. My Uncle Solomon then told me, "He is eighty-three." I was fascinated. I wondered if he would get 83 candles. It was all very exciting. Solomon said that since the Emperor was over 80, he had the right to have fireworks for his birthday. My birthday was coming up, and in the back of my mind I was wondering what it would be like to have fireworks. "That would set the whole neighborhood in ecstasy," I thought, "at least I can have lot of firecrackers, because I doubt I will get fireworks."

In September, school opened, and the next thing I remember is that the kind of messages and news on the radio changed. The voices on the radio changed, and the way that my father would listen to the radio changed. My father would pick us from school at lunchtime every day to have lunch at home. The sun was really hot, cracking hot, so we were usually tired. By the time we went home after the morning, had our lunch and were driven back to school for the afternoon, we were just as tired. As we drove home, up Churchill Avenue, around and up the hill next to the Mezegaja Bet [Addis Ababa Municipality building], a certain very strange music came on the radio—each time this music came on, my father

---

[25] "Janehoy" is also a way of referring to the Emperor Haile Selassie; other Ethiopian names for Haile Selassie include Janhoy, Talaqu Meri, and Abba Tekel (http://en.wikipedia.org/wiki/Haile_Selassie_I).

would sit up straight, grip his steering wheel, and lean toward the radio to really listen to the news read by a most monotonous and ghostly voice. The announcer would start listing the names of people who had been arrested that morning, as we drove around the circle with Menelik, passed Saint George's church, and drove up on Mesfin Harar road to our house. Unlike before, we now hardly spoke in the car. Boubiye was lost in his thoughts, and the voice of the man on the radio was taking up too much space in the car.

As soon as we reached the house, my father—usually a calm person—was a little bit more hectic, and I could see the stress in him. He was not very talkative with us children, and we just went in the house. The first thing that he did was to turn on the radio, one of those huge ones used in the 1960s or 1950s. It was almost as big as a table, and it literally was a piece of furniture. So he played with the buttons to tune it to continue listening to the news, and I could hear along with him that it was an announcement that the Emperor had been put under arrest.

I saw the face of my father completely change, in a way I had never seen. That's when I started to get worried. Soon after, we heard that many things happened. We couldn't go out anymore after a certain time. This new thing was called *Se-at Elafi* (curfew), and the whole neighborhood would go quiet early on. At times we would hear gunshots, and we would be told to stay on the ground. Many nights we had to sleep on the ground because of heavy shooting going on. It all changed overnight. Many years later, a morbid joke emerged of two soldiers patrolling the streets at curfew, and about 20 minutes before curfew time, they see a young man walking home. Then one soldier takes aim and shoots the young man. The other soldier, in shock, asks: "What is your problem? It's not yet curfew!" And the other responds, "I know this guy—he lives very far. He'll never make it on time."

There were many roadblocks on the streets, and masses of people would demonstrate, shouting "land to the people, land to the people, land to the farmers" and "down with the imperialist, down with the bourgeois, down with the capitalist." This went on and on, day in and day out. "Down with the capitalist and long life to the people." I was not very sure if we were part of "the people" or not, and anytime these demonstrations were in the street while we were on the street driving, we would have to stop the car and let them pass. The people in these demonstrations looked angry to me. I sat in the car, just looking out. At times I noticed that the veins on many of their necks were just bulging out. They were shouting until they became breathless. Sometimes one or two of them would look at us sitting in the car, and the way they looked at us had nothing friendly in it. It made us cringe and curl back into the vinyl seats of our little car.

For my neighborhood and community, 1974 was a strange year. It saddled both regimes, and I think that people thought things would go back to normal and were still hopeful. When 1975 kicked in, the revolution was taking on more speed and the future was looking increasingly bleak. Students, especially from private schools (meaning the children of the so-called well-to-do families), were being shipped out to the rural areas to teach literacy to the farmers; houses were being nationalized; and business and factories were being nationalized. There were also many people detained, executed, or gone missing.

It is with this backdrop that around July that year, my father took Fofi and me to Harar, his hometown. Fofi and I were not fully aware of the political and social deterioration that was taking place. Actually, things were not looking so bad yet—a lot was happening under the surface that was not yet apparent. We were so excited to pack up and go visit our paternal grandmother, to finally visit this special place that we had heard about all our lives—this city where children grow up with abundance. They used to tell us that in Harar, fruits like mangos, papayas, oranges, pomegranate, and peaches were falling all over the place. People from Harar used to say that when a child fell because she slipped on a mango or papaya, all they had to do was pick up another papaya to rub the scab and make it better. Of course it was all fantasy, but we took pride in this fantasy because we associated with the identity. We felt strongly about Harar just because Boubiye was from there. In fact, later on in my life, I talked about Harar so much that during a meeting a colleague asked me: "By the way, when did you leave our beloved Harar?" I had no answer, because the only time I was there was when I was 8 years old, and only for about a week. So I just smiled and told him, "It's a long story—we'll talk later." Thankfully, he never brought the subject up again.

This was the first time that Fofi and I took an airplane flight. We were very proud. We flew from Addis Ababa to Dire Dawa, and then took a car from Dire Dawa to Harar. Boubiye had organized the car, and we waited for it at the Ras Hotel, sitting outside in the garden. Fofi was very happy. She was playing and singing at the same time. She sang the "Que sera sera" song of Nat King Cole. Boubiye was sitting with some men and talking. We didn't know if the men were family or people that he worked with. Eventually the car came, and we started our journey to Harar, driving along the winding road in the high mountain range to reach my paternal Grandmother's place. We called her Emama; her full name was Beshewamel Metaferia.

The road seemed endless. I don't remember how long it took us to drive; it must not have been more than a couple of hours, but to us it seemed like a lifetime. Fofi and I had never been in a car for such a long time. As the car drove around an escarpment, the driver was commenting to Boubiye that this was the place where most accidents happened, especially with the passenger buses that carried people going to the Kidus Gabriel pilgrimage. We just listened and looked down the cliff, and hoped that we didn't overturn to the bottom of it.

It was pouring rain. We left the main road and drove onto a side road that was not paved and was a bit rocky. The driver followed Boubiye's directions and stopped in front of a whitish gate made of corrugated iron sheet. Someone peeked out of the gate that was barely cracked open. Then, once he realized it was us, the man went back inside and opened the gate for us with difficulty. He had to open the gate while at the same time lifting the doors slightly to dislodge them from the grooves on the ground. We drove in. The compound was on a slope, so we drove down a bit until we reached the veranda.

As we finally arrived at Emama's house, she was waiting for us with Mimi, who back then must have been 4 or 5. Mimi is the daughter of our Aunt Lishan, Boubiye's youngest sibling and only sister. On the veranda, Mimi Lishane (as we called her to distinguish her from me, who was also called Mimi, and many other Mimis in the family) was standing with her pullover turned over her head to guard her from the rain. She was wearing flip-flops and was just so excited to see us. Emama was standing at the entrance of the house, and she too was smiling and was happy to see us. We ran from the car to the veranda and enthusiastically kissed and greeted everyone.

Emama lived in a nice little house, with a veranda spacious enough for people to sit for coffee. The floor of the veranda was tiled with tiny white pieces of ceramic; the walls were also white and the house was mostly white. The windows had wooden frames painted in a brownish burgundy with oil paint that shined. Emma's house was different from Laïbet—it was much smaller and much more intimate. Inside, the furniture was proper but modest: a set of sofas, some coffee tables, and a TV suspended on a high table covered with a crocheted square. The dining room table was very close to the living room and had six chairs and a beautiful tablecloth with embroidered flowers. Mimi took us to our room, and meanwhile, Emama was serving a great festive meal. This was the very first time that Fofi and I had set foot outside Laïbet and traveled this far. We had never really spent the night anywhere else, so there was a lot of excitement in the air. We felt grown up. We felt exhilarated to be in Harar.

I could not believe that we had finally arrived in Harar, this Harar that I had heard so much of and that I so identified with. The country of my father. Yes, we were finally here! I felt right at home, right away.

Emama had a small cottage garden with various kinds of vegetables and also a small corn field. Past this vegetable garden, she had another little house that she rented out to a small family. We could not go out because of the rain, but we looked out the window as Mimi explained it all to us. Later on in the evening after the meal, we headed to our bedrooms to change into our pajamas ... and that is when we heard the howling of the reknowned Harar hyenas. We were startled, scared, and also excited to hear them finally.

Harar was famous for its hyenas, and in fact there was a man who made a show of the feeding of wild hyenas. Of course, hearing the howling of the hyenas, we rushed to the living room to tell Emama. Boubiye had already left because he was staying at the hotel, as Emama's house was too small for all of us to stay there. Emama laughed and promised to take us to the place where the hyenas live. She took us back to our rooms and told us the story of her mother, Emiye, who was famous for the hyena traps that she used to make in her youth. Apparently, Emiye—a tiny lady—used to be the one to rid the community of the hyenas. She knew how to make the traps and had no fear in going to the traps to check whether the caught animal was safe to release (dead), whether to leave it still in the trap until it died, or whether she would call someone to shoot it.

We went to sleep in the little bedroom. Mimi, Fofi, and I shared the same bed. It was fun! For me, it was like a great adventure. The next day, we woke up early in this new environment. It was the first time I had ever woken up not in Laïbet or in our own house. The smell around the house and the neighborhood was different. It smelled like the earth, because it had just rained and the soil was still wet. It was chilly. I could smell the burning firewood from the kitchen area and also hear the crackling of the coffee beans being roasted. Emama was up already, and she came to see us on the veranda. She told us she would take us to the market later, after we finished breakfast, which was something called *chipchipsa*—comparable to thick Indian Naan cooked with *berbere* (our paprika powder). We drank tea with lots of sugar.

We went to the market by foot. Emama would stop and greet everyone on her way. She was very popular in the neighborhood, and in the market a lot of the women knew her. Many women were veiled or wearing very colorful *Drias*, a long, loose-fitting gown made of thin and colorful fabric and worn on top of another dress or pants. The Dria is the traditional or common dress for women of the Hadere Ethnic group in Ethiopia, as well as women from Somalia, Soudan, and Djibouti. Hadere women wore a lot of jewelry, mostly gold or golden necklaces, bracelets, bangles, ankle chains, and earrings. Emama bought us bracelets and ankle chains. She spoke fluent Somali, and she would chat with the market women while we listened. She bought us Hadere shawls, and the woman who sold them to us wrapped them around us. The shawl is wrapped around the head and the body together, and then a knot is made with the two top corners of the fabric behind the head, holding the shawl on and also covering the head very well. One of the market women put nail polish on our little hands, which reminded me of the family of Haderes that lived near our very first house in Addis, before Fofi was born. They used to come by our gate regularly. When I saw them, I would run to the gate and slip my hands out, and they would put polish for me on my nails. I must have been one or maybe two years old. Now I was in Harar, and the Hadere ladies did the same—they took our hands and painted them with glittery polish.

Emama bought more fuel wood and contracted a porter to carry it to the house. Fofi, Mimi, and I walked in front of the porter, and Emama was walking all the way behind us—we felt so thrilled to be walking "alone" in town. The sense of freedom we felt was almost intoxicating. We were just jubilant. As we walked with such pride and such a sense of freedom, we encountered Boubiye and Gashe Ayalew (my father's paternal uncle) walking toward us from the other side of town. They were shocked to see us "alone." (They could not see Emama.) "*Ende, menew, men tiseralachew,*" we giggled, telling them we came out to buy wood. The look on their faces was great, and it confirmed to us that we might indeed have managed to take a small piece of freedom and independence, even just for a minute.

When we returned to the house, Emama and I walked down to the neighbors' little house past the corn field. Emama took me by the hand and introduced me to the wife of the family. The greetings were endless, as are most greetings in Ethiopia. "Emama, *dena not?* [How are you?]" "*Endet not?* [Are you well?]" "*Dena not?* [How are you?]." "*Dena, dena.* [I am well, I am well.]" "*Irso dena not?* [How about you, are you well?]" "*Dena, dena.*" "*Lejoch dena nachew?* [How are the children?]" "*Dena dena.* [They are well, they are well.]" It went on and on.[26]

---

[26] In Ethiopia, greetings can go on for several minutes with each person asking how the other is, and then the other can ask about the children, the husband or wife, the parents, the house, the job—the list can go on forever. Each time, the answer is usually, "*Dena Dena*" for "I [or

Finally, the lady of the house said to Emama, "Oh, Emama, you have a drop of water near your nose." Emama replied, "Please remove it for me, my child." As the lady stretched her hand toward Emama, Emama closed her eyes—and when the hand was close enough, she made a growling sound as if she would bite the hand off. The lady was so startled that she fell back and fell on her bed. Emama was laughing so hard at her own prank, she could hardly breathe. Her tears flowed from laughter. The lady, on the other hand, could not get up from the bed and remained there holding her heart, and she mumbled out, "Emama, *Menew, menew, menew...menew, menew?* [Why? Why? Why? Why?][27]" That was all she could mumble. We left the house and walked back to Emama's place. She still could not stop laughing.

That night, Boubiye got another driver and they took us to see the hyena man. This man would hold meat in his mouth and the hyenas would come from the woods to take the meat from his mouth. We rolled up the windows and stuck our faces to the glass to see. It was amazing. I had never seen so many hyenas in my life. In fact, I had never seen a hyena in my life, and now there were some fifteen or twenty of them roaming so close to this man. (Many years later, I heard that this same man was attacked by the hyenas, and died.)

Our time in Harar ended quickly, and before we knew it, it was time to say goodbye. We were crying and

---

they] are well." When people know each other more, the replies can then contain more explanation as to whether a person or their family is well or not and give any kind of new updates.

[27] *Menew*, which literally means "Why," here implies "Why have you done that?" or "How could you do that to me?"

little Mimi Lishane was also crying on the veranda. Boubiye took us to Harar because he already knew that we would be leaving the country, and it was his way of showing us his place of birth before we had to leave.

Even though I have never lived in Harar, I have a lot of attachment to it, probably a reflection of my attachment to my father. Even now, when I am with friends from Ethiopia, I always say that I am from Harar. One time, someone asked me where I lived in Harar. I said, "I live next to the *mesguid* (mosque) and the big market." I know that there was a *mesguid* and a big market near Emama's house, so often that suffices to claim my Harari heritage. One time, someone at a meeting asked me: "But when did you leave Harargue?" and I had to laugh and tell him that I only visited once when I was about 8-9 years old.

PART II:
THE ETHIOPIAN
REVOLUTION

In Amharic, revolution means "change"

In Amharic, the word *revolution* is *Abiot* or *Lewut*, and *Lewut* means "change." During the early years of the revolution, all we heard was that *Lewut* had come. As a child, I could not understand the kind of change they were talking about. I had no idea what was changing from what. But as the days and months passed, I started noticing the things that changed around us. We could not get wheat-flour bread anymore; it was now corn-flour bread. The bread made from wheat was labeled an "imperialistic bread," a thing of the bourgeois, or the *Ad Hari*,[28] as they were called. The corn bread did not taste good at all. It was rough and had no flavor. The prices of everything changed as well, and little by little we

---

[28] *Ad hari* refers to counter-revolutionaries or individuals who were "against the people," mainly referring to the aristocracy or previous regime's middle- and upper-class people.

started seeing lines for supplies. There was no way we could go and buy something in the supermarket. The government had rationed everything; all basic needs such as flour, oil, soap, and so on, we were to get from the *Kebeles*.[29]

Trying to understand but not knowing where to go

No one was telling us children what was going on. I wanted to understand, but had no one to ask. I could see that even the grownups did not have answers. The usually energetic compound of Laïbet became quiet, looking more and more like the kind of energy we see a few days after someone's funeral. It was a mood of undefined sadness. But now, the faces of the adults around us also took on a spirit of anxiety, like a perpetual question was tormenting their minds.

Witnessing the change from peace to fear

Little by little, fear seeped into our lives—not just our own lives per se, but the lives of the entire community. Between what we saw in the daytime, the rumors we heard, the things we experienced, and the new sounds of the night—tension started mounting. I could see that people were increasingly wearing the black of mourning that is usually worn for forty days when a close family member passes on but can be

---

[29] The *Kebele* was the smallest administrative unit established by the Derg in 1975. Although *Kebele* means "neighborhood" in Amharic, this new form of administrative organization allowed the Derg regime to reorganize the city into a new administrative grid. A *Kebele* could consist of about 500 families or about 3000-4000 individuals. Although the Derg supposedly established this new system to encourage development and land reform, *Kebeles* evolved into one of the main tools for the Ethiopian Red Terror.

worn longer to reflect the loss one feels. It seemed that there was a loss every other day because the black of mourning was becoming the norm.

Shots in the night, shots in the day

The newest thing and the more remarkable change was the sound of gun shots in the night. At times it was single shots, like shots coming from a pistol or a rifle. At other times, it was shots that ripped through the night like a drum roll—the firing of automatic shotguns and Kalashnikovs. No matter which it was, we learned quickly to dive to the floor when we heard it. Soon, we just started to sleep on the floor. Our beds were left only for sitting during the daytime.

In a way, as children, we felt the presence of our families even more during these times because the escalating gravity of the situation brought the family closer. No one went out in the evening anymore. We started all staying in one or two rooms together and not spread through the house. All conversations were quiet, and even though there was a lot of anxiety in the air, the care and love within the family was palpable.

Feeling vulnerable

For me, though I felt the presence of my family even more during these days, I also felt very vulnerable. I thought that any day my father or my mother could be taken away—or maybe it would be Almazesha or Ababi, or one of my uncles or aunts. It is difficult to explain the anxiety that I felt as a child. It was a sense of not having security anymore, of feeling that the gates of our homes no longer protected us because the people of the *Kebeles* or the soldiers of the *Abiot* (revolution) could come barging in and create havoc.

I felt there wasn't much I could do to help the situation. My biggest fear was that my father would be killed. I had such an attachment to my father that even the thought of him being in danger was enough to destabilize me.

When I saw military trucks or soldiers on the street, I could not get anything from their eyes. Their eyes were cold. I was afraid to look at them; I thought they were unpredictable, similar to wild animals. It is better to look down and avoid eye contact, I thought.

The greatest feeling of vulnerability came from not understanding everything around me. It came from not being informed or explained to. I knew inherently that things were going from bad to worse, I just did not know how, why, and until when.

At home, we could not run around as we did before between our house and Laïbet. Now we had to ask permission to go here or there. We had to be accompanied, and the spirit of bubbly fun and mischief just disappeared a little at a time.

At school, the dynamics also changed. Children who had been quiet before started emerging and commanding the playground; they were the children of the new powers of the country. Some were children of cadres in the military, and others were children of the new ministers or, as they were called, *Derg*[30] officials. I had no idea where they emerged from. Even in school, even at our age of 6-7 years old, we

---

[30] *Derg* means "committee" or "council" in Amharic, and is the name used to refer to the communist military junta who took power in Ethiopia after the overthrow of the monarchy.

compiled rumors and tried to make sense of how the dynamics were changing. I could see that some children who were all bubbly and joyful before had become became quiet and withdrawn. They were the children of those who were supposedly labeled as "*bourgeois*," "imperialist," and "*Ad Hari*"; some had already had family members detained or even executed.

I observed all this but did not become part of one or the other of the cliques. I just went on my way as I always had. I was not sure where my family stood. I figured that we must be part of the *Ad Haris* because we had two cars, we had a home, my parents spoke English and were educated abroad, and many more reasons. On the other hand, I could not believe that we would be *Ad Haris* because Almazesha was helping so many people and so many of our relatives in the countryside were farmers. I just could not imagine how anyone would say that Ababi and Almazesha were part of the *Ad Haris*. It was a time to be quiet and not say anything, and I became very quiet in school. I even became quiet at home.

The Kebele people entering our home

Once while we were playing in Laïbet, a number of people we didn't know suddenly walked into the compound. They came in with such a sense of entitlement—their eyes were all over the place, as if they were assessing or calculating the value of the house or the size of the compound. Under the new communist way, if a house was deemed "too large," they would just cut it up and give the subdivided parcels to others. Many homes were cut up this way.

For now, this group of people just walked straight up

to the entrance of the living room, the *salonbet*. They were led by a woman with a big ledger; she had eyes that were slightly crossed, and she looked mean. Her lips were thin and curled in. She did not look good in any way. She did not even take note of us standing there—there was a group of us children standing right by the big manicured bushes leading to the stairs to the living room. The woman reached for the pen tucked behind her ear and opened the big ledger. One man took out a black ink marker, and on the yellowish sunset-colored wall, the man stretched up and wrote the numbers that she was dictating to him. She was writing the same numbers in her ledger, I assume, because it seemed that she was listing the houses.

I will never forget this moment when they wrote the numbers on the houses. It felt the same as being branded with a hot iron. It was as if I could hear them loud and clear, saying, "Now we know where you are and how to find you!" Any and all sense of safety and security fled away from me.

As the first two wrote and dictated the numbers to each other, another two or three were standing next to them, watching them, watching us, and looking around all over the place. They never said hello, or goodbye, though now I think they may have told the person keeping the gate that they came to list the house.

It felt as though they came in to bend and twist our lives, to make us comply with their rules and their games—with their way. We all knew very well how much disobedience could cost, so as children we said nothing. We were very scared and stuck together as a bunch, standing very closely together as if the staying close would keep us safe.

The *Kebele* people left as fast as they came into Laïbet, still led by the woman with the curled lips with her pen back behind her ear. They walked with a defiant posture, as opposed to the culturally accepted norm of walking with slightly forward shoulders to reflect humility. I suppose humility was now a thing of the past, since the communists did not allow religion or spirituality.

A demonstration at our gate

One day, Enaniye was driving us back home from our weekly shopping at the grocery store. We loved to go to Bambis, which was owned by a Greek family.

As the car turned from the main street, Mesfin Harar Road, to the Medhaniyalem Road that led to our house, we faced a massive demonstration coming our way from the other side of the road. There were masses of young people, *temariyoch* or students in high school or university. They feared nothing and shouted their slogans very loudly and in cadence with their steps.

"*Meret Larashu,*" they shouted, "Land to the Tiller!" Or they shouted "*Enashenifalen* [we shall overcome, we shall win!]." As our car reached our gate, Enaniye started tooting the horn for Hussein (our gatekeeper at the time) to open for us, but he was nowhere to be found. I think he could not hear the honking because of the noise from the demonstration. Then Enaniye saw a friend of hers across the waves of people approaching us, and she got out of the car and called, "Suzy, Suzy!" But Suzy could not hear her. Instead, some of the student-demonstrators who had reached us started staring at us and making fun of Enaniye's voice. They started imitating her calling her friend. The situation was about to escalate when the gate finally opened. Fofi and I were in the back seat and did not say anything. I felt bad for Enaniye, but I did not know what to say to express my feelings, so I said nothing. She got back in the car and eventually we drove in, and that ended our day.

The flock of students marching was scary. There were so many of them, and they were so loud. It is ironic that as much as the students supported the revolution, working to help it take place and gain momentum, the same revolution turned against them very shortly after—during the Red Terror era, thousands of students lost their lives to random, lawless imprisonment, torture, and executions.

There is something very powerful about rebellion and about the swell of human bodies through such demonstrations. Like a flood, it cannot really be stopped or contained. If I were of age, I would have probably joined in—whether or not I was conscious of the risks. Such floods and waves of people draw more people in, inexorably—somehow, it drags you in. These youth carried pictures of the Emperor along with defamations and complete assassinations of his character. Of course, there were banners with "down with imperialism" or "down with capitalism." They all shouted. I thought they were so loud. Then in unison, they would raise their fists and shout "*Enachenifallen* [we shall overcome, we shall win!], *Enachenifallen*, *Enachenifallen!*" I had never seen this raising of fists. I did not understand intellectually what it meant, but inside I felt it must mean something completely new, something in contrast to the lives we were used to.

Among the students, there were sons and daughters of families from all social strata. There were those from the upper class who rebelled against their own families, those from the middle class who rebelled against the Emperor and his ways, and of course those from the working class who demanded new ways. The demands the students were making were not out of line: they demanded land for the farmers, work for everyone, justice and equality, and so forth. Basically, they were asking for the basics of socialism.

It is true that back then in Ethiopia, life was not always fair. There were landlords who owned immense plots and farmers had to work for them, keeping very little of the crops for their own families. Such lands were passed on from generation to generation—an outsider could buy the land if they had enough money, but there was still nothing in it for the farmer. It is also true that the aristocracy and those linked to the royal family dictated how things were done in the country; for example, when my father returned home from his studies and early career abroad, trying to start a life, it was close to impossible for him to get a proper job. Despite the fact that he had received his doctorate in law, and despite the fact that he came home after turning down a relatively high post in the United Nations, still he was not "good enough" because he was not the son of anyone within the circle of aristocracy. On the other hand, while my mother's family was one of the old families, my mother was subjected to isolation or even ridicule at times, because she came home and married a man without a name. Boubiye told me that one time, about a year or so before the revolution, he had tried to buy land to build a home for us. He went to see the land, owned by someone from the nobility, and tried to negotiate with the landowner. He tried to negotiate the price a bit, and the answer he got was beyond disrespectful: "How about a 25-cent discount?" said the man, with disdainful arrogance. Boubiye was then a young man trying to make ends meet to feed and make a home for his new little family, and this answer left a bitter taste of knowing that anyone not with the "in" crowd would be left out in the cold.

My father got this same kind of treatment in most jobs he held. Boubiye must have been in his early thirties by then, with all that comes with that age, such as eagerness to work, lack of patience, wanting to stand up for justice, lack of diplomacy, a potentially naïve perspective on what's right, and so on. He must have held several jobs from which he was asked to resign or leave because of his response to how his superiors treated him.

Once he was the General Manager for Meta Birra, a local brewery. I remember him telling me how hard it was to work there because the main competitor was Giorgis Birra, which was owned by the Emperor. Boubiye's marketing strategies worked very well and sales soared—but this meant that sales of Giorgis declined. Apparently, his board of directors also included members of the Giorgi management and some relatives of the Emperor. Whatever marketing strategy he came up with, he soon found Giorgi doing the same. Despite all this, sales were good. One day, Boubiye told me that a message was sent to Almazesha to tell her son-in-law to "watch himself"— word had reached the Emperor that some young guy that had come *Kewuchi* (from abroad) and was telling the people to buy Meta instead of Giorgis because Giorgis would have the Emperor's urine in it. Of course, Boubiye never said such things! It was just another way of forcing him out of his job.

He also worked at the Ethiopian Airlines for some time as Director of Human Resources, and it was equally hard. He noticed that preference was being given to white people sent by TWA to train local staff and then to the Indians who came along with TWA, which was helping the country set up Ethiopian Airlines. Ethiopians came last for promotions and job opportunities; in fact, even the way that some Ethiopians were treated was far outside the professional ethical norm. Again, Boubiye tried to right the wrongs, not giving due attention to the fact that one man, alone, cannot change the system. He was asked to resign.

After many such letdowns in his own country, he literally lost his dream of working and living at home. At some point, things got so bad that he decided to leave the country and find a teaching job elsewhere. I was already born and life was tough. An old friend of his advised him to go into business for himself. Boubiye did not know much about business but took the advice and opened an office in Addis Ababa with the hope of getting involved in some kind of trade. His office had a great location on the second floor of a building adjacent to the Ethiopia Hotel in the center of town, right in front of the National Bank Head Office, the National Theater, and the Ministry of Defense. Months after his office opened, some of his uncles from Harar came to visit, and looking around this empty office with its conference table, phones, and file cabinet, one of his uncles asked, "*Mamo, sheketa sheketu yet ale ... negade nejn alalkim neber?* [Mamo, where are the goods and the stuff?....Didn't you say you were a merchant?]" There was no *sheketa shekete* (goods or items for sale, often in small shops)—his uncles did not understand what, exactly, he was going to trade since they didn't see the goods.

By the time the revolution happened, Boubiye had been working on getting his business started for 3-4 years. Things had started to take shape and we were living well—we were not rich by all means, but we had what we needed. My sisters and I were in school, and once in a while Boubiye and Enaniye would go on trips abroad or take us out to the outskirts of Addis to Langano or Nazaret for a long weekend. Things were really okay.

Given my father's experiences, when I look back now, the demands the students were making were not out of line with some of the injustices. There was also a lot of abuse of domestic staff. It was not uncommon for the employers of domestics to beat, overwork, and abuse their domestics—not in all families, but it happened. There was not much difference between domestic help and slave labor; in fact, it was only in 1942 that slavery was officially abolished in Ethiopia. Housemaids or domestic personnel (male or female) were called *Ashkir*, which literally means "servant" in its absolute sense. Slaves were called *Baria*, which often also means "Black" because the slaves were often those abducted or sold from the Southern regions of Africa. To this day, some people still use this derogatory term, referring to all people of dark-colored skin as *Baria*. For years there has been an undercurrent of discrimination and unfair access to human rights subject to ethnicity and skin color.

There is one thing, however, that the marching students may not have realized—while they were fighting for justice, human rights, and social equality, those within the government had a different outlook on how things would or should unfold. It was about equalizing everything. For the new government, it was not about creating justice but rather about razing all forms of established justice to erect one dictated by the "good books" of communism. The goal was to equalize everything. It was not about alleviating poverty by distributing land or availing capital, but more about making sure that no one stood out with wealth. Everybody was to be poor and that was the righteous way. And forget about freedom of speech—the revolution would not tolerate that, of course, that was something from the imperialist past. One of the major "intolerables" for this new system was, of course, religion, and this for a country as old as both Christianity and Islam, with devout Christians and Muslim populations. The forbidding of religion would be the source of great distress.

All of this would not come until a few months later, when the new regime would start to impose itself on the people first through terror and then through forced re-education. Then, it was clear, one could choose to be with the system or not; all those who did not line up on the side of the new order were considered to be against the system. In which case, they would be executed. But for now, we were still in the early days of the People's Revolution along with all that entailed: the exhilaration of the masses for the change to come, the tension and anxiety among the establishment for not knowing how long they would last, and the stunned witnessing that many of us were reduced to.

The one thing we all knew was that change was coming and there was no stopping it—what we did not know was that this change would substantially affect the lives of every single Ethiopian.

Executions have started

One day, the news jingle changed, the little piece of music advertisement that played right before the news—it was no longer the usual news-sounding jingle but rather a very old Ethiopian war song. The voice of the man reading the news also changed. I don't know if it was the same man reading the news or not, but I could feel that the voice was completely different. Now the news was a series of announcements, as opposed to news of what was going on in the world. There was something fatalistic about it, and it spread fear in all of us.

Everything stopped when the news started. Everyone listened with undivided attention—we children, too, except that I did not understand much of what the man said because he included so many new words and was talking too fast for me to follow. I just know that at the end, he would often list the names of those who were newly detained, were executed, or were to be on trial. There was something almost Old Testament, a kind of Biblical fatalism in the voice of the man reading the news. He would make announcements of the latest *Awaj*, new law or directive. Each day, it seemed, a new *Awaj* came out. It was best to remain informed, as some of the *Awaj* concerned the curfew or some other restriction that, if violated, could cost someone time in prison or possibly life.

The man kept on reading, day in and day out, and each day, his voice was more fatalistic than the day before. It was hard to think that this man was a human being—even then, I thought he sounded like a machine. He read without a single sign of emotion. The emotions were on the other side of the radio, on the side of the *yeferedebachew*[31] listeners. These listeners were our parents, our neighbors, our friends and family, each of us. The listeners were the people of the country, those subjected to the new *Awaj* and the new ways of this People's Revolution. There was no telling who would be next, whose name would be read among the list of executed or newly arrested. There was just no telling which one of our families would next be subjected to the wrath of this "great people's revolution." Anyone was at risk, and there was no guarantee that one would remain on the good side forever. Things could turn at the whim of people from the Kebeles, or worse yet, the whim of those referred to as *Kadrey*"— members of the politburo or the higher levels of the hierarchy, men mostly but also some women. In Amharic, the emphasis on the "K" and "R" gives the word a jagged edge, in line with the jagged spirit of those who carried the name.

Often during the news, the adults listening would start weeping or crying out loud with their hands in their heads, or would start beating their chests as they recognized the names of those listed. Of course, as children we did not always know the official names of people—we just knew to call them Gashe so-and-so, or Etiye so-and-so. This made it close to impossible for me to find out who the listed people were.

I noticed something—after a while, the spark in people's eyes had disappeared. There was a certain feeling of dullness, lethargy, surrender. There was no

---

[31] Those on whom "He" (meaning God) has passed judgment or allowed to be sentenced—it means those without choice.

more energy, and it seemed that everybody had a sort of surrendered, or given up. Their faces were resigned.

One day I came to Laïbet, running breathless to talk to Almazesha. I told her that I had seen a dream, and she said, "What dream did you see?" She was always listening to my dreams, and she always took them seriously. I trusted Almazesha, and I told her, "Well, I saw my godfather being chased by people, and at the end they killed him." She was surprised, and said, "What are you talking about?" and I said, "Yes, they were chasing him till the end, and they killed him with their spears." She was upset and said, "Well, it is not possible. This is just a *Kijet,* a nightmare, and it doesn't mean anything. Let me finish my work," she added, basically telling to go play and leave her alone. I was disappointed that she didn't listen to me. I was telling her what I saw in my dreams—she always used to believe me, but now it seemed she thought very little of my dreams. So I went away pouting. I did not realize that in fact she was listening.

Almazesha's house and my godfather's house were two big compounds adjacent to each other. Walking from one compound to the other was a big, big journey for us as children, even though it was less than 50 meters away. From Laïbet, standing right outside the living room on the veranda, I could see the house of my godparents, General Deresse and Emama Ethiopia, or "Hopee" as we used to call her. I could go down the steps, run into the garden, go up to the main gate, cross the field that led to my godfather's house, and then curve to the left to find myself standing in front of their gate. I knocked on this gate with my little hands. I remember the big gate—it was always a reddish color and heavily guarded by men in military fatigues. I felt so small standing next to them; they looked so big and so unbreakable. At times, I thought they looked like cars or some sort of machines. Another set of guards peeked through their security window with its tiny opening. The guards were not mean, but they were also not kind. They just never warmed up to us. Now I think maybe they changed regularly, but I never realized that as a child—I thought it was the same old men just being unfriendly. My godfather was the head of the police, so he always had military people guarding the house.

Once the gate opened, the house could be seen on the left side, a bit far away from the gate and set back for privacy. The path sloped, and I always walked down with apprehension because they had tiny dogs that liked to chase after visitors. I was afraid to go his house because they had so many dogs in the compound and I don't like dogs very much. So, I would always plead with the guards to keep the door closed until the dogs had been put away, and then once they opened the door for me, I quickly ran to the living room. As I walked up the steps leading to the living room, I would always look down the steps—and right under steps there was a crocodile always laying in the same position. At the time I was terrorized to see this monster. I did not even question whether he was alive or not. To me, he was a monster and it was best not to look at him too long. In fact, it was a crocodile that the General had brought back from a hunting trip, dried and stuffed. But I didn't know it, so after being scared of the dogs, then I had to manage gain my courage to go over the steps even though there was a crocodile under them.

By the time I reached the living room door, I was

exhausted. Hopee would welcome me warmly. The main living room had a green, kind of earthy color. It was wall-to-wall carpet with Chinese rugs on top, very soft. There were a lot of sofas everywhere, and it was just very comfortable and plush. It was always a treat to go there because I thought my godmother was just so beautiful and she treated me with so much love every time I came. Of course it goes without saying that each time I went there, I went with Fofi. Hopee would give us cookies, and we could have soft drinks—Fanta, Coke, Mirinda, or whatever other soft drink—all we had to do was ask and it would be brought. Our visits never lasted too long. We stayed for a bit of conversation as we munched on the cookies and slurped the Mirandas down, and then we had to head back. The same ordeal awaited us as we left. First the crocodile, then the dogs, finally the military guards, and once we were out of the compound it was a home run to Almazesha.

We visited back and forth often. We knew their daughters Adelahu and Mulu-Alem, and their son Dubale, who were friends with Koky, Essayas, and Solomon. Mulu-Alem got a job at the Hilton through Enaniye who put her in touch with their Human Resources department.

Yes, it was my godfather I saw in my dream that night. I saw him being chased by armed men with spears and other sharp weapons. He was running for his life. It was happening in the rear yard of our house, back near the kitchen area, and finally they caught him and took his life. This is what I wanted to report to Almazesha, but she shooed me away.

What I had seen in my dreams was not too far from the truth. My Godfather was a cabinet minister, in charge of the police and security. A few days later, after I had told my dream to Almazesha, I learned that he had been arrested and was one of the 60+ men from the Emperor's cabinet who were executed all in one day, in a small cabin somewhere behind the building of the Organization of the African Union. Many if not all of these men must have come so many times to the OAU to attend conferences or hold meetings. Many must have had the escort and motorcade that comes along with the prestige of the positions they held. Now, in this same area, they were just plainly massacred. They say that some of the soldiers lined up as part of the execution squad tried to resist shooting these men, and that subsequently, they were executed along with them. Most of these men were in their forties, maybe fifties—they were young men in their prime. As children, we thought they were old, of course, but today I realize the gravity of this mass execution of the cabinet.

Now that I myself am in my forties, I can only imagine how tragic this was not just for the men executed, but for the whole nation. Basically, what the Derg did was to decapitate Ethiopia in one night. In one night they took the lives of the men an entire nation depended on. Why? It would have been possible to just put the men in prison and keep them there for as long as needed, but no, the Derg decided it knew how to better "serve" the nation.

There were many family members, family friends, and relatives among these 70 men who were executed. Hundreds if not thousands of people were mourning the next day for the loss of these men—in silence, of course, since overt mourning was no longer allowed. We were not allowed to mourn because, supposedly, getting rid of these men was a good thing for the revolution. If we were found mourning, it would mean that we were not with the revolution, meaning one would risk going to prison or risk one's life. So it was a silent mourning.

That was one of the most tragic days, the day we heard the entire cabinet of the Emperor had been executed with a firing squad, my godfather among them. I felt betrayed. I felt that things could have been different if Almazesha had believed me and paid attention to the dream I reported to her. Almazesha had seemed to ignore my dream, and now he was dead. Of course, it was naïve of me to believe that something could have been different, but I felt guilty—as if I had held back vital information that could have saved his life. I doubt it could have been different. There was no escaping the new regime's claws. The day we heard the news, I thought everyone around me had lost their minds. I realize today that had I been conscious of what was really happening then, I would have lost my mind too. Many years later, Boubiye told me that it was the only day in his life where he drank himself to sleep. "I drank almost an entire bottle of gin...nothing could numb the agony I felt," he said to me.

On this day, the entire country was shaken, broken, beheaded in fact. Cut the head off and do with the body as you wish—this was it, really. These men were the head of our homes, families, society, and certainly the country. What better way to take over a nation than to do away with those who are the mind and brain of the country? This is exactly what happened. In one night, over seventy men in the prime of life were brutally and savagely murdered, ironically enough, right next to the building housing the Organizations of the African Union (now, African

Union), the organization established for human rights, justice, pan-Africanism, and freedom in Africa. The Derg Regime had finally managed to decapitate the previous government and take over the land. Sadly, the worst was yet to come in the years that followed.

After the news of the execution, Fofi and I were brought to visit Hopee. As usual, we walked from Laïbet. As we arrived, however, the usual guards were no longer there. The gardener opened the gate for us, and the compound looked eerie. We looked out for the dogs, and they barked as usual, and under the protection of our nanny and the gardener, we scampered along to the main door that opens to the living room. The crocodile was still there under the stairs, inanimate but so threatening to us. Hopee opened the door for us and welcomed us warmly as she usually did.

We sat in the living room. There was a large painting of General Deresse on the wall, over the mantel, with a black shawl over the frame of the picture. The mood in the room was very sad. Despite that, Hopee invited us to drink Miranda and have some cookies. She had changed, in just a matter of days—her gorgeous face had become stricken with very deep sadness. I don't remember the conversation we had. It must have been the usual. Actually, both Fofi and I are very shy, so it must have been an exercise of pulling the words out of us. I remember we were very happy for the Miranda and the cookies.

Yet, I felt very sad for what had happened. I did not know how to express it, but it was inside of me. I knew very well that Ababa Deresse was not coming back. His death stayed with me for a long time, and I often hoped it all went quickly, as opposed to my dream where I had seen him harassed by people trying to hunt him down.

The times were challenging.

Eventually, Hopee was also arrested along with some of her children. They were in and out of prison. Almazesha was active, sending food to prison each day. We did not know who the food was going to but we just knew that it was being sent to prison for family, friends, and relatives who were detained. Almazesha had several cars, none of which were new really—they were just cars that had found their way to Laïbet. And the drivers who delivered the food, each with their very particular characters, dedicatedly took orders from Almazesha and often returned with news about the welfare of those held behind bars. Almazesha would listen with her eyes looking down and her head tilted to one side. She listened with empathy and sadness. Yet, the resilience in her was also visible through the glances she would throw once in a while when she looked up. She never surrendered. She just listened, and I know today that she worked with strategy and wisdom to be of the most help.

Everything changing, and not for the better

The general situation was very, very overwhelming—things started deteriorating, and you could hear shots in town by day or by night. My parents did not explain anything. No one said anything to us, so I would try to get information from the people we spent our days and lives with, the cooks, the gardeners, and the caretakers of either our home or Laïbet. Some of them spoke to me; others just told me not to worry and to go play. It appeared that many people were being killed and life had changed completely.

One particular situation I remember is that we used to be able to buy nine wheat rolls for 25 cents from the Shoa bakery right above Laïbet. We could smell the bread coming out of the oven and run up and get the rolls. So for about 50 cents, we could get close to 20 rolls. The rolls were warm and tasty, and it was great. We used to stuff the rolls with sugar and eat them while sipping tea (brewed the Ethiopian way with cinnamon and cardamom). After the revolution, the government decided that only 5 rolls were possible for 25 cents, and rather than "imperialist" wheat flour, they were made of corn flour, as if corn flour represented the people and farmers. The taste of the rolls was not comparable. But we had no choice; this was the way it was going to be.

Little by little, the supply at the grocery shop dwindled and declined. The Bambis grocery we visited before the revolution was nationalized and renamed *Misrak* Grocery, or "Eastern Star" grocery. But there was nothing in it—all the aisles were empty. Before, we could buy cheese, sausages, meat products, corn flakes, peanut butter, Jell-O, and all sorts of things at very reasonable prices. After the revolution, these items were considered "counter-revolutionary" products, only good for the capitalist and imperialist, so they had to disappear from the shops.

Now, one could hardly find anything. There were no canned tomatoes, or *conserva*[32] as we used to call it.

---

[32] We often called tomato paste cans *conserva*, I suppose borrowed from Italian.

The aisles had soap, and you could also find some strange marmalade in great big tin cans, or corn flour. That was it.

Nonetheless, there were always many people at the cashier. I guess they worked there because they had uniforms. But there was no work to do—there were hardly any shoppers. So, when we approached the cashier, one person took our cart, another took the items out and handed them to a third who read the price aloud to the cashier, while another started preparing the receipts with carbon copy included, and another piled the items in a box...and so forth. Finally, before leaving the shop we would have to show the receipts to someone at the door, and as he read out the list, another person would check the contents of the box, to double-check, I suppose.

I understood that you could not complain, because that might cost you being labeled as a bourgeois or imperialist—an *Adhari*. Now the "People" were in power. I learned that we were not part of that group. It felt strange to be hated. The hatred and bitterness was very visible in the eyes of those counted as the "People." If they could have, I think they would have enjoyed packing up everyone they considered imperialist and doing away with them. The only trouble was that the line demarcating the "People" was very subtle. Who in Ethiopia did not have a family member or relative among those considered imperialists? I can see now that it was a lot about betrayal; out of conviction, ignorance, or just even fear, many sided with the revolution, and to prove it they would make as many denunciations as possible.

No one could be trusted anymore. All conversations were just whispers, and even the whispers were careful whispers. The only loud voice that was to be heard was the voice of the Ethiopian National Radio news broadcaster who would come on air regularly with his piercing voice shattering the silence, listing the names of those who had been either arrested or executed that day. That voice praised the Revolution and the Chairman, Comrade Mengistu, and his cadres.

During this time, I learned about prison and about the process of taking food for incarcerated family members. I think the process might be the same for prisons all over the world, especially in Africa. There were special bowls we used just to take food to the prison. They can keep the stews, the bread, and the varieties separate, while at the same time, the whole thing is easily transported back and forth between the house and the prison. Five or six bowls could be put one on top of the other and be held by a rod that bent around it; called the *mesa ika*, this was also used by schoolchildren to take food to school. Usually we had several sets because once you bring one set to someone behind bars, you have to use another set until the first set is returned. And then, of course, we didn't just have one person detained—there were several of our family members, friends, and relatives. So as children we would just watch as Almazesha had the food prepared and ordered someone to either take a taxi or drive out to deliver it. Whoever was sent would then come back and report on how it all went. At times, the food was refused, and this meant that the person might have been executed or that they might have died. The authorities were so cruel that they did not notify families consistently, so one just never knew. The welfare of the prisoners was always a mystery.

In a community that had previously been so open and carefree, it was a time of hushed conversations. I could feel that change in what was happening around me, but there was no one to confirm what I felt. Each time I engaged in a conversation or in questions that were considered outside my league, my inquiries were gently rejected. As I write now, I am coming to realize that maybe they thought I had become a child informant, as many children had. I am not sure— maybe. Or perhaps they thought that by not answering me, they could protect me in a way from whatever might come ahead. I tried to find the explanations for myself, but I did not get very far.

I tried to put parts of conversations together and make sense out of it all, but that did not happen, mainly because many new words had entered the vocabulary, and I had no idea what they meant. People spoke of the *Abiot*, but at the time I had no clue what the *Abiot* was. They spoke of the *Abiot Feneda*, which literally translates to "change burst"—I could not comprehend. In fact it was all about the revolution coming to be and how it opened a new day for the country. They spoke of *Fendata, Adhari, Cadre, TsereAbiot*, and so on.[33] I could not make sense of it. This disturbed me—I wanted to know but no one was willing to explain.

On the television, all of the cartoons we used to watch disappeared. Instead, there was endless news and other programs where we could only see people

---

[33] *Fendata* directly translates to "explosion," but in this case the word refers to the "explosion" of the old system—to a radical change. *Adhari* means "bourgeois" or "imperialist," and *TsereAbiot* means "counter-revolutionary," but I did not learn these meanings until later.

sitting and talking endlessly. We started seeing the map of Ethiopia at the beginning of the daily evening broadcast, with a picture of a bulging single eye like the ancient Cyclopes of Greek mythology. The image was strange to me. I much preferred the familiar Great Lion of Judah that we used to see before programs started—little did I realize that the two images represented two worlds that were completely opposite.

At times, we children of Laïbet just sat together and wondered what was going to happen. One day as we sat like that in the courtyard, Mama Berhane came running at us and chasing us away from the courtyard. She was screaming, and looked upset and unsettled. "You better go away before *tebarari tiyit* [a "running bullet," i.e., a stray bullet] gets you! Go away, go inside! You might end up dead out here!" she yelled. There was shooting that day. We had heard the machine guns, but we thought we were safe at Laïbet. The whole concept of a "running bullet" was a new one on us—yet another word we did not know.

We still thought Mama Berhane was crazy because she was very old, she could hardly see, and we had never seen her running around this way. We took our conversation inside and continued exploring how we might manage to escape if the soldiers came to Laïbet to shoot everybody. For the first time, we started talking of death. Maybe we were not all conscious of what we were talking about in terms of the end death represents, but we had a sense of the pain that would be involved if shooting took place as we faced our death. What bothered me the most was not the death per se, but the pain that it might cause to be shot. I kept on racking my mind about ways to avoid it, but none of my plans seemed to hold water. There were so many questions. Who will take care of you? How about all the pain? How does one take care of oneself in such a situation? How big will the bullet hole be? As someone who was still unable to get an injection with calm, the thought of having a big bullet hole in my body terrorized me.

We dared not bring our questions to any adults. We knew that there was a lot of death around. In those days it seemed that black was the only color women and men wore, day in and day out. We knew death was around also because nobody was really dressing in the beautiful white traditional clothes with intricate embroidery anymore. No one was really laughing out loud anymore; no one was crying loudly anymore. There was a morbid kind of silence.

There was a collective pretense that everything would be okay and life would go on as normal very soon, while there was also a collective and subtle knowledge that there were worse days to come before we would see better days again. The grownups tried as hard as possible to remain normal with us children, but I could clearly feel that things were not okay. I just wished someone would explain or tell us what was going on. But that did not happen, so I remained in this space of anxiety. An anxiety that was new to me but one that has remained in my bones for the rest of my life.

Everybody was just very quiet, guarded, and almost secretive. In all of this, I did not stop going to Laïbet. Before the revolution, we could either walk to Almazesha's using the main road or someone would give us a lift. After the revolution, I felt my movement to Almazesha's was becoming restricted, so I carved out a path between the houses—a path that did not use the main road but just cut across gardens and landed me right at Laïbet. So despite the trouble in town, despite the unrest, the curfews and all, Fofi and I kept on coming to Laïbet using our special path. We would come after school, do our homework there, and go home after dinner, escorted by one of our uncles, caretaker, gardener, or nannies.

Signs of departure

One particular night we stayed longer at Laïbet. As usual we had dinner and then we started watching television. I rested my head on Almazesha's laps as I always did when I watched TV with her. She would massage my head and my skull and run her fingers through my nappy hair. As the TV went on, she would sometimes carry on conversations or answer the phone. For me, this was my place of comfort. I just gazed at the TV; I did not really watch actively. What I enjoyed the most was to be in this place of safety. If I fell asleep, someone would either carry me to Almazesha and Ababi's bed to sleep, or they would let me sleep there with her, or they would wake me up and take me back home to bed. This particular night, I was not sleeping yet but my eyes were closed. I think I must have just started to sleep but I could still hear the conversations that were going on. Then, I heard them asking one another if I was sleeping.

They were speaking in English, and at the time I didn't officially speak English. I was going to the French school and we had very little English. I had, however, picked up enough of English from my parents, aunts, uncles, and the TV programs we used to watch to understand. In fact, I understood English very well; I was just too shy to speak. I used to feel it was the language of "others," not mine. I spoke

Amharic and French officially.

When my family was now whispering in English, I felt betrayed somehow. What were they trying to hide from me? They spoke very quietly. They were discussing plans to leave the country. During this time, many families tried to flee and go abroad. It was difficult. It was very difficult to leave. It is on this particular night that I learned that we too were to leave soon. Eventually, I understood that it was "us" that were going to leave the country. I heard them speak of places I had never heard before. Two things were disturbing me. First, I felt let down that they consciously kept me out of the conversation. I was demolished by the fact that my closest family members didn't trust me anymore and had to know I was sleeping in order to talk about confidential matters. How could they even question my loyalty? Didn't they know how much I loved them and what they meant to me? Second, I felt a sudden sense of rupture of my world. I had never thought of leaving Laïbet, and now it was happening. I heard them speak of *Aropa* (Europe) but at the time I didn't know that it was Europe—I had heard of a place called Nairobi before and I was confusing Nairobi and Aropa. I wasn't sure if it was the same place or a different place, I didn't know how far we were going, and I didn't know if it was a country or a province or some other place in Ethiopia that they were talking about. I just continued to pretend to sleep.

And so on this day on the one hand, I learned that I didn't have my family's trust anymore, and on the other hand I learned that we were leaving. This incident, this night, remains in my memory as if it was yesterday. Throughout the whole process, Almazesha's hands did not stop running through my nappy hair, over my shoulders and back again to my neck, gently massaging me. Despite the growing sense of not knowing and the insecurities and anxieties that came with that, being near Almazesha always gave me a sense of security. As long as I was near her, I knew I had a refuge.

My family's behavior that night was normal, considering that the government had started recruiting children to denounce family members for counter-revolutionary acts. Many children became informants without really knowing the kind of tragic and fatal trouble they were getting their families into. Many families suffered through that; many were imprisoned and, worse yet, executed with nothing resembling a trial. Children were recruited by the local districts officials, *Kebele Astebabari*, to come and sing revolutionary songs; required to attend and learn about the revolution, in the same process they were brainwashed, one song at a time. Eventually, the local district official would pressure such indoctrinated children to become revolutionary informants and denounce members of their families, regardless of whether those family members did or did not have counter-revolutionary tendencies. At times, the process of denunciation was initiated so someone could get even and settle a score from some old grudge; other times it was just a show of power and ego from the newly appointed Kebele officials for the community members. If a person was targeted by local officials, there was rarely a chance to escape the consequences of public humiliation, imprisonment, torture, or even execution.

I suppose my family wanted me to spare me the trouble of knowing anything about the direction the family was headed in, just in case I should one day face the unfortunate situation of being pressured by local district officials. If I did not know anything, then there would be nothing to confess to the new masters of the country.

To this day I remember how I felt that night—there is something utterly shattering in being excluded from the family's circle of trust. I was just shattered. Interestingly, while all this conversation was going on, Almazesha's hands and fingers did not stop for a second, moving through my hair in a rhythmical way. The way that I lay on her lap did not change, her breathing did not change—none of that changed. She has always been my silent source of comfort, throughout my life. While I have seen life change its textures and contours, and everything is changing, something will always remain same—this is the constant she has been for me all my life.

Not long after this night, Boubiye started packing up his things. No one said anything to us about him leaving because information about family movements was shared by very few within the family, for the sake of protection. With such lack of information, we had to guess things based on what we saw going on. For me, even though Boubiye didn't explicitly tell us that he was leaving, I could see from his behavior that he was getting ready to go. No one said a word about anything, for fear that it would leak to the *Kebele*'s newly appointed officials. Selected and appointed from "the People," many of these officials fell into the ego trap of power. As "the people's representatives," some made it a point to sport their newly attained positions by harassing and terrorizing—with threats of imprisonment or execution—selected members of the community. Their eyes were on those who were educated, those who might be from the nobility, and anyone who did not look or behave like them. These targets the *Kebele* officials, duly or unduly, considered part of the "bourgeoisie," the capitalist imperialists that the government was continuously condemning through marches, radio, and TV propaganda. Often these same *Kebele* officials took their positions to pursue a personal vendetta—it was their word against whatever victim they had their eye on. Of course, their word won out, unless by some miracle someone from the new government intervened to save the person accused. Taking the life of a person seen as counter-revolutionary was a way to pledge allegiance to the party in power.

Many families tried to leave the country at all cost. We all tried to leave. Some families managed to get visas and flights and leave that way; others had to leave the country by foot or through a network of people who trafficked them out. It was very dangerous. When families left by foot or by road, if it wasn't the new government partisans who harassed them, then the farmers could be quite cruel and denounce them; or worse yet, just the environment, the weather, or the wild animals out there could make the trip close to impossible to survive. I had heard rumors of some people who left under such difficult conditions. I was always wondering if we would leave that way. I was grateful that Boubiye would be flying out as opposed to using the road. It gave me hope that I might see him again sometime in the future. I knew that he was leaving a good week or ten days before he said anything to us children, but I kept that information to myself and didn't tell anyone.

The day before Boubiye left, he called together Fofi, Noela, and me. He finally told us he was leaving and that we would see him in one month. He used to travel a lot before, for business, so we were sort of used to him going. But this time, I knew there was something different about his traveling. He would have to leave early in the morning, before dawn. He kissed Fofi, Noela, and me in the evening when we went to bed. Lily was an infant, born a few months before. I wasn't there when he said goodbye to her; she was still in the crib made of beautiful bamboo and decorated with many cushions and tiny little curtains that made her look like an elf in a nest. I think that Lily might have spent the night with Boubiye and Enanaye, as they passed their last hours before the great departure.

Just as soon as he finished talking to us, I rushed to my room and just stayed there, because I can't stand to say goodbye. I was not sure I would see him again. That night was very short—I didn't sleep much. In the very early morning before leaving to go to the airport, I remember he came to our room, where we were supposed to still be sleeping. He walked in quietly and bent down to kiss us goodbye. I was very conscious he was leaving and that this marked the moment of his departure. I kept my eyes closed as if sleeping because I couldn't bear to see him leave.

Right before he walked out the door, I opened my eyes. I wanted to hold him back or say something to make him stay. But I had nothing to say, and even so, I was too shy to say it anyway. I wanted to ask him to stay or to take us with him—not to leave us behind. None of that came out of my mouth as I tried to speak out. Instead I just said to him, "Can I have fifty cents to buy a crochet and some cleaning material for my room?" I was hoping he would ask me to explain, to make me tell him why I need a crochet and why I couldn't use the cleaning material in the kitchen.

Instead, he opened his wallet and handed me a one-dollar bill, one Ethiopian dollar. Back then, the currency had not yet changed to Birr; it was still called the Ethiopian dollar, worth about USD $0.50. A full dollar just for me was quite a lot of money. Then, without a second more, he smiled, told me to try to get some sleep, and walked out of my room. It all happened so very fast—one minute he was there, and then he was just gone. I could hear the car engine start up, the gate opening and creaking as usual, and then it was over. The gates closed again. I could hear when the two sides of the gate came crashing together and the middle rod was lowered into place, passing through the loops that kept the two sides of the gate closed and anchored to the ground.

He was gone. I felt empty, I felt vulnerable, and then I felt nothing. Complete void. The scent of his cologne lingered in our room. Not knowing was hard; for me it made me old before I aged chronologically. It made me think of things that a child should not have to worry about. I stopped all my pranks, my gangs, and my running around Laïbet. Something inside just shut down—it's hard to explain.

Eventually, life went on without him. What should happen in a month? What would we do for 30 days, for one full month? It seemed like such a long time. Soon, Enanaye put all of our belongings on sale. She sold the furniture. She sold the record player. She even sold the radio, the table-sized one Boubiye used to listen to when he got home from work—that famous radio as big as a table was now no longer with us. The audiotapes were also sold, and so were the carpets and all the glasses, the dining plates, forks, knives, spoons, etc. She also started putting aside the things we were supposed to take out of the country with us. The house looked more and more chaotic, and as the days went by, the echo in the rooms got louder and louder, because the house was getting emptier and emptier. People would come at all hours to look at our things, people we knew and others we didn't. They would all pick up one item or another. Some would stay a bit and have a drink or have a bite with Enaniye. Her friends loved her dearly; they used to call her Sally.

Eventually it was time to engage the process of getting our passports and travel documents. We had to get passport pictures, so we were taken to the hairdresser. In fact, Almazesha took us to Ato Hailu, who had a shop around Arat Kilo. The last time I had been in his shop, he had closed the curtains and made a cubicle by the place where they washed hair. He had used some funny tool on my head, and then, with a very proud voice, he said to me: "From now on, you will have gorgeous hair!" He swiveled me around and put me in front of a large hand-held mirror. To my shock, I could recognize my face, but something was missing from the picture. He looked so proud of his work that his golden tooth was flashing out the side of his lips each time he smiled at me. He looked over to Almazesha, and told her, "Emete [my lady], I have not left a single hair, and from here onwards, I know your granddaughter will have the loveliest hair." That's when it hit me—Ato Hailu had shaved my whole head. There was nothing left. To make things worse, my birthday was a few days later, and as if being bold was not bad enough, I was also missing my front teeth. It was all such a nightmare at the time.

Because of this previous experience, I was a bit apprehensive to go to him again. Each time he saw us, especially with Almazesha, he got so happy and smiled so much that all I could see was that flashing golden tooth each time he laughed. "*Dehena note, Emete* (Are you well, my lady?)" he repeated as he ushered us in. Fofi and I followed Almazesha like kittens following the mother cat. The hair washing attendant picked us up and sat us on the big chairs. Now we could see ourselves in the mirror, right above the counter full of rollers, combs, brushes, etc.

"Please make their hair, they have to take pictures," Almazesha said. "*Minew, be dehena* [Why? I hope all is well]," he replied. Almazesha had a way of turning her head away when she had to speak of something that weighs heavily on her heart. "They are on their way out," she sighed.

And then we did not talk anymore. They brought us each a bottle of Miranda and one sugar doughnut. Ato Hailu called the man who would be washing our hair, and asked us to move to the washing station. He had put cushions on the chairs so that our heads were level with the headrest. Once he had washed my hair, he rolled up the towel that was on my shoulders and wrapped it around my head, and added another fresh towel on my shoulders. He then gently asked us to move to the table where we had sat at first, so the process of rolling our hair could start. They called the rollers *bigoudine*. There was a difference between just getting your hair rolled up and dried, and using the hot curling iron (*beh isat*). They suggested rolling my hair first and then using the hot iron to straighten it. Fofi did not have to go through that as she had beautiful hair that did not need straightening.

Soon, we were sitting under the dryers with rollers all over our little heads. Fofi's head was bigger because they used bigger rollers for her much longer hair. I just looked like the old ladies that one sees in European hair salons with tiny rollers working hard to grasp the little hair I had. In the dryer, it got hot. I was getting uncomfortable, but was too shy to say anything. It was only Almazesha who realized that I was not okay, and asked one of the guys to fix the cushions for me and to reduce the heat. Once my hair was dry, it was time to go over it with a curling iron. Back then there was no electric curling iron—it was literally heated with fire. They would put lots of cotton in a device that held the curling iron, then dash some alcohol on the cotton and light it. Then they would put the curling iron on the fire and wait until it was hot enough. It was quite scary for a child. They had a way of playing with the handles of the curling iron to make it sound like tap dancing. Then, the man blew on the iron as if to cool it a bit and gripped my hair from the root, going towards the top of it while beding the curling iron to make hard-earned curls. Some smoke came out of it, but they told me not to worry—it was only due to the oil they applied to the hair earlier. It got trickier when they came close to my hairline by the ear; nine times out of ten, I ended up getting burned one way or another.

Fofi was luckier. With her long beautiful hair, it was easy to use the curling iron on her. The man working with the iron didn't feel obliged to start right at the root with her hair, because her hair was smooth. For me on the other hand, it was nothing short of gymnastics. It took a skilled hairdresser to manipulate the tool without burning me up. After a couple of hours, we were all done and finished. Our cheeks had turned red or pink from all the heat in the hair shop and all the stress of getting our hair pulled on one side and then another side. Fofi's hair dangled down her back—me, it was a bit different. They did the best they could, but my hairstyle was not far from that of James Brown's. It was like a smoothed out, slightly curled, puffy thing. For the first time, I could feel the wind on my skull. I felt very light.

Abdul Aziz was the driver that day. We got in the car and drove straight to the photo shop to take our passport pictures. We also stopped at the clinic for a load of vaccinations.

Now it was dawning on me that Boubiye was not coming back, but rather we would be leaving. Nobody really said it out loud until the very last stage. It is as if we carried on preparing for somewhat of a departure, but we remained silent—almost worried that words might jinx it. The scary part of our leaving was that we were supposed to be happy and grateful to leave, but I didn't know where we were going. My heart and soul filled with anxiety about what waited for us next and what would become of those we left behind. But again, that wasn't to be discussed; we should just be grateful to go and find a new life. I wasn't sure about this going business. It was a no win; you're damned if you go and you're damned if you stay. In a way I felt, good that we were leaving, getting a chance to leave like everybody else. On the other hand, I was feeling such discomfort from the whole idea of departure because no one told me where we were going. I didn't know.

Now there were just a few days left. Most of the items in the house had been sold or packed in the shipping container. Only minor furniture remained, or household stuff we would use until the last day and then probably give away.

They come to search our house

It happened a few days before we left. Fofi and I had shared a bedroom since she moved out of the crib next to my mother's bed. One day, in the middle of the night, the gatekeeper of our house, Hussain, banged senselessly on our windows. "Wake up! Wake up!" he shouted. "You have to open the door!" He could hardly breathe.

We did not know what time it was. Koky's husband, Yigezu, was an Air Force pilot and sometimes he would drop her off at our place before he left for a flight. So, we thought it was Koky and we rushed to open the main door. We did not want to wake up Enanaye and just walked to the living room to open the door. Once in front of the door, we tried to look a bit through the glass tiles embedded in the main door, but we couldn't see clearly because the glass was too opaque. I could sense that there were more people than if Yigezu was dropping off Koky. There were several people outside. As soon as they heard our movements, they started shouting at us, saying, "Open the door! Open the door! *Fetasha, Fetash Newu, Kefetu!* [This is a search, open up!]."

I opened the door—I didn't know whether I did right or not, but I opened the door. I was standing there with Fofi, both of us wearing nightgowns that we had just received from our uncle Daniel who sent them from London. These were little white nightgowns, very cute with pictures of the Strawberry Shortcake girl and writing that said: "Good night sweetie." We froze as we saw what we saw when we opened the door: a group of soldiers standing there with their shot gun barrels leveled right at our eyes. Panic and fear are far too understated to describe how I felt.

There were many of them. We were too stunned to count. They pushed us to the side and entered without asking. Of course, soldiers never ask when they come and search a house; now I know this, but back then it was my first time to learn this important lesson.

It was too late to close the door on them. It was too late to back up and return to our room. We just stood there, waiting to hear what they would say. For some reason as scared as I was, I didn't react in a way that showed fear. I remained there with a straight face, staring right back at them. One of the soldiers spoke out: "This is a search, step aside!" He must have been the lead soldier. They came into our house with their big feet and big boots, and all I could see was the dusty footmarks their boots left on the parquet of our living room. They came into our house, and their mere presence was violence to our peace. It was aggressive. They did not care to be invited. They didn't need to have a warrant. The mere fact that they were in service of the revolution gave them every right to do as they saw fit, especially with people who could potentially be part of those called *Ad-Hari*.

They turned things inside and out. They looked everywhere. Then, from the living room into which they had entered, they walked into the hallway that led to the bedrooms. I ran in front of them and knocked on my mother's door. When I think about it now, I realize how horrific it was for me to walk to my mother's room with four or five soldiers following me. I thank God that at the time, the soldiers were disciplined and very proper to their duties; so many things could have happened in a house without a father. It was just Enanaye and myself and my sisters in the house, other than the helpers like Hussain the gatekeeper—all girls, all women, and no one to protect us. The worst could have happened. But all things remained proper at least in the sense that the soldiers did not abuse their power on us for anything else other than searching the house.

The soldiers spread out a bit through the rooms and continued the search. Unfortunately, my parents' bedroom had wall-to-wall carpet that had just been installed a few months ago, a beautiful, deep burgundy color. This carpet and its color did not go over well with the soldiers that day: They said something to my mother, that these colors were Imperialist and that should she have anything to declare that might be considered counter-revolutionary, she had best say it now. They threatened her, telling her that if they found something that she did not declare, it might cost her dearly. Enanaye told them that we had no guns and our only protector was *"Menfes Kidus* [the Holy Spirit]." They hardly listened to her answer, and resumed searching the house, turning it inside out and upside down.

While the soldiers were searching, Hussein was just standing there like he was frozen in time. He was so panicked that he moved like a zombie. He tried to help them search, but it was very odd, so he just continued to stand there.

The soldiers went through every single room, even searching the bathroom at the end of the hall. The last room they searched was the room where we kept all our suitcases, at the end of the hallway. No one really slept in that room except for the occasional relative visiting from the countryside. Often played in that room, as it was mostly used for storage.

There were piles of suitcases on top of the cupboards, and in those suitcases we kept many household things that we didn't always need, such as Christmas or Easter decorations or party decoration material.

As soon as they entered the room, they seemed to get excited, like they had finally found a room where for sure there would be something to incriminate my mother. "*Ante, Ante, Na!* [You, you—come here!]" they shouted to Hussein. He came forward into the room, shaking more than ever. They ordered him to go up to the cupboard and bring all the suitcases down, and then to open them up. He did as they ordered, but he was shaking a lot. In fact, these were old suitcases that still had a leather strap to close them or some kind of silverfish buckle. As he pulled the suitcases from the top shelf, standing on a stool and stretching as best he could to get a good grip on at least one suitcase, he must have pulled on the wrong thing because the entire pile of suitcases fell on him. To his demise, some of the cases opened up as they hit his head and unfortunately or fortunately for him it was the Christmas decorations. So now in the midst of a search, in these wee hours of the day, up on a stool with a suitcase half falling on him, Hussein stood there with Christmas decorations hanging from his head down to his feet. I remember that even as children we thought the situation was sadly comical, but no one dared to laugh. Nobody laughed because we were just so stressed out—we were even more worried that the soldiers would get upset and that it might lead to something else. Hussein was equally stressed and hectically plucked off the decorations hanging on him and came down from the stool.

The soldiers kept on searching, but they didn't find anything because we didn't have anything. They headed out the back door of the house, toward the service quarters. There was a big staircase leading to a backyard. As we all stood looking down the stairs, waiting to hear from them which way they wanted to proceed, their eyes fell on one room that was built under the house. This room was like a basement with an entrance to it from the backyard. It looked a bit conspicuous because there were steps going down, leading to a small door that looked as if it was guarding some hidden treasure in a mysterious room under the house. Of course, they asked where that door led, and Enanaye told them it was where we kept our grains and other supplies for the house, like a root cellar. They said they wanted to see the room. As we rushed down the steps to open the door for them, in mid-stride we realized that the person who had the keys to that door was not there with us. The keys were with the person in charge of cooking, and that day she was not there. As Enanaye explained that we didn't have the key, the soldiers became agitated.

They were getting very agitated and were certain that this was the place where we might keep any ammunition we had. To try to help Enanaye and to create a distraction, I told them that until we found the key, I could take them to my grandmother's home. They were not planning to search my grandmother's home. I don't know why I said what I did, because it could have been a very dangerous situation. Instead of them going around on the main road, I took them through the path we had built for ourselves and the other children. It was a tiny passage that went between the houses and reached Almazesha's in 2-3 minutes. I was almost very proud to take them to Laïbet, because I felt it was my kingdom, my country, and the place where I knew each and every part of the compound like the back of my hand. Somehow, I think I wanted to show these soldiers what Laïbet was all about. It was very naïve of me. I had no idea what I was doing and Enanaye could not stop the situation as I had already engaged these men to follow me. Even though I was only about 8-9 years old at the time, they listened to what I said and decided to follow me.

It could have been dangerous, because Almazesha had a lot more going on than we did in our little house. She was the daughter of warriors and a warrior in her own right, so she had no qualms about having her own set of arms to protect her family and be ready for the worst. As I led the group of soldiers through this little passage, Enanaye must have called Almazesha to warn her that I was on my way followed by a group of soldiers. Almazesha had five minutes to prepare for their arrival.

The first thing they did was go through my grandparents' bedroom. At that time Koki had just delivered Timmy, who must have been just a few days old or a couple of weeks at most. Koki had been sleeping in Almazesha and Ababi's room since the delivery because Yigezu was traveling so much. It was very early in the morning, just before dawn at most, and most people in Laïbet were still asleep. But because of the call, Almazesha and Ababi had time to get up and get dressed. By the time I arrived with the soldiers behind me, both Ababi and Almazesha were calmly sitting in their room waiting for our arrival. Once inside the bedroom, the search continued. They searched all the closets and cupboards; they even looked in little corners of the room. Finally, almost disappointed that there was nothing to be found, they continued their search in the various warehouses Almazesha had built in the house and also searched throughout the house.

For sure there were arms in Laïbet, but I don't know how Almazesha managed to allow the search and at the same time be sure that the soldiers would not run into the items we were not supposed to have. I later learned that she had a small pistol in her bedroom, and when the soldiers came she just tucked it under the baby, so they never found it.

This was the beginning of the revolution, the first few years, so I suppose the soldiers hadn't yet gotten as vicious about their searches as they would later on. This may be the reason why they didn't lift the baby up or anything; they just left the room as fast as they had entered and continued the search throughout the rest of the compound. If weapons had been found in the house, it could have cost Almazesha or Ababi or both—time in prison for sure and possibly it could have cost them their lives. Thank God nothing was found and the search episode ended without complications. It left us shaken up. For days we did not speak about it; we all just kept quiet.

The search of both homes ended, and they did not find anything. They left as easily as they came. But after they left, something changed in Laïbet. Something changed in our lives and in the way we carried on living—everything came to a standstill. We felt violated. It is strange when people come to search your home. There is a sense of vulnerability that words cannot explain, something in being subjected to someone's caprice or whim at your family's expense. Everything just sort of stopped, became still. In just a few days, we were preparing to leave the country. We had to leave and go to some other place to set up a new home and hopefully make a life until the situation back home returned to peace and stability.

We are leaving tomorrow

At last the day came when we said, "Tomorrow we go." It was a very long night. The flow of family and friends coming to say goodbye was endless. Almazesha kept dishes carefully prepared at Laïbet and sent them to our house with a steady flow in sync with the arriving friends and family. Everyone tried to be casual about our departure, despite the uncertainties we all faced. Inside our hearts, we each knew that this might be the time we left never to come back again, never to see our loved ones again, never to live this way again.

The inside of our house was eerie. With all the furniture sold or shipped for our next home, voices were louder—it felt the same as when a funeral took place. People sat on an assortment of chairs brought from Laïbet, stood around in the hallways, or just sat on mattresses laid on the floor. Whoever arrived late would be spending the night with us, as the new government had established a curfew.

The conversations that night were a bit strange, at least with us children. People made fun of us and said that where we were going there would be no food like we have in Ethiopia: It would all be burgers and pasta. Isn't it ironic to say there would be no proper food when we were going to Europe, because there would be no *injera* (Ethiopian staple food/bread).

None of us slept well that night, if at all. There was too much going on. We got dressed very early in the morning, and lots of people came to say goodbye again. We were almost shiny from being so properly washed up and lotioned-up until we shined even in the absence of the sun. We got dressed up, properly booted and suited. The getting ready process was done so fast that our bodies were not really fully awake—I remember sitting around a little table soon after being dressed, still drowsy with sleep, doing my best to stay seated and behave. A huge plate of breakfast was brought, with the usual fried eggs and a bit of *Firfir* and *Kinche*. Many people were running up and down in the morning rush, but many were around us, feeding us with *Gursha*'s.[34] We just ate, the three of us, Fofi, Noela, and me (Lily was a baby so she was not with us). They were feeding us like there was never going to be food again for many days to come. I couldn't eat anymore, but they insisted—the usual argument with adults and children when it comes to the topic of food. No matter how much they pleaded with us, it was not possible to accommodate any more *gursha*'s. We had no appetite given the circumstances, and also it was so early in the morning.

On any other day that many people came to our house, there was some function like a wedding, a funeral, or some kind of celebration. This time there was no wedding or funeral; it was more of a send-off with an uncertain return. People were standing around the entire compound. It was cold, dark. The last time I woke up so early was for Koki's wedding where Fofi, Noela, and I had been bridesmaids; other than that, I had never been awake at that time. I had

---

[34] *Gursha* refers to the bite of food given by another. In Ethiopia we eat by hand, and traditionally meals are shared among family or friends. At times, an older person, a caretaker or close friends make a bite of food and feed the one next to them, to show love, friendship, and care.

never seen such a dark night. The fog had not yet lifted, and it was all very hazy.

A lot of people were crying and I was not very sure how to handle it. Because they were crying I thought, "Well, it seems we are never coming back." I wanted to cry as well, but I was afraid to cry because I was afraid that if I started crying that I might never stop. So I resisted crying until the last minute before we got into the cars to leave the compound and go to the airport.

My tears began flowing when I saw those with whom I spent my days, standing there wearing their *gaby*'s or *netlas* (an Ethiopian throw). What got me was the look in the eyes that words can never say. It's the intuitive messages that pass among us in spirit that unleash the tears.

Of course, the departure was to be from Laïbet. Some people walked to Laïbet, and others got rides in this or that car. Once we reached Laïbet, the number of people in the compound was far more than at our house. I remember the tension that day. I could hardly breathe. Standing in front of us and all around the house were the caretakers, the uncles and aunts, the neighborhood friends, and just about everyone I had spent and lived my life with so far—and now, I had to say good-bye. It is a very hard process to say goodbye without knowing when you will come back again. For the first time in my life, I thought of the possibility that I might not see some of them again, and maybe I might not see any of them at all. Noela did not really go around to say goodbye, at least I don't remember her; I think she was just sitting in the car with Lily and Abaye waiting to leave. Fofi and I tried to say goodbye, but by the time we reached the third or fourth person, we couldn't hold it anymore and broke down in tears just like everyone else. Everything from then on is like a nebulous dream. I just remember the kisses smacked on our cheeks. The worst farewell was to those standing on the veranda. People were mumbling blessings as they kissed us: *Yzger yitebikish* (May God be with you), *Mariam tiketelachew* (May the Virgin Mary protect and keep you), *YeIsrael amlak Ayelaychew* (may the God of Israel never leave you), and so on. It seemed endless.

Koki was standing on the veranda; she had left the baby Timmy inside Almazesha's and Ababi's bedroom. Both my uncles, Solomon (aka K) and Pastor Daniel, were standing there too. Pastor Daniel was standing with Tsehay, his first wife and Deborah and Kidist's Mom. She was always so nice to us. She stood there with a great big bandage because just days before she had fallen with a bottle in her hand and had seriously cut up her hand. She looked angelic, standing there wrapped up in a Gaby. She had plucked eyebrows that arched in a way that made her face look melancholic.

Then there was Almazesha and Ababi. Almazesha was pretending to be very casual about it. She smiled to us, joked a bit, and told us we would be back very, very soon. But I could see in her eyes that it was all a lot of talk to avoid admitting the reality in process. Ababi was also very sad. He stood there very stoic. He didn't feel like he had to say goodbye quite yet, since he would be coming to Bole along with the convoy.

The lumps in my throat were literally choking me to death. I couldn't control my hands from shaking. This was my entire life, and now, it was time to walk away.

The only comfort was that Fofi and I were still together, Essayas was to come with us as well as Abaye, and once we arrived we might see Boubiye again. The end of my life in Laïbet came too abruptly. I was afraid that I would never again come back. The level of anxiety I felt was beyond what a child could handle.

The cars left the compound in a convoy, loaded up with so many suitcases. The engines made a lot of noise and a lot of smoke as the cars started up and drove up the hill that led from Laïbet to the main road. I know well this little road that goes up the hill along the side of the Laïbet compound so that by the time the hill reaches the main road, you have passed the delimitations of Laïbet. At the time, you could just take a left onto the main road (that's not possible anymore) and drive down Mesfin Harar Road.

The last image I have of the life we left behind is everyone standing on the veranda that morning and all the people standing around in the courtyard, wrapped up in long Gabys, most holding their hands over their mouth in disbelief, looking like ghosts in the mist. All those who had raised us, all those we played pranks on, all those who pinched us or gave us the famous *Kurkums*—all were now lined up in almost the same position. They stood with their shoulders almost lifted up to their ears, hands crossed and almost with their hand over their nose and mouth as if to contain their refusal to accept the reality that our entire family was leaving. On this day, Enanaye left the country with all four of her children as well as Abaye whom she adopted and her brother Essayas. This was a tough day, especially for Almazesha who just had to stand there letting her oldest daughter and her youngest son go with all of us.

Isn't it strange that once you know you are leaving, as you drive down roads that had been the roads that you saw every day, everything takes on more detail. It all passed in slow motion for me. As I looked at the roadside, as I looked at people we passed, everything seemed to be standing still and I could only sense my body, my life, moving further away from what I had known to be my world. Everything just disappeared, passed away, and I wanted to look back from time but I didn't. I just looked forward.

When we neared Meskal Square, now renamed Abiot Square, there were a couple of roadblocks. We stopped the cars to allow the soldiers to check us and to show permits. It was very scary to me. I did not know what the soldiers wanted. I didn't know exactly how many cars we had and who was in which car. It was obvious we were leaving the country. If the permits were not in order, the soldiers could ask us to check every car and possibly even every suitcase—they could even send us home. It was not easy to go through the roadblocks. We knew that the soldiers also had lists of the names of people labeled anti-revolutionary; no one knew whose name they had. Being on the list meant one was suspect and could mean immediate arrest. The mere fact of not knowing whether our names were on such lists was a source of extreme anxiety.

If you have ever been in front of a roadblock with armed men whose intentions you are not sure of, you will understand the kind of anxiety I learned on that day. When we speak of basic rights, of human rights or justice or peace, it takes on a whole new meaning when one has experienced firsthand the lack of it. I did not know what they wanted. I only saw them armed and knew that these men might have taken the lives of many people so far. Even as a child, I knew. These were my first moments of existential fear. The feeling has never left me since—I learned a new kind of fear. I felt like my skin had been pulled off, exposing a raw vulnerability. It is so scary to look into the eyes of another human being and not find anything but darkness. The soldiers had no expression in their eyes. Just looking at them terrorized me.

The worst roadblock was yet to come, the one right by Bole Airport that had not only armed soldiers but also a line of nails on the ground. Should the car fail to stop, the nails would rip all the tires. This roadblock was harsher than the others. They checked every single thing; I think they even had us open a few suitcases. They had a way of peeking through the window and looking at you from top to bottom. It felt very odd. I felt so unwanted and almost a sense of being handed out or assigned shame. We were not part of the "people," obviously—the people's revolution was against people like us. We were now part of the unwanted. Being unwanted is a strange thing; knowing that you are unwanted and despised for who you were born to be is even more difficult to understand. The tragedy is there is nothing you can do to change who you are. We are who we are. When you are unwanted, they make you understand clearly that your life has no value. They make you understand that to them, you and scum are one and the same. They make you understand that you are just a "thing" they cannot wait to dispose of.

Finally, we arrived at the airport. Back in the day we used to go to the airport to watch the planes take off and land. We used to go the airport to receive people, get ice-cream, or as an outing. This time it was no longer an outing—we were trying to leave. It wasn't easy to leave, and everybody was just dead serious. The entire mood was very austere with adrenaline running the show.

Looking back now, I wonder how we all managed to get through those days. How did those who left manage to leave, and how did those who stayed behind manage to survive the years of brutal communist dictatorship? My mother, Enanaye, could not have been older than her late 20s when we left. She showed such courage to take the six of us with her. Essayas and Abaye may have been about 17 or 18 years old, and the rest of us were under ten years of age. I suppose she had the courage you get when there is no other way to go. We say in Ethiopia that smoke will always find a way out, as we refer to the audacity that some people engage when faced with a critical and life-threatening situation. And, as Almazesha always said, everything passes and nothing is forever.

The whole process of saying goodbye started all over again at the airport, right outside the entrance where passengers and accompanying family get separated. I remember the rest of them stayed standing outside the airport entrance in the cold, and we followed Enanaye into the terminal. All the men of our family were there wearing their dark coats, the same coats they wore for funerals and serious events. Ababi was standing there with Ababa Bistate. Many friends of Boubiye and Enaniye were also there. Yigezu was there, running up and down to help Enaniye as best as he could. Mesfine, Boubiye's youngest brother, was also there. He was with the Air Force.

There were soldiers and strange-looking security people all over. We had to be searched. The girls went into one cubicle with a woman soldier who frisked us inside and out. Her hands were rough and she was not gentle at all as she ran her hands up and down our bodies, squeezing us everywhere to the point that it was uncomfortable and embarrassing. We had to stand straight with arms and legs spread out. The usual Ethiopian gentle hospitality was nowhere to be seen, not even for us children. The one boy, Essayas, went into a cubicle with a man soldier. I guess he had the same treatment as we did. It was possible to be sent back from that point—they could find anything and make it a reason to forbid anyone from traveling. People have been known to be pulled out of the aircraft itself. So, until the aircraft left the ground, the tension was unbearable.

Once that was done, I suppose we had our boarding passes and all. I don't remember that well. Before we even realized it, we were seated on the Lufthansa plane. All I remember again is when Yigezu, Koki's husband and Timmy's Dad, came onto the plane to say goodbye to us. He had a special permission to board planes because of his affiliation with the aviation field.

We were all seated at the front of the economy cabin, and I could see him coming from the steps up into the plane. He smiled to me and I smiled back even though it was a very strained smile. He had a way of talking to me like I was a soldier myself, like I was so tough. He grabbed me by the shoulder, shook me a bit, and said: "Mim' are you ready for your new life?" continuing, "I am sure you are and we will come and visit you soon." Then he did the same with Fofi who was sitting just next to me.

The plane took off shortly after, and we were still

busy crying. I just remember that at one point, I was very conscious and realized that we were about to take off from the ground. We were now no longer on the ground of our country—we were airborne. There was a sense of relief in being airborne because now there was no way anyone could stop us from leaving the country. Fofi and I were sobbing, so deeply crying that we had hiccups. Now it was over; we were gone. Maybe one day we would come back, maybe we would not come back. I had no idea.

All I knew was that I felt ripped open. I was going into unknown territory. What made it partly so hard is that I had never lived with my parents: I only used to go home to sleep, and otherwise, I was always with Almazesha and Ababi in Laïbet. But I only had a chance to say goodbye to them like everyone else; there was no processing or acknowledging of our unique relationship. We are just so good at being strong and pretending not to be weak. Of course I loved my parents, but that intimate relationship of parent-to-child was with Almazesha, especially. I had such complicity with her that for me, leaving her was tearing my heart out of my chest. As a child there was no way for me to express it—I just had to bear with the pain of separation and make do as best I could. In fact, as I write these words, Almazesha has been gone for exactly 35 days. I write these memoirs and I not entirely certain it was not all just a dream of a life. I cannot believe that I left her then, in the 1970s, and now about three decades later, she is the one who has left me.

Everything happened very fast. From our days of running around in Laïbet to now, I look at the life we had and I can't believe how fast it all went. I can play back the memories in my mind like a slow-motion film. I suppose we know we have aged when we start reminiscing too much about days long gone, when the number of people we know is less than the number we once knew that have passed on. In times like this, you can look back at an era and wonder how it could all have passed so quickly—was it all a dream or did it really happen? Was there really a Laïbet with an Almazesha and an Ababi, or was it all in my head?

The flight attendants on Lufthansa were kind to us. I suppose they were aware that many Ethiopians were in the process of exiling themselves and leaving their home. I suppose they may have empathized with us and the way that we were just so heartbroken to leave. "Don't cry, it will be okay," said one attendant to us as she tried to caress our heads and console us, and then she gave us some juice. I don't remember having a *Ferengi* (foreigner) talk to me so directly, ever in my life, except maybe the teachers in school. I was so distracted by her that I didn't even listen to what she had to say. Little did I know then that Lufthansa would be so much a part of my life, like all the airlines I have ended up taking throughout my life. I have met people on Lufthansa who remained close and dear friends, like Pierre Pioge and Claire Noelle Jamoulle, and certainly met my husband, Matthias, on one of their flights. But this would come some twenty or thirty years later.

This was our departure from Ethiopia and the beginning of the next phase of our lives outside Ethiopia, a phase in which I learned about my country from the outside, looking inward. More than that, though, it was the beginning of a phase where I became conscious of tradition, conscious of race, conscious of ethics, and conscious of the enormity of culture. I became conscious of what it means to be part of a lineage, and put into action all that I had been taught in such subtle ways through play, stories, and witnessing how life was taking form around me. I was to become so conscious of how Almazesha had raised us.

As the plane took off, I believe I took off as the 8-9 year old that I was, but as it landed hours later in Europe, I had morphed into a little adult. This was the end of my childhood and the beginning of the rest of my life.

PART III:
LIFE IN PSEUDO-EXILE

Ferengi Ager[35]: Landing in "Aropa[36]"

As the plane landed, Fofi and I were still sighing deeply, recovering from the tears and weeping of our departure from Addis. As these deep sighs shook our little bodies, we just stared at each other. We were staring at everything that on the plane, at the people, at the cabin, at our seats—just staring randomly, looking in vain for something familiar. Thankfully, this was not our first plane ride: we had already been to on a plane when Boubiye had taken us to visit Harar. The flight to Harar was a short ride, and it was fun. We received candies, a choice of Miranda or Fanta or Coca-Cola, and even a small tuna salad sandwich. That small plane had landed in Dire

---

[35] *Ferengi* means "foreigner" but implies a white person, and *ager* means "country," so *Ferengi Ager* translates to "country of the foreigner."

[36] At the time, I did not know how to say "Europe" and thought that it was called *Aropa* as that is how it sounded to me when adults said the word.

Dawa—how great to still land within Ethiopia. Even though we were relatively far from home and Laïbet, we still had felt comfortable. Now, however, things were very different. The Lufthansa flight took perhaps ten times as long as the flight to Dire Dawa, and then to make things even worse, it did not land within Ethiopia but outside of Ethiopia. In Amharic, when we talk about going abroad, we say "going outside" or "going toward the outside"—*we de wochi mehed*. As the Lufthansa flight landed, I realized that I had reached the "outside" and it was an outside where I didn't know anybody. It was an "outside" where later I would learn that I was the "outsider."

That first time we arrived in Europe, what hit me first was the smell—it smelled completely different from what I was used to. The Luftansa flight, of course, first landed in Frankfurt and then we transferred to another flight to continue on to Brussels. But instead of flying to Brussels as intended, we had to divert to Amsterdam because a snowstorm in Brussels made it impossible for flights to land. We landed once more, this time in Amsterdam in a deserted airport late in the night. We had to take a bus all the way to the Zaventem airport in Brussels. The bus ride was endless and the smell inside the bus was too overbearing. I felt nauseous from the smell and the swinging bus motion. We reached Zaventem airport in Brussels a little past midnight. We had had a long, long journey. We had boarded the plane in Addis under a lot of stress, saying goodbye to everyone back home. There are no words to describe how very emotional our departure was. It was like being snatched away. As I sat in the bus, I was hypnotized by the highway. It made me dizzy. Everything looked so straight and so repetitive, and it all moved so fast. I don't think I had ever been in a vehicle that moved so fast and for such an extended period of time. We were quiet children. Even Lily who could hardly talk or walk was quiet. She didn't cry at all, not even once. The rest of us—Noela, Fofi, and me—didn't utter a sound. We just looked at each other and did with precision whatever Enaniye, Abaye, or Essayas asked us to do.

We had finally left Ethiopia. The sense that we had departed was slowly sinking in. Reluctantly, I was trying to imagine what our lives would be like from here on. I had nothing to for my thoughts to clasp onto, so my mind was just spinning and jumping from one thought to another. I was worried for some reason. Many things kept preoccupying me. As I reflect back now, part of the preoccupation was because I could not think or act independently anymore. We left our home as a group, and now my thoughts and actions were defined by how this group continued the journey. I didn't like to wait to get instructions on what to do next. It was not easy to become dependent on directions from someone else when all my life, until then, I had done things very independently. I had gone wherever I pleased, done whatever I wanted, and had the option of being at home or running to Laïbet. Now, there was no more Laïbet. I felt confined to this bus that was flying down the highway. I remember being so quiet that my lips sealed together, and each time I wanted to say something I had to clear my throat and unstick my lips.

My mind was wandering and back and forth, between the compound of Laïbet with all its drama, action, and life, and the thought of the unknown that was waiting for me ahead. As much as Laïbet is an institution of its own, I found myself thinking of it as my grandmother's home. Maybe this happened because I was trying to process the fact that I was separated from her. I am not sure, but I remember making that distinction. Often they referred to me as *Ye Woizero Almaz Ye Lej Lej*, "the child of the child of Woizero Almaz." That used to make me feel so very good—I was proud to be Almazesha's *Ye Lej Lej*. It was my opportunity to behave in a way that would make her proud, like I inherently knew that whatever I did under that identity reflected on her. So I always tried to surpass my limits and do things much beyond my age, all to just be able to look back at her and see her approving smile. It's strange that I only realize these things now, as I write some forty years later.

So much is clearer now as I sit and reflect on what happened; so much of what happened has so made me who I am today and has branded me with all the responsibility I feel. It has also brought on the constant the anxiety that is always lurking in the background, and paradoxically, it also shaped me to behave as we had been raised: *Gobez, Tchewa Lejoch* (brave, polite children). I also felt the need to not be afraid and move forward regardless of the fears I might feel within. I have learned to contain my fear and leave it to the side, as if I had no longer had the privilege or space to entertain being afraid. This bus ride was one such moment. I was not afraid per se, but I was very concerned about what would come next. I was worried that I would never see all of the people we left behind. But there was no one to tell this to, so I kept it inside.

We arrived in Brussels, and the airport was completely deserted because there were no planes landing at that time. It was close to midnight. There was only this bus coming from Schipol, the airport in

Amsterdam. As we disembarked from the bus, we were a big group: me and my three sisters, my uncle Essayas, Abaye, and Enaniye. Essayas helped the driver take our suitcases out of the bottom of the bus while the rest of us stood on the curb. It was freezing cold. I had never been so cold in my life. All I remember was that Fofi, Noela, Abaye with Lily in her arms, and me were just standing there with our teeth chattering and bodies as stiff as tree trunks. We could not move. We were stunned by the cold. Nothing we were wearing helped even though we had our new coats, the scarves that Etiye Kelemoi, Boubiye's cousin, had made for us, and handmade caps (which didn't really help, but it was good to have them). My fingers and feet were so cold that it burned.

Meanwhile, Essayas lined up the suitcases one after the other from the bus to a small area next to the entrance of the arrival hall. We had the most suitcases by far—at least 15. Essayas still had his afro and was wearing his white long coat with fur on the inside; he looked as jazzy as jazzy could be, like one of the African American singers of the times. We were all very well dressed, but in a fashion much different than what other people were wearing. It was almost as though we were too dressed, too proper, too much attention to everything. We looked picture-perfect, yet on the inside we were all entertaining immense turmoil, in silence.

Inside, the airport seemed even more deserted. It was still freezing cold despite the heater that hit us as we stepped through the entrance of the arrival lounge. None of us had ever been so cold, and we were all shaking. Noela was freezing more than any of us, maybe because she was so skinny: Her teeth were literally making a lot of noise. Lily had turned bright yellow from the cold. She had a little beige leather jacket with lots of fur on the inside layer and also on the collar. It was a funky jacket, but I could see that it did not help; she was just stunned by the cold. It was actually her birthday that very day. On the day of our arrival, she turned one.

Fofi and I, unlike our younger sisters, were semi-conscious of what was going. We were clearly conscious of the discomfort of traveling and the discomfort of not knowing, even if we didn't recognize it as much as the adults.

Finally, at this airport with a completely empty arrival hall, Enaniye told us to sit down on a bench. There, we waited and waited while she and Essayas collected all the suitcases from the bus. We could see Enaniye and Essayas help each other line up all the suitcases. We, the children together with Abaye, behaved and sat on the designated bench very quietly. We sat on that bench with our feet suspended in the air and our hands crossed together and resting on our little laps.

We were lined up like the sparrows that used to line up on the electric line in front of the veranda at Laïbet. I remembered that at 5 o'clock in the afternoon, every day at Laïbet, the sparrows lined up on the electric lines and Ababi came to sit on the veranda; someone came to give them grain and they all flew down to the courtyard to eat their grain and go. Now I felt that we, too, were sitting like sparrows on the bench. Our feet were certainly not touching the ground; they were just dangling down, pulled by the weight of the new, heavy, shiny leather shoes we had all received for the trip. We were seated very nicely with our backs all the way to the back of the bench and we just behaved as best we could, because that's all we could do to support my mother at that time.

As we sat there, I suddenly heard a lot of commotion outside. I heard voices with a familiar sound, and I realized Boubiye had just arrived to pick us up. Sure enough, when we looked toward the entrance of the arrival hall, we saw him coming in. I can't explain what a sense of relief I felt to see him there. As most children, I always felt a sense of security when my father was around, this sense that now that he was there, everything would be okay. I believed that Boubiye could always sort any problem and find solutions, so I was really excited to see him. We were all excited to see him. At the same time, we were overwhelmed to see him—I wanted to tell him everything that had happened back home but I couldn't. I wanted to tell him about our house being searched, about how there was a line of nails blocking the road as we drove to the airport, about how everyone showed up to say goodbye to us; I just wanted to tell him so much, but not a sound came out of my mouth.

My sisters and I were still too shy to run to him and wrap ourselves around his neck. Instead of rushing into his arms, we just remained frozen on the bench, hesitantly sitting. He is the one who came to us. He kissed us one by one, holding our little faces with both of his hands and moving our heads left to right and right to left as he kissed us over and over. He took Lily in his arms. Actually, I passed Lily to him. It was an emotional moment and baby Lily was a good distraction from the emotional tension we all felt.

So that's how it started, this pseudo-exile life of ours. Moments later, he went back outside to load suitcases into his car together with Essayas. Of course, there was the with the usual commotion—I think it must happen in most families—of people arguing with each other to lift the suitcase alone or to allow another to help. Everybody wants to carry the suitcase alone without help, and of course, everyone else wants to help. So instead of actually loading the car, we spent a substantial amount of time arguing about who should lift which suitcase and who could help whom, not to mention the whole thing of trying to make all the suitcases fit in the trunk of the car. Boubiye had come with a man called Mr. Dininger, a former colleague of Enaniye's from the Hilton hotel in Addis. He was German but he spoke Amharic fluently. For us, it was very funny to see a foreigner speak our language, and it made us giggle. Once the suitcases were loaded, we were asked to get in the car. Boubiye asked Abaye and Lily to get in the car first and the rest of us followed. We had a taxi also follow us and we drove into Brussels toward our apartment.

Everything looked new. The roads were completely deserted; of course, it was now way past midnight. Everything was white because it had just snowed heavily and that was the reason we had to land in Amsterdam. Needless to say, we had never seen snow—all we knew was the hail that used to come crushing down on our heads as we ran for shelter, the fun of the rainy season in Ethiopia. There was no school in the rainy season from June to September. When it hailed or rained hard, we would often be in Laïbet snuggled up in one room or another, sipping on tea with loads of sugar and eating fresh Gifilfil that would come covered up with a layer of Injera. It was the time for stories, the time for the collective nostalgia that the older people would contaminate us with. I guess this was their way of linking us to the past and imparting what used to be in contrast to how it is now.

This white snow made no noise. It was mute. I learned later that it is unusual for Brussels to have so much snow, but on that particularly exceptional year, it was full of snow. As the car drove through the town and I looked at the empty street, I wondered where everybody was. I could only see buildings, and all the houses were lined up in a very straight line along the road. Back home, you can see compounds and shops, and some compounds start right at the road while others are set back a bit. Oh yes, it was very different. Everything was very linear. The road seemed smooth; I couldn't see any *Korekonch* (potholes or rough road). It took about 45 minutes to get to our apartment, but back home it only took a few minutes to reach the airport.

The great adventure of life was opening a new chapter. I knew, even then, that this would be a new and completely different phase of our lives. I was not so concerned about the new life: my concern was about living without the community of Laïbet. I could not in my wildest dreams imagine having any life at all without running to Almazesha and Ababi and without running around Laïbet setting the compound ablaze.

Finally, Boubiye pointed to a building and told us this was where we were going to live. It looked like a big office building to me. It was impersonal. There was no *Zebegna* (guard or gatekeeper), no gate, no one standing outside waiting for us. I didn't know exactly what that meant. I was used to having a compound, to blowing the horn in front of the gate and having a guard open the door so the cars could drive in. But this time, we all just jumped out of the car, lined up on the sidewalk, and followed Boubiye as he walked toward the apartment's main door.

He pulled out a key from his coat and opened this big glass door. We followed him in one by one, like ducklings following the father duck. The first thing I sensed was the scent in the air—a clean but particular scent that smelled like a hospital, the only thing I could associate this new building with. The entrance hall defiantly reminded me of some of the hospitals we had back home. The floor of this apartment building was sort of marbled, and it was extremely quiet.

We followed Boubiye into this new hall toward what looked like an elevator, but I had never seen such an elevator that opened like a door. You had to go inside and close the latch so that the elevator could close, and then press a button to reach the desired floor. Boubiye pressed on the number three and said this was where we were going to live. "Don't touch the walls," he said, "it is dangerous in case you get your fingers caught."

There were two apartments when we came out on the third floor, ours on the left and the Dan family's on the right. We came out of the elevator and all huddled tightly in the dark. There was no light in the hallway until Boubiye pressed a button, and to our relief we could now see. It was the first time we entered what would be our home for the coming four decades, though at the time, we didn't know we would be around for so long—we thought the situation in our country would improve within some months, maybe a year or two maximum, and that we would be heading home shortly. Again, the scent on this floor hit me. It was different than the hallway at the main entrance; now it was more of what I would later find out was cat food. We stared at the door Boubiye was pointing to. He then pushed another button right by the door and the bell rang. We heard a loud "diiiing doonnng."

The usual commotion we were familiar with in Laïbet when someone arrived from abroad was nowhere to be found, and I found that very odd. But when the door opened, I was delighted to see my aunt Lishan, Boubiye's younger sister. She had come from London to help us settle in. She did the best she could to make us feel welcome and received us with a lot of enthusiasm. One by one we kissed her as the men went up and down the elevator bringing the suitcases to the apartment. Us children, remained in our buttoned-up coats for a while until someone realized that we still had not taken them off. In time, I learned that when you live abroad, you basically have a much smaller number of people around you. There is no such big community of people waiting for you to welcome you after a trip—sometimes no one comes to pick you up or no one waits for you at home. It's a lonely life. I missed home tremendously. I missed everybody there.

Life in our new home

We had never lived in an apartment before. In fact, the only apartment that I had been in was that of my Great Aunt Terry, Almazesha's youngest sister. She was working at the O.A.U. (Organization for African Unity), drove a sporty white Mazda with only two doors, and she lived in an apartment. Had I known the phrase "jet set" then, I would have thought of her at the time, but I did not know about it. I just thought my Great Aunt was living a great life. Her apartment was in one of the few condominium towers built during the time of the Emperor, right behind the United Nations Economic Commission for Africa (UNECA) building and not too far from the Royal Palace. Today, the top floor of that building is a restaurant; in fact, it always had a restaurant on its top floor, even during the Derg time. I am not sure, but I reckon this must have been our first and probably only sky-view restaurant in Ethiopia other than the one on the top floor of the Wabe Shebelle Hotel in Addis Ababa.

Anyway, now it was our turn to be in an apartment. Fofi, Noela, and I were still very quiet; even Lily did not budge. We did not realize the magnitude of the change in our lives—for the sake of sanity, possibly. The apartment had its own kind of scent, a smell of wood and wax because of the parquet floors. It was very foreign to us. I know I felt very confined. I often became very edgy because I could not go out and run as I used to.

For months I would just look out the window onto the small street of Rue de la Fouragere that cuts perpendicular to Avenue Brugman, the main avenue. I would stare at the corner of Fouragere and Brugman and fantasize that the *Comby* (the VW Laïbet used for delivery) would turn the corner, the door would open, and out would come all the children and grown-ups of Laïbet that we grew up with. The logistic of fitting so many people in one van never occurred to me—I just missed them so much that my only hope was that if I stared long enough out the window, they might would show up.

Almazesha would try to call us often. At first, we did not have a phone, so we would have to go to the ground floor to the apartment of the building concierge and speak to her through that phone. The concierge was a nice, kind woman who worked very hard cleaning the stairs, parking area, courtyard, and so on. She would start her work by about 5.00 AM, and by the time it was 7.30 AM she was already at the pub in front having her first of many beers and first of many cigarettes of the day. Her son, Michel, lived with her. He was a big guy, I thought. He was blond and kept his hair long. They both smoked in the apartment, so did the father. The entire place smelled of a mixture of cigarettes, cat litter, and lack of proper flow of air. When Ababi and Almazesha called us from Addis Ababa, the concierge would ring our bell from the intercom downstairs and would shout loudly: "*c'est la famille au telephone, c'est la famille!*" with a nice thick Belgian accent. We would stop everything and rush to the elevator and flood her apartment.

In retrospect, I think she must have been a very kind person to let all of us come in and speak with our families. We all came to the phone, from Boubiye all the way to Baby Lily, eight of us in total, including Abaye and Essayas. This concierge must have had a big heart to let eight people into her small living space. The son, Michel, was kind too. Each time we came he changed the TV channel and put on cartoons for us children. We were extremely shy and as we sat on their old couch, we couldn't really bring ourselves to watch the TV "*Be Mulu Ayen* [with our full eyes]" and instead peeked at it from the corners of our eyes. Even though all of us could not get on the phone, listening to the others talking gave us a bit of Laïbet. Many times, there was not much talking possible. Hearing the voices of Almazesha, Ababi, and all the others back in Addis just made us cry from the emotions of wanting to go home. For me, I could not bear to hear the voice of Almazesha. It cut me to pieces. It made me miss her exponentially more, even more vividly. I had so much to tell her, but it is as if I had a tennis ball stuck in my throat. Nothing came out. I could only answer her back with single word answers, "yes" or "no." Even these single-syllable words had a hard time leaving my throat because of the lump that almost choked me. Each time I spoke with Almazesha, the lump in my throat remained for hours after the call.

One thing bothered us, however, and that was the dog the concierge had, a white French poodle that was very hyper and jumpy. It was nothing we were comfortable with. So, each time we went to speak on the phone, she had to either lock the dog in another room or have her husband or son walk the dog until we finished our call. We grew up with dogs in Ethiopia, but they were security dogs rather than pets. In our house, there were always three to four German shepherd dogs that only Boubiye and the *Zebegna* handled. They were tied or kept in their doghouses most of the day, and let out only at night. Whenever they were let out, none of us would come out. On the weekend, Boubiye would let them loose and play with them in the garden while we stayed inside glued to the living room window watching him play.

Now, in this new country, there were dogs everywhere. The worst part was when someone came into the elevator with their dog. It was horrible. The lift was small, and there was nowhere to go. There was one lady in particular, the wife of the son of the owner of the building, who never managed her dog.

The leash was always too long. And this silly dog would run and jump—as any dog would—toward us. On a lucky day, she might pick up the dog and keep it in her arms; this gave us some relief. Otherwise, we just lived with the terror. What we found most curious was that people would treat their dogs as their children; they even kissed them and let them lick their faces. I couldn't understand; knowing where the dog snout must have been, how could they kiss that? For some reason, the concierge knew our issue with dogs. She and her family were also very conscious of our situation and went out of their way to make us comfortable during the calls from Ethiopia.

Telephone calls were always monitored on the Ethiopian side, and all international calls had to be made through an operator. The operators were, of course, government agents (*Selayi*) who listened to the conversation; one operator in particular was the one who always connected us. I know that Enaniye and Almazesha tried to befriend her and connect to her as a human being rather than the agent she was. She was more or less okay, but we were never to forget that whatever we said on the phone would be reported. So, we started inventing some kind of code to communicate, hoping that they would get the meaning on the other side. A few years later, we started sending gifts to this lady phone operator to thank her, I suppose, for doing her job and connecting us. Even the phone operators were playing with their power to connect or not connect families, to give us confidence in our conversations or spread insecurity and force us to limit our conversations to the usual *"Dena na chew? Dena, Dena. Enanete dena nachew? Dena, Dena* [Are you well? We are well, we are well. And you are you well? We are well, we are well"—*Eshi Addis Ababa, Berasles Mesmer kift new* [Okay, Addis Ababa, Brussels, the line is open]." The line is open—like taking off one's clothes in public, we carried on our conversations aware that someone else was listening. It's strange. It makes it hard to talk when you know someone else is listening; it is even worse when you know the person monitoring the call. It's just weird.

I look back now at our path and journey, and I cannot believe that my parents took the risk to take four small children and two teenagers to a country where they did not know anyone, with less than USD 10,000 in their pocket and no employment at hand. Once more the saying in Ethiopia that "Smoke and determined souls always find an egress (*Tchiss ena Korate mewutcha Ayatam*)" remains true and true.

A new school: L'Ecole du Centre

In this new apartment, we used a small, grey, square folding table about 1 meter by 1 meter or a little bigger. The chairs were also grey with black lining; there were only four chairs, and it was just right for the children to have breakfast. I suppose that the grown-ups had their meals together once we had gone. There were also only four of them, so the table worked fine, except at dinnertime when we had to revert to using the living room area and make a combination of the table and the sofas. There were small side tables in the living room, such as we had in Laïbet and in our home in Addis Ababa, little nesting tables that we could move here and there and use to put our plates or drinks next to the chair or sofa where we sat.

Anyway, the grown-ups set up that grey folding table

right in the hallway, just before the bedroom section started (*dans le hall d'entrée* as they said in Belgium). In the morning, all of us children would squeeze around this table to have some kind of breakfast. I don't remember consistency in the kind of breakfast we had; at times it was eggs, at times it was French toast, and at times, it was cereal. Basically, breakfast was whatever was available in the house. It was so different from the breakfast we used to have back home. In this new home, we were served whatever was available and it was not possible to ask for something else. Back home, we had the privilege of entertaining childish caprices, choosing whatever we wanted, and Almazesha would just order it for us. Minutes later, the chosen dish would come from Tachbet on a tray, all covered up in a colorful lacy cloth.

Back home, we had time to wake up with the sun. We could wash up and dress up, and in the meanwhile, the table would be set. When we arrived at the table, breakfast would be sitting there, gently covered with a napkin or cloth like a bride veiled before a wedding. At times we would have pancakes with real maple syrup; toward the time we were preparing to leave, we started having cereal. Enaniye told us that we had to used to it because that is all we would have when we went abroad. There were so many people around us at home, taking care of us and making sure that we ate properly. Sometimes Almazesha would send some Gifilfil or Kinche in a bowl with a lid. Just looking at the bowl, our imagination alone would make us all excited about what was inside. Sometimes the Gifilfil came covered with a fresh injera, and all the pleasure was about uncovering only bits at a time and digging in the warm Gifilfil with our little hands almost snooping around the injera cover to discover bits and pieces of meal inside.

Alas, now in Brussels, we faced a reality far from that. Now we had to get ready for school when it was still dark outside. The sun never came up in time for us to see it before we went to school. Breakfast was rushed, and forget the kind of breakfast we had back home. On top of that, now we even didn't come home for lunch anymore. In Ethiopia, we came home every day to eat at our own place or have lunch at Laïbet. The table would be full—not excessive, but full. Depending on whether it was a fasting day or not, there would be a variety of dishes like Ye Atkilt Alicha, Ye Miser Wot, Shiro, Ye Timatim Firfir, Ye Assa Wot or on a non fasting day we would have Ye Beg Wot, Tibs, at times Ye Doro Wot or Ye Doro Alicha. Those were the days! Now, lunch was a sandwich. In fact, the bread that we bought for the sandwich came from Jose Epicerie, the one down the street from our apartment. It was not fresh—it was pre-packed bread, meaning processed from a factory. Jose called it "Toast Bread" and said the words with an attempted English/American twang. We never talked back to him; we just nodded, paid, and left with the packet of bread. I did not like the taste of it, and in fact, I didn't even like the smell of it. To make matters even more complicated, Abaye and Enaniye, who prepared our lunches alternately, often made a fried egg sandwich with a bit of ketchup (the ketchup, I think, was to reflect their Love). By lunchtime, this poor sandwich was in no state to stir up an appetite. The eggs were cold, the ketchup had sort of dried out between the bread and the cracks on the eggs, and the bread was limp. I didn't eat. I just stopped eating lunch. I would only have the apple or the banana that was in my lunch box. We never said anything back home. They thought we ate, and we didn't say anything.

Around 4:00 PM when we returned home, we just were so happy to be home that we munched on anything we found and then did our homework until dinnertime. At dinner we would all sit together and have our meal, and the spirit around the dinner table was not too far from that back home in terms of eating together. We did our best not to pay attention to the hardship we were going through. Dinnertime was the only time we re-connected to our identity as a collective. No one complained and everyone tried to be of good cheer, even though we all had our own respective challenges; our daily burden of making it through the day was not to be shared with one another. I think we did not share in order not to bring down the spirits of others or add unnecessary worry for them. Each one of us tried to share uplifting stories. Subconsciously we knew that only encouraging stories and events of the day or that were anticipated in the coming days would be good for us. Essayas is very good at cheering people up. He always has a few jokes up his sleeve and always finds a way to create jokes with whatever is happening in the moment.

At school, it was arranged for us to have some beverages. For 20 Belgian Francs (about 1 US dollar) a month, we got milk every day, but again, milk is one of the things I just don't manage to drink. I think I must have overdosed on it as a child. Almazesha told me that I would drink two liters of Milk per 24 hours until I was about a year old, when on a fatal day I contracted a severe infection from unboiled milk. This infection and the month I spent recovering from it marked the end of the "Milk & Me" story. At school, the milk came in triangular tetra containers along with a straw with a sharp end. For the first few days, I just dragged my feet about drinking the milk, holding the straw to my lips to look like I was sipping it until I found a dust bin far enough from everyone to toss it out. Eventually, the teacher caught up with my trick and confronted me about it. I told him I just couldn't stand it. He was kind enough to have my ration switched to orange juice.

In the first few months after our arrival, Mr. Dininger would often visit us with his family. His wife, Angela, who was half Italian and half Eritrean, would come and cook something special to cheer us up. One day, she made lasagna. I have no idea what went into that lasagna, but almost forty years later, I still recall that it blew us away. She made the lasagna sheets from scratch; she brought her pasta machine with her. She made the sauce with ground beef, but then there was something else she added that made her lasagna out of this world. We ate the leftovers for about a week, and as the Goddess of Lasagna would have it, the older the lasagna gets, the less of it is left, the more excruciatingly delicious it tasted. We just ate the pan clean. Not even a crumb was left.

That's how our lives in *Ferengi Ager* started. We all thought that our days there would be limited to a few months or maybe a year or two, but we ended staying for decades more—it has become our home. My parents still live in Brussels and I go there several times a year, no matter where I am in the world. My two daughters were born there; Rosi and Leoni spent the first few days of their lives in the same apartment that received me and my sisters on that snowy and cold end of December back in the mid 1970s.

My time at the Ecole du Centre was not too bad. I had a good teacher, Mr. Rossels. Impeccably dressed from head to toe, he always came with some cologne like Brut. He was a chain smoker and for some reason I liked the smell of his clothes, a mixture of cologne and cigarette smoke. He was very kind with me. He took his time to explain things, to let me understand. Fofi was not so lucky—the teacher she had, Madame Black, was a serious racist and gave Fofi a hard time. So, Fofi's first year was not pleasant. For the second year, we found her another school (the Ecole du Val Fleuri) where she finally had a competent and balanced teacher, Madama Natkil. Fofi and Noela attended there, and I remained at the Ecole du Centre.

Lily eventually joined the "Petit Poucet" Pre-School and Kindergarten and would leave the house before all of us, accompanied by Abaye. Lily had a little red coat bought from Marks and Spencers in the UK. The coat had an "Empire State" cut, a tight fit on top and then bubbly from under the breast until the knees. She had her little glasses on and her little school bag and a pair of tiny gloves. With that, Lily would go to school each day very early in the morning. She was the first one to leave the house, earlier than anyone, without any complaints whatsoever. Her school started earlier than ours because it also served as a daycare center and had to be open early enough for parents to drop the children off before heading to work. Petit Poucet was about five minutes' walk from our apartment, at the junction of Avenue Brugman and the road that led to the Park du Wolvendael. Abaye walked her there and back each day.

During our second year in Brussels, Enaniye was hired

as Executive Assistant to a Director of one of the Centers for Industrial Development (CDI), an institution based in Brussels for the development of "ACP" (African, Caribbean, Pacific) countries. This new job changed our lives—now we had a regular income to sustain our family. In addition, the job also came with education allowances and even home leave. Suddenly, the prospect of returning to Laïbet for vacation changed the sense of uprooting that had sunk into every cell of my body. I felt better all of sudden—just knowing that we could go home to Laïbet gave me a great sense of relief. Her new job also meant that we could attend the French International School of Belgium. Things seemed to return to normal after all, I thought.

For Boubiye, Enaniye's new job was also a relief. He was working very hard. He had changed one of the bedrooms in the apartment into his office, and every morning without fail and with discipline, he would get dressed for work, have breakfast, and go to that room to work. For us that room was off limits. We did not want to disturb him. We could hear the Telex machine bringing in messages, the phone ringing, and the typewriter click-clacking away like a mad tap dancer. Because Boubiye worked with people all over the world, Telexes arrived at all hours of the day. Sometimes in the middle of the night, we could hear Boubiye returning to the office to check the message and reply to the Telexes or phone messages. Sometimes, we would see Boubiye emerge from his office to go to the post office or somewhere near the train station to send telegrams. He never flinched. He kept at his work with utmost discipline and determination. Despite all the stress that he must have been experiencing, to us his children, he never changed his smile. He took us out for ice cream once in a while; at times, he gave us some office supplies to play with or make drawings. We liked that a lot.

We used to sneak into the office and play on the revolving chair. Once, Lily sat on the chair and Noela started spinning her. Lily was still very small. The chair was spinning so fast that Lily ended up falling off pretty hard. We were all shocked to see that the fall made her spit blood. We picked her up and begged her not cry. We all quickly ran back to our rooms and never played with the chair again.

Before she got her job, Enaniye also had a desk in Boubiye's office from which she maintained a close watch on the family's administration, as she still does to this day. She followed up on our school fees, vaccinations, doctors' visits, shopping, meals, and so on, keeping a record of everything and of all our expenses including what we spent on groceries. I guess that allowed her and Boubiye to keep things under control. She arranged for a petty cash box, like in any office. We loved to see her open the little box and take out or put money back into it. We didn't really understand the purpose of the box; we just thought it was a treasure box or her piggy bank.

The day Enaniye heard that she was recruited, we had a small celebration at home. I remember we all sat around her and she was telling us that this job would allow us to have a normal life. It would even give us a proper resident permit. Until then, we had been staying with temporary permits that had to be renewed every quarter or so, an anxiety that brought a lot of stress. We were conscious that it was always possible we might not get renewed. What would happen in this case—do we go back home? Do we live illegally? So many questions haunted us.

The story of the permit was not a simple thing, and we lived in constant anxiety and lack of basic security. For example, Abaye's permit did not get sorted out until almost three years after our arrival. It was so difficult that eventually, Enaniye and Boubiye adopted her officially as their own daughter, she changed her last name to Tessema, Boubiye's last name, and things got easier. Before that, the police would harass us regularly, according to a routine. The policemen would ring our intercom bell from outside. We knew it was them and not anyone else because they had a way of ringing that was very persistent and invasive. The sound of the ring would be poignant, as if sending in the sound to dig us out of our hole. They would just keep their finger on the intercom and make the phone inside the apartment ring literally off the hook. We never replied to intercom. We just kept quiet. We did not know if they were going to take Abaye away or what else they would do. We were always so startled each time they rang. Sometimes they would find a way to come inside and then would ring the doorbell in front of the apartment. "*C'est la Police* [It's the police]," they would shout and again, while we remained quiet as church mice. "*C'est la Police*," they would continue to shout at the door. Sometimes we opened, and they would ask for "Abibich"—Abaye's official name is Abebech, but I suppose they did not know how to say it. With a hesitant voice we would just say: "*Elle est sorti* [she went out]," knowing very well that we had her in the furthest bedroom in the apartment (the master bedroom). And the Police would go away, leaving a convocation paper. We played this cat and mouse game for three years until finally her status became stabilized.

The privilege of citizenship can only be understood in

full through the experience of what it means to be without—I am not referring to citizenship in another country but to our human rights to citizenship. It is because this right is taken away that many of us flee our homes and try to make a home somewhere else. These "other" places are often not necessarily friendly places where we are taken for the human beings that we are, with human rights, but rather seen as immigrants who need to be dealt with. But what about our rights to live somewhere with dignity, freedom, and opportunity? When do we demand this right? Is the world ready to listen to our voices or is it still not yet time to discuss these uncomfortable issues? The story of immigration changes with the seasons and with the flavors of geopolitics: One year it's us, the Ethiopians, another it's the Rwandese or the Afgans or whoever. It doesn't really matter—what matters is that depending on what we allow to happen at the geopolitical level, families, fathers, mothers, and children get displaced and are the ones who pay the price of this displacement, not the supposed leaders (elected or otherwise). No, most of those leaders responsible for the mass exiles they cause never pay the price of exile: They remain comfortably in the kingdoms they created. They speak of freedom, democracy, and whatever else, traveling with their private jets, strutting their stuff at conferences or high level meetings. No, they never pay the price.

It is this right to citizenship I am talking about, because most of us people of the South do not have this right. We have to stay quiet when the police come along. Because we don't have this right, the police can come and dance on our heads, and when they leave we are relieved that we have survived this time around. There is no audience to take our grief to—we have to just swallow it and be grateful for the day. We have to hold on tight to the hope that maybe by tomorrow our papers will be in order, but our papers never will be. The same circuit of cat and mouse will continue. At times, some of us might break, some might cry, and others might fight back. But where should the fight be if the war is to be won? Is it a battle on the grounds of someone else's gate, asking to be letting in, or should it be back home at the gates of the homes of our forefathers asking to be let be? I think the latter, but maybe we need more time or more pain to truly get on it and make it work.

New job, new school

Enaniye's new job landed us in a new school, and we entered the French International School in September 1978. In the months before, we had been working all summer long with a tutor, so we were very ready to get started.

The French School, Le Lycée Français as it was called, was huge—massive compared to the tiny Ecole du Centre or Ecole du Val Fleuri. It could accommodate preschool (3-4 years old) until the terminal grade (13th year of high school), as well as graduate students with a Baccalaureate (18-19 years old). It must have had over 500 students, maybe more, with a fleet of buses to pick up and drop off students. The Lycée was a whole new phase of our lives, a time of evolution and integration.

Finally we were among students from all over the world, most of them children of diplomats, civil servants, and private sector families. Enaniye brought us to school on the first day. There were so many students in the courtyard that it was overwhelming. The tutor that had been working with us emerged out of the blue and came to give us some guidance on how to find our classes. I was to enter "*La Sixiéme Année*," equivalent to seventh grade. I had to go find my name on the lists of classes posted on the wall, and—thank God for a name that starts with the letter "A"—I found my name in a short time. I was to enter "*6eme B.*"

Once we found the class, we had to go find our group under the "Preau" (the open area on the ground floor of the buildings). There was another girl standing right there. She was African, and that made me happy. I felt I had found someone from my country. We introduced ourselves. She was Alice Birara, and she would be one of my closest friends for many years to come. Alice was from Rwanda. She told me that her father was the Governor of the Central Bank and that she and her siblings were sent to Belgium to study under the tutelage of Belgian guardians. They went home to Kigali every summer, but during the school year they lived independently, commuting between school and the home of their guardians. I was very excited to meet Alice. I had not spoken to anyone my age and from Africa in almost two years. She reminded me of Almazesha because she was so small and also very calm and reserved.

Within minutes, more students came to line up and shortly after that we found ourselves in the classroom. It had that new classroom smell of school supplies, like the smell of new plastic book covers, UHU glue, and ink from markers. I love that smell. I could just sit there inhaling big breaths of it and almost levitate.

I stayed at the Lycée for about five years, until 1983. A million things happened during this time. We grew up together, we evolved and learned life together, and most of all I think that most of us emerged in our characters.

Among my peers, I was more the one who studied all the time—I had close to perfect grades except in sports. Sport is always a challenge, still remains so in my life. I was not much of a sportive person, and I am still struggling to find my way to the gym and get some exercise. Any other topic or class was perfectly fine for me. My time at the Ecole du Centre had prepared me well for the Lycée. I understood the mechanics of French grammar so well that my worst grade in that topic was never below 17 or 18 out of 20, while most of my classmates were hardly breaking 10 out of 20. I knew it was important to learn the mechanics rather than memorize as the others insisted on doing. In the French system, grades come as Felicitation, Encouragement, Tableau d'Honneur, Blame, or Refus, equivalent to the grades of A, B, C, D, or F. In fact, Refus is worse that an F—it means more complete and absolute failure. Along with that the grades, we got the average scores of our tests and also our class ranking. My rank was never below third, and often I was first in my class. Most of the grades I received were Felicitations or Encouragement (except in sports, where I could hardly maintain a Tableau d'Honneur).

I was happy about my performance because I took it as my job to get good grades. It was my way of contributing to my family's life. I did my homework and also helped my sisters to study with great discipline. This was so different from my understanding of school in Addis—back in Addis, I just could not understand school. I didn't like the school or the people in it. The teachers scared me to death and each day I counted the minutes until it would be over and I could come back home. Now, in Brussels, something had clicked in my head. I knew that education was the only sure way out of hardship. Intuitively, it had clicked in my head and I gratefully took this opportunity to learn. Through learning, I hoped that one day I would be in a position to help my family and all those we had left behind in Addis.

I was not prepared to discover that the other students would eventually start to resent me because my grade distorted the curve for the class. There were only two or three other students with similar grades. Of course, I became friends with them; when I think of our bunch today, I smile at how nerdy we looked. I had my Afro and my very conservative clothes from Marks and Spencers. Enaniye liked that store so much, it was the only place we shopped. There was a Japanese student, Masako Kawamichi, who was nice to all of us. She put a lot of stress on herself to score the highest possible grades. There was also a German student, Marcus, and another French student, Eric, whose last names I forget. None of us had fashionable clothing. None of us were invited to the parties thrown every other weekend. Of course, none of us smoked or did anything outside what would be expected of a good student. But it wasn't really about good student or not—we just had no interest in the other aspects of school social life that involved skipping class, smoking, drinking occasionally, and dating.

I witnessed how much fashion was stressing the students around me, but I did not have access to it, so I didn't bother about it. I was conscious that my parents could not afford to buy us the so-called designer clothes. I knew how much they worked just to keep us alive, fed, and in school. Given our circumstances, fashion was the least of my concerns. But most of the other students would die to be seen with a Millet (puffy ski jacket) and a Benetton scarf. Back then and even today, Benetton scarves were so expensive, the number of scarves a student wore was a direct reflection of the wealth of their parents. We had some wealthy students, like the daughter of the late President Mobutu Sese Seko of Zaire, who would change her scarf every day and sometimes twice in the same day. In fact, she never wore the same thing twice. We had other children of Mobutu regime officials, and they too tried to match their President's daughter.

Then there was the green military bag that everyone used as a bag for books and notebooks—That was the thing to have. Without fail, most bags had the following written on them: "Zimbabwe, ACDC." I did not know exactly what that all meant. I had such a green bag as well, but bag did not have anything written on it.

First business attempt in Brussels

Despite the fact that Enaniye had her new job and we were in a better financial situation than before, things were still hard. After we entered the Lycée Français, witnessing how hard my parents were working to keep everything together was weighing on my heart. I knew that that biggest hardship was financial, and I decided to do something about it and try to also make some money. I had no doubt I could make money, because I had already made so much money back in Laïbet. I knew things would be slightly different here, but nonetheless I started racking my brain for possible ways to go into business.

What could be my contribution and how could I make it? After weeks of thinking and ruminating on the idea, one day as we watched TV all together as usual, there was a commercial break. The one commercial that hit me was the one for Colgate—something about the whole family using Colgate and how they all now have white teeth. I thought, I also have white teeth and maybe I should call them to suggest that I make a commercial for them. Of course, I had no idea about the whole machinery of marketing and the numerous processes involved in making a commercial. I had always heard Boubiye's stories when he was working for Meta Bira as head of marketing and how he would pick people from the street and train them to make commercials for Meta Bira.

As always, I consulted with Fofi about the idea of calling Colgate, and she seemed to agree with me that I should give it a try. For the coming days, I really focused on teeth. I checked my own teeth and looked around in school and in the neighborhood to check the teeth of others. All in all, my observation concluded that very few people had white teeth and many had teeth that were crooked or yellowish. I also started remembering how many times, since we arrived in Brussels, people had been saying to me: "*que vous avez les dents blanches*! [what white teeth you have!]." I thought of possible skits I could propose to Colgate and practiced in our bedroom (the audience being Fofi, Noela, and Lily who were being supportive and coming along with the idea).

With this little reflection done, a lot of enthusiasm, and a bit of getting ahead of myself in planning how I would allocate the money I earned, I took the phone book and looked up the number for Colgate. I felt some joy and a bit of butterflies in my stomach as I found the number. I wrote the number down on a piece of paper and kept it until I found a time when the house would be empty, or at least not have so much commotion, so that I could have a quiet conversation with Colgate—my first business call. The opportune time came. I took a deep breath, picked up the phone, and dialed the number. It rang about four times or so, and then I heard the voice:

« *Colgate? Bonjour*! » I said.

« *Oui, bonjour Madame* » the receptionist answered.

« *Je vous appelle a propos d'une publicite* [I am calling to propose an ad]. »

« *Comment* ? [What ?]»

« *...er, une publicite* [...eh...an ad]» I insisted.

« *Vous dites* [You're saying... ?]»

« *Je dis une publicite, parce que vous savez, j'ai des dents blanches et je ...* [I said, an ad, because you know I have white teeth and I...]»

She interrupted me, asking, « *Vous avez quoi ?* [You have what ?] »

"*Des dents blanches* [white teeth]."

"*et alors* [and so ?]"

« *et alors je suis prete a vous faire une publicite* [and so I am suggesting that I am ready to make an ad for you].»

There was silence on the phone for a while. I think the receptionist must have thought this was either a prank or a mentally deranged person on the line. "*Oui, merci. Nous ne faisons pas de publicite* [Yes, thank you. We don't make any ads]" she replied and shortly after hung up. There was no time to say thank you or ask any further questions. Only the deafening sound of a line gone dead rang in my ear.

Oh, well, there went one attempt. It failed, but I did not give up. I did not even get offended; I just thought it was their loss and went back to the mirror to check my teeth, and they were still white. "Too bad for Colgate," I thought, "I will find another toothpaste company that knows a good thing when they see it." Fofi was also a bit disappointed, but she agreed with me that it was their loss. How different than in Laïbet where I could make money so easily with all the pranks and mischievous things we did.

The challenge of adolescence

By the time we were in eighth grade (*cinquiéme année*), a lot of my friends started dating one another. I did not date anyone and did not plan on doing so for a long time. At the beginning it was okay—not dating did not bother me and it was not even an issue. However, very soon almost everyone was paired up, and only very few students remained without dating. Again, it was the same click of Marcus, Eric, Massako, myself, and a few others who did not date. The rest of them were busy. In the wintertime, they would all stay against the heaters in the bathrooms and kiss for the entire morning and afternoon break. You could just see them stuck to each other. I always wondered how they managed to breathe. I certainly could not do that, I thought—how would I breathe?

I knew no dating would be happening in our home. What would I even tell Boubiye if some guy started calling me? It would be embarrassing for everyone, I thought, so best to remain focused on my studying. As soon as all the dating started, the gap in grades widened, and resentment increased toward the few of us who still got high grades. It's funny, on one hand they were not willing to study, and on the other, they got upset if others studied. I didn't understand their issue well. Little did I know that this would continue throughout life, even in professional settings: Some will not work and will be pretending to work; these same ones who don't work give those who work a hard time.

Those days brought something else new: copying during exams. Each time we had a test, the same students who spent their breaks kissing in the bathroom against the heaters would charm us into letting them copy during the exam. At first I didn't mind, really. At times, especially in math, I had enough time to do the exam in two different ways so that I could give them a way of finding the right answer, one that was different than what I had on my exam sheet. It worked well and no one could accuse us of copying. This went on for a while until I got tired of the nonsense—I was doing double the work for nothing at all. They took it for granted, and I was putting in too much effort to make two tests in a limited time just so they could have the grades without us being busted.

In fact, one day, we were in *Histoire-Geo* class sitting for a mid-term exam. No one was sitting next to me; I was sitting next to the heater to keep warm and ready to get going with the test. One student came in late, a boy called Francois, the "man" of the day. He was "it," the man every girl wanted, tall and skinny with his Millet jacket adding lots of shoulder volume. And for only God knows what reason, he came to sit next to me. I could hear the chatter behind me of the hip girls talking about why he would sit next to me. Why would the coolest guy in school sit next to the least cool girl when there were so many others he could sit next to? The guy had it going so well that even girls from higher grades were after him. Me, I knew the only reason he sat next to me was, of course, to copy. He was so pushy. I could not concentrate. The desks were made for two students, and he leaned in so much that I was stuck between the wall with its attached heater and him. I was very uncomfortable. With the combination of him being pushy, the heat from the heater, the anxiety of being caught cheating, and running against the clock to complete the exam, I was close to fainting. This is the first exam I failed badly even though I had studied and knew my material. Later as we received the exams back, the teacher asked me if I was ill and whether I wanted to take it over because my performance was far short of the usual. I let that pass and told her I would make it up during the final exam. Something changed in me after this episode. I swore to myself that I would not get involved in all this copying business anymore. And since I was sure they would not stop asking to copy me, I just decided I would pass them the wrong answers until they gave up sitting next to me.

The first major conflicts I had to handle emerged. When we received the test results, they wondered why there was such a difference between the grade I had and the one they had. I didn't care. I found them rude, but whatever they said rolled down my back—I did not let it reach my heart. Back in kindergarten, the children didn't want to play with me because I didn't have pigtails. This time it was because I didn't let them copy anymore. It didn't matter to me; I had one thing in mind and that was to learn as much and as best as I could, and possibly go back home to Ethiopia to work. Whether the other students wanted to be friends or not was irrelevant. The interesting thing is that even now, I don't mind whether I am included or not. I am happy to live my life and do my thing regardless of whether there are others coming along or not, whether I am included or not. I realize that this marginalizes me and that often people who don't really know me think I am antisocial, but it's okay for me. As Almazesha always told me: *"If your heart and conscience are clear with God, then don't worry about anything else—the main thing is not to hold grudges and issues in the belly. It is unhealthy for you and unhealthy for those around you."* For me, it was very clear. My heart and soul belonged in Laïbet. I had all I needed within, so there was little reason to look externally to find something to complete me. I knew where I come from, and I knew where I wanted to go. It was very clear in my mind.

Maybe it's a blessing in disguise to deal with peer pressure early on; it forced me to make choices. At the end of the day, we are the only ones in charge of the choices we are willing to make and are committed to keep. Although it is human to want to belong and be part of the community, whatever that community is, it is also equally important not to allow ourselves to be subjected to the pressures of belonging. Back home, there is something we call *yelunta*, which might be best translated as "social or peer pressure," or even the fact that we do things not because we want to, but because of what others might say if we did otherwise. So, for example, we say "yes" when we would rather say "no"; or we fast for Easter, when in fact we don't really care about the meaning and purpose of the fast, but are worried about what others might say of us or our family should we eat animal products during Lent. I think the *yelunta* robs us of our freedom. Although there is always an appropriate dosage of *yelunta* that has to exist in order to live in a society, at times—and this is especially true in

Ethiopia—we overdo it. *Yelunta* keeps us trapped in a behavior that we don't want.

What I have learned is that if one holds one's ground long enough, usually, others will eventually stop trying to influence or subject one to peer pressure. That is the point of freedom and the more such points of freedom we reach, the easier it is to exist fully as we are without having to bend in ways dictated by the majority. I was lucky to have been forced to make such choices since my earliest age. Whether those around me thought I was nice or strange, I lived my life and continue to live it in the way that best works for me.

Rite of passage

In the summer of 1978, Almazesha came to visit us in Brussels. The entire family was so excited for her anticipated arrival. Sleeping arrangements were made: Enaniye and Boubiye wanted her to have their bedroom and moved to one of the children's bedrooms; in turn, us children moved small beds and mattresses around to make sure everyone had a place to sleep. When Almazesha arrived, she moved into the master bedroom as planned. There was not even a discussion on who would share her room with her—it was me, and that was not negotiable.

As usual, our conversation routine got re-established right away. We would start chit-chatting right when we got ready for bed, as we each put on our nightgowns, brushed our teeth, and washed up. Once we were well tucked into our bed, then the conversation reached a new level of depth. It always started gently and dived into the depth of the stories of life. We talked about everything. We talked of old times, the present, and also the future.

For me, this was like having Christmas, Easter, and New Year all at the same time. I felt alive again. I felt resurrected.

This time, Almazesha spent quite some time talking to me about boys and men. I was eleven years old, going on twelve. I suspect she came to Brussels specifically to prepare me for my transition from childhood into adulthood. As tradition required, she traveled to share with me the message of life and for life that her grandmother, Emama Gessu (the one from Adoua) had passed on to her. She did not lecture me; she just told me stories interlaced with examples and colorful illustrations. I listened to her with absolute attention.

They will call you one day, and tell you that unless you promise to be theirs forever, their life will stop and they might die. Some might even tell you that they can't breathe anymore. They will say that you are the only one they think of when they wake up and when they go to sleep. Others will tell you that they are just not eating anymore because all they can think of is you.

Lejay Tetenkeki [my child, be careful]. These men, who are often really just boys at heart, only want one thing and that is wode alga guday [the matter of being in bed with you]. Once that is done, they will just move to the next one. We are like games for them. They are boys who just want to play. If you do not understand this, you will be headed for much heartache and possibly unnecessary complications with your life.

If you refuse to see them, they will complain some more, but when they know that there is no way to get with you, they will just move to the next phone number of the next girl in their book and try their chance there. Don't think you are special to them. In a man's world, the woman is often just a sex thing and nothing more. No matter how serious they look, ultimately most men have only one thing in mind. And that is wosib [sex]. Don't blame them—they can't help it. It's biological. We are just made differently.

Of course, there are those who might be genuine about how they feel about you. You will hopefully be able to make the distinction. Those who are genuine are not so sweet with their tongue; maybe because they are truly in love, they end up fumbling a lot. In any case you will feel it in your heart whether it is the right one or not. You might be dating a few before you find the one you marry. Back in our time, there was no dating—girls were just presented to their husbands and that was it. It is true that often these girls grew up to be women and in the process they learned to love the man they had to marry. In our times we just prayed that we were presented with a man of ethics, discipline, and manners; so many turn to be violent or drunkards. I have been lucky with your father [that's how she referred to Ababi]. He has always been dedicated to his children. He has always paid school fees first and taken the children to school himself. For that I am lucky. But don't ask him about money. The accountant that he is, he never spends a dime for other things, other than school fees and expenses related to his children. Of course he didn't have enough extra money, but I had to work and get my own business going to supplement our lives. He doesn't really know that. He is a good man overall and I think he has done a good job at raising the children.

Should you fall in love with a boy, my child, be cautious about what you do with the boy. Soon you will see your Yewer Abeba.[37] Every month, about 28 days, you will find that you are bleeding. During the days that you are seeing

---

[37] *Yewer Abeba* translates to "monthly flowers," and is how classical Amharic refers to menstruation.

the Wer Abeba, change your pads regularly and throw them away wrapped up in paper or plastic. There is no need for everyone around you to know that you are seeing Yewer Abeba. Make sure to always wear dark colors from the waist down during these days. I say this because at times you can have accidents that leave blood spots on your clothes. If this happens, don't be ashamed—this has happened to all women throughout the world and throughout history. Just find a way to cover yourself and go home to change.

Yewer Abeba is the sign that you have started the process of being able to carry a child. I say be careful with boys because they rush to put their privates into yours. Sometimes they try to fool you and say that they just want to lie with you naked or they might even say that they will not penetrate you but just touch your thighs. The problem is Fireyachew[38]—they flow out and before you know it one will reach your womb and depending on the time of the month, this can cause you to conceive a child. Conceiving a child is a beautiful process, but if you conceive too early this might bring you to make unwanted compromises in your life. You still have a long way to go with your education.

You know when they gave me in marriage to your father, I was only nine. Your mother was born when I was just about your age. I didn't know what was going on and how my body was changing. The delivery was hard. Emiye helped and there was just the two of us to manage the whole process. So, don't think that because you are so young, you can't have children. It can happen.

When and if you date someone and even if you are proper each day, make sure that you have always showered and washed and dressed impeccably from head to toe. Have

---

[38] From "seed" (*firey*), *fireyachew* in this case refers to sperm.

always a bit of cologne on you and especially in small parts such as behind your ears, in the heart of your elbows, your wrists, and even the back of your knees, especially if you are going out on a date, a dance or dinner or something. You should always be clean and fresh like a flower. Men are funny, tenkolegnoch nachew [tricky]—before you can stop them, they can just fall on you and kiss you in parts that you did not expect. For this, you have to make sure that you are always perfect inside and out. You don't want a man to kiss you to find that your beauty is only on your face. You have to make sure that you extend that beauty to every inch of your body.

If men ask you out and you want to refuse their invitation, do it gently; don't be like a bad-mannered animal. They have feelings too. They have the right to ask anyone out—it is just for us to make a distinction with whom we want engage or not. No matter who they are, what they look like, or where they are from, be polite as I have raised you. Remember to consider that even if their only intention was to get you wede alga. No matter what, in whatever situation remain graceful, polite, and courteous. You have to know that the world is small and whatever inappropriate behavior you have will emerge to haunt you later in your life.

Wake up early each day. Take a shower and get dressed before anyone. Make your bed and make sure that your room is spotless. Spend time in prayer and in silence before the day starts. You are to grow up into a lady and not remain as the tomboy that you are. Be graceful and elegant. When you laugh, don't do it like a horse and show all your molars; keep your lips reserved and laugh with poise. Keep your voice gentle—don't shout like a market woman. You are living your life, but as you go along remember that you are representing the entire family and all the ancestors who have brought us so far.

I absorbed all of what she said like a sponge. I didn't fully understand every detail, but I got the overall message. This summer was like an initiation in its own way. I think Enaniye felt more comfortable to have Almazesha explain all of this to me, rather than her. A few weeks later, I was introduced to pads and told that when the my periods came, this is what I would have to use on a monthly basis. No one said how odd these pads would feel and how strange it is to have wear them, at least for someone that has never used them before.

I think of my children now, and I wonder how we will make that transition from being a girl child to entering the age of womanhood. I suppose I would have been very happy to have Almazesha explain it all to them. It's always so much better when such advice comes from a grandmother.

The first thing I did after listening to all these words of wisdom and guidance was to gather all my sisters and tell them what I had been told. I couldn't always explain in detail because I didn't understood all the detail, but did my best to convey the message to them. It's funny—it's all related to the sense of responsibility the oldest child often feels. I have always felt responsible for my sisters and all my cousins, as if I am a bridge between them and our parents and elders and life in general. If harm was to come, I wanted to take that on myself instead of seeing my sisters or cousins subjected to it. I wanted to be a shield of some sort. Of course, thinking about it now, I realize how naively idealistic my attitude was. Still today, I feel this sense of responsibility even though most of us have grown into adulthood. There is a something about being the oldest child. In a way, the oldest child never really gets a chance to be a child—the minute there is a younger brother or sister, we are expected to provide an example. It is unfair, but so life goes and we have to do with what is so.

True test of time and coming of age

If I had to point to one part of my life in terms of difficulty (short of saying hardship), it would be adolescence. On one hand, I was very conscious of the importance of education: I concentrated on my school work fully and did my best to perform at the highest level. I needed to contribute to our family's life, and I could not conceive the thought of being a difficult child or going into the usual adolescence crises that remain very common for the teenage years, especially in Western culture. I though these crises were at the will of the child—I did not understand that at times they could result from the physical changes or even the cultural context in which the child was living. At the time, I still thought that adolescents chose to be one way or another, andI just felt it would be selfish to subject my family to whatever they called "teenage stuff," so I kept myself to my books and studies. I tried to help my sisters study as much as possible, and in whatever extra time I had, I tried to help in the house with cooking, cleaning, or shopping.

Although we were in Brussels, inside our house we lived within Ethiopian culture and ways of being. This culture included many things, such as respecting our parents, never answering back (whether to a parent or another adult), being always ready to help out as much as possible, and most of all, behaving properly as we had been taught.

Outside our apartment, we lived in another world.

People spoke their minds, regardless of age. Adults and youths mixed in ways I had never seen, speaking and exchanging as equals without any deference for age or maturity. As our ages pushed through the teens, I could see my friends changing the way they talked, the way they wore their clothes and hair, and especially the way they related to the opposite sex. I observed all this from afar, and though at times I was tempted to join them, something in me refused to go along.

Most of my classmates were now couples, which might last for months or just for a weekend. I tried to ignore this wave of change that was happening, remaining one of the few not dating. It did not bother me until others started making a big deal about it. The challenge, of course, was not only that I was quite shy, but also that I was living in two worlds. At home, I lived in a culture that despite modernity, would not accept dating other than dating with marriage in mind; in school, it was about how many dates, boyfriends, or girlfriends one could claim. Among my girlfriends, the entire conversation at school revolved around boys. Week after week, I had nothing to report. I knew very well that my girl friends thought I was a bit strange. Day in and day out, they saw me alone, never glued to the heaters in the bathroom stuck to some boy or out in the park next to the Lycée skipping school and making out with a guy.

I knew that if I didn't do anything about the situation, the pressure on me would continue to mount. I was conscious that they were wondering why I hadn't been seen with a boy yet. Unless I did something, the lack of being seen with a boy combined with my grades put me at risk of being isolated and left alone. I knew I had to take some action, but I certainly did not want anything to do with the boys. I couldn't be bothered, and plus, how would I manage that with the dynamics at home? So, the next best solution was to first learn what needed to be learned about sex and sexuality and then embody that learning.

My challenge was to find a source for this learning—there was no way I was going to ask anyone to tell me about sex. Almazesha was far away, Fofi didn't know much more than I, and the movies on TV did not go into explanations of how things worked. Each evening as we watched movies, if kissing started on the screen, we would quickly change the channel, or the scenes were too obscure to understand what was exactly happening. The biggest mystery for me was how people managed to breathe and kiss someone at the same time. I found it gross to have someone so close to your face. I tried to understand, but no matter how I thought about it, I could not help the feeling of disgust of the mere idea of it.

The next best thing was to turn to books, and I rushed to the usual newsstand, the one at the Globe roundabout where we used to stand to wait for the school bus. The newsstand was right next to where the concierge had her daily beer after finishing her work. I went to buy one of these pocket books of the SAS series: The stories in these books are often quiet steamy (I had been told), and I figured I could start by studying such a book. I bought one.

For about a week all I did was study this one book, the story of the main character, Marco the spy, and his adventures in various developing countries, written as a raunchy novel. Of course these adventures were about one-fifth work and four-fifths adventures with the local women. With the dictionary in one hand and the SAS book in the other, I read, and read, and re-read. The greatest challenge was being able to understand the double or implied meaning of every normal word that was now being used in the sexual context. That was not easy—it took me forever to figure it out, if at all. Once I had the book completely studied, I felt a sense of confidence about my newly acquired knowledge. I sensed that I might even know a lot more than my girlfriends, though they probably had experienced their knowledge and I had just read about it. But I was certain that my reading took me to greater knowledge of sexual boundaries than my girlfriends would ever be aware of, unless they read the same book.

Now I was ready to put my plan into action. Just as I had decided to kick the biggest guy's ass back in primary school to establish my turf, now I had to do the same ass-kicking in a slightly different way—I had to share what I had just learned in a way that would get them off my back, once and for all.

I knew exactly the day I would break the news to my girlfriends: a day we skipped PE as usual, and ran out to the park behind the school. It was Spring. We sat on the bench and the usual suspects started reporting on their weekend sagas—how they kissed this one, how that one looked at them, how they broke up with another one, how they hoped to get the next one, and further details that I would rather leave out. Everyone talked. Between the sounds of chewing gum bubbles bursting and matches or lighters striking to light cigarettes, with the sun beating down on us, time went sort of quickly. We were in a zone where life revolved only around the dating scene. And then it was my turn to talk or report something. As usual, my girlfriends expected nothing from me, since until then the only reputation I had was for scoring high grades and being a "boring-good-girl."

To their surprise, I started asking them questions about their guys based on my newly acquired knowledge. I had very specific, sexually advanced questions, much of which they might not have understood. I asked them if their guy did this or that when they were together. All eyes were on me, and in sync I heard their voices echo, "*QUOI ???* [What???] Since when do you know all this stuff?" This was news. Now finally, the one person they never thought would ever come up with a guy-story was asking questions insinuating that I had actually some experience in this so-called sex thing. They could not wait for me to talk more. But I didn't. As a seasoned trader with a scarce commodity holds the stuff back to push prices up, I played on that and lingered with each word. I didn't want to say too much. After all, what I knew was limited to the book I studied, so I didn't want to put out all the merchandise at once. I had to say enough to tickle their attention, but not so much as to sink the value of my newly acquired knowledge. I left them wondering how much more I knew.

They were stunned, to say the least. I had managed to make their jaws drop—mission accomplished. My reputation was instantly upgraded from "boring-good-girl" with high academic scores to a mysterious question mark. Since that day, the girls were left wondering how much more I knew. They were never sure whether I had done the stuff. They always wondered how in the world I knew what I seemed to know. In fact, as the days passed, some of them would come asking for advice or asking questions about their relationships.

Although this got the girls off my back, I still didn't start dating anyone. I didn't want to. In fact, the truth is that the opportunity also never really came up. The good thing was that I had successfully established my street credit; I was free to continue my life fully engaged in my studies and remaining the *Tchewa lej* (polite child) my family and culture expected me to be.

One night that changed everything

A few months after that, I decided to take further action. The girls would always report on the nightclub scenes they lived on the weekends. I had never been to a nightclub, and I resolved to deal with that as well. I had two good friends, Patricia and Alexandra, who were also perceived by the others as the "boring-good-girls." I suggested to these two friends that we had to take action and deal with this nightclub issue. It took us a few days of "intelligence work" to find out where the nightclubs were and which one to try.

Le Pied was a nightclub in the Forest area, thankfully not too far from home, and we picked a day to engage this new frontier. Patricia and Alexandra and I made our plans. Patricia's mom would drop us off, and Alexandra's mom would pick us up. In preparation for this night out that would prove to be a turning point in my life, I went shopping for appropriate clothes—except I didn't know what would be appropriate nor did I have the money to shop. I went to the Chez Julie shop on Chaussée d'Alsemberg, owned by a Jewish family. An entire family, generations of women, owned the store: The grandmother, the mother, and all the daughters worked together. They knew our family well. They always had loads of clothes and at very reasonable and affordable prices. I knew that my little budget would somehow fit the prices in their shop. I bought a pant/jacket suit made of velvet. At the time, I thought the color was okay. Thinking about it now, I smile at how much I had no clue about fashion. I still don't have much fashion sense, but that's okay. The outfit, a strange greenish color, had pants with huge, brown, outside pockets similar to the leather pockets on cowboy pants. To add to this, I bought a black turtleneck sweater. I thought it looked all right. My point of reference for choosing this outfit was the clothing I saw groups like Cool and the Gang or Earth, Wind, and Fire wear on TV.

I told Enaniye and Boubiye that we were invited out somewhere. Of course, no one had invited us, but I just could not tell them I was actually going to a nightclub, *nitekelebeh* as they would say in Ethiopia. I was fifteen. Shortly before I went out, Enaniye did my hair: My lovely nappy Afro was tamed with a hot comb that she heated on the stove and ran through my hair. As she applied the comb, the sound of crackling and the fumes of hair oil invaded the room. She tried the best she could to make me some curls. My ears got a bit of the hot comb a few times but I did not complain. Finally at the end, I had somewhat of a hairdo. Well, to tell you the truth, I looked more like a female James Brown impersonator. The tight curls framed my face. All the oil and hair cream petrified the do, and no wind could have changed its shape. It looked like I was wearing some kind cushiony brown helmet.

Then, of course, the make-up, another thing I had no idea about. Fofi told me that I should use the lipstick as eye shadow and as blush as well as to color my lips. I did everything she said. Then, I added a thick layer of eye-liner. By the time I left the house, I am not exactly sure what I must have looked like. It was creative, to say the least, and completely out of sync with the fashion trends of the day. I thought it was fine and tried to keep my conviction that this was how it was all supposed to look. My new outfit, my turtleneck, my new James Brown do, and my make-up in place, I left the apartment like a big girl. Fofi, Noela, and Lily were excited for me. In fact, at this time, our cousins Ahmed, Mohamed, and Fana were staying with us, and they too were happy for me. I left the house as a brave soldier goes to the war front. Regardless of my doubt and anxiety, I put my worries to the side and walked out tall. I took a deep breath right when I opened the main building door and stepped out into the night. There was slight drizzle and the sidewalks were slippery. The street was deserted. I felt exhilarated to finally tackle this nightclub issue. It would be good once that was sorted and dealt with.

We had agreed to meet in front of the little church on the way to Drogenbos, right on the Rue de Stalle, a 10-minute walk from our apartment. I bravely walked the way, in the dark, taking a deep breath once in a while to renew the courage I needed. Patricia and her mom were already at the rendez-vous in the mom's little Peugeot. I hopped in and we drove off to pick up Alexandra. Before long, we had arrived near the famous Le Pied.

Patricia, Alexandra, and I asked to be dropped off a few blocks away—we didn't want to be seen with a parent. That would be way un-cool. We walked up to the club as confidently as we could. As we got closer, we saw the others. They had this cool-ness as they stood chatting, kissing, intertwined like Egyptian snake drawings with the music from Le Pied blaring out the door. It was loud. We couldn't let people see that we had no clue which way to go or what to do. It didn't matter. It was too late now—we had to move forward. There was a short moment when we stared at each other, and then we were hit by a sudden surge of unexpected confidence. The three of us walked in with a demeanor that oozed self-assurance as if we knew it all (although we really had no clue).

As we stepped inside, we kept tripping on each other. No one had told us that nightclubs are dark inside. We couldn't see and kept bumping into everything. We followed the music, paid our entrance fee, and managed to find a wall to stand by. There were so many people dancing. "Oh shit," I thought, "I forgot all about the dancing part." I had never danced before, not to mention that even the thought of it embarrassed me greatly. We stood there for a while. We got some sodas and took a cool stance against the wall (trying to emulate what we had seen others do or what we had seen on TV). We stood there, ignoring the nagging voices of our minds. The truth is we didn't know how this whole nightclub thing operated. Before long, someone came and asked Patricia and then Alexandra to dance. Patricia had pretty bad teeth and wore serious braces that protruded. She also had pretty bad acne, but none of that stopped her from being asked to dance. Alexandra was the tallest, already about 1.75 meters if not more. I guess because she could not own her height, she developed sort of a hump on her back from not standing straight. She had thin blond hair that struggled with static. She, too, went to the dance floor. I was left at the wall, sipping on my soda—five minutes, fifteen minutes, half an hour passed, and still no one came to ask me to dance. Patricia and Alexandra never came back either.

I hate to be defeated by circumstances; I refuse to be subject to a situation and not do something about it. So, once more, I took to action. I scanned the dance floor to try and understand the dynamics there. If boys were not going to ask me to dance, then I would do the asking. This club was 99% full of white kids, and I knew my chances to dance with a white boy were low. So, with calculated risk, I spotted one African guy. He must have been mixed because he was of a fair complexion. The target identified, I moved straight to him with military precision. I thought that for sure this brother would not let me down, or so I hoped. I walked straight up to him. He was busy wiggling his body with a short little skinny white girl. The girl was very BCBG (preppy, Benetton style). She was certainly up to date with fashion that I could not even dream of. I tapped the guy on his shoulder as if knocking on a door. He turned to me. "Do you want to dance with me?" I asked without any hesitation, straight to the point. There was no need to beat around the bush; best go straight up to the matter. There was a split of a second of silence and non-action. He looked at me with puzzlement. The look on his face was like he had just been confronted with an alien from another planet. Then without even responding, he turned back and continued dancing with the girl. Hmm. I was not going to let this incident affect me. I remained there and did one or two little dance moves, just to be tough I guess (like the time we didn't react when Emama Berhane planted mega-Kurkums on my head), before gracefully sashaying my way off the dance floor and straight to the bathroom.

I wanted to check what was wrong with me that he didn't even have the courtesy to reply to my request. He had just turned around and continued dancing without even saying yes, no, later, or whatever.

The bathroom was full of girls glued to the mirror, fixing their hair, adding make-up, and fixing their décolleté so that their breasts would bump out a bit more. I too came up to the mirror, and to my surprise I found someone I could not recognize. My little curls, so dearly curled with the hot comb, had shrunk into an unrecognizable thing. My hair had receded from my forehead as the sea receded from the beach at low tide. It's hard to describe what my hair looked like. It wasn't an Afro, it wasn't curls—it just looked like a broccoli was on my head. The eyeliner, well, that one had melted off and run down my cheeks. And because of the velvet suit and wool turtleneck sweater, I was drenched in sweat and my face looked like I had just left a steam room. Basically, I looked like a baby raccoon with big black circles around my eyes and a black broccoli on my head. Well, I thought, I could not blame the guy. Despite the shock I had when I saw my reflection in the mirror, I too stretched up to the mirror and tried to fix myself up a bit just like the other girls, using my little fingers to bring the eyeliner into order. There wasn't much I could do about the hair, so I just patted it here and there and walked out very tall and very straight like nothing had gone wrong.

Something changed in me as I stepped out of the bathroom. I somehow sensed that it was not about how I looked per se, but rather about how others perceived me—and about attitude. "Who gives a shit what they think," I thought to myself. I knew who I was and what I was about. A monologue started in my mind. "If they don't like me, that's their choice. It won't be the first time in my life I get rejected, so I don't care," I kept repeating to myself. "Who are they to tell me what I can and cannot do, who I can and cannot be with or dance with?"

I felt a clear and new sense of rebellion emerge in my heart. I felt the shy girl retire, and a side of me I was not very familiar with emerged. This new self was tough, almost hard-core. "If it's going to be like this, then, I too will change and not give a f—?!? Shit!" God good, I could not believe my train of thought. Was it really me? I had never known this side of myself.

I knew that though I didn't look ugly per se, I also didn't look "cool" in the context of what was cool at the time. But I also knew that a lot of other kids who looked a lot worse than I did were having their fun. It was all about attitude—that was very clear—and I could change my attitude. As one would switch the lights on or off with the touch of a button, so my attitude instantly transformed. Of course, as always, I didn't have a reasonable measure or moderation in my change of attitude: enough with this nice-girl bullshit. As always in my life, things were left or right, black or white, super shy or not shy at all.

With my new monologue playing in the back of my mind, I walked straight to the bar, pulled myself up on a bar stool and sat there with a demeanor that would make a gangster look like a pussy cat. Okay, if they wanted to play tough, I would show them that not only can I play tough but I invented the game. I rested one elbow on the bar and the other on the back of my high chair. My whole body was tingling from the revolution I felt inside. As much as I felt at peace, there was also exhilaration like that of driving full speed on a windy road—I did not know what I would find behind the next curve, but I did not care and kept going full speed.

There was a rugged, tough-looking guy sitting next to me. He had a short glass with what I believe was whisky on the rocks. Thanks to the books I had studied, I had picked up some of the hardcore street lingo and without even an inkling of doubt, I nudged him with my elbow and said: "*file moi une clop* [give me a cig]." (I had learned that *clop* is the street word for cigarettes.) He offered me his pack with a few cigarettes poking out, and I selected one. He held his lighter for me. I leaned closer and lit the cigarette. I didn't say thank you—I just gave him a slight nod of the head. Inside I was praying that I would not collapse from the smoke, because I had never smoked before. I held that cigarette like Al Capone and started rambling with this guy. He rambled back. Eventually, just to show him that I didn't give a shit, I got up and left in the middle of the conversation, telling him that I had to go. I didn't say goodbye or that I would come back; I just gave him another nod of the head.

As I walked away, I felt satisfied with this change. My stride was different. Everything was different now.

However, deep inside my heart, for the first time, I felt terrible in a different way. I was sad, and my inner bravado crumbled. What happened to the tough girl? Where did she go? I had no idea. This time around, I felt hurt. It was nothing short of my first day in school when the little children didn't want to play with me because I didn't have pigtails. Only this time I was grown and it wasn't about pigtails anymore: It was about fashion, sex, and being cool. I knew the fashion wasn't going to happen—my family couldn't afford it. The sex wasn't going to happen, either, because I didn't want to and my chances of getting involved with someone were close to nil. The coolness was also not going to happen because all I knew how to do was get top grades in school, take care of my sisters, and help at home, none of which was at all cool. I decided to end the night. I wanted to go home—I had to move on. Patricia and Alexandra stayed, and I took take a taxi home.

To my surprise, my sisters were waiting for me and wanted to hear how it went. As the oldest sister, I didn't want to share my despair and sadness with them. Why should I? They thought I could manage anything and I wasn't going to let them down, I thought, so I decided to tell them that I had a swell time. I danced throughout the night and came home early because I was tired of dancing. As I went to bed that night, though, I lost hope. My spirit collapsed and a deep sadness took over my heart. I could not understand why—given that I did everything expected of me (e.g., help out at home, have the best grades, and be good)—I was still on the outside of life. It hit me pretty hard. "If it is going to be like this," I thought, "life is not worth living. It's better to die and end it right here." I made the decision to take my life.

As usual, once I made a decision, I created a strategy to implement it in the most effective way. Some months ago, I had seen a neighbor jump out the window in an attempt to commit suicide;

unfortunately, she didn't die. She ended up being extremely hurt, possibly paraplegic. On another occasion, I witnessed the police and ambulance personnel trying to dissuade another woman from jumping, so I thought jumping out of a window was not a good strategy. Not only was it not very effective, but it was also pretty embarrassing and distressing for the family. I had to find another way. Beside, who would clean up the mess if I jumped? We lived on the third floor so I might actually manage to die, but what if I didn't? I had to find another solution.

For weeks I tried to determine how best to go about it. It's interesting how once one is resolved to do something, even suicide, there is a sense of peace that emerges. I didn't care about anything anymore—nothing mattered. I had an agenda, and that's all that mattered. I withdrew emotionally from my family and friends. Some weeks down the line, I came to the conclusion that the best way might be an overdose of medication, but the medication had to be the right one. Each day, I would search in our family pharmacy, bringing each packet I found to the bathroom to read the instructions. I found one medicine, one day, that finally said an overdose could cause death; strange, how satisfied I was to have finally found what I was looking for. I kept the package and looked for another, and once I had collected enough of it, I set a date.

The next step was to investigate the process of death. Again, I did my research, and found out that when a person dies, all the fluids come out of their bodies. I didn't want to leave a messy body, so about a week before the appointed date, I stopped eating, and a couple of days before the date, I took laxatives to empty my bowels. Obviously, this made me fatigued, but no one noticed. On the day itself, I came home, took a bath, and washed every part of my body. I wanted to be found clean. I then sat down and wrote a letter to my family. I sat with my sisters and just stayed with them, giving them some words of advice on various things of life. They had no idea that these would be my last words. I remember kissing them each and hugging them, telling them that no matter what I would always be with them on earth or from heaven. As much as I was ready to end my life and at peace with the decision, I felt sad to take a last look at my sisters. I stood there watching them play and hoped for the best for them in their lives. I didn't linger too long—I didn't want to change my mind. I went to my room. Once I made all my planned preparations, I quietly sat in my room and I took all the tablets. I prayed and then lay in my bed hoping to never wake up again.

It's strange how relieved I was—I felt I had made the right decision and also that I had chosen the best way to go about it. It would be gentle, nothing rash. I had no way of expressing how I felt in those days. There were so many contradictions. I did everything expected of a "good" child, and I tried to stick to our culture. Outside, in school, I remained focused on my studies. I could not get myself to entertain all the dating, sex, drinking, partying, and whatever else everyone was doing. I just couldn't do that. What would Almazesha say if she saw me behave like that? I wouldn't want to disappoint her. At the same time, not doing what the others did kept me excluded from social life. There was also guilt—yes, I even felt guilt for having difficulty with life, since I had a roof over my head, I was fed each day, I had something to wear, and my school was paid for. What in the world could be my problem to not want to live anymore? I knew that everything my parents provided was a privilege that many did not have back home in Ethiopia. How could I possibly ask for more? There was a lot more than I could explain, and a lot I could not understand. There was some inner pain that was unbearable: No matter how hard I worked and how tough I was, I felt myself cracking inside from the pressures of the environment.

I questioned our way of living, this picture-perfect life that is so common to many of our societies, especially our Ethiopian ways. We say nothing. We just live, and no matter what happens, we insist on maintaining this picture perfect life on the surface, refusing to allow ourselves to mirror the discomforts that we might feel within our hearts, deep inside where the true self exists. And so, we end up having split realities—there is the reality that we present to society and that which is true to ourselves. I would not be wrong in saying that some of us don't even make a distinction between these various realities, as we all believe in the illusion of the life we live. Sometimes—in fact, more often than not—the disparity is colossal and hence creates an existential dysfunction we experience in many different ways.

This picture perfect surface life, especially in our Ethiopian society, is our strength and our weakness at the same time. In my experience, in this environment there is no way anyone could have a straight conversation or get a straight answer to sensitive questions—it's all in layers. Peel, peel, and keep on peeling, and maybe one day you might land on something that is genuine, or you might find yourself still peeling. It's absurd, surreal. No matter how hard I worked, or how hard I tried to understand and be understood, nothing ever changed. My efforts seemed to be in vain. That is always dangerous, but for someone like myself going through the tough teens, moving between an array of cultures within the same day, this duality or duplicity was just too much to bear.

In the morning, my sisters found me lying lifeless in my bed.

I remember hearing voices from afar; I wasn't sure if I had died or where I was. I learned later that our family doctor rushed to our home and injected me with something (I don't know what) and then I opened my eyes. To my great disappointment, I realized that my plan had failed and now I was stuck with having to explain. But maybe my decision to end my life was a blessing in disguise, because it allowed me to crack part of the unease I felt. It opened a way to speak to Boubiye and Enaniye about some of the difficulties I experienced. At least they listened, and wanted to know why, and how come I came to the decision to take my life. What was not okay? They wanted to know.

For days I was not allowed to leave the apartment. I remember my parents watched over me with extra attention. I had never had that much attention before, at least not since before Fofi was born, I suppose. It was understood that I would not tell anyone what I had done. This unfortunate incident was to remain at home.

One idea from my parents and family at large was that it might be better for me to move and live in the United States where I could go to boarding school or live with Etetila, at least until I finished high school.

My mother was very often on the phone with Etetila, and I suppose they were discussing how to arrange me possibly moving to the US. My other aunt, Zene, who was visiting at that time with her family, insisted that I write Etetila a letter. We wrote the letter together—I wrote and she dictated what I should write. It was not the kind of letter I would have written, but I thought that I had better write as she said if I wanted the move to work out.

Some weeks down the line, the decision made: I would move to the US and live with Etetila until I completed high school. I didn't mind so much leaving my school, but leaving my sisters was just unbearable. I had never lived without my sisters. We were very close. We were friends. The move would be okay, but how could I ever survive without sisters? It was hard.

PART IV:
A NEW LIFE IN THE US

I was bought a brown suit, jacket and pants, along with boots to wear on my flight to Washington. I would first land in New York and I take a connection to Washington National Airport. My uncles and aunts who lived in the Washington at the time came to pick me up. I felt so good seeing them. It was like old times. Because I grew up in Laïbet I could better relate to my aunts and uncles, almost like a younger sister. They came in my uncle Dawit's big car that had enough space to seat three in front and three or even four in the back. His car looked like those American cars we saw so often on TV, like in *Hawaii 5-0* or *Colombo* episodes. And the streets were so wide! I had been to New York and Washington once before, but this time, I noticed things a lot more. They had three, four, even five-lane roads. People were driving not as fast as in Europe. Many were slouching as they drove, and I saw people eating and drinking out of large cups as they drove. I was puzzled. My uncle's car did not have gears; you just had to put it on "D" and go—I had never seen such a car. The drive to Etetila's place took about forty-five minutes to an hour. It was dark when we arrived. There was snow here and there; it was winter. I did not realize how much my life would change in ways I never expected.

I was about sixteen. In my head, I had decided that although I would continue to work hard in school, this time around, I would decide how and with whom I would spend my social time. At that time, I was still called by my middle name, Heran. Some people suggested that I change it and introduce myself as Karen to make it easier for Americans. I thought it was odd—why should I have to change my name? I didn't disagree; I just let the conversation die out. Sometimes, I knew, it's better to sit things out, and when things don't have a proper basis they die out anyway. Almazesha used to often not react to some of the things that would happen in her life. She would just say, "let it be and it will sort itself out." Of course, you can't sit all things out, and I suppose the wisdom lies in knowing what to sit out and what to take action on. She always knew what to let be and what to address—I suppose it was about perspective and her ability to see further to the horizon and not be stuck to what is just on the surface.

High school in the US was okay. I was enrolled at the Lycée Français of Washington at first, but it didn't really work out because it was too far from Etetila's house and the commute was too much. My cousin, Etetila's son Samson, was attending a small Montessori school, Barrie School, not too far from the house. Eventually I left the Lycée and enrolled there. I stayed there about two years and graduated with honors. At graduation the school director told me that I was valedictorian, but I did not know until later that it meant I had the best grades in the graduating class. Although there was no family pressure to come home with high grades, there was always an underlying expectation of performance. Almazesha and Ababi always encouraged us, their grandchildren, as they had also encouraged their own children. But even with their encouragement, there was no exaggerated celebration when one of us earned high grades; Almazesha would just smile and gently let me know that she knew what I had achieved, and that was it. As far as I know, she did the same for all her grandchildren. I was happy that I had finished high school, and I knew Almazesha was happy for me, too. Of all the people in my family, I knew that she knew exactly what kind of growing pains I had gone through. It felt good to know that she knew, even if I didn't talk about it much with her. I knew she knew, and that was enough for me.

The students at Barrie were very different than those at my school in Brussels, with a much milder level of social activity, yet I did not understand how they came to school in what they wore or how they behaved. At times, I thought they were quite immature and unpredictable. They called teachers by their first names and turned in assignments that my old teachers wouldn't have considered good enough for the trash bin—assignments written in all sorts of ways, sometimes on wrinkled paper or full of scratched-out words. It was not uncommon to see homework done with pencil instead of pen or ink pen. I was always amazed at how they got away with that; for me, even out of the school context, I was shocked at such behavior. It was entirely outside the *Sene se-erat* (etiquette/manners) I had been taught by Almazesha. But as she also said, *"Min tadergiwalesh...lej be abatu bet bimolakek, engida minem mallet ayechelem* [What can you do about it? If a child has spoiled manners in his father's house, a guest can certainly say nothing about it]." She advised me,

"*Anchi zem belesh serashn keteyi* [you just remain quiet and continue doing your work]," and she was right. I was a mere guest in their country, and they were in their own fatherland home, in their school. But I was still often amazed.

Applying to college was a process I did not understand. I didn't have any guidance on going about it nor did I understand the importance of applying systematically. I did as best I knew. I asked for application forms for various colleges that I chose randomly. When the application came in, if it asked too many questions or looked too thick, I just tossed it out. In the end, I decided to only apply to schools in the area, and I applied to most of the big schools in the Washington area. American University admitted me first—I forgot about all the other applications and geared my life to join AU.

Life in AU was closer to that of Brussels, as there were a lot of international students. I felt very comfortable and found friends who also spoke French and knew of other parts of the world. What was interesting and strange to me was the clear divisions between students. The Americans stayed to themselves, and within them, the black and white students also stayed to themselves. I learned of sororities and fraternities, and their strange rituals to admit freshmen to their groups. I befriended some black students at first, but soon found that they were very racially biased and had issues with me also having white friends. I never really chose my friends based on their color, and found it very bizarre that this would be an issue for the black students I had met. I heard for the first time the expression "Oreo," which meant someone that is black on the outside and white on the inside.

Why would we have to choose friends based on race? I had never encountered this kind of attitude before. I could not make sense out of it, until I spoke to Almazesha about it. She took the explanation to another level, and brought in the reality of overall racial tension between white and blacks. She spoke of the history of the country with its background of slavery, racial segregation, and the struggle for equality. She spoke of the fact that it will take many more years if not generations for this racial division to disappear. Sometimes, she said, it was more than a racial division—it was an economic division. Often, she said, this division comes from ignorance and narrow-mindedness on both sides. She mentioned many such reasons, and then she spoke of how in our own country and many African countries, the same division exists between ethnic groups. The message she shared with me was that racial division was nothing exceptional. It exists and will continue to exist until people awaken to the need to address the fear and ignorance that is within—only then can we truly live in peace within our own communities and the greater societies.

As the months went on in my first year, I slowly settled in with those who would be my friends for the rest of my life. Many of them were from Europe, the Middle East, Africa, and also South America. I had some American friends as well. And of course, there would always be my friend Bob Rieger, whom I had met at the Montessori high school.

Some of my friends met Almazesha, either when she came to visit in the United States or when they visited my family in either Brussels or Addis Ababa. She was always kind to them, and I know they have appreciated her. There was always, however, a cordial distance that had to be kept—that is just how my culture is. So, while my friends met her, I doubt they knew how much she acknowledged them, how often she asked about their well-being, and how much she always wished them well. When she asked me about them, I knew how sincerely she meant it. She was not just asking to be nice or for protocol; she really wanted to know how they were doing. I always told her, though I never managed to explain to some of my friends how genuine and sincere her asking was.

What I didn't understand in college was how to study and how to choose classes—I had absolutely no clue whatsoever and soon got completely lost. As much as I was always first in school throughout my life, this time around, I could hardly manage to get the grades anymore. I didn't understand the assignments. I didn't understand the system and soon found myself floating on with average to low grades. Needless to say, there was also a lot of social life and I think I am guilty of giving it more importance than the academics.

By the time I graduated from AU, my grades were very average, and I realized the cost of that when I tried to enter graduate school. It was now too late to try and raise my scores. Not performing is a mistake that cost me the possibility of entering the kind of schools I wanted. Never again would I make this mistake, for school or in life in general.

Almazesha shared her own wisdom on mistakes and judgment. She always told me that mistakes and bad judgment are interesting, and that "*Manim ke Enatu hod ewoket yizo ayfeterim* [no one leaves their mother's womb with knowledge in hand]." Therefore, the goal is not to avoid mistakes or bad judgment—"*sewu sewu newu; anide yemaysasat yelem. Ya temiheret newu* [A human being remains a human being. No one lives without making a mistake, once; that is a lesson]." However, she also counseled, "*yesewu lej, gin, hulete ayesasatim. Lej, hulete atesasachi* [But a child of man should not make the same mistake twice. My child, don't make the same mistakes twice]." As the years went by, she would tell me "*leje atchekuyi; eski rega beyi* [my child, don't rush; please pace yourself]," and even today I know that I make the poorest judgments when I don't pace myself, when I don't remain mindful of the moment and instead rush into things. As she also always told me, I have learned not to beat myself up over a mistake or a poor choice—that is being human, as she told me. The challenge is not to make the same mistake twice. Although not making the same mistake twice sounded simple at the time, I have learned that there lies the ground of true testing and character building. I want to say to Almazesha, "*Eyawokesh! Lemin? Endet?* [But you knew! Why? How?]" More than making the same bad choice twice, making the same bad choice a second, third...tenth time is also possible. Some bad choices do not come from simple, straightforward things— some bad choices are habits, some involve relationships, some involve others, and things quickly become neither clear nor straightforward.

So the challenge is to still make appropriate choices and know how to move forward while remaining mindful of all that I know, all that I have been taught, and all that I have come to understand in life. Back at University, I was able to follow Almazesha's teaching without much trouble—only later did I begin to see that her teaching held more depth than I thought. Following her teachings has been a constant struggle, for me, between choosing what "I," the flesh and blood, personally want to do, and having the strength and wisdom to make the right choice as per the teachings and principles I learned from her. It's not always easy. Often, when making a poor choice, I have to admit that I am conscious of it. Sometimes I do it anyway even though in my heart I can see Almazesha just shaking her head in disapproval. It was easier to make poor choices while she was still only a phone call away, because I could always call and talk to her. Now that I cannot call anymore, I have become a willing hostage of the principles she taught me; maybe this is the part that makes me feel so much older.

Finally, the friends I had made found their way to either graduate school or marriage, but I certainly didn't have marriage in mind. As for graduate school, I struggled to find a school that would accept me. In the end, I entered the University of Maryland, a good school by all standards, and I was happy to be able to finish my graduate work. I worked for hours on end and my results came back in line with what I had been used to. Things were back to normal: I had high grades again.

As all this was going on, my only aim was to finish school as fast as possible to return to Ethiopia to work. I took fully loaded semesters and continued my classes throughout the summer. The greatest joy for me when I finished my master's was that I had turned 22, which was in my mind a good age to return home and start my life. I thought the toughest part of life was behind me. Little did I know that the next years would be even tougher than trying to finish school.

The school of life

Going through school was like a mad race with lots of ups and downs, but finally it was finished. I had now my master's completed, and the only thing I wanted to do was to go back to Ethiopia and start working there. Once more I was on a plane flying back to Addis, this time glowing with the relief that at last I could come back home and live near my family—and especially near Almazesha. Finally, I could work in my own country.

It was not so simple, however. With my family's advice, I accepted the fact that I should not start as an independent entrepreneur right away, but rather work within an organization for a few years first. I wrote up a CV, but no matter how wide the margins or how large the fonts, it did not add up to more than a page or two. I applied for work over and over, but nothing came through. Even my parents tried to help by calling on some of their friends to arrange interviews for me, introducing me to people, and trying everything to support my efforts to secure a job. For each interview that came through, I borrowed one of Enaniye's suits and headed off like a good trooper. The suits felt odd. They would sort of hung on me. The size was okay, but I just wasn't used to wearing a suit and wasn't able to carry myself accordingly. The interviews always ended up feeling very odd, too—I don't know if it was because I was just starting out or because I just felt so weird in the clothes I wore. I did not know what was expected of me at the interviews, and invariably the questions they asked were too vague to suggest to me a clear or precise answer.

Nothing came through, and it was very discouraging.

The people I spoke with or had interviews with sat behind their desks and asked such broad questions that, without fail, I ended up in an endless river of rambling. Without fail, the interviews ended with, "Thank you for your interest (or thank you for coming). Good luck, we will call you." But they never called. Almazesha never gave up on anything, ever. She kept encouraging me to keep trying, to keep going, and I tried to listen as much as possible and draw patience and persistence from her encouragement.

After six months, I came to the conclusion that I might not ever get a job. If I was not going to receive a job offer, it was up to me to create one. I had always wanted to work in development, and I knew I could do good work—I knew I brought enough commitment and dedication to give whatever I started every chance of success. With this in mind, I changed gears and started looking at what was already in Ethiopia and what was "not" there. What was not there that was needed and that I could provide? Gazillion ideas came to mind, and I took each one back to Laïbet and to chew it over with Almazesha or Ababi. Whatever idea I came up with, they always listened to me until I was through explaining. They always tried to see my perspective and help me work out a feasible plan. Whenever the plan involved something related to farming and cows, Ababi was the most supportive; if the plan was about small-scale manufacturing, then Almazesha would be the main person working with me.

My conversations with Ababi were about creating a dairy industry. In his own way, he loved the fact that I might have his love for farming and working with dairy cows. With Almazesha, it was more about looking into other industries, such as starting up a candy factory or producing manufacturing goods that were in everyday use. She knew exactly what I meant, and her questions often led to more reflection. She was different in that way from all the people I spoke with—she asked questions to deepen my thought process, not to tear down my plan. Others would ask questions that pointed to the holes in my plans and highlighted how unfeasible my plans were, whereas Almazesha could point to the same holes in the plan and discuss them as shortcomings to be dealt with. We sat for hours on end in her room or on the veranda when the activities at Laïbet were slow, around mid-morning or late afternoon. At the time, Almazesha's work was booming. She was one of the first coffee roasters and provided many restaurants with her coffee; she also packaged tea and salt. The whole thing was set up within the compound of Laïbet, and most people in our immediate neighborhood were working in her various lines of business.

Almazesha knew that business could be started with a bit of capital and a good idea. With me, she believed in what I wanted to do. Her faith in me, support, and encouragement allowed me to overcome the deflating attitudes from everyone else. We settled on two ideas: an artisan candy factory and a small dairy farm to provide milk and other dairy products to the market. With this in hand, we agreed that I should return to Brussels to get more information and pursue potential partnerships with European companies.

A dream deferred

So I went back to Brussels to look into these projects we had in mind. It took a few months to gather all the information and learn more in depth about the industries I wanted to get involved in. After much discussion with Ababi, Almazesha, Enaniye, and Boubiye, I decided to look into the dairy farm in the first phase. I went to visit several farms and spent time with the farmers learning about the dairy industry. I was confident that a modern dairy farm in Ethiopia would work well. I was even thinking that I would have to do some cross-breeding between Belgian or Dutch cow breeds and the Ethiopian ones in order to increase milk production. I was also looking at ways of improving the grazing area in Ethiopia. At last it was time to look for financing: I needed start-up capital of about $800,000 U.S. dollars to start a modern farm with about a hundred cows, pasteurization machinery, and packaging machinery for the milk, yoghurt, and other byproducts. My plan made sense to me. I still believe that it could have worked well.

Initially, I didn't think it would be too difficult to get the funds. I had a proper study to support my argument and a well formulated, well thought-out business plan. The innovative part of my project was the idea of producing both for local consumption and for export. I presented my case to sources of funding, but nothing came out of it. At times, the meetings ended abruptly. Sometimes the men or women I met at the various institutions seemed to ask more about how my parents were doing or tell me how much I had grown since they last saw me, instead of allowing me to present my project. At times, they just took me to lunch and wished me good luck—in any case, the answer was no.

I was quite convinced of the project I had in mind: I wanted to boost the dairy industry in Ethiopia, encourage local consumption of dairy products, and produce export-quality milk, yoghurt, cheese, and so on for export to neighboring countries. The land was available, the cows could be acquired, and to increase production I was intending to cross-breed Ethiopian and Dutch cows. Maybe I was emotionally attached to the possibilities that the project held—it would have made Ababi so happy to have cows again and for him to be on a farm. I wanted to have the farm at any cost.

Since I was not getting the funding from the financial institutions, I had to come up with another way of getting the money. Racking my mind for ways to come up with the $800,000, I finally came to the conclusion that only one of two options would allow me to make this money in a short time. The most effective way would be to win the lottery or make a best-selling music album. I could see how much singers were making for their albums or even their singles—some of the songs didn't even make sense, but they soared in sales. Many of the singers that were making serious sales did not have extraordinary voices; it was more about the beat of the song and the way it was presented. I thought I could try my luck. I told Almazesha about this plan, and I have never seen her laugh so hard. *"Bilesh bilesh...zefen assebish—esti engedih mokeriwu?"* [And now, after all, you are thinking of singing? Well, then try it]." I know she laughed not at the plan per se but at how farfetched it all was.

So, I embarked on a completely different boat to move toward my goal. My baby sister, Lily, has a beautiful strong voice and is the kind of person who can just pick up a microphone and sing like a diva. For some reason, I thought I might also be able to sing if I tried. I kept repeating to myself: "After all, we have the same parents and we also look very much alike—it is very likely that there is a voice in me that is hiding somewhere. I just have to find it and bring it out, sing, make my money, and get my cows." It was very simple and straight-forward. But alas, I soon learned that gifts are not necessarily genetically related.

For my first appointment with the studio, I asked Lily to come with me. At that time there was a famous group produced out of the Washington DC area, so I made an appointment with the producer who worked with them. What makes it obvious that I had no idea about the music business was that I made my appointment for 8:00 AM.

Once at the studio, the producer asked me what kind of music I had in mind. My answer was simple: I told him I wanted something that had blues, reggae, house, and world music—all at the same time. The man just looked at me, baffled, not knowing if I was serious or if I was pulling his leg. When he realized I was not joking, he got up and left. "I have to smoke a cigarette," he said, and left. When he returned, he asked me for the song. I didn't know I had to come up with a song. I had no song in mind. Well, since I had booked my studio time and they would charge me anyway, I just sang an old Ethiopian folk song: *Sheb Ereb Yiwodal Betu*. "Let's work with that," I said to him. It was disaster—not only did I not know how to sing but now this poor man had to sort a folk tune into blues, reggae, house, and world music. I spent the little savings I had and he put a bad tape in my hands.

Now I knew I could not sing, and I learned that

studio fees were expensive—therefore, there must be a market for affordable studio time for artists who were just starting out. Changing gears, I thought that if I could not sing, then I could open my own studio and try to make the money I needed for my farm by offering affordable studio rates and also by managing artists.

Getting deeper into the rabbit hole, now I was borrowing money to open a small digital studio with the aim of offering affordable recording and production rates. I knew Almazesha would support the idea of opening a studio because it would allow me to take things in to my hand, but at the same time, I also knew she would question my getting into a business about which I knew so little. I wanted to try it out—I knew this might be a costly venture, but I had to try it out.

Once more, little did I know what lessons life had in store for me. I met a number of musicians, producers, and artists, and together we launched a studio on Wisconsin Avenue in Washington, DC, right by the entrance to the Tenley Town Metro Station. We had a good space. Fofi came to spend some time with me to help me paint and arrange the place. Within a few weeks we opened shop. And there I was, coming in at the crack of dawn to clean up the mess of the night sessions, open the business office, do the admin work, take calls, and so on, while musicians slowly started trickling in.

Lesson 1: My biggest mistake was engaging in a business where I was not the expert. Not being an expert—in fact, not knowing the ins and outs of a business—prevented me from understanding what exactly was going on. On paper, it seemed that the hours we charged would allow us to break even; in reality, we never broke even. The rates for recording and production were different, but I often did not know whether a session was recording or production.

Several years later, I had maxed out my credit cards, I was working seven days a week, putting in as much as 16 hours a day, and nothing was happening. My dreams of a farm and candy industry slowly faded. At one point things were so bad that I would pay everyone and then borrow back money from them to buy petrol or buy some McDonalds. God bless McDonalds and their 2-for-1 deals! God only knows that for a while, I only survived on that. I had to find a job to subsidize the studio.

With an MBA in finance and all the language competences I had, for some reason, I was still not able to get work. Out of frustration, I started applying for receptionist jobs, but even those I couldn't get because they would ask me if I knew how to handle their multi-phone systems (which of course I did not). Finally, someone hired me, and the place was close to the studio, so that worked well. They paid ten dollars an hour, which was great. My job was simple: I had to take incoming calls, but there was only one phone and one line. Once in a while, I had to make a letter or two, and other than that, I just had to show up.

I was the new secretary of the Saint Mary Armenian Orthodox Church of Washington, DC. My job was to assist and support the work of Father Kolagian, the priest of the Church. As broke as I was, with hardly any money to eat, I would drive in with my sporty BMW, the only car I had and a complete paradox given my situation. I spent the morning answering the few calls that came in and doing very small administrative choirs for the Church office, and then headed back to the studio by noon. The money I earned from the Church allowed me to pay our office rent and eat more regularly.

Of all the part-time jobs I could have had, I was happy to be working in a church and even happier that it was the Armenian Orthodox St. Mary Church. Ababi had many Armenian friends in Ethiopia, especially the ones with jewelry shops in the Piazza in Addis Ababa. Once in a while, Ababi would come home with play jewelry for Fofi and me, which we loved, or buy us dolls from the same shop. The fact that it was St. Mary's church made me very happy too. "*Enatachen Emebetey Mariam* [our Mother Lady Mary]" is what Almazesha called her, and her bedroom was full of Virgin Mary icons from Greece, Russia, Ethiopia, or Israel. I remember Almazesha was somewhat surprised that I had taken a job at the Church. She was proud that I did not just give up on the studio but that I tried to make it work. "*Emebetey Mariam, teredashalech* [Our Lady St. Mary will help you through]," she often said to me when I called. She would also ask "*Abba*[39] *dehena nachewu?* [Is the priest doing well?]."

I worked as seriously as I could for the *Abba*, Father Kolagian. More than ever, I felt that maybe this was the start of a new path in my life, one that would take me into the work, the profession, and the service I am meant to do. I prayed a lot. All her life,

---

[39] *Abba* is the term of respect for a priest in Ethiopia, especially an older priest. When speaking of a priest or to a priest, it is also protocol to use the respect-form, like "*vous*" in French.

Almazesha woke up each morning at 4:00AM and prayed until 6:00AM, so in these months of challenge at the studio and my work at the church, I too woke up at 4:00AM and prayed. I prayed for direction. I prayed in the name of the God of Israel, as Almazesha prayed. I did not ask for anything in particular, just for guidance to help me take the right next steps.

The life of the studio took a turn for the worse and I knew that sooner or later we would have to close down. While I worked for Father Kolagian, I kept looking for work and landed a job with a French company based in Bethesda. The pay was much better, the environment was professional, and to make the deal even sweeter, I had an outstanding man for a boss—Michael McMurphy.

Working under Michael was like working under a guru. He had a way in the office. He was sharp and hard-working, he demanded results, yet he also listened to people. He was tolerant and although he ranked in the top ten of a company of 30,000 employees, his humility, humor, and kindness were exceptional, to say the least. With Michael I learned how to apply what I had learned from Almazesha, in terms of work ethics and human relations, to a modern work environment.

It felt so good to work under such leadership. The short time I spent working for Michael allowed me to come full circle with all that I had learned in school, in life, and through Almazesha. When I spoke on the phone with Almazesha, I knew that she knew this also; and felt how I felt. She told me, *"Gobez aleka astemari newu; edelegna nesh lej, temari. Beterash antchim astemari tehognalesh. Kote na lebu alesh, endawu tinish ketigistu betchmirilish. Gin yelejenet guday newu...begizewu yimeta* [A great leader is a teacher—you are lucky my child. Keep learning. When your turn comes, you will also be a teacher. You certainly have the head and the heart—if only God could give you a bit of that patience you lack at times. But that's more of an age factor; the patience will come in time]."

These were good days, months when I would often talk to Almazesha and reflect on the years that had passed, the obstacles I had had to learn to deal with, and the mistakes I had made or not made. We spoke of the recent past, and at times she told me stories from when I was a toddler, stories from her own past, or stories of her ancestors. Such discussion anchored me more and more into the principles she taught me. More and more, I understood—and as I understood more and more, my aspirations started to change, moving away from the private sector toward work creating welfare for the destitute and underprivileged. I wanted to share what I had. All the privilege I had from having an education and a loving family, I wanted to put in service of others who might not have been as fortunate.

The call of home

About a year down the line, although I was happily working and living quite well in Chevy Chase, Maryland, something inside my heart started ticking again. I had this urge to go back home, but I remained with the urge unattended. I was tired of starting up life a gazillion times over. But then, one evening, while I was driving home from work, a young girl drove through a stop sign and crashed head-on into me. The car was totaled. I was not harmed, but every single bone in my body was shaking from the shock. It was time to go home.

I had spent almost eight years after graduating from college going in circles, and even though my job with Michael could have meant a career, I knew that I had to go back. It had to be now or never.

By the time I went back, things had changed a bit in Ethiopia. I still had the farm in mind or the candy factory, but something else emerged: In combination with my own experience of testing for HIV/AIDS, I realized that the epidemic was ravaging the country. It was not as bad as some of other nations that suffered from HIV severely, but it was pretty tragic. I felt that all my going around in circles may have been a learning process, and that through this process, life had taught me more than I would ever learn in school. Almazesha told me, "*Yezger sera behiwetachin min endehone fitchiwun lemawek gize yefejal. Idelegna gin be gize yegebaawal* [It takes time to understand the lessons of God in our lives; the lucky ones may understand in time]." I was not sure whether I had learned what I was supposed to learn, but more than ever, there was lightness in my heart and clarity about how and for whom I wanted to work. Conviction brought me commitment and gave me the courage to articulate my plans, to embrace innovation, and to accept being different and leverage that to be creative. I have learned that sticking by what stirs my heart allows me to go through thick and thin—it is not possible to remain committed to anything unless that thing stirs our hearts and thrills our minds.

So, once more, I resigned from my job. By now the studio had closed and the only thing that almost held me back, a little, was my relationship with the man I was dating at the time. In a life where the few men I dated were comparable to buffaloes in their behavior and their character, this guy was unreal in his kindness, his behavior, and everything else you can imagine. Sometimes I feel that my relationship with him was part of experiencing and knowing all the dimensions of love and intimacy. It was like being given a chance to see how good *good* could be.

This relationship was particular, almost obsessive— we were together 24/7 and time didn't matter anymore.

He would refuse to let me do anything. Almazesha smiled with complicity when I told her about this relationship, and said that such behavior is not common to men. Almazesha was never one to pass judgment on men who cooked or were ready to roll up their sleeves to take care of their women. She would just say that often only men who had a very close and loving relationship to the women in their own families, could be so loving to their girlfriends or wives. I knew this relationship was not common. I was always well aware of that.

All he wanted was for me to sit in the living room while he cooked up a storm. I would sit on the couch with some jazzy music in the background, and he would cook, whistling and mumbling some lyrics, then pop out of the kitchen with his apron and a tiny spoon holding a sampler of the simmering thing in the pot. At times, he would come out with colorful cocktails that he made up with whatever juices and liquor he had in his closets. Some days we just stayed in, with him painting my toenails or telling me fairy tales as I sat in a bubble bath that he prepared for me. I remember he had these natural sponges that he soaked with water and let the water trickle down my back. I couldn't even tell anyone about what I was living—who would ever believe that there were still men like this around? When we went out for dinner, his etiquette was nothing less than perfect. There were times I could sense that people around us felt odd about our relationship because it was not so common to see an inter-racial intimate relationship of that kind. But I didn't care and he certainly cared even less. We laughed a lot—there was such complicity. We hardly slept. I have no idea how the days, weeks, and months with him passed.

There are times when things are so good that the only wise thing to do is to just soak in it and enjoy it for what it is. There are times when someone comes into our lives, and no matter what else is going on, the person lights up the stars in our skies and tucks the sun in our hearts. Such was this relationship to me. I never felt he was my boyfriend per se—I had no title for him. He just was, and for the time that we were together, we lived as one entity. There was no expectation; we had no constraints on each other. We just lived one day at a time, maybe even a moment at a time. It was surreal. It is as though we had made a subconscious commitment to just love the other unconditionally and in the most unselfish way.

The urge to go back to Ethiopia emerged in the midst of this relationship. I was hesitant to go, but I knew in deep inside that I had to follow my heart. I shared my desire to return with him, and we spoke at length. I wanted him to come to Ethiopia; he wanted me to return to France with him. We were both stubborn despite the love that kept us together. We agreed to disagree. I would go back to Ethiopia and he back to his country.

If tears of separation-sadness could be compared to a waterfall, then saying goodbye was nothing short of Victoria Falls after the rainy season. We were both heartbroken to have to say goodbye, even though we both knew it was the right decision. With loads of tissues and sniffles that lasted days, I finally purchased a ticket for the flight that would bring me back home, back to my country.

Oh, but life had more in store in the week before departure.

PART V:
FROM THEN TO NOW—
THE MORE RECENT
JOURNEY

Out of kindness, Michael gave me permission to stay in the corporate apartments for a few days before my departure, as I had vacated my apartment. The corporate apartment, a two-bedroom penthouse in a posh building in Georgetown, had a breathtaking view overlooking the Potomac River.

Enaniye had come to stay with me to help me organize my trip. I was living my last days in DC with all the exhilaration that last days often carry. I was out all the time, dining, shopping, romancing, and what have you. It was almost too much.

As the days dwindled, I wanted to spend as much time as possible with this man I was dating. With my final departure planned in about a week, I remember telling Enaniye and Fofi that I would go out for dinner on one particular night, and that they should not expect me to come home early.

An unexpected surprise

That night, Enaniye and Fofi also came in as late as I did, about 11:00pm or so. They were giggling. I asked, "What's all the good mood about?" "We have great news," Fofi said. "Did you win the Power Ball?" I asked. "No, but do you remember Enaniye's picture of when she was at the hospital?" I knew exactly which picture, and I nodded, prompting Fofi to continue. "Well, it was not a kidney problem—she had just delivered a baby. We have an older sister!" she shouted. Then, just as quickly, she whipped out a piece of paper and gave me a number. "Her name is Jessica. Here, this is her number. You call."

What in heaven was all this about now? What? We have an older sister? My head was spinning from happiness. I couldn't make sense of it. I joined in the joy and giggles and picked up the phone to call this new sister of ours.

I went to the bedroom, changed into comfortable clothes, got something to drink, and sat on the floor with the phone. I dialed the number, and each time it rang my heart jumped. Finally, she picked up. The conversation was interestingly natural. "How strange," I thought. Although I was speaking to someone completely new in my life, someone that I had never met, knowing that she was my sister created an instant bond. We spoke for hours. She told me she was planning on coming to Washington, DC on Saturday to meet Enaniye and reunite with everyone on our side. It's hard to put what I felt into words.

In the midst of all that, I could only think of Boubiye—he had to come and be with us on Saturday. After hanging up with Jessica, I called him and told him the story of this young lady living in California. I told him how much she was like Enaniye, how she also ate oatmeal in the morning and took loads of vitamins. I told him that she, too, was into real estate investment. I even told him that she was also into arts. Finally, he interrupted me and asked why in the world I am telling him all this. "It's because she is coming on Saturday to meet us and you have to be here." He was in Brussels at the time, and Saturday was just three days away. He was at a loss. "Why should I come? What does it have to do with me?" I was out of my league and passed on the phone to Enaniye for her to explain. Boubiye took the next available flight and stood right by Enaniye faster than anyone could ever imagine.

The three days waiting for Jessica to arrive had all the tension of a long awaited event—it was an unbearable drumroll rocking our hearts. Each moment and minute seemed to last forever. We decided to meet in a neutral place, and booked ourselves into a hotel in Chevy Chase. On "the" day, our entire family—my parents, my sisters, most of my aunts and uncles, cousins, and family friends—filled the room in the Holiday Inn. Some of us had to wait in the hallway because there was just not enough space in the room. We waited impatiently, pacing up and down, looking through the window, going to the lobby to check. We were just so restless. Then, as a caravan escorting a bride would raise the dust of the desert as it neared, she finally arrived.

Jessica came with her mother and friends and family. The corridor on our floor was bustling with emotions. Some people were snapping pictures, others were filming, and all were crying, hugging, or just standing stunned by what was taking place. Enaniye was weeping. She kept thanking *Fetariye* ("my Creator"), as she called God. Fofi and I were frozen, happy, moved—everything at once. We called Almazesha right away. "*Metach eko* [She's here]," we kept repeating on the phone. I only wish Almazesha could have been there that day. She kept saying that finding a child and being reunited is a true gift of God, and that we should be very conscious of how lucky we all are. Some months later Jessica went to Ethiopia and had a proper homecoming at Laïbet, and it was a very moving moment for all of us, and especially for Enaniye and Almazesha. In that moment Almazesha's and Enaniye's relationship, which was already very close, took on another dimension of closeness. Almazesha felt sad that the cultural and societal pressure had brought her eldest daughter to carry such a heavy heart all her life. There was no way of undoing the past, though, so the best they could ever do was to make a better future. There was a conscious and subconscious collective decision adopted by all of us as a family, which was to live life in a way that doesn't leave anyone to carry alone the events in their lives.

On that day in Chevy Chase, none of us knew what to do or how to process the emotions of joy. Some cried, others laughed, others just busied around—there was a lot of movement. Nothing made sense, and it all made a lot of sense all at once. In a society that is so conservative, and in our family in particular that is even more conservative, it was unfathomable that we would be having such a situation. In my parents' generation, no young woman in her right mind would even dare have a relationship before marriage let alone conceive a child. It was unheard of.

I was so happy to have an older sister. We were all so

happy. At the same time, the math did not add up in my head. I could not imagine how Enaniye could have lived with knowing that she had a child living somewhere in the world and have the strength not to tell anyone about it all these years. I could not understand how she even managed to have a child without anyone knowing about it. What surprised me most was Boubiye's reaction. To the contrary of what would have been expected of him, at one point he said that it was his daughter—just to protect Enaniye.

Of course, there was a lot of drama as usual. There was a lot of speculation floating around in the grapevines of our greater community. Enaniye is a highly respected person within our community, known to be poised, conservative, and kind. No one could ever think that she might have had a child before marriage. Everyone was trying to add up the years and do the math to figure out the "how" of Jessica. It was all a mystery. As usual, instead of asking Enaniye directly, many were just fabricating different scenarios around the context in which Jessica was conceived. Enaniye was so happy about finding Jessica that she was just there stunned, grateful and thankful to God.

In all of this commotion, I was still due to leave for Addis in a matter of one or two days.

A new chapter in Addis Ababa

It was Meskal when I arrived in Addis. The flight arrived in the early evening and the bonfires had already been started around town; there was the familiar scent of burning Eucalyptus wood and a festive atmosphere. My girlfriend Benedicte Ausset (Bene) was already in Addis and waiting for me. Bene and I met in our first year of college at American University and have remained very close throughout the years. Bene always sensed the times when I needed to have someone on my side. On this trip, she had called me a few weeks ahead and offered to spend my first month in Ethiopia with me. "Let me stay with you until you get used to it," she had said. She had just started her career as a photographer and being in Ethiopia would also be an opportunity to explore the country with her camera.

The first month in Addis was good—full of new things, new people, new dynamics, and new possibilities. It was good to have Bene with me, so there was someone I could really talk to. She helped me get properly anchored in this new setting. I stayed in my parents' home near Bole Airport in a residential area called Bole Rwanda (because the Embassy of Rwanda is located there). Almazesha loved my friend Bene; knowing that Bene was an old friend, she was both surprised and very much appreciative that Bene came to be with me for a month just to help me get settled. Almazesha was concerned that Bene was too thin and would try to send me all types of dishes to get Bene to eat more. She would always tell me that I should never call Bene a girlfriend but that I should introduce her as my sister.

Just for adventure's sake, Bene and I decided to go up country into the north to visit the historical sites. We spent a couple of weeks travelling by plane, bus, and foot. To my surprise, I was shocked at how my people treated foreigners. There was substantial racism. As I walked around with Bene in Addis and up country, I cringed at how people behaved. I had never before felt so self-conscious as I experienced each day a side of Ethiopia I had not known before. Children would follow us, shouting *"ferengi, ferengi* [foreigner, foreigner]" and an occasional *"ferengi* fuck you....you, you, fuck you." I don't think they knew what they were saying, but it was annoying. None of the adults reacted to correct the children; in fact, some adolescents and younger adults joined in with the children. It was worse in Lalibella when one of the young guides insulted us viciously inside the monasteries because we refused his services. I wondered, "Is this the country that I am coming back to?" Things were different in Axum, up in Tigrae—it is as if there was discipline. People went on with their lives and their ways; no one insulted, harassed, or provoked us. In fact, I found that people there went out of their way to be helpful.

Almazesha was as disappointed as I was about the bad behavior we encountered. She found it shameful that our society had reached a place of displaying such manners in Ethiopia. In her day, she would tell me, such behavior would have been severely punished. On the other hand, when I told her about the people in Axum, she did not seem surprised; she said that the people of Tigrae are dedicated Christians who not only exercise their faith but also enact it in their daily lives. Discipline is part of their norm, she told me.

On our return to Addis, we were relieved to be back in the comfort of modern life with hot running water, food, and a proper bed. The short adventure out in the living conditions of rural Ethiopia was a bit of a shocker—the level of poverty I saw was shocking. There was such a gap between how people lived in the rural areas and how we lived in the cities. I did not know anyone within my immediate circle who had traveled up country and in the way that we did. People tended to just remain in Addis and reduce

Ethiopia to the capital, not caring to know the situation in the rest of the country.

Now that I had been in Ethiopia for a couple of weeks, it was time to turn my focus to settling down and finding a job or setting up an organization. We set out to visit organizations and embassies to connect into the world of NGOs and see how I could join in the work. Interestingly, although I was the one making the appointments and talking to the individuals, most of them ignored me completely and focused on responding to Bene. She kept pointing them back to me, but in vain. Most of the time she was getting all the response and possibly the respect as well, because she was a white girl; at the same time, on the streets, she was the one being insulted and harassed more because, again, she was a white girl. I was ignored in the offices by people who tended to give more attention to foreigners rather than Ethiopians, and outside on the streets, I was insulted by boys and young men because of my association with Bene.

This was all an absolute shock for me. I never remembered any such thing in my country. As I relayed my latest experiences, Almazesha would only shake her head in regret that a country formerly known for its hospitality and manners had reached levels of such disrespect for guests and its own people. She lamented, "*Min yederig, temehirt ha hu mekuter bitch ayedelem...seletane belewu endih sihonu min yederig? Yezger yirdan, Etchi meskin ager wodet eyehedech yehon. Ay fetariye.* [What can we do when they think that education is reciting the *Ha-Hu*[40]? What can we do when they behave this way in the name of

---

[40] Ethiopian alphabet.

civilization? May God help us. Where is our poor country heading? Oh, my Lord.]"

I didn't let this discourage me, however, and kept on pushing forward. Finally, by chance, at the Hilton we encountered some people working with Médecins Sans Frontières. One thing led to another, and before long I was presenting myself as a candidate for a new project in service of women working in the red light district.

One last interlude

It took a few months to work out the logistics of my hiring, during which time I decided to fly back to Washington, DC for the end-of-year holidays and to visit once more the man I was dating. I was hoping that the intensity of our story would have died down, since I had been gone for a few months. But I stayed in DC for about 10 days and for 10 days, I can say that we hardly slept—as if sleeping would steal time from us, we stayed up watching TV, going out at night, dining, walking, etc. Far from having died down, our story was more alive than ever. For a while, I reconsidered my decision to move to Ethiopia, but in the end, I stuck to my decision.

This was back in the days before 9/11, when non-passengers could escort passengers all the way to the boarding gate: The drama as I boarded the plane was unbelievable. Although we had already said our goodbyes at his apartment, with the usual flood of tears and sniffles, although I had taken my cab to the airport...as I was about to board, waiting in line to hand my boarding pass to the flight attendants, I heard him calling my name from afar. He was running, swooshing between travelers like a skier swooshes in curves around the poles of the ski slopes. Drama from heaven, or hell, or whatever you may call it—it was drama for sure. As shy as I am, especially in public, this time I got caught up and "swooped" into it.

When I think about it today, I can only shake my head with a smile and know that these were good times, the good times when we were young and for a minute maybe considered living *"d'amour et d'eau fraiche* [on love and fresh water]." As he ran to me, his coat was flying off his back. His hair was all over the place, and he could hardly breathe. With words that he tried to speak as he caught his breath, he scooped me up like the *amora* (the eagle) we knew so well in Ethiopia. I was swirling in his arms, turning and turning in an endless waltz. It was as if the rest of the airport did not exist—it was as if he pressed the pause button on time. "Miss, miss, the gate is closing. Miss, miss, the gate is closing." Finally I heard the flight attendant, restarting time for me. Why are last moments so full of drama and so heavily loaded with emotion? Why does time in last moments seem to go in fast forward?

I boarded the plane, albeit ruffled up from all the commotion, crying, kissing, hugging, and uncertainty of the path ahead. I had chosen a path of my own, and now I had to take up the reins of my decision. The agony of saying goodbye once more ripped my soul into thin slices. Walking away from a man I knew I could have loved for the rest of my life, it was unbearable.

A long time ago, Almazesha had told me about *"ye kenfer wodaj* [a lip lover]"—a lip lover, she said to me, was a young boy who would be introduced to a young girl before marriage. They would be allowed to remain together in the daytime and would only be allowed to kiss. She told me that most of the time the pair would go up to the prairies or fields to sit covered up in the girl's *netela* and spend the day kissing and being together. The two would be close in age, and the boy would never be allowed to do anything else with the girl other than kissing her lips, hence his title "lip lover." The relationship was sort of a prelude to marriage, perhaps an initiation of sorts. Shortly before the wedding of the girl, there would be a ceremony to bid the lip lover goodbye. Despite the celebrations taking place, this would be a sad moment full of tears. I have never asked Almazesha whether she had such a friend. Maybe she did; maybe she did not.

This man might have been the kind of lover that Almazesha told me about, the *ye kenfer wodaj* or lip lover. I once told Almazesha about this particular relationship. We were alone in her bedroom, and I was sitting at the foot of her bed as usual. It was one of those quiet mornings in Laïbet. I remember she smiled as she heard me go on and on about what I did, how it went, and so forth. She smiled and her gaze flew out the window in the direction of the mountain range. I knew she was listening to me, but with the background of my voice; I also knew that she was traveling back to a time long gone where fact and legend become one and the same. There are times we talked yet few words were spoken—it is as if the silence spoke for the heart more than words could ever manage. This moment was one such moment where I was conscious that our conversation was beyond words. It was almost as if the story I told her allowed us both to enter a different dimension.

On the flight back to Addis that day, I felt completely broken. My thoughts were blurry, mixed up, and I was not so sure anymore. I was uncertain about life, ready to throw in the towel. Was I making the biggest mistake of my life or was this the right decision? I did not know.

Almazesha always said to me, "when in doubt, talk to God." So, I wrote a letter to God on the plane home, I remember. (I can't pray mentally because I get distracted, so I usually write out my prayers.) In this prayer I remember telling God three things: 1) that I knew there would never be anyone else in my life that I would feel so strongly about, so if he could please just allow me to have the kind of work where I could fully invest myself; 2) if he could please make me like the gym because I needed to exercise but I didn't like it, so if he could just do something about that; 3) if he could for the hundredth time help me quit smoking once and for all. I left a little P.S. for him: I told him that if he thought that there was someone else for me, he should let me know. I stashed the letter in my wallet, disembarked from the plane, and walked tall in the spirit of the new future I would start in Addis.

A new calling

The past was past, and now I had to look forward and keep moving with faith, despite all the doubt and uncertainties that still haunted me. I started work within days, as the communication and education person for an HIV/AIDS project for women surviving from prostitution. I experienced an instant connection with the community that our project was serving.

I was both shocked and saddened by the life

conditions of the women and young girls I encountered. The world of the sex trade was new to me, and it is a hard world. Our team worked through the night several times a week to meet and work with the women of the various red light districts in Addis. By day, we did our paperwork and all the other activities that accompany running a project. I saw women of all ages working and selling sex; the hardest for me was seeing very young girls start out in this line of work. One thing was evident: these women were surviving, but they were out there because there was demand for them on the market. For a country that is rather conservative on the average and where sex is a taboo issue, I couldn't make sense of the number of women working and the number of clients they had each day. The clients were from all levels, from the lowest social class to the highest, including the international and expatriate community. Witnessing this double existence of my society was hard to process—as usual, I turned to Almazesha almost every day to get some explanation, to make some sense of what I saw at night.

Often when I spoke to Almazesha about what I saw on the street, she would be as distraught as I was. She would look away, take her gaze elsewhere, and quietly say, "*ye set lij mekera* [the burden of girls/women]." She, of all people, knew that the women on the street did not enter the street by choice but by misfortune. She, of all people, allowed me to understand that critical fact and enabled me to relate to the women I served. She, of all people, gave me hope that just because the women were in such a predicament today, it did not mean that such would be their lives forever. Change is possible. When we can put judgment aside, when we can relate to another's pain, when we can see a brighter horizon despite the challenges, then we are also in a position to change lives—our own as well as that of those around us.

Among the toughest things I saw was the violence against these women. They were beaten by the police and often raped in detention or just right there on the streets. Clients also beat them regularly or walked out on them without paying. If a client left without paying, the girls would say "he used me for free"—this was how they referred to rape. There were times that the police or soldiers beat the women right in front of us. A few times, they threatened to beat us too. We could not do anything to save the women; we could only take care of them after the fact. What is one supposed to do when those meant to impose law and order are the same ones who violate law and order? In the night, it seemed there was no law—the strongest, the toughest, those armed and in uniform ruled the streets. That was how it was.

At some point I found out about the traffic of virgin girls. Clients would ask the usual women they used for sex to bring them virgins, for which they would pay about ETB 1,500 (USD $200)—a colossal amount compared to the meager ETB 30-50 per sex session that the women usually earned from well-to-do clients. So, a trend was starting where women were bringing in their younger sisters, friends, and relatives to the sex trade so they could collect the bounty of ETB 1,500. Of course, clients who could afford such a price for sex were certainly not those from the lower income levels: they were the men who ran the private sector and those who held high positions in the public sector or in international organizations. I once met a girl with a slashed cheek, a terrible scar disfiguring her pretty face. She was only about 13, maybe 14 at most. She explained to me that she had been knifed by another girl a bit older than herself because she had refused to be a "virgin" assignment for the older girl. Later on, when the older girl found out that she had given her virginity away to a random boy (never mind that it was her lover), the older girl slashed her with a knife to teach her a lesson and make her an example.

As much as I was shocked by the situation, I was equally if not more inspired by the resilience of the women. They were strong women, proud and courageous despite the reality of their lives. They were generous women with a great sense of humor and immense empathy for others.

Matthias

It might be that God received the letter I wrote to him on my flight back to Addis. The first time I saw Matthias was while I was waiting in line for the Ethiopian customs officials when I arrived back from Washington, DC. It was normal that all arriving passengers opened their suitcases and were checked before being allowed into the country. He was standing right behind me, the line was long, and we struck up a conversation. He was holding some strange-looking long tubes, similar to those used to store posters. He had a very dark tan, which made his short, blond crew cut stand out more. I couldn't tell what color eyes he had—at times I thought they were green but then again they looked blue. (Later I found out that his eyes tend to be green or blue depending on the light or the colors he wears.)

That day, he was wearing a particularly old leather jacket, like something from old black-and-white movies. We started just chatting as you would in any queue, and found out that we lived on the same street, "Bole Rwanda." We had some friends in common as well—it was the usual airport/expatriate conversation. I learned that he had been in Ethiopia for about a year or so and that he spent most of this time in Bahir Dar completing his master's thesis research. As we blabbered on, my turn came to be checked. We exchanged numbers for eventual parties or social events, and I continued on my way. I didn't hear from him or he from me for 2-3 weeks.

Eventually we met again by some coincidence at the "Torerro," the primary night spot at the time. It was good to see him again, but I didn't think much more of it other than just seeing someone I had met earlier. We had the usual courtesy conversation and made plans to have dinner in the coming days. We went out for dinner on two occasions. Matthias was very sweet and nice, more on the conservative side despite the hard-core leather jacket he had on. Sometime in this couple of weeks, I had a dinner party at my place, and as usual, it lasted into the wee hours of the night. It was actually my parents' place—the house was built for entertainment and receptions and we made good use of that, especially since my parents were not in the country. I had the house all to myself for a few weeks. Time to have a party!

I sensed that a slight romantic adventure was getting started, and I went along with it. It would not be untrue to say that we both thought of this romance as a little romantic escapade, nothing more.

A few weeks after the dinner party, he had to go out to the south of the country for his work, to the surroundings of Jinka for about 2-3 weeks. He suggested that I join him for the last few days there and we would drive back to Addis together. I took off from work, got a stamp for the yellow fever vaccination in my vaccination pass, and booked my ticket. I asked where I would meet him. "When you get off the plane, look to the left, and I will be sitting at the terrace of the only café there," he said. "What nonsense!" I thought. I didn't believe him—how would someone just get off the plane and look to the left?

The airplane headed to Jinka was a tiny plane, 8 seats or maybe 10, and it seemed more like a minibus with wings than an airplane. It did not fly very high so of course the flight was bumpy, and with each bump, I thought it would be my last moment in this world. Finally, there was an announcement that we were about to land and to put on our seat belts. I looked through the window, but I did not see tarmac or even an airport for that matter. I was too shocked to panic. As the plane descended, I could see someone in an airline ground crew uniform shooing cattle away and asking the merchants to get off the road. "Lord, Jesus," I thought to myself as I realized that the tarmac was the main street of this little town and that in the absence of an incoming aircraft, this road/street served as the main market. "No, no, this can't be," I was thinking. But it was so. The cattle were diverted, the merchants picked up their goods and moved to the side, and the plane landed in the road/market. I heard the usual flight chime indicating the green light to disembark. I left my seat, still a bit crouched as the plane was so small. Through the small door of the aircraft, I looked out to the left and to my surprise, there he was sitting at the only café—just as he had said.

If one were to judge or guess the location of the café,

from Matthias's demeanor, you would think that he was sitting at one of the terraces in Paris or Brussels, with his dark glasses and khakis. Except, this time, it was Jinka. I took my little bag and walked across the street to join him. That was it. This was the "airport." I was still in disbelief about the entire journey. He ordered a beer for me, a Bedele beer. We didn't say anything much. He seemed tickled by the entire thing and was giggling at my shock or reaction to the entire thing. "Ethiopia is not only Addis...it's also places like this," he said. As we finished up the beer, the driver from his project came along and joined us.

In the car, we headed to where we would stay for the next few days. I assumed we would be staying in a small hotel or whatever might be available around this place, but I was wrong once more! We drove down the dirt road, bumping as the road swerved and curved. "We're almost there," he said. I looked to the left, I looked to the right, but all I could see was savanna. I was not sure if this was his definition of humor, but at this point, I was beyond being even upset. I was furious at myself for having agreed to come on this trip. I just looked him dead in the eyes and said, "Glad we're there...can't wait to freshen up and rest." The car took a right turn into the bushes. There was no road—the only path was probably what this very car had carved out in the past few days. We drove through the bushes with branches scratching the windshield and windows of the car. I could see a sort of camp, a number of tents. Although I knew that this was what was waiting for me, I was still hoping that there would be something else around the corner, maybe a small lodge or a hotel or something. I could not believe that I would be stuck in the middle of the savanna.

Unfortunately for me, there was no hotel, no lodge—just a tent. We were to spend the next days in this camp. Matthias was happy and proud to tell me that we had been given a special tent, one with a floor! In my head I was thinking, "Why would that be considered special? What else were we supposed to sleep in?" At this point, Matthias had not yet realized how much I am terrorized by anything from the creepy crawly family. I tried to be brave and went into our new little home, the special tent.

The next days were tough, for me. No one else seemed to care about the legion of insects going up and down everything around. At night, we all gathered around a campfire to eat the dinner that one of his colleagues cooked. I didn't know where to put my feet, as the traffic of insects swarmed on the ground. No need to think of showers—it was just a bucket of cold water. Privacy, you say? Oh, yes, no worries, just stand behind the cars, basically butt naked in the middle of the high grass of the savanna. Toilet, hmm, no problem—the bushes are there for that! Oh, yes, don't forget to take the toilet paper and the shovel with you. I must have lost 3-4 kilos in those few days. I could not be any happier than the day we packed up to drive back to Addis.

A week later, Matthias's birthday was coming up on April 21st. His roommate and I planned a surprise party for him; to allow her to make all the party arrangements in peace, I thought I would have a pre-party and take him out to Menagesha Mountain for a picnic. We stopped by Fantu Grocery in Bole and bought all sorts of finger foods, snacks, croissants, coffee, juice, cheese, fruits, etc. Matthias had brought a huge bottle of Moët Champagne. We drove out early in the morning and reached the mountaintop around noon. Once we found a nice little corner to park the car and still have a view, we opened up the trunk and set somewhat of a table with the food and drinks. We sat on the edge of the truck. The picnic was going well. It was drizzling, but I was almost happy about the drizzle as this meant I would not have to force myself to climb or hike up the mountain.

In the midst of it all, Matthias asked, "Can I ask you something?" "Ask me anything," I said, "but please don't ask me to climb up the mountain. Anything else is okay." He paused for a moment and replied, "Would you spend the rest of your life with me?" "What?" I was shocked. I was expecting him to ask me to hike, walk, climb up the mountain, or even make plans to come back next weekend to climb up this mountain or another. I must have remained stunned for a while, because he asked me again, "Would you?" For some reason, I knew I would spend my life with this man, so I said "Yes." We had known each other for about three months. We had spent maybe a good 3-4 weeks together and now I was agreeing to spend the rest of my life with him. I knew it was the right decision, deep in my heart, but my mind could not rationalize my decision. What in heaven was all this about? Matthias pulled out two champagne glasses (which I didn't know he had) and opened the bottle of Moët. It was amazing to be out there in the mountains, under drizzling rain, sitting in the back of a truck, drinking champagne as we giggled and laughed. I still can't believe it when I think back.

Well, it was one thing to agree to spend our lives together and something else to follow the entire protocol of making this decision reality. I explained to Matthias that if we were to marry we would have to abide by the traditions of my culture. This means that the decision was not only mine but also involved the elders of my family. He would have to find *shemageles* (eligible elders) to represent him and his family, to come and ask my elders for my hand.

The wedding and the ceremonies

Ethiopia has very intricate wedding ceremonies and the ceremony's form and details depend on the ethnicity of the bride and groom. In my lineage and according to the culture of my family, the wedding starts with elders from the groom's side coming to ask for the hand of the bride. The parents of the groom are never involved, because should the bride's family refuse to give the hand of their daughter, then the groom's family would be able to keep face.

The groom's elders make an appointment to see the bride's elders, and on the day of the appointment they all come together to the house of the oldest member of the bride's family. In my case, the *shemageles* that Matthias appointed came to Laïbet. They drove in, and then walked solemnly toward the main house, coming up the steps one by one to reach the entrance of the living room. They were not invited to sit, but had to remain standing. For a few minutes, it is normal that the bride's family ignores their presence a bit. This is part of it. Then, the oldest or the leader of the bride's family asks: "What can we do for you?" or "Why are you here today?" Traditionally, they reply, "We have come to ask for the hand of your daughter for our son." In my case, everything went accordingly, except the answer Almazesha gave to their statement was not really what they had expected. "I have many daughters," she said, "which one did you mean?" "Yene is the one we mean," they replied. "What is her

Christian name?" Almazesha asked. The Christian name is the name that we are given at baptism, and prayers for a person are done using the Christian name. As they heard this question, the *shemageles* looked around at each other and realized none of them knew the name. "It seems you don't know the name," Almazesha continued. "Best we talk to you once you find out." And on this note, they had to leave the living room and drive away.

The truth is that *I* didn't even know my Christian name. The *shemageles* reported the question to Matthias, Matthias then asked me, I asked Almazesha, and then I told Matthias the name. In turn, he informed the *shemageles* who now had to make a new appointment.

On their second visit, they knew the Christian name and when asked for it, they were able to give the answer. The living room in Laïbet was full with all the senior members of my family. Every seat was occupied, which means there were a good twenty or so members of my family: my aunts, uncles, parents, some older cousins, and of course Almazesha and Ababi. Once the *shemageles* gave the right answer about my Christian name, Ababi took the floor and asked the *shemageles*, *"Ye ma lej New?* [Whose son is he?]." "Werner Reusing, sir," they replied. Ababi repeated the name to himself as if checking in his memory. "I doubt we know each other," he finally said when he could not find the name in his memory. And he continued, "I am now in my old age. I don't know the family of the young man. I believe they live in a country far from here. If this young man were to take my daughter and mistreat her, I could not come to her help, given my age. So, I would like to ask you to bring us a letter from the municipality of the city where they live, stating and confirming that this family is one that is law abiding and has no criminal record and a promissory note from the family stating that they will treat our daughter as their daughter, in the same way that we would be treating their son as our son." With this new assignment, once more Matthias's ambassadors left Laïbet without even being offered a seat or water.

In parallel, I believe that Matthias's parents were a little concerned that he was to marry an African. There were no Africans in their village and what they expected of Africa might be more in line with the exotic National Geographic programs rather than what actually Africa is. It must have been a surprise for them to receive this request from my family asking that they send their elders to my elders to ask for my hand and to present their son as a suitable young man. They may not have known that on our side, my family was equally concerned that I was about to go and marry someone from a foreign country, someone whose history and family reputation we did not know. As much as they were concerned for their son, my family was very concerned for my welfare. We say in Ethiopia that marriage is not just between a man and a woman—it's a whole family linking up with another family.

On the third visit of the *shemageles*, they came with the letter from Germany. This time, Ababi asked them to have the letter translated officially as he does not speak German. He promised to them that in the meanwhile they would talk to me, and if my response was favorable, then the next time they came we would be able to reach some conclusion.

It took another couple of weeks to have the fourth

and last appointment. On this day, Ababi and Almazesha had already discussed it with me, and my parents had also given me their approval. I was told I could attend the meeting and that Matthias could come and introduce himself. So, on the fourth appointment, the *shemageles* were finally invited to sit and were offered the usual Laïbet hospitality with food and drinks flowing throughout. Matthias was there too. One of my great-great-uncles, Ababa Bisate, asked him the last question before the deal was sealed. Ababa Bisate, who is Almazesha's father's brother and a refined man with a sharp sense of humor, saw that Matthias had an earring, a small gold loop. "I see that our young man is wearing a loop. In our culture, only warriors and those who have fought lions are permitted to wear such loops. What war did he fight or what lion has he fought to feel that he earned wearing this loop?" The question was translated to Matthias. My poor sweetheart was against the wall, but finally I could see his face brightening up and he said: "Sir, I have not fought a war, but I believe I have found my lion!" Ababa Bisate loved the answer—he and I shared some affinity and he glanced over at me with his usual mischievous smile and finally broke the silence with "Somebody, pour my new son some whiskey!" This was Matthias's last hurdle and Ababa Bisate's way of telling him that now he was no longer an aspiring groom but a full-fledged son to my elders.

We had a simple wedding. I refused to spend more money than the total of my monthly salary and that of Matthias. As in most countries, in Ethiopia families often end up spending so much for weddings. I didn't believe in that kind of spending, especially while I worked and saw each day the hardship of so many women in the red light district. Despite all the kicking and shouting from my parents and Almazesha, I insisted on having only about 150 guests. Fofi offered to bake our wedding cake. I refused to have unnecessary car decoration fanfare and only used Boubiye's Mercedes as the bride and groom car. As for bridesmaids and all that jazz, I refused once more because I did not see the value it would add, other than additional headache. Instead, I had cute dresses done for Essayas and Gueni's children (Maheltt, Saron, and Rediyet) and that was it—my sisters and close cousins could each have a rose pinned on their collars. The food was to be prepared at Laïbet and we would keep the menu to something simple and traditional. The day of the wedding, I saw that there were a number of people I had not invited and when I looked to Almazesha, she laughed and confessed that she had Xeroxed the invites and invited her close friends and family also. We had a great party. It was only after the wedding that Almazesha, my parents, and my aunts appreciated and admitted that after all they were happy with our choices to avoid the usual high-cost wedding.

Real life kicks in

We did not go on a honeymoon, as we could not afford it. We didn't take time off after the wedding, but both went back to work on Monday and resumed our lives. Going on honeymoon was more a Western tradition, anyway; in Ethiopia a traditional wedding did not really involve a honeymoon. So, the fact that we went straight to regular life did not cause any comment. We first lived in my house, the one I had rented when I started working for MSF. It was just around the corner from my parent's home, and it was not unusual for me to call and have supplies or meals sent over.

Since a number of our friends, siblings, cousins, and so on had flown in from the various corners of the world for the wedding, we continued the festive mood for a few weeks. Then, just about 3-4 weeks after the wedding, Matthias fell seriously ill. He was unable to leave the bed. He felt extremely weak and dehydrated, and drank up crates of Ambo water (local sparkling mineral water). I had no idea what was wrong with him. After a visit to the doctor, we found out that he had diabetes. It was a tragic moment. We knew what it meant because his father had diabetes. Somewhere in my mind, although I knew Matthias would handle it, I was worried that this would change our lives and especially his life. Today, I can say that our life did not change a bit and he takes care of his sugar level with precision, discipline, and surrender. But that first time, we had to fly him back to Germany and have him admitted to a center where they train people living with diabetes. Almazesha was concerned by the news, and sad because she loved Matthias like her own. She kept calling and asking me about his well-being. She had as much faith in Matthias as me, if not more, and was confident he would handle the situation well. In fact, in later years, she always called on him to come and explain to other people who had diabetes how to handle their diets and lifestyles.

Juggling work and family: A structure of life

I had never really envisioned getting married one day; marriage was simply not part of my plans. I never thought I would meet someone with whom I would want to spend the rest of my life, or a person who would want to live forever with me. A hundred questions always ran through my mind when I thought of marriage: what if we don't like each other anymore, what if I change my mind, what if this or what if that. The questions never ended. It certainly did not help that most of the men I had known behaved mostly like buffalos, so it was hard to think that there were other kinds of men out there.

These events may be one reason why I had such a rough time finding the new balance in my married life. I didn't really comprehend the nature of marriage. When the oath we take states that we now live not as two bodies but as one, I took it lightly. At least I know I didn't understand at the time—it took me many years to really know what that meant.

A few weeks before the wedding my old friend Fouad Ismael told me: "Once you marry him, he will not be your boyfriend anymore; he will be your *husband*. Do you realize what that means?" I shrugged it off. I had no idea what Fouad was talking about, but then again he was such a radical rebel that I thought he was once more going on a philosophical tangent in the middle of the day. I had to get back to work, so I smiled and left.

He was trying to explain to me that we might not be fully conscious of what we were getting into when we decided to marry. At that time, how much do we really know about relationships? How much do we really know about what it means to love someone? Is it about how that person makes us feel (i.e., focused on the "me") or do we also take into consideration what we might offer to the other (i.e., focused equally on the "other")? I suppose we all have our reasons to choose to marry a person; it's personal choice, difficult to discuss. For me, however, I just felt like spending my life with Matthias. I hadn't known him for that long, but from what I knew of him, I thought that he was a great man and that together we could build a family and make a good little life. Almazesha had often alluded to the fact that marriage is not always easy and that the relationship we have with our spouse is not comparable to one we could have with a lover. But on the other hand, she pointed out, the relationship with a lover does not involve the daily aspects of running a household or raising children, so it is easy to think it is less stressful or more fun.

Although there were a number of sources of conflict between Matthias and me, the first source was punctuality and time. I was laid back about time, so I expected him to be as laid back. I really didn't mind what time he came home or whether he was held up at work or out with his friends. It didn't matter to me. For Matthias, however, that wasn't so: If I came home late and did not call, he would worry about car accidents or unexpected health problems. My blood pressure was extremely low at the time and I would faint regularly. And being me, I would often forget to call ahead or plan ahead and tell him that I would be coming later. This would come to be a source of unnecessary stress. Then there was the particularity of my work—I not only worked during regular office hours but also at night for fieldwork in areas known to be amongst the worst areas in Addis. This didn't help the situation.

Instead of appreciating his thoughtfulness, I took it as his attempt to control me. My reaction to his worries was less than graceful, and I often regret it when I look back at my behavior. I know that when I die and go to heaven, St. Peter will keep me in the waiting lounge for years before he allows me to enter heaven because of how I conducted myself in the early days of our marriage.

If I thought the beginning was hard, though, it only became tougher when our daughters were born. As much as babies are cute and adorable, people sort of never give you a warning as to what else to expect. They never really bring your attention to the fact that your body changes and morphs into something that is hardly recognizable; they never tell you that it takes months to recover if at all; they never tell you about the sleepless nights, about the wet bras, and the fact that none of your clothes really fit anymore. . . Of course, I knew a bit about all this, but you never really get it until it happens to you.

Almazesha knew very well what I was going through. She often just took my hand when I came to visit her, and as she kept my hand cupped in both her hands, she would gently ask: *"Ena enedet nesh yene lej?* [And how are you, my child?]"* I knew she knew the challenges I was facing, and I am certain she knew I felt her understanding. So, this conversation was not really in words but more in gazes, and without saying much more, we moved on to drinking coffee or talking about something completely different. I felt comfort in knowing that at least one person acknowledged some of my challenges. I was happy that I did not have to pretend all was fine and dandy to at least one person.

I was delighted when Rosi was born. I had the most beautiful pregnancy. I didn't really gain that much weight; I was swimming about 2km each day, at times more, so I was quite fit. As long as Rosi was in my tummy, I loved it. But then, when she came out, I had to share her with everyone—and this didn't fly well with me. Everybody had their two cents as to how I should feed her, how I should dress her, and how I should do this and that. My nerves were most sensitive if Matthias made comments on what I *should be doing* or, God forbid, what I might have done wrong. There was a she-monster about to burst out each time he said anything at all. Everything he said, I took as an offense on my ability to assume my role as a new mother.

My life had expanded beyond just me and included two more persons, Matthias and Rosi. The quality of responsible life took on a whole other meaning. It's not that I was irresponsible before, but I had gotten used to making decisions alone and going forward with my decisions without ever looking back. I had a hard time changing gears to learn to live while involving others in the decisions I wanted to make or had made. As usual, the more we resist or constrict ourselves in the process of change, the more the change is tough, often leaving cracks marking the confrontation between the way we used to be and the new way to be. But, eventually I learned, even if that took years on end. I learned.

Once, in a conversation with Essayas about marriage, he gave me a word of advice in story form.

There is a story about a Mr. Porcupine meeting Mr. Rabbit somewhere in the forest. And Mr. Rabbit, after the courteous greetings, approached Mr. Porcupine gently and said: "Mr. Porcupine, if you don't mind, I have a question I have been dying to ask you. But it's a personal question, would you allow me?" Mr. Porcupine replied: "Yes, please, we are such old friends that I don't mind anything you ask." On this note, Mr. Rabbit asked his questions: "Er, it's about you and the Missus. How does it really happen? You know what I mean. I just can't figure out how you would go about it." Mr. Porcupine smiled and with a chuckle said: "Oh, my old friend, we have learned to go about it very carefully!"

Although the story of Mr. Porcupine and Mr. Rabbit might make allusions to a particular aspect of married life, what I learned is that marriage in general is an institution that needs to be handled with care. And this care must be sourced in respect, compassion, and understanding. It might not necessarily be about romance but about having the true mutual foundation of communication with understanding of ourselves and our spouse based on love. At times I felt I was losing myself in the process of creating this whole. There is no need to mention that I must have been unlivable in the early days as I was confronted with new dynamics I was not prepared for. My behavior was neither compassionate nor loving.

Little by little, by some grace of God, I learned to communicate, to actually listen to the core message and also communicate clearly enough to be understood. A self-made therapy kind of communication, if I may say, but it worked. It started out rough, but in the long run I learned to express myself such that my husband and my child could understand the whole message I wanted to pass on, including how I felt, why I felt that way, the state in which I was, and the intentions of my reaching out to them.

The greatest lesson was not in the loving moments but in the times of conflict and confrontation. Compassion, to me, is being able to fight or handle conflict without hatred. Although this may sound like a paradox, in my experience, I found that I was less hurt and was less harmful to others, especially my loved ones, when in times of conflict I dealt with the situation with a softer, less judgmental gaze—as opposed to having the other positioned as a target in the bull's eye of my virtual bow and arrow. I learned that even in the heat of a fight, my loved ones and especially my partner are not to be targets. It sounds so simple when I say it now, but it took me such an emotional roller coaster to finally come to understand this. Almazesha used to say, "*Sewu sibal, yemayetala yelem...honom manenim saneskefa, hulunim bekiber yizen gudayun mastcheres alebin* [As long as we are human, we are bound to encounter conflict; however, it is our responsibility to resolve all matters without offending anyone and with full respect for all involved]."

I have had my share of mistakes, and more times than not, I know I have screwed up in colossal ways. Despite all that, one of the vital lessons I have learned is that there is always a reason to get up again, no matter what mistakes happened. Forgiveness starts with me, and through that, I can make it possible for my heart to truly forgive others. Should the ghosts of fear and insecurity take over my heart, it would be an uphill struggle to have any kind of forgiving, whether of myself or others. It is in forgiving myself, first, that I can forgive others and make reconciliation possible. We are human, nothing more and nothing less.

Through the years, my relationship with Matthias evolved, despite the initial turbulence of two stubborn people coming together. Did we get old or did we get more mature? Maybe it's a mixture of both combined with having lived full speed, sometimes to my detriment. The lessons lie in the felt texture of life in real terms and in the choices we made about how we reacted to these textures. I still have a hard time coming to terms with compromise, but I am learning each day.

Married with children

A few years down the line after we married, I found myself married with children. Fofi and I would sit together at times staring at Rosi and Leoni, and wonder: "Are these babies really ours?" Has Fofi become an Aunt and I become a Mom? It all seemed so unreal. I couldn't believe how fast time had passed. Good Lord, so we had now grown up, adults with our own lives. In Ethiopia there was a song we sang as children, a song that most children sing. The lyrics say: "*Lejineet, lejinete. Mar ena Wotete* [My childhood, my childhood, my honey and milk]." The song speaks of the sweetness of childhood, and I remember adults around me tsking and saying, "make sure you sing it well, because it will be gone before you know it." Incredible how time passes. It's very strange to look at my own life from the outside in, as a witness peeking through the window.

I was fortunate to have both pregnancies go without complication. It seems that sometimes God signs you up for courses in life that you didn't elect, and once more this was the case with the pregnancies. Although there was no health complication, my greatest challenge was to live the months of anticipating a baby with all the excitement that I felt. I was so happy about my tummy growing each day. I did not change my lifestyle—I kept on going to my sports, mainly the swimming. I felt so good in the water, I had to find time to get in the pool at least once a day. When time allowed, Matthias and I did laps together. Despite my tummy, I kept my usual speed.

The interesting thing was the reaction of some of my compatriots at the pool. As if having a well rounded tummy with a baby inside was a sin, they gave me looks of such indignation. They might have been less indignant if I had walked out naked. At work, I got comments all the time about how I should wear loose dresses so as not to show the tummy too much. Working in a project that spoke about sexuality, condoms, sex, sex trade, violence, reproductive health, and what have you, I just could not believe that the same people I worked with had an issue with me not wearing the kind of dress that looks more like a tent. My clothes during pregnancy were normal pregnancy wear, designed to make the tummy obvious as the central reason for joy and celebration. In Ethiopia, my pregnancy clothing did not work well for the people around me. They seemed almost embarrassed. Eventually, their comments and attitudes became too much to bear, but Almazesha just laughed when I came to her complaining. She laughed and laughed. "*Metchess min lebel?* [What can I say?]" she repeated, and just continued laughing. It was not that what was happening around me was funny to her, but more about how much they did not understand me and how much I did not understand them.

Unfortunately, the moment of enough is enough fell on an extremely conservative woman—I liked her a lot, but she said the one comment that broke the camel's back. She had taken me aside after the weekly management meetings and whispered in my ear that she could take me to a good tailor to get bigger dresses and that my tummy should not be that obvious. "Is the issue truly my tummy or what my tummy represents?" I asked her. "I think you are all uncomfortable. You still deny that babies are born as a consequence of sex." I knew I was not being graceful and that I spoke like a foul sailor, and I didn't care. "Other than the Holy Virgin Mary, everyone else on this Earth had sex to bear a child, except maybe in our good country—because we don't do that, do we?" I was furious.

How do we ignore a pregnancy and then come to celebrate a birth? We do not condone dating, but we expect people to find a husband or wife. What kind of double or triple reality do we create? It's as if there are parts of ourselves or our bodies that don't exist or have no right to exist. Yet at night, when I went out to the red light districts to visit the women of our project, none of this hypocrisy existed. It was business as usual, with the main product and merchandise being sex. The streets were full of conspicuous men looking for it and women selling it. Almazesha often told me that I had no business being upset by other people's behavior, that I was only responsible for my own way of being and thinking. If others behaved in one way or another, maybe there were reasons for them to be that way—maybe there were factors I did not understand that led others to think and be the way they were. She counseled me that it was certainly not my place to either be upset or be judgmental about others. Of course, I never understood what she meant, until many years later.

To add to my frustration with these double standards, I found out that the medical scene was no better. I tried to get find a gynecologist to follow-up with until I gave birth. But I never made it to the doctor—my endeavor stopped at the receptionist who found it normal to treat women like cattle. Well, that is, until he found out that not everyone would allow him to be so despicably rude. Maybe I was able to speak up for myself and leave because of how the women in my family raised me or maybe because I knew I could always find someone else, or better yet, fly out to my usual doctor; whatever the reason, maybe it was essential to me that I did not allow this man to bully me. It's about not allowing others to treat us like dirt just because we are women, and pregnant women at that. There is a minimum respect that we all deserve, and in particular, that expecting women deserve.

In the end, Rosi and Leoni were both born in Brussels, in the country that received me as a child so many years earlier. There I was giving birth to the next generation in a place where my ancestors did not give birth, which implied of course that none of the cultural and traditional practices of birthing would be offered. When Essayas' daughter Mahlett was born, I remember that the entire Laïbet community was occupying the lobby of the Filowuha hospital—there was literally no one home. We all just sat there, waiting for her to come. Yes, this was our way of welcoming her. Maybe it's not a cultural thing, but I knew that in my family, the arrival of a new member doesn't go without a remarkable level of commotion.

In Brussels, however, things were different. Although I grew up there and despite the fact that Brussels is as much a part of me as my own country, things would not be as we would have had it in Addis. For starters, I had my own plan for the birth and wanted to be alone at the hospital. I wanted to be there with Matthias and have the experience of my first child fully, without interference from anyone. So, when Enaniye suggested that she come to the hospital with me, I refused. I was not very tactful in my way of expression and I am certain that I must have been hurtful. I can only understand now that I have my own children. She felt excluded; if I felt excluded by Rosi or Leoni, I would be quite hurt.

But the other side of the story was that I did not want to be patronized. The anticipation of the birth was stressful enough without adding more stress from having Enaniye there, especially since at the time, we had a difficult relationship. Later when I asked to borrow the car to drive to the hospital, she refused. Whether she then refused to lend us her car as a result of my refusal for her to come with me or otherwise, I don't know.

I was equally stubborn, and picked up my suitcase and took the tram to the hospital. It was the number 55, the one that goes up and down the Chaussée d'Alsemberg on one end and all the way to the Gare du Midi on the other end. I hopped on at the junction of Avenue Brugmann and Chaussée d'Alsemberg. Hôpital St Pierre was somewhere towards the other end. The tram was cracking full. Matthias carried the suitcase and helped me get on the tram with my belly that was just about to pop.

At the hospital, as I sat in the lounge waiting for Matthias to fill out the admission papers, I felt lonely. All I could think of was that things would have been different if Almazesha had been there. In my heart, I knew she would be thinking of me. I knew she would be praying for my fate, back home in Laïbet. She is the first person I told about the pregnancy after telling Matthias. The thought of her made me feel even lonelier, and I wanted to cry. Here I was, once more, true to the proverb that Almazesha often repeated, "*Ye Abay Lej, Wuha sitemawu* [when the child of the Nile went thirsty]."

For Leoni's birth, I felt like a veteran. I had been there, done that. It was a lot easier. Matthias did as usual and spent as much time with me as possible, and at regular intervals went to the church to make a prayer, light a candle, and come right back. Even in terms of my relations with Enaniye and my family, I was much more inclusive and open for their visits. I felt I knew the drill. I was less stressed and actually was more mindful and present.

As much as I was in awe when I held Rosi in my arms seconds after her birth, there was a part of me that couldn't quite process what had just happened. At Leoni's birth, it was different—I wasn't scared of holding her or afraid to make a mistake. It must always take a first time to appreciate the second time around. Had I had more children, the births would have been more and more mindful. It is such a miracle that takes place that it is overwhelming. It is just overwhelming. The privilege of giving birth bestowed on women is a sacred one. Part of the gift, for me, was Matthias's extraordinary participation in the birth process. This was not common in the history of our family. It made Almazesha chuckle with pride and also amusement when I told her.

After each birth, I returned to Addis within a few weeks and resumed work. The little ones were good. They were not hard to take care of, and only cried a bit here and there. Matthias was always there to help anytime; he took care of them, at times, more than I did. By the time I fell asleep I was often so run down by a full day at work and the evening routine at home, I could not manage keeping up at night. Matthias got up and paced the house with one or the other baby in his arms. More often than not, we all slept in the same bed. It was nice and cozy, but by the crack of dawn, the entire dynamic would change. The girls would be up. No matter how tired I was, I would just drag myself out of bed and bring in the nanny, get ready for work, and leave for another long day. If I had to do it all over again, I would have set the job aside, and I would have opted to stay at home with them. I know for a fact that Almazesha gave her entire life to her children and grandchildren. It is not that she did not have opportunities to pursue her passion—she did—but each time, she gave priority to her family. I never really had a chance to talk about my change of heart with her.

I was torn between continuing my work and also being there for Rosi and Leoni. In the end, I spent my life on the road, shuttling between work and home three times a day, morning, lunchtime, and evening. Rosi and Leoni grew steadily. Matthias's parents visited regularly from Germany. My parents also played a good part in the first few years of the girls' lives. But most of all, I have to say that other than their father Matthias, Fofi played the biggest role in their lives. She was with them possibly as much as Matthias and I. To this day, they have such a close relationship to her—to all my sisters in fact, but Fofi is particularly special.

everyONE

Juggling a working life and trying to give my full attention to my home at the same time was not easy. When I first came to Ethiopia in 1997, I had intended to start an organization to do community work but in the process of finding my way, I ended up getting sidetracked. I worked with so many different organizations, from MSF where I spent most years, to GTZ, to UNDP, UNAIDS, and more.

After a while, I was disenchanted with what I experienced. We worked on reports, proposals, budgets, and launching conferences here and there, but in the end few of us had actual concrete improvements to show at the community level and in the lives of the people we worked for. At times I thought we didn't really work for the community. That was just development jargon—we worked for ourselves and we made careers. It didn't matter how much we worked or didn't work, because there would always be another project as sure as the sun would rise the next day. Moreover, hard work was not always appreciated.

I had become bitter and extremely cynical. The one time that we organized a regional HIV/AIDS conference through one of the UN agencies, I asked to hire people living with HIV as ushers instead of hiring the usual college students. It took weeks to get permission. Once the permission was granted, the day they came to meet with me at the office, all dressed up with whatever they could afford—well, a couple of secretaries almost fled the office. They didn't mind having part of their salaries charged to the HIV projects or attending whatever reception was organized for the cause, but to be in the same room as people living with the virus was asking too much, apparently. To make matters even better, I asked one of the young ladies if she would help me to get refreshments for the team of ushers that had just arrived. Out loud, she replied, "There is no budget line for that." We had raised a quarter of a million dollars for the conference and there was not ETB 10-15 (about USD 2.00) to get some sodas? Even if there was no budget line, would it be asking too much to just buy it and ask me to pay her back later? It was all too much for me. When I came to Laïbet for lunch or dinner and spoke about such issues with Almazesha, explaining my frustration, she often just told me that everyone was entitled to their own bouts of fear or courage. If some colleagues of mine behaved in discriminatory ways toward HIV-positive persons, it was their fears that emerged. The only remedy then, she said, was to find ways for my colleagues to better understand HIV instead of living in fear of it.

The process of registering a non-profit organization in Ethiopia is not simple: Instead of having to show the worth of the organization through results, one must first jump through all the hoops of the registration process. It took me about four years to get a license for the organization I wanted to set up. I was about to give up when I finally received the famous license and the green light to start working. We had already secured substantial funding; all I needed was the permission to get started. The day I learned we had the license, it was as though my cage had been opened. I knew the organization would face its own set of challenges, but for once, I thought, I could do what I had set out to do—what I intended to do when I had first come home back in the mid-1990s. Almazesha listened, as she always did, during these years, but she let me pursue the registration on my own; I think she wanted me to learn what the bureaucratic reality was all about.

Things moved quickly after that. I had enough money to recruit about 15 team members including field officers; after interviews, I ended up recruiting 62 persons. I had never planned to employ that many people, but the kind of young people who responded to our call were outstanding. Each time we completed an interview and I found a great person, I asked them to wait to hear from me, over and over, until I realized that I had way too many on the waiting list. I decided to hire all of them. We would just have to spread the salary budget around to make sure everybody got paid. In exchange for a modest salary, they would have the opportunity to run their projects themselves without having a control-freak manager breathing down their necks. The ones who accepted my offer, to whom I am forever grateful, are the founding members of everyONE, which is still running strong today.[41]

Rather than thinking that we were coming with answers for the challenges of the community, the idea behind our organization was to support the community in their thinking process as they formulated solutions that they saw as most suited for their needs. Just as this process was getting started and I finally exhaled, Matthias informed me that he had an offer to take a post in Lusaka, Zambia. I was not ready to move. I did not want to move. I had just gotten the license and funding to launch the organization. We agreed that I would stay and we would see how things went for a few months.

We had a budget for about 200 community workers, but given the need on the ground, we ended up having close to a thousand. Again, we changed our ways to make the budget work, and instead of paying community workers per diem, we bartered. For the youth, we paid for a training or school of their choice, and they in turn gave time working in their community. For the elderly, we gave them a monthly stipend of ETB 50 and they kept an eye on the youth and children of the neighborhood and met each other at least once a week for a coffee ceremony. This small amount of money allowed most of these destitute elderly women, who had often lost their adult

---

[41] www.everyonesworld.org

children to AIDS, the choice to stop begging on the street and stay in their homes. We focused on communities that we considered the most underserved and underprivileged. We worked with those who had disabilities. We worked with the women of the red light districts, mostly women I knew from my time in the MSF project. We worked with the community of people affected by leprosy. We worked with those who were way beyond the poverty line and lived in the outskirts of the city.

All in all, it was a powerful group. We not only worked together but also learned from each other—we are still learning today. Soon after the organization was launched, we also started supporting children orphaned by AIDS (a whole other story, which comes later). Once everything was set up, once the team was recruited and the community brought on board, we organized an inauguration ceremony.

Something in my heart was telling me to go all out for the inauguration. I thought that for once, we wouldn't open a community project in a community hall—we would go bold and bring everyone over to the Sheraton. Of course, it took negotiating with naïve faith that the Sheraton would help us accommodate about 1,200 persons. I also had a condition I wanted them to work with: for me to afford the event, they would have to promise to use short glasses and share each soft drink bottle between at least two persons. I just wanted to bring everyone in and have them, for once, have a Coke or Fanta standing at that large window outside the ballroom, looking down at the pool.

I knew in my heart that Almazesha would be happy about my plan. She always loved celebrations, and especially celebration that raised the morale and spirit of the community. She would often say to me: Honor those whom society might forget because most them are angels and more so the children of God, and in time when you honor the people of God, remember that angels will keep note of your deeds.

At the community level, everyone was excited. We rented busses, the usual government Ambassa busses. The most excited of all were the grandmothers from the ALERT: "After today, I don't mind if I die now," said one of them, insinuating that setting foot in the Sheraton would be the highlight of her elder years.

The day of the inauguration, I went to the Sheraton Hotel very early. The room was set up, and it was impressive to see 1,200 empty chairs. I had shivers down my back, both of excitement and of anxiety that we might not be able to fill the room. Then, right on time, I went outside and saw the best scene of my life. There were a dozen buses if not more driving in, one after the other in an urban caravan tracing from the palace down the hill and around the circle to reach the Sheraton.

Although the buses were old, they seemed to shine that day. I saw that people had taken the initiative to make banners, and as the buses swirled down the curve leading to the entrance of the hotel, the banners quivered almost in sync to the traditional song emanating—booming—from inside the busses. I have had many great days in my life, but this one in particular was a day of hope and a landmark in my life. I heard them hum and sing the oldest traditional songs of victory. One by one, they each went through the security check. There were people of all kinds: those in their wheelchairs, others dressed like models in high heels, toddlers or grandmothers with their traditional *Habesha Kemis* (Ethiopian dress). Even the grandmothers from ALERT who are often so rejected because of the scars of leprosy walked in proudly.

The security staff was baffled at first, but then, I think they just appreciated it and made it as smooth as possible for people to come in. It was magic. I doubt there will ever be a day to top this inauguration day at the Sheraton. To see the Ambessa Buses descend the hill one after the other, with banners flying in the wind and chants of *"ehem newu"*—I felt absolute joy and gratefulness.

Matthias had come back from Lusaka to be with me on this day, the day the organization was finally officially born. As I spent four years trying to get the license and secure funding, he was one of the few who helped me substantially in making this organization a reality. In fact, he is the one who came up with the name. Initially, I wanted to call it Candlelight, and he immediately said that sounded too much like a church organization. He knew the idea I had in mind for the organization, so he suggested I call it *everyONE* because it involves everyone and every person.

It was December 2003, and Matthias had moved to Lusaka in September. With our little family straddled between Addis and Lusaka, I had no idea what the next steps would be.

We were struggling to keep our lives together. Life was not easy with Matthias so far away from the girls and me, and the girls asking for their father every other minute. It was tough. I insisted on remaining in Ethiopia and continuing my work, but I saw how much it was costing us emotionally, especially the children. Almazesha urged me, "*Lej Abatun yinafikal, beteleye set lej! Endaw meftay agigni* [Children miss their father, especially daughters! Please find a solution]." We spent that holiday season together in Addis. The girls were so happy to have their father back; we were all glad to have him back in our little house. Once more, I was conscious that while I was fully engaged with all the running about in the house, I also found myself detached and just witnessing it all from afar. It was nice to see Rosi and Leoni wrestle with Matthias. They would roll around in the garden, take baths together, make cookies, take naps together, spend time on the playground, and it was all giggles. The thought first entered my mind that I could not aspire to support children and women in the community fully, while not fully being there for my own children. I kept the thought to myself for a while, letting it simmer.

Matthias returned to Lusaka after Ethiopian Christmas on January 8, and I was left with a difficult inner conflict to resolve. I had worked so hard to put this organization together and now that it was finally up and running, my personal life seemed to take a different turn. How long could I remain in Addis with Matthias in Lusaka and the girls torn in the middle? I could last another few months, maybe a year, but then what? I had to come up with a durable solution for the sake of my children and family as well as for the sake of the organization. Some weeks down the line, after discussing with my teammates how I might be able to work from a distance, I decided to take the girls and move to Lusaka. I did not have the heart to tell Almazesha that I was moving indefinitely. I did not know when we would live in Ethiopia again, if ever, and I could not have moved if

I had admitted to anyone that I was not intending to come back. Instead, I presented it as another visit to Matthias, knowing darn well that this would be it.

Our flight was scheduled to leave Addis at the ungodly hour of 3:00am. That very afternoon, I went to Laïbet with my Rosi and my Leoni, to be with everyone. As soon as I entered the compound, I saw Almazesha getting into her car, sitting in the back seat, opposite the driver. She summoned me to come and told me to wait for her; she said she would be right back after attending a funeral. I told her I would wait, but I knew I was lying. This would be the last time I would live in Addis Ababa for many years to come. I knew it, and it was heavy on my heart. But at the time, it was easier and gentler on me to just deny it all and pretend that I was just going for a quick visit to Lusaka. I stayed in Laïbet for a couple of hours. Eventually, I decided to drive home to pack and get ready for the flight. The children had to get some sleep before I woke them again in the middle of the night. As I drove out of Laïbet, it felt like the first time we left Laïbet back in the 1970s in midst of the Communist Revolution. Everything went in slow motion. The children got in the car. Essayas and his children were in the compound playing. All the children—Samy, Babyshoe, Mahlett, Dodi—were there. Each kissed Rosi and Leoni, stretching into the back seat. I watched, and did not say a thing. Finally, the doors of the car slammed shut. It was time to leave. Rosi and Leoni's nanny, Nigat, was there. She did not realize how heavy my heart felt. As I drove up the hill from Laïbet to the main road, I was conscious that it would be many years until I returned.

Once on the main road, on the opposite side of the road I saw Almazesha's car driving back home. I saw her clearly, still sitting in the back. I didn't realize that my tears were rolling down, until Nigat said: "*Mamy min denew? Enday? Min new?* [Mamy, what is it? What's wrong?]" I wanted to tell her to leave me alone, but I remained quiet. In my tears I found comfort. I knew it was one of the few times I would leave Almazesha with options to come back. When I told her I was leaving, she just said to me, "*Lejochu Abatachewun nafekewal...wusejiachew isti!* [The children have missed their father—please take them to him!]"

I was hoping we would move back to Addis after Lusaka, but that never happened. After Zambia we moved to Sierra Leone, and after Sierra Leone, to China. I was getting further and further way from my organization and teammates.

In retrospect, I think it was a good thing for the organization, allowing it to get past "founder syndrome" very quickly. everyONE had to stand on its own without my interference. As with any start-up organization, it went through ups and downs. It came close to being shut down many times, but it survived. Today, it is still running and the community is being served—actually, the community is not only being served but it has also evolved to serving itself.

Zambia, Sierra Leone, China

Moving to Lusaka from Addis was quite an adjustment. I was coming from a buzzing professional life where I would often leave my cell phone with the receptionist or our administrative assistant asking that they take a message unless the call was from my immediate family. My phone was ringing off the hook. At work, appointments and meetings were planned far in advance to have proper time management.

Then, we landed in Lusaka where I spent most of my day at home. I had the same cell phone, but it stopped ringing. At times I would stare at it and even check whether it was still working or not. That phone never rang for the first year or two—the only time it rang was when Matthias called to check in, or when Fofi called me from Addis. Agenda? No, well, I didn't need one. There were only hardly one or two activities, and the highlight of my time was going grocery shopping at Manda Hill on Saturday mornings.

I was bored to tears. No, boredom is even too light of a word. Not only did I not know anyone, I had left the work I loved behind and found myself stuck at home trying to assume the "can't wait to bake you a pie, honey" kind of woman role. I didn't know how to play *wife* or how to play *Mom at home*. All my life, I had been raised to be independent: to have my own job, to earn my own income, and manage my own life. Married or not, this teaching was about the way we were raised to live. Now, things changed—I was in a position where I had to depend on Matthias. It was difficult. All that I could remember, at this time, was how Almazesha always had her farms to supplement her life.

In the midst of this I got two job offers, both of which were close to my ideal work, within progressive international organizations and with the potential of moving substantial projects. The first offer I declined because Matthias thought it would be difficult to maintain our family if I took the job. The second one I hesitated to decline from a professional perspective; I knew, however, that if I accepted the job, my family life would be subject to serious hardship. The post would be in Addis, which meant we would have to split the family again. I was not even sure that our marriage would survive it.

It was time to have a serious conversation with Matthias and sort the situation out. "Four years down the line, when you have moved on with your work and the girls are in higher grades, I will only be able to possibly bake better pies. And I don't plan on spending my life baking pies," was the main message I had for him. Now it was about negotiating my life and how my own life would fit into the life of the family we had made together. Short of getting back to work, the next best option was to go back to school for a doctorate. This would allow me to be with my family, especially with the children, and also not waste away doing nothing to continue the path I had started long ago. I knew in my heart that Almazesha would always be supportive of education. Even if I could not get right back into my work life, using my time at home to not only take care of my daughters but also gain another degree would help me in the long run.

We did not have the means to get me back in school, but thanks to student loans and credit, I started my doctoral program. I felt better. I could be home with the girls on weekends and evenings. During the day when the girls were at school, I had something to work on, something that would lead me to continuing my work in general. I spent all of the rest of my time in Zambia working on this degree. I thought I would have finished it by the time we left Lusaka, but it did not happen. It took several more years. Each time we spoke, Almazesha would gently ask me how far along I was in my program, and each time I would tell her I was almost through. And each time, she just graciously told me: "*Gobez yene Ambessa* [Well done, my brave lion one]."

As much as I had a hard time getting used to Lusaka, leaving was just as hard. It's funny how we get used to places and then we don't want to leave them anymore. I had never expected to live in Zambia—it was never on my radar, and now it has taken its own place in our lives. Rosi and Leoni made long-lasting friendships, and both Matthias and I also enjoyed an intimate community of friends. It was good to be there. Leaving Zambia for Sierra Leone was not easy. The two countries were so completely different, not to mention the relocation hardship.

I certainly never thought of living in Sierra Leone, either, and as life would have it I would spend a good four years in Freetown. Once more, going from Lusaka to Freetown was not simple: There is such a difference between the two cities in every possible way. To start with, we were right on the shore of the Atlantic Ocean in Freetown and life was always around the beaches and the sea. As much as Lusaka is quiet and reserved, Freetown is buzzing with life, with hardly ever a moment of silence. If it is not the church choirs blasting out in the neighborhood, then it's the mosque sharing the prayers, or the discos, shops, or boom-boxes spreading music. And if none of that was happening, possibly in the very early morning hours, one could be sure to hear fights, dogs barking, some child crying loudly, or people giving loud directions to whatever vehicle was snaking through the streets.

Just as much as I had a hard time adjusting to Lusaka, now I had to find my way in Freetown. Again, it took a good year or more to get started. In my experience, it takes at least two years to be fully anchored in a new place before one can spend the third and fourth years actually enjoying the place—before leaving once more.

Freetown was wonderful. I met many expatriates who hated every single moment they spent there, but there were an equally large number who loved it as I did. And then we left Freetown for Beijing, China—Jesus, can we get starker changes? We will be in China for another four years or so, before we move again to God only knows where.

There is a recurrent pattern about relocation. We learn to be at home wherever we put our bags down. We learn to leave when it is time to leave. We learn to keep in touch with friends and know that relations last only as long as they are genuine. We learn about impermanence and the ability to enjoy the moment while it lasts. And to me, no matter where I am, I remain close to those I love because when night falls, we share the same moon. When I shared these thoughts with Almazesha, she said, "*Mechess segdet segdet newu. Sewu kebetu keweta, balebet bet memesret alebet, bianes le lejochu!* [Well, exile is exile. Once a person leaves their home, they have to find a home wherever they are, if nothing else, for the children]."

In all this moving around, my daughters changed schools many times. They made so many friends around the different places and saw so much, and for this I am grateful. Matthias worked in different environments, each with its respective challenges and opportunities.

And as for me, I have finally found a rhythm that works. I lived through the years of bucking the confines of marriage where I felt locked in and gagged, and then moved into a stage of introspection that lasted years. At times this introspection was dangerous as I experimented with life regression, shadow work, and various religions and spiritualities. At the end of all this introspection, I ended up facing a health crisis: I came close to losing my life to cervical cancer. In fact, a girlfriend of mine who had the same illness at about the same time as I, never made it through. She lost her life. Almazesha was less able to be with me during this time because she, too, was experiencing many health issues including a cervical tumor; of all the synchronicities between us, this was the least pleasing.

This escape from cancer was a major wake-up call. Regardless of all the philosophy, spirituality studies, reflection, retreats, and so on, this call brought me face to face with what was at stake. Is life not precious enough? Am I not to count my blessings no matter how many challenges I face at the same time? Am I not to be grateful for the man in my life and the children we have together?

Since recovering from this health crisis, I see the world with a different eye. I am just grateful for waking up with all my loved ones. I am grateful for everything—everything including the good, the sad, the ugly, and the beautiful. I am thankful and I am committed to making the most of life while we have it and while we have each other. "Each other" is not limited to the people I know or my family, but is the greater each other: It is more about the collective consciousness to be thankful for the environment, for the earth, and for all the living beings around. It's about recognizing the oneness that keeps us linked from within. It's about knowing that forgiveness and love are remedies for any challenge, no matter how great. Nothing can surpass love and forgiveness. It's about finding the peace to live a day at a time, and even a moment at a time.

Looking ahead

I have reached a time and place in my life where I wonder what it's all about. It is a blessing to realize how finite our time on this earth is. What's even more interesting (and often sad) is to notice how we still manage to get caught up in hurtful behavior, in conflicts and fights about who's right and who's wrong—as if a few years later, it would still matter who was wrong and who was right. Does it really matter? What matters is finding in our hearts the compassion for one another, the compassion for our own selves. It is more about our ability to understand the world in which we each live. They say that we each carry our own burdens and that each burden is comparable in the weight it subjects us to, yet we slip into burden-comparison. If we feel that others have it harder, there is a tendency to feel better about ourselves. Yet if we feel that ours looks like a heavier load, we might feel shorted by life. Fortunately, it's not like that—it's not about the burdens we carry but how we choose to handle our load. While we all live in a collective consciousness, the choices we make define the quality or flavor of the life we inherit.

It's all about the choices we make, from something as simple as choosing to smile rather than pouting, to something as serious as rebelling against oppression and injustice rather than behaving like a doormat. It's the choice between loving in many ways, and making the walls around ourselves so thick that we end up isolated and barricaded in our self-made prison.

If there is one thing that I have learned from Almazesha, it is the value of living life with my heart in the pilot's seat and my gut feeling or intuition as co-pilot. We have this inner intelligence that knows—it knows because it is the eternal self that is linked to all who have been before us, all who will come after us, and all who live with us. Our willingness to think with our hearts might not always be supported by society, but it is the way to transform lives, both our own and those around us. In fact, the heart is much more intelligent than the brain because the heart goes straight for the solutions.

Almazesha could connect with all persons. She could see beauty in everyone. That starts with seeing the beauty in ourselves and being able to see the beauty in others, no matter whether it is apparent or hidden under layers of various behaviors. Somehow, she could see through everyone. She could sense the vulnerabilities, the strengths and weaknesses in people, mostly because she was very clear about her own humanity. As much as society often judges people, she never judged. For her, our faults or weaknesses were just part of our humanity, and this is what allowed her to forgive so easily no matter what.

I remember that during the Derg regime, one of the men working for her went to the local authorities to denounce her and Ababi. This man had been living and working at Laïbet for years. His children had grown up in Laïbet. We were family for all practical purposes, yet he decided to denounce her for whatever reason made sense to him. At the time, it was illegal to have firearms, but Almazesha always had firearms. It is something that she inherited from her elders who were warriors throughout history; she was trained by her grandmother to handle firearms. In fact, it was not only about shooting with firearms but also about knowing and respecting weapons and knowing how to use them for the sake for peace, justice, and human rights.

Being denounced at that time could literally mean a death sentence. His denunciation could have meant that she, Ababi, or both might have been led to the execution. What unfolded in the days following this denunciation was an immense lesson for me. The local authorities knew her well and respected her. They came to Laïbet and explained to her that one of her employees had denounced her. They suggested that they should arrest him and do away with him, because if this man denounced her to others in the system, it could cost her life. I think that anyone else would have agreed with them and had the man killed, but her reaction was different. She told the men not to harm him and to leave him alone. I remember that she told them that only God can decide the lives of people. "I don't want blood on my hands. Please let this man go," is what she said to them. The men were surprised in a way, but in another way, I don't think they were surprised—her decision was nothing exceptional given her track record of life. The man ended up returning to Laïbet to continue working, and she continued to pay his salary and support his children. She never spoke of this incident again, and I believe that she truly forgave him.

At the end of the day we are only human, and human beings cannot be faulted for lack of judgment. Human beings are beautiful because our weaknesses live along with our strengths. These same weaknesses are the foundation of our humanity; it is not only our strengths that make us great. Greatness comes from living with our weaknesses and our ability to own up to our faults and working toward overcoming the weaknesses or leveraging the weaknesses to evolve to greater levels of consciousness.

From the very beginning, I was always a believer in possibilities. At times this was more of a curse as it led me into more trouble than I would have had otherwise. There were times that I could not see the possibilities anymore, as if I was blinded by my own constrictions. It took effort and time to peel off the layers I had allowed to obstruct my ability to see. Now I am at a time where I can see again. It's funny: I see again, and this enables me to say that the key to life is compassion. It's love, authenticity, and also forgiveness. It is certainly hope and our ability to be gentle with ourselves and each other. I have no shame in saying this, no matter how clichéd it sounds, because to me, this is the only truth that is—the only truth that ever was and that ever will be.

In Ethiopia we clean windows or glass surfaces in a particular way, with either soapy water followed by drying with newspapers or soapy water with a piece of rough leather. We call this piece of leather *ye-wowsha coda* (dog skin), but rest assured that no poor puppy was scalped—it's all cow hide. The most prized *ye-wowsha coda* is not the stiff, brand new one that is just out of the package, but the very old soft one that has served many times over. To me life is comparable. We start out as a stiff *ye-wowsha coda*, straight out of the package. If we are lucky, life gives us opportunities to serve, and the more we serve the softer we become until we are so flexible and malleable that there isn't any surface we cannot envelop and touch with love.

I have reached a place of surrender and acceptance. I

am grateful. My conscience allows me to follow my heart no matter the repercussions. This is no green light for being irresponsible, though; it's more about finding in myself the silence for our energy and that of those around us. It's a good place to be, free of expectations and full of gratefulness for what is, while constantly working to let go of my expectations and hold on to the treasures of life. If my life had to be over tomorrow, I would choose to live fully today. To leave this life with no regret, it's best to live in the moment.

I listen to the whispers of my heart. Sometimes it tells me things I am afraid to do, sometimes it tells me to do things I don't want to do, and sometimes it tells me things that make my head spin. But no matter how I feel, be it fear or excitement, I try to follow this heart of mine and trust that it knows best.

When we hear such whispers emerging gently like tiny sparkles dancing to the surface, what then? Don't we have a responsibility to manifest them into our reality? Whispers of the heart are not random occurrences—they are how we intuitively connect to the whole that we are and remember our existence as a sacred one-ness.

Texture of life

It is not that we ever reach a time in our lives where there are no problems; problems, challenges, tragedies, and drama will always be part of our lives, as much as joy, surprises, and miracles. The important thing I have learned is that it is the choices we exercise and how we handle the ups and downs of our lives that allow us to go with the flow or resist the flow. It's like riding a wave—things are bound to go up and things are bound to go down. Nothing is permanent except this eternal movement and the flow of the river of our journey in each lifetime.

Fofi said to me one day: "The day will come when it will be my last day. Our days are numbered, and it's up to us to make our stay on this earth as meaningful as possible. Meaningful to ourselves first, and then also to those that are around us and that we love." It is often when we find meaning for our own life that we can allow harmony to surface all around us. Do we have a purpose to wake up for? What is it that just makes us jump out of bed?

This is my life journey so far, and as much as my childhood was rooted with Almazesha, she continues to be my safe place and my thought partner though she has moved on from this world. The next section presents the letters I wrote to her after she passed on. I was not ready for her to leave us. Are we ever ready? As I described earlier, I was in Freetown, Sierra Leone when I heard of her passing. I was so far away. I could not run home; I could not shout out my pain. There was no way to express my loss. My shouting sounded muffled to me and remained loud in my heart. If there is such a thing as a "closet griever," maybe I was one for a while. I did not dare share my loss. I knew many would not understand and would say things that would spoil the purity of my love for her and the sacredness of the texture of my loss. So, I remained silent. I kept it for myself—I almost found comfort in keeping my grief to myself, in my heart.

As I wrote the letters to her, I found time to be alone with her again. I found time to talk about all those things we did not have time to talk about. I know there is still so much to say. Maybe when we meet again across the other side, and we have eternity in front of us, we can sit together again and talk in silence forever. Maybe then, there might be enough time.

Each day for about a year after she passed on, I wrote to her. In my letters, I spoke with her. I met her again in my thoughts and in my dreams. I slowly found my bearing again and came to peace with my life without her physically around us in this world. In each one of us that she touched, family and friends, her legacy lives on. I hope that through the stories and the letters, I can share further what she has meant to me. I wrote the letters to her because it was my way of being alone with her. It was my way of praying and finding time to meditate and find my peace. When I started writing these letters to her, I had no intention of making them part of this book; only at the end did I realize that including the letters would give me peace and a sense of closure.

In my letters, I often call her "Emaye" as I sometimes called her when we sat and talked. I sign as "Mimi," which was her nickname for me.

PART VI:
LETTERS TO MY
GRANDMOTHER

From the things we used to do and the way
we used to be, here are letters for you with
the conversations I wish we had—
the conversations we would have had
if we had the time I thought we would.

October 27, 2009

Emaye,

Do you remember the day you invited all your uncles and relatives? It was a great dinner you made; I don't remember what the occasion was for, but I know that it was an important dinner. That day, the compound of Laïbet filled up with cars—there were cars even outside the gate. There was a sense of festivities in the air and everyone scurried along working.

Half an hour before the guests started arriving, the living room and dining room looked impeccable and all things were already set. The small table was ready by the sofas to allow the guests to rest their glasses and plates, along with the small bowls of *kolo* (roasted wheat seeds), the lined-up drinks for the aperitif, and the glasses that stood shining on the table, lined up like foot soldiers on the day of a parade.

It must have been 1970 or maybe 1971, when things were still good in our country. That day we did a big mischief I never told you about before, but I guess it's okay to confess now. Well, you know Emama Berhane was very mean to us children. She used to pinch us on the flesh right under our arm, where it is always soft, and twisted the pinch so much that we ended up going onto our toes until she stopped. Well, one day we got fed up with it and together with all the children in the compound we decided it was time to implement revenge.

Well, in fact, the truth was that I used to sell or barter a kind of insurance. I promised all the children in the compound that if they paid me 25 cents a week, I would ensure that revenge was taken out on all adults who beat us or pinched or did whatever to us. It was in this context that the case of Emama Berhane was brought to my attention. We sat together and thought very hard about the kind of revenge that would make us feel justice was had. It took lots of thinking, and then the day you had your dinner, I thought it was the ideal day to actually move into action.

Emama Berhane, bless her soul and may she rest in peace, had no idea what was coming her way. So, once all the food was served on the buffet, I managed to drop a few raw, unpeeled, unwashed onions into the *wot*. The onions dove right in and disappeared. Then we just all stayed around the little living area behind the buffet to watch the unfolding of our action. You led your guests to the buffet, started passing out plates, and started serving. Everything went into slow motion. I could only see you plunge the spoon into the *wot* and as you raised that spoon out, it brought some of the raw onions that had sunk to the bottom. They looked like some strange animal that accidentally fell in a pool, emerging all red from the sauce and with their roots a bit bent. You should have seen the look on your face—it was a face of disbelief. All I then heard you say was: "Berhane, Berhane, *min alkush enate?* [Berhane, Berhane, what have I done to you, for you to behave this way?]." Poor Emama Berhane had no idea what happened. She was as shocked as you were. She put her hands on her head and just started mumbling things we did not understand. For us, the revenge was done and we were quite proud of it. Now that I think of it, though, I can't believe how cruel it was. But we did not know. We were only children back then. Forgive me.

Love, Mimi

October 28, 2009

Emaye, it's now a day and a month since you left. Wherever you are, how are you? I am well, though I am still very sad about your departure. I think of all the conversations we had before, all the laughter we shared, and it warms my heart. I feel less lonely when I think of the good times we had.

Do you remember when I called you to tell you that I was pregnant? You were very subtle in gently asking how long I had known. Of course it was super early— I had been just pregnant for about a month, and you almost fell back into your chair. "*Ay ye lej neger, ay good, ay good; menew mimiye, be weru ko ay woram enate.* [Oh dear, the things of children—my beloved Mimiye, you can't speak about it just in a month.]"

Do you remember the conversation we had?

> You asked me: "Are you sure you are pregnant?"
> "Yes of course, I am. I just came from the doctor."
> "How do you know?"
> "I missed my period."
> "I can't believe that you say you are pregnant and it's only been a few weeks. This is child's play."

I did not understand why it was not appropriate to tell about the pregnancy as soon as I knew. I know you always say that so much can go wrong and that we should only talk when the tummy talks for itself, but I knew I was pregnant, I was so excited, and I wanted to tell everyone. I didn't really know about our tradition of keeping it all hushed until the tummy is impossible to hide. But I am sure you were happy because I was carrying your first great-grandchild. Emaye, don't you think that it's beautiful we were able to have such a generational gift? You have seen four generations.

But not telling until the tummy shows, why do we do that, Emaye? Isn't it good to just be happy in the moment? Life is so short—why can't we be happy and celebrate right there and then? I know you will say that we can't celebrate something that is not yet given to us, but you know, even if the child is not yet ours, I think there is due reason to celebrate the pregnancy. It is such a pity that we spend so much energy suppressing our joy and our excitement. After all, what's the point of life if we can't be excited and share the excitement? What's the point?

I have never been as happy as when I was pregnant. Do you remember? I used to go swimming at the Hilton till very late in the pregnancy, and then I continued in Brussels and only stopped swimming about four days before Rosi was born. For Leoni's pregnancy, I stopped six days before she was born. You should have seen the faces of the people at the Hilton pool. Many of them were almost offended to see a pregnant woman strutting along the poolside.

I really still wonder how we got such a culture of denial. You know, when I was pregnant with Rosi, I was wearing really cute pregnancy dresses and skirts. My legs did not get fat, so I continued wearing short skirts. I swear it looked good; I would not lie to you. But then one day, an older colleague came and told me that I should wear a bigger dress that did not show the pregnancy so much. I was offended by her comment. I was wondering why I should have to hide something that I was happy about. We all seem to celebrate weddings without acknowledging the dating period, and then after the wedding we wait for the child, but we refuse to celebrate the pregnancy?

Emaye, you need to tell me more about this, because I don't understand. In fact, the colleague who suggested I wear a bigger dress insinuated that showing a tummy might imply a woman had been intimate with a man. I thought it was such nonsense! I told her that as far as I knew, every pregnant woman had been intimate with a man, without a doubt, with the exception of the Virgin Mary's Immaculate Conception. My colleague left our discussion with such speed, you would have thought I was speaking blasphemy.

I was so happy with both my pregnancies. I was lucky not to have any complications, and so I had the chance to enjoy each and every day and remain mindful of the baby's movements and growth.

The funniest thing of all was when Rosiye was born (and the same with Leoni), you just could not believe that I had milk. You kept on asking me: "Do you have milk?" and "Are you sure there is milk coming out of your breasts?" and when I said "Yes," you just said, "I don't believe you?!" I guess you didn't think my breasts could make milk. Emaye, just because I have very small breasts, it doesn't mean they can't make milk. In fact, I wish I had showed you the picture I took when Rosi was just born. You would never believe it—I had breasts so big that I couldn't see my feet. I swear to you. I was even teasing Matthias about it. There is this one actress called Pamela Anderson who is very famous for her very large breasts, so I used to tease Matthias and tell him that he had married the Ethiopian version of Ms.

Anderson. But alas, mine were real and pregnancy-related, so about three months down the line, they disappeared into thin air. But I still have a couple of pictures for the record. I knew no one would believe me, so I wanted to have something on hand to show that "Yes, my breasts were that big, once a upon a time."

You are so funny sometimes, not believing that I could make milk. Well, I did, but the milk did not last long; at about 3-4 months, I had to start the bottle to supplement, and by six months it was all done. Nonetheless, let it be known that I did breastfeed. But you know what? Because I exercised the whole time through, I did not get a single stretch mark. I think it was due to the swimming about 2km a day each day until the very last moment. In Brussels, Boubiye drove me to the pool in the last days of my pregnancies. He sat reading his newspaper at the coffee shop while I did my laps. He was so worried that the babies would come out in the water.

You always said that I am lucky to have found a husband like Matthias. Yes, you are right, 100%. He was fabulous with the girls from the moment they were born until today. I told you that he went into the delivery room with me. It was good, except that at one point I was a bit upset because there he was, not speaking much French, with the midwife from Morocco and not speaking much English, and the doctor was Belgian and preferred Dutch to English. I was on the delivery table trying to interpret and translate for each of them. At one point I told them that it was too much to expect me to translate and that they should figure out how to communicate alone, without me. The truth was, I was really jealous that I could not witness the baby's birth. I was so busy working on it rather than being able to see it. At one point the doctor brought a mirror for me to see the baby through the reflection, but it didn't help.

Finally when Rosi was born, it was Matthias who cut the cord and gave her the first bath. He did the same for Leoni as well. I loved the feeling of giving birth—what a gift. If modern life were not so expensive, I would have loved to have more children. I think they are like angels among us.

You know I am not one for bravery when it comes to pain. Do you know that I fainted on the delivery table when the nurse brought the syringe and needle to use for the infusion? First, since I told her that I didn't like needles, she said she would try to only stick me once and use that same needle to draw blood as well as to give me the infusion. But then she could not find my vein. As usual, I think it is a genetic thing; they can never find our veins. And so, the nurse tried many times over. At one point I could not take it anymore, and I just told her, "Excuse me, I think I am going to throw up." She stuck a bowl under my chin, but then I said to her, "No, I mean, I am going to faint." And before she could do anything, I had fallen backwards and passed out. It is very odd to faint with a belly that is nine months old and ready to pop. They managed to awaken me, but then the anesthetist came with a needle even bigger than the last; I just wish they could have done what they had to do before they woke me. This time, the syringe had to deliver a shot right into my spine, for the epidural. Gosh, I wish I could have run out of that room. I hate needles. No, correction—I don't hate them, they just scare the hell out of me. Yes, even at my age. And I have no shame in admitting that I am scared of needles.

When I think of how petrified I can be of needles and shots, I think of you and all the women of the world who had to give birth in very natural conditions, and I can only bow to you in awe. I don't know how you did it, because me, well, I asked for painkillers even before I felt contractions. I just didn't want any kind of pain. My doctor was great; he showed me a little button I could press on the intravenous line. He whispered to me and said that if I needed more painkiller, all I had to do was press the button. Well, you know me—I pressed on that button in anticipation of any kind of pain that might think of arising in me. I just did not want to take chances.

In the maternity ward, I could hear the screams of some women who had decided not to have painkillers. I felt terrible for them. I also did not understand why they would choose against the painkillers, when they knew clearly that the entire process was interlaced with high levels of pain. Emaye, how did you manage with the birth of all your children? And then, to complicate matters, they were all born at home, so I am not sure how you sorted that out.

The good thing about being at home is that after the birth, you are in your own house so you are very comfortable, but as it happens, I can't imagine how you would go about it. I know that birth is nothing new, but I tell you Emaye, all the theories go up in the air as soon as you go through it personally.

Love always,
Mimi

November 1, 2009

Emaye,

I know in spirit you can hear me, and even if you don't read this letter per se, I know that you can hear the message that is in it.

Fofi finally flew to Addis, following Enanaye. They are there now, to celebrate your 40th Day. It seems everyone is gathered, but I could not go, you know. I am just too far way. Coming to Addis from Freetown is a saga on its own. There is still no road to the airport and the saga starts with boarding the ferry, the speedboats, or the helicopter to reach Lungi. And then, the hustle and bustle at the airport—you just get tired before even boarding the aircraft. I tell you, we don't know how good we have it in Ethiopia to be able to drive to the airport.

I am still very sad. Koki told me I should know that you are in a great place together with Ababi and somewhere in Heaven. I know that, and I believe her. But I am still very sad.

Last night I had a dream that I had checked into a hotel and that Fofi, Noela, and I had gone on vacation. We checked into our hotel, which was a really nice resort, only to reach our room and realize that the suite they promised us was not really a room—it was like an outdoors room built like a duplex. We still took the room to give it a chance, but then realized there was a snake inside. In fact, there were three snakes. The snakes were on the top level and we were on the ground level of the room so we had no way to get out. It was very bad. We tried to find a way to leave the room, but it was difficult.

Finally, Noela managed to call the reception desk and they rushed to help us. They were not much surprised by the snakes in our room and just removed them. Fofi killed one of them, the green one—she squashed it with her foot. It bent up and swirled like the dragon that St. Gabriel killed. Then they gave us another room even more beautiful than the first one.

I don't know if this is just a random nightmare or if it has any meaning at all. I know you were my roof. You were my shield and my anchor. I know that these days I feel extremely vulnerable because I can't call you or come and see you any more, except in my dreams and maybe in prayer and meditation. Does it mean that even though the room is gone, we will have another way to continue living, shielded from all the dangers of life?

Emaye, who will I call now to talk about my dreams?

Did I tell you that Leoni and Rosi come to me in the morning and often tell me the dreams they had at night? Well, it reminds me of what I used to do with you back in the day, and it makes me reminisce.

They made a drawing for you yesterday. It's supposed to go in the brochure Fofi is preparing for your 40th. I emailed it to Addis and hopefully you will see it along with all the messages from all your grandchildren and great-grandchildren.

I have to go now; I will write you later.

Always with love,
M

November 3, 2009

Emaye,

I thought of you this morning. I'm not sure if it is a poem, but here are the words that came to me.

Comme un soupir	As a sigh
suspendu devant moi,	hangs before me,
je te regarde.	I look at you.
Et tu es la,	And you are here,
présente et prés de moi ;	present and close to me ;
tu es belle	you are beautiful
juste comme tu es,	just the way you are,
dans toute ta majesté,	in all your majesty,
resplendissante comme jamais.	resplendent as ever.
Et je me vois.	And I see me too.
Et j'essaie en vain	And I try in vain
de te rejoindre,	to join you,
de te ramener a moi.	to bring you back to me.

Emaye, I feel a sense of surrender and reverence to you and the life that you have had. I am in awe at the work you have accomplished, the lives you have touched and changed, the love you gave so unconditionally. How did you do that? How did you so love everyone just the way we each were, with all of our weaknesses and flaws? It amazes me.

As long as you were there, I felt a sense of safety and security; I knew that no matter what, I would always have a home to come back to. I am not so sure about having a home anymore. Did I already tell you that I feel the roof has been removed from over my head? Well, that's how it feels. I feel exposed. Who will I come to for comfort? Who will I go to for guidance? Who will I go tell about my latest drama?

I am closing down from here on. It's no longer important for me to tell my stories and reach out to hold someone close. It was once with you, and it stops there. You think I am being foolish? No, I am not foolish—Emaye, I am shattered and heartbroken. I know there are worse things in the world and that I should feel grateful to have had you for so long, but I am not there yet. I am still in my world, that world of mine that has been so shaken up, like when the Queen Bee leaves the hive. What are the foot soldier bees to do? Was I not your foot soldier?

When I told Rosi and Leoni, it was hard. I only told them after I came back from Ethiopia because I wanted to be with them in their mourning process. Here is what I told them: "Do you remember that I told you Almazesha was not well?" They nodded a yes. "Well, she is really not well," I continued, "in fact ... in fact, she has now become an angel." Just when I said that Leoni cried bitterly. You know that she really gets very deeply sad and cries tears from the depth of her soul. Rosisha was not as outspoken as usual—she just turned completely red and curled up under the sheets with a stream of tears running down the side of her face, across her nose, and onto the other side of the pillow. Emaye, I didn't know how to comfort them. It is difficult to comfort them when I myself am not yet back on track. I felt I was giving them a bitter pill to swallow, the bitterness of separation. You are the first person they lost who was so close, someone they know well and loved—you, their great-grandmother! How lucky we are. I will never be a great-grandmother; I will be happy to even make it to grandmother.

I am sitting at this nexus of such gratefulness and the bitterness of the separation. Did I tell you about my friend Rita? Well, she still has her grandmother, in Asmara. She sent me a picture and her grandmother was sitting in the same posture as you in her bed. Today, I thought how lucky Rita is. I don't have you anymore but I trust one day we will meet again. I suppose we will all meet. In fact, we will always be together anyway.

Have I told you how much I love you? It doesn't flow out nicely when I say it in Amharic. Sometimes I just wanted to tell you how much I love you. I know I told you many times, but have I said it recently? Well, in case I have not said it, I am saying it now. I love you, my Almazesha. I love you so much and we all love you forever—this I am sure you know.

I was thinking that if we could have made you stay to debrief us before you left, we would have kept you here for another 50 years because the debrief of our lives would have taken at least that long. But you just left without too much warning, so I am doing my debrief in writing Emaye. I hope you hear me and hear my words as they tell the stories through these pages.

I love you,
M

November 4, 2009

Emaye,

Tomorrow is your 40th Day Celebration.

Can you believe it's already been 40 days since you left? I have been in such a special and strange space in these past days. I sing a lot and then I cry as I sing. I am always humming the same song that I made up, a mixture of old tunes I know and some words I made up; at times it rhymes and at times it doesn't.

It's been strange since you left. Did I tell you that I am reluctant to tell people that you've moved on? Well, yeah, I don't want to say it. I feel that you go further away each time I tell someone. So, back here in Freetown, I have just kept it to myself. When I have actually admitted to friends that you are gone, I have cut the conversation short. I don't want to talk about it. I am afraid of the comments people will make. Sometimes people talk without being mindful and I don't want any such words to stick in my memory, so I am very quiet these days. Maybe I am even slightly depressed. Okay, I am very depressed.

I think you can't blame me for being sad. When I spoke to Koki the other day, she said that I am stressing out your spirit and that I should stop being sad. Well, that's easier said than done. I am actually almost happy to be sad, because in my sadness I am in your presence. I am afraid that the memories will fade away the minute I move on with my life. Do you realize that you have been the one and only for me, all my life?

You know, I have always been conscious of that—all

the times I used to call you or the times that we spent together, I was soaking in it because I knew, one day, you might not be by my side anymore. Yes, it's very selfish to dwell on your departure. I should rejoice, as they say, for the life that you have had. But don't make me lie; I am so not there yet. I am just not there.

I thought of Wolde today—you remember him. We were dating for several years until I decided to come home to Ethiopia. I shared great moments with him and to this day he has remained a true friend. Anyway, I thought of him today for some reason. Do you remember how we went together to his mom's funeral. Gosh, I was shocked that she had passed and I was very sad for him, but I never realized the depth of the pain that he or his family must have felt. I called him to pay my respects and give my condolences, and now I wonder whether my words were enough. You know, for me, I don't even want to hear condolences from people who just say them for the sake of protocol. It makes me feel like running far away so as not to hear them. In my heart, I know who means what they say and who is just fronting the usual words to conform to our traditions.

Today I thought of all those who have lost their mothers; I can't imagine the pain that it represents. If they too felt like I feel, then, my God I am ashamed of not being conscious of this pain earlier. I guess I could not have known, without having experienced it. The other day, a friend asked me where I was in the grieving process. I was not sure what to answer, so I didn't. In fact, I don't see it as a process, even though I know that is what they say. This friend is very dear to me, so I took what he said seriously, but for some reason I could not relate to the loss in relation to a process. Process, for me, is something work-related, not heart-related.

If I could take back time, I would not do anything differently in the way that we have lived together. Maybe the only thing is that I would have made sure to come and see you more often, even if I am on the west end of the continent and you are all the way to the east side. I know we spoke a lot on the phone. I just loved to call you.

Me, I miss you; well, I am sad for now, and that's okay. Every day that goes by, it's as though you are going further away and I still want to hold on. You know what I miss? I miss "us." What will this "us" become now that you are no longer here to hold the other end of the story with me? What will our "us" become without you in it to make it complete? Even as I write this I swell up with tears and then I can't see what I am writing, so I have to take my glasses off and get some tissues, take a deep breath, and continue to write. But enough about all that now, let me tell you about other things.

You know, I still stand up when an older person calls me on the phone; I even bow and give my respects while on the phone. I know they can't see me, but I just can't manage to sit and talk. You know what else—I still wave goodbye when I hang up the phone. I find it funny. Some things never change. I remember you used to tell me that I waved like that when I spoke on the phone as a child. I stood up every time when I spoke with you as well. For you it was out of love and admiration, and respect. Now, I am forced to sit when I speak to you, because instead of the phone, I am speaking to you through these letters I have been typing. Now, I have to sit, Emaye, when I talk to you. I have to sit.

I have that old picture we took together, back in the day, of me and you sitting in the garden near that big rock. Do you remember? You must have been whispering something to me because I look so concentrated and my ear is pressed to you. Well, I have put it in a beautiful frame that sits right on my desk. I don't know who took the picture, but I love it. I had the frame for so long just sitting in my cabinet; I didn't know I would use it for our picture, me and you, when I bought it. In fact, it never had any pictures in it—I couldn't find a picture that would fit it. Now, I am surprised how custom-made it looks with our picture in it. It is as though they made the frame just for you and me. I love to write to you because then it is just you and me, with no one to interrupt or disturb my conversation with you.

I have been listening to the same CD for about a month now, the one I bought on the flight back from Addis after your ceremony. I love it. It is all instrumental music and at times it makes me dance a bit of "*Eskesta*"[42] all by myself in my office. I feel that I am dancing for you, for all our loved ones gone and those still here, for the entire world and all the beauty in it. I dance in gratefulness and in celebration of humanity and the essence of the bonds of community and family; then, the gratefulness and deep joy overflows in a meltdown and sometimes I break down in tears. It's been like that. I am overwhelmed by emotions. I feel engulfed by the love you gave us all and the magnitude of the void I feel without you in this world.

---

[42] *Eskesta* is the Ethiopian traditional dance.

Do you remember how we danced at my wedding? I have never seen you dance since. It was great. Do you remember how Etiye Almenesh dances in such a subtle and elegant way? Those were good days. She was there at your funeral. I know she was your best friend for many years; I always thought she was a gorgeous woman, with so much character. She looked tired when I saw her at the funeral. She had lost a lot of weight. I stayed with her a bit but didn't tell her jokes and stories as I used to.

The other day, I had some tears again. Rosi and Leoni were there, so I told them it was probably pepper in the air. They are both so sweet, they sort of accepted my statement without questioning it. The windows were wide open and the air was clear—there was not even a trace of a scent, let alone pepper. Then a few days later, I had tears again and Leoni was with me. We were eating a small lunch after school. "It's that pepper again, hmm?" she said to me as she continued to work on her plate of rice and curry. "Yes, it's the pepper," I confirmed, and that is the way we have been.

I am not using make up anymore for a while, not by choice, but I just can't do it because each time I cry, the eyeliner smudges and I look like a raccoon. Since you left, I have put on a lot of weight, a good 5-7kg. I am not eating more or anything; I just stopped running in the morning. I think I will lose it when I get a bit more stabilized about you, if ever that is to happen.

The good news is that I don't smoke anymore. I have been on and off the cigarettes, but I think this time is for good. You remember the summer I came to stay with you a couple of years ago? I would wake up so early, just to be able to have coffee and a cigarette in the back kitchen before the house started buzzing. And when I told you, "Sorry Emaye, I am up early to catch up with my work!" you just smiled and said, "Don't lie—I know you're just out there for a cigarette."

I remember your hands and the little circle you tattooed on each hand. It's hard to think that I will not hold your hand again. I can't even remember the last time we were together. I know it was this past Easter, but still it's only a vague memory. Thank God for the pictures Matthias took, at least we have that. What would we do without pictures?

M

November 5, 2009

Emaye,

Today is your 40th celebration.

I cannot believe it has been 40 days since you left. Usually when you travel out of Ethiopia, this is about the time you come back home after your treatments; I guess you are not coming back now.

You know what I remembered today? Just about the time I had Rosi and became a mother is when you became a great-grandmother. I was a mother at 31, and you became a grandmother at about the same age when I was born, and coincidentally right about the same season. Remember? Rosiye was born on the 21st of September and I on the 18th of August—about 4 weeks and 31 years difference.

I called home today, about three times. I know they must think I am flipping out here in Sierra Leone. But I am not, don't worry. I just wish I was back home today. I miss being at Laïbet. I miss you, of course, but I also miss the fellowship.

Yeshiye and I are trying to make sense out of this. We are both pretending that we are okay. But we are not. We cry alone and pretend to be strong so that the other is not sad or doesn't give in to the grieving.

Emaye, Fofi said to me that Kidist said that Ababi looks happier in his pictures on his Epitaph. Is it true? Are you together again?

I can't say that I am over you yet, but I am seeing some light at the end of the tunnel. Today I explained to Rosi and Leoni what the celebration of the 40th day means. I explained to them that although we are all sad that you have left, this is a day when we transition from mourning to celebrating your life. On this day, we officially inherit the flame you carried all along your beautiful life; we pass on responsibilities from one generation to the next; we are grateful for the time we had together and the joy, the love, the compassion, and the tribulations we shared together; we celebrate you, and we officially acknowledge the lineage. Yes, this is the day. At least it is so for me.

I am coming to accept the fact that you are gone now, at least for now. I might not see you in flesh and blood, but you have been with me in spirit throughout these days. I also believe that you will remain with me and us all forever. At times, I can't wait till I myself pass in order to be reunited with you and the rest of the family. But then I think of Rosi, Leoni, and Matthias as well as Fofi, Nono, Lily, and everyone, and I can't just leave like that. What to do? I miss you.

On Sunday I go back to Bo, up country, a few hours' drive from Freetown. I will be staying in the same room where I stayed when I was there to complete my assignment, even though I had heard that you had passed on. Would you say it is full circle? What a place to go full circle! Of all places in the world, it will be in Bo, Sierra Leone, at the Imperial Hotel.

I will miss you forever, as Leoni said. I will miss you forever.

You know, somewhere in me, I still think that you are around somewhere on the planet and that one day you will come. And so, I am waiting for you. Yet, I know inside that it is futile to wait because you will not be coming back; rather, it will be me who will join you one day.

Yours always,
M

November 8, 2009

Emaye,

I have come back to Bo, where I am staying in the same hotel as before I traveled to Addis for your ceremony—I am even staying in the same room. How funny, how time passes. Just a few weeks ago, I was in this room preparing myself to come and bid you farewell; today, I am in the same room, contemplating the ways we can continue talking. I love to write to you even though you are not here. I trust that my letters reach you in Spirit. It eases my mind and lightens my heart's sorrow to be in these conversations with you.

I am here to moderate a workshop for organizations working on the issue of gender-based violence. I feel ready and strong for the workshop because you stood so much for justice, human rights, and especially the rights of women. It is the first time I have done work without you in my life. During the sessions, I kept you present and in a way I felt your influence in the way that I did things. My moderation was very gentle. I told the participants I would be compassionately demanding excellence, as you have demanded of yourself and us throughout your life.

It is the first time I left a workshop with such a satisfaction and sense of accomplishment. We put dates, we put deliverables, we assigned roles and responsibility, and we committed ourselves to results. It was fabulous. I have to tell you, it's all because of you and your presence in my heart.

I love you always,
M

November 12, 2009

When I came home from Bo, I found an envelope on my desk containing a CD with your voice on it. Laura sent it to me—you remember Laura Johnson? She is the one who came along with the group of people from Seattle that had come to Ethiopia to explore the possibility of Integral Africa.

When we were all at Laïbet, talking to you, she started recording your voice. I stopped her in the middle, saying that she did not get your permission to record. Then, later in the conversation, she put the recorder back on and I did not say anything. I thought it would be okay. Today, I wish I had not interfered when she started recording. I would have had your full interview.

The whole audio is about your thoughts on governance. Remember when Dana Carmin asked you about how you felt about white people from America coming to Africa, to train Africans on Leadership. Do you remember what you said to him? You said to him that it is not about color but rather about finding the right people, with a mind open for learning and a heart ready to serve. There is nothing worse than trying to teach or train someone with a closed mind—it is a waste of time and effort. You told him that whether we are talking of a white man or a black one, the blood is red, and in the blood banks, it has the same market value. There is no difference between us in terms of the color of our skin; all the difference lies in our individual willingness to service, to seek the welfare of others, and to work for justice and human rights. "Does a blood transfusion from a white man to a black one make the latter lighter in color?" you asked him. In the same way, learning is learning and if you have something to teach, share, or impart, you should not be concerned about the color of your skin but rather be concerned with the intentions of your heart and the content of your mind.

It seems such a long time ago that they all came to see you. Dana was very touched by the meeting he had with you. I was so proud to sit next to you. I felt like a small tiny potted plant, next to an ancient baobab. I felt so honored by the conversations that we all had together that day. I have pictures, you know, thanks to Laura. There is a nice picture of you and me together, and it says everything about our relationship. The funny thing is that the tone of the spirit in the picture is the same as the pictures we took together back in the 1960s.

Are you really gone? It seems that you are still here somewhere, in a place where I might not be able to call or visit but where I know you can hear my voice and witness my thoughts.

I feel so blessed to have been raised by you. I feel so privileged for all the hours we spent talking about all things. I don't know anyone else in the world with whom I can talk with such frankness and on such a broad range of topics.

Do you know that I feel so free to ask you about anything, even very personal things? I don't mind, and I know you don't mind me asking as well. Like the days everyone was so worried that I would never marry and the old aunties were setting me up on blind dates so they could see me married, alas all in vain. Do you remember? I just did not want to get involved with anyone that I was not in love with. I was hoping to fall in love and then marry, so I resisted all the attempts to be set up to meet possible partners. I know you think I am stubborn, but I am not stubborn, Emaye—you taught me to stand my ground and convictions. I didn't like going on blind dates. Why were people so worried? Why couldn't they give me time to find my way?

Have you ever been in love? I know you loved Ababi dearly, but I wonder if that was comparable to being in love. I have only been in love a few times. First, it was back in the late 1980s, I thought I was in love with the young man from Ivory Coast. We stayed together about four years, until he got involved in drugs and started dealing cocaine. With cocaine in the picture, I could not stay with him, so eventually I let him go on his way. I figured that if he screwed up with those big dealers from Florida, they might come after me or my sisters, just to spite him. There were rumors that his parents kicked him out of the house and that he was homeless in Georgetown. I can't believe how life changes like that. We were only about sixteen when we met. He had a bright future ahead of him both academically and also in athletics. He was a great soccer player. All that went down the drain when cocaine appeared on the scene.

You know what pissed me off? Well, one day, the big guys asked us to try some cocaine. I refused because I knew that if I ever got addicted, it would be the end of me. I also knew that many women addicts end up compromising themselves to keep up their addictions, and I knew that the same fate would await me—plus, how could I ever face you in such a situation? So, I refused. That's when they came and asked us to sell for them, as if it was an alternative. As he had diplomatic status (due to his father's job at the embassy) he could carry the stuff and not be searched by suspicious police. So, he got involved—what a fool. Me, I still refused. Then, this fool tried to convince me again to try some. I still refused and came very close to breaking up with him. The last straw was when we went out one night, and at the nightclub, he pointed to a man and told me to be nice to him because he was the big boss from Florida. I was shocked. Do you realize what he was asking me? Yes, now and today it was to "be nice," and then tomorrow, the niceness might turn into asking me for more, like for example, asking me to provide sex. Can you believe that? Well, I walked out of the nightclub and told him that not only would I not entertain such demands from him, but that this was where our relationship ended.

I walked out and drove home. I never saw him again, except once when he came by my apartment at about 4:00am. In fact, he just called from downstairs and asked to come up; I refused and told him I would come down. When I went down, I saw him with a powdery nose. He had consumed the cocaine he was supposed to sell and now he needed money to pay. He thought I could advance the money or give it to him. At the time I did not have much on me, so there wasn't much I could do for him. I was sad to see him in such a state. He had lost a lot of weight. When I asked him about the powder on the top of his upper lip, he said that it was flour from his night job at some bakery. He had never lied to me before, at least so I chose to believe...now things were different. Anyway, I have not seen him since. I am not sure whether he is still alive or not.

You know that at the time, the only thing that saved me from getting involved with this troublesome crowd was the fact that I did not want to disappoint you. I wanted to live up to your expectations and even strive for more than what you would expect me to achieve. Anyway, so that was the end of my story with my first-ever relationship.

Matters of the heart got really complicated after this episode. I ended up meeting many new people, and along with them, many different characters. For many years, I did not want to commit to anyone. I wanted to stay alone. Of course, once in a while I would have a crush here and there, but nothing more. I went on about my life and my studies.

In fact, when I stopped going to parties and stopped initiating gatherings, outings, and so on, many of those around me, whom I had thought were friends, just turned on me. All I wanted to do was to stay home and be left alone to study. They could not understand. I lost a lot of weight by the sheer fact that I did not have much money, so I was not eating out as much. But you know what? Some girls that I thought were girlfriends spread the rumor that I might have AIDS and that was why I lost all the weight. I was heartbroken. I cannot imagine that friends would be so cheap. Maybe it was my misunderstanding to assume they were friends when they were merely acquaintances.

This is about the time that you called me one day and asked if I was okay. You said you had seen me in your dreams and that I was in great distress. Well, you had seen right—I was in bad shape. I did not have my old friends, I had broken up with my long time boyfriend, Etetila had moved on to Boston for her course at Harvard, and my friend Bob had moved to California. It was such a time of loneliness. I felt so separated from you, from my parents, and from my sisters. I felt lonely, but I also felt strong. I think it was about this time that I started building my own path. This is the time that I got hardened, almost like pottery fired in flames. I knew that when I came out the other side, I would be the same in some ways, but I also would be a different person. I would be a woman of my own.

Gosh, do you remember the resistance I faced from all angles? I know that back home, Enanaye and Boubiye just did not know what to do with me. Of course, some people I will leave unmentioned thrived in the situation and made me the scapegoat for all the ills we experienced as a family. As you always say, this too shall pass, and it passed. It did pass, Emaye.

So many years ago, and yet it all seems like yesterday. We don't realize as human beings the impact of our actions and words on others, especially on those whom we claim to love. I think that the greatest pain I ever felt came from within our family. It was the pain of betrayal, of abandonment, and of making choices whether to stay in the reality in which I lived or go my way even if going my way meant a brutal emotional uprooting.

Many years later, I fell in love again, this time with a French man. It was a year of passion, if I can put it this way. The man was just out of this world. He would cook for me, and while he cooked, he insisted that I just relax in the living room. He would put on some jazzy music, come with a tray of tropical colorful cocktails, and then paint my toenails. He played with my braids. I felt like I was back in my childhood again, like I had found someone to play with. If he made a bubble bath for me, he had candles all over the place. He sat on the rim of the tub, often leaning on the wall. From there, he told me stories and trickled warm soapy water down my back. Emaye, I think I must have called and told you about him. Whenever he told me fairy tales, he made up the story as he went. At times we went out for dinner and then dancing until dawn. Can you believe that I managed to stay up so late? Well, it wasn't too hard to stay up so late—we danced the whole night through.

When I first met him, I did not think I would be dating him; it never even crossed my mind. We were sent out to sort of chaperone. Well, the chaperones soon forgot about the ward put in their care. I can't say that there was any kind of preamble to this story. It all unfolded with the music, the dancing, and the rest of the atmosphere. As we started dancing, one thing led to another, and before I knew it, it all just happened.

But guess what? Remember that when I came back home to Addis, I told you I had ended a relationship to come back home—well, that's the one. After almost a year of dating this beautiful person, I felt I had to leave and go back home. I asked him to come with me, but he responded by asking me to come with him to Paris. We were both a bit stubborn, so I insisted on going home and wished him good luck. Do you remember that year, I said I would fly back to Washington to see Fofi, Noela, and Lily? Well, I was planning to see them of course, but my intention was to see him. I was hoping that our story would be finished and I just wanted to confirm that.

I spent 10 days in all in Washington, 9 of which were all with him. I guess my sisters understood my situation and did not give me too much trouble about it. To my surprise, it seemed that nothing had changed between us; if anything, it was even more intense than before. Again, we discussed his coming with me or my going to Paris with him. I was not going to give up on coming home, so we agreed to go our separate ways.

The farewells were tough. It was hard. I had never cried like that before, for anything or anyone. I wasn't crying, even; I was just so sad that the tears welled up from somewhere deep inside. Emaye, I promise, I was not crying for me. He was crying too. We were both crying. We were both so sad. While we realized that the choices that we made were the right choices in terms of the directions of our lives, we also knew that such a story, as happened between us, doesn't happen every day. We had to say goodbye. It was better this way. We both inherently knew that we were never to forget the year we spent together, and that the memories of these days will always envelop us with warm memories of a summer love story.

Did I ever tell you about the letter I wrote to God? Well, I wrote it on my flight back from Washington to Brussels. It was January 5, 1997. I made bullet points in my letter and I told God I had three requests for him. 1) I told God that I was no longer interested in having relationships, since it appeared that was not working for me. I asked him if he could please direct me into a career path where I would be happy, where I could use my skills to serve those who needed to be served and also to bring hope, happiness, and possibilities in communities where such hope or possibilities did not really dwell. 2) I asked him to please make me like sports and exercise. 3) I asked him if he could please intervene and help me quit smoking. After the closing of the letter, I had a PS that said: "Dear God, but if you see someone I might like come my way, please give me a heads up—only if you think he would be a good match for me."

Almazesha, I can't tell you whether it was fate or the letter I wrote to God, but I met Matthias the very next day. He was on the same flight back to Addis from Frankfurt, but I had not noticed him. Back then it was still allowed to smoke on the flights, so I was of course in the back with some friends who were on the same flight. We were having a great time and were completely lost in our philosophical conversations, slightly tainted by the nicotine and the red wine we consumed.

Upon arrival, Matthias was standing behind me at customs. And although they often irritate me with their paranoid attitudes, this time, the paranoia of the customs officers delayed everything so much that Matthias had the chance to strike up a conversation with me. Again, there was no particular intention or inclination to start dating, let alone get married. You know that he also lived at the Bole Rwanda *Sefer* [neighborhood], so we exchanged numbers and promised to call one another sometime in the future. Eventually we met again through the social circles. The social scene was not as widespread as now, so you always ended up seeing everyone at the same parties and gatherings.

The day I met him again at one of those parties, I was out for dinner with some friends, so I asked him if he wanted to come along. It was a French crowd, and you know how they never make an effort to speak anything else but French. He spoke some French, so he followed the conversation, but I think it was not the greatest evening for him. We then met a few days later for dinner, just the two of us. This was his initiative and he took me to Blue Tops—you remember that restaurant I liked so much, the one that opened next to Kidist Mariam Church by Arat Kilo. I had the usual spinach soup and he ordered carpaccio. It was a nice evening and possibly the only evening where we had a calm conversation without much commotion or noise.

I found him to be very charming. I was conscious of just being out of a relationship and did not want to bounce into another without being mindful about it. We had the greatest evening talking about life and how we hope to spend our lives. As the evening turned into night I must admit that there was a new energy that emerged. The kind of energy, when you know something is about to happen between two people. It was magical. I tried not to think of it and just continued enjoying the evening. After dinner, we ended up at the usual Torero nightclub and called it a night. Soon after that, I was off with some friends for the weekend at Lake Langano; we invited him and his roommate to join us. It was a great weekend.

That was the first time I thought there definitely was something brewing between us. Then Enanaye traveled, so I had the house all to myself. Do you remember how I called you once and asked if I could have party platters prepared at Laïbet and you sent me loads of food? Well, that was for this party. By the time the party ended, people had started their morning jogging. Emaye, we were just young and still had energy to spare. I couldn't do that now. I am so tired. You would laugh at me if you saw me now. I am in bed by nine and up before six in the morning. Would you say that these are signs of aging?

Going back to Matthias, not too long after the weekend at Langano, he took me to the mountains for a picnic. It was the 21st of April. I remember the date not because I have a good memory, but because it was his birthday that day. We were sitting in my truck and as we started nibbling the stuff we brought for the picnic, he said to me, "Can I ask you a question?" It was raining outside, and I was afraid he was going to ask me to start hiking in the rain, so I replied: "You can ask me anything as long as you don't ask me to hike in the rain." So, he looked up and said, "Will you spend the rest of your life with me?" Good God, what? I didn't expect such a bombshell of a question. What? Emaye, I was shocked and stunned. A voice inside me started shouting: "What did he just say? No, way, I am not getting married. No way!" I was surprised—he hardly knew me, and I hardly knew him. We did have a bit of a fling, but nothing serious, I thought. Now, this question blew my mind away. The voice inside subsided and I heard whispers from my heart... Inside my heart, I felt that "yes" was the only answer I could give him. I have no rational reason; it was all intuitive. Did you ever think that you would one day see me all settled down, married with children? I certainly never thought it would happen. It has not been easy, though.

Emaye, marriage is great, but you never told me how much effort it takes to keep it running smoothly. I just had no idea about that. I had never seen you and Ababi argue or disagree radically; I had never seen Enaniye and Boubiye fight or argue. So, when I married, I didn't know how to handle it when arguments or disagreements came along. I had never learned to argue without fighting. It's strange. We didn't fight too much though, rest assured. It was just once in a while, mostly early on. Now, there is hardly any argument. Things are just fine. We are happy to have made it this far and hope that we will have many more years to come. It's been quite a journey.

I have to go, Emaye. Tomorrow I get up early—I better get some sleep.

More tomorrow. I love you,
M

November 18, 2009

I arrived in Amsterdam yesterday morning. It always seems to be an adventure to travel out of Freetown, and this time was no exception. Once I checked in, I tried to go find something to eat, but you know me—I can't really sit and eat alone. So I brought some crackers and cheese to my room and had that.

I was so exhausted I fell asleep around 7:00pm, but then throughout the early evening I had so many calls coming in that I lost my sleep. I tossed and turned until I finally fell asleep. Now it's about 1:00am and I can't sleep anymore.

My thoughts are going all over the place, jumping from work-related things to family, back to my research and again about family. I am thinking of you and all the things that have been going on since you left. In a way, I am sure you are proud of how we have handled the entire situation. As you always told us, *Alte Zrekerekinem* (we were not disorganized). All of us from the oldest to the youngest member of the family were very proper and did all things according to your tradition.

Before I left Freetown to come to Amsterdam, I spoke with Fofi. She is still in Addis with Enanaye. You know, she is the one who prepared the English version of your brochure. I think she did a great job. But from the conversations I have had with her, she didn't feel like she had everyone's support on it. It goes back to the usual drama and underlying dynamics—everyone is so sad about what happened that there is serious misunderstanding happening. I hope it passes. It all makes me very sad. I am not sure who we will go to for mediation from here.

At your *Seleste* (third day of mourning), we all sat in the tent outside early in the morning. There were not many outside guests; it was all the family and close friends. Zene asked that some of us get up to speak about what you have meant for us. The first person to speak was one of your old friends, and I guess she was very sad because her speech was not very kind to those of us sitting there. After she spent some minutes praising you, she took a sudden turn in her talk and said that unless "we"—meaning the remaining children—want her, she didn't want us either. I wonder if someone hurt her feelings. It felt like payback for something that someone may have said or done, but even so, I did not feel that it was appropriate for her to say that. But who am I to say? You can't possibly say that you love someone and then turn around to overtly reject that person's children and family when they pass. Wouldn't you agree? I am sure you would say that she had her reasons and we should make an effort to make sure she is always welcome. In fact, I know you would say that.

Then an older lady from your village, Gurene, spoke. She looked very old from her appearance, but I am sure she is not that old—she might have had a rough life. She was really sweet. She was hardly dressed properly; she didn't have shoes, and I don't know if she left them outside or if she walked barefoot. As I write these words, I am thinking that I should have gone to find out and I should have made sure that she got some proper shoes. She might have had some old Converse tennis shoes on, I am just not sure. She was so distraught about you that her speech was interrupted many times by the knots in her throat. She was upset that the men from your village only sent a few horses to receive you on your way to Debre

Libanos. I think they did the best they could, and there were many horsemen who came to mourn. But this lady was upset. And as she put it, "these fools only sent some scraggy old horse or two...how can they do that when our most honored mother and daughter of all of our forefathers comes home....let them wait until I get back home....I will sort them out." I felt sorry for those men. I think they are going to get a piece of her mind when she reaches home. The whole time she spoke, she was standing, and then she would put her hands on her head and twirl around and then squat down and then get up again to twirl with her hands on her head. The sadness she had was so deep, we all felt for her. Many of us wept as she spoke.

Zene was still up, being the master of ceremony for this session, if we can call it a session. She said, "Maybe we can have some words from her grandchildren. Mimiye, come and say some words." I had to find the courage to swallow all the tears and stand up and talk in your honor. I remember I read out a speech in English at Ababi's ceremony in Debre Libanos. That was not so hard because it was a larger audience and it was more formal. I had it written out so all I had to do was read. Now, here it was just us— the usual Laïbet crew, family and friends. All of those sitting in that tent were people with whom we all have lived closely and all of us knew you very closely. I didn't want to just ramble, so I took a moment of silence to ground myself and then I let it flow.

Initially, as I started to speak, my voice did not cooperate. It seemed to have stayed in my throat and was not willing to come out. I wanted to say what you meant for me. But nothing came out. All I could do was swallow, as if I could swallow the sorrow I felt, as if I could have swallowed my grief. Finally after a few tries, I managed to blurt it out: "To me, Almazesha was my best friend." What a relief after I said it. It was out and I had said it. Then, my entire spirit took a turn and I did not want to dwell on the mourning or immense loss we all felt. I wanted to speak about the good days, I wanted to speak about the future, and I wanted to be a voice in which we might hear your words.

So, I explained to them why you were my best friend. I told them that you are and will always be the one person to whom I could speak to about anything under the sky. I told them how during my work at MSF on HIV/AIDS, I would call you daily to find out the various words in Amharic relating to reproductive health. They all laughed when I told them that you would take my calls, and then jokingly tell me that you had done your communion and why should I call yet again to ask you about all these words about sexuality, reproductive health, and the body parts we don't talk about in Amharic. It was funny. I still think it is funny, and those sitting there had a good laugh. I think it was the first time they had laughed since they heard of your departure.

I also told them that you are my best friend because you were always the first person I would call when I got a good joke. In fact, I wonder if you heard what happened to Boubiye this summer. He was supposed to meet me in my hotel in Brussels, but I was going to be a bit late so I called him on his cell and asked him to pass me to the receptionist. I told the receptionist that he should let my father into my room and not have him wait in the lobby. Because the receptionist knew me well, he kindly gave Boubiye the key. Once in the room, Boubiye made himself comfortable: put the TV on, got some snacks, had something to drink from the fridge, and just waited for me. There was a chocolate muffin in the fridge, but he hesitated to take it and finally left it because he thought I had saved it for Rosi and Leoni. He took his shoes off and just started zapping the channels and enjoying himself.

Suddenly, apparently, the door opened and as usual, he just said, "Mim, *gosh metash* [good, you're back]." Only to see that the person who entered was a tall blond woman. That didn't faze him, though—he assumed she was my friend, so he just greeted her and sat back down to continue watching TV. He even offered her some chips and invited her to sit and relax until I returned.

But then, when the woman remained stunned—she apparently just stood there staring at him—he added, "why don't you sit and relax? She will be back soon." "Who will be back?" the woman asked. "Mimi—she is just out shopping," he replied, but from the look on the woman's face, he felt something was not adding up. "Are you friends with my daughter?" he asked. "I don't know your daughter," she replied. "Then what are you doing in her room?" he asked. "What do you mean *her* room—this is *my* room!" she retorted. So, to make a long story short, he had been given the wrong key and had been making himself comfortable in someone else's room. Anyway, by this time, I had reached the lobby and we had a good laugh.

So, going back to the jokes, the first thing both Boubiye and I thought was that we should make sure this story reaches you. I hope he told you.

But as you always do, I also wanted to pass on a

serious message along with the humor. I told everyone sitting in the tent that the time was finished in which we had the luxury of entertaining drama and chewing on issues among us, because we no longer had our mediator among us. Now, the time of internal, unnecessary disputes was over because we no longer had a higher body to bring our grievances to. The time for being unkind to anyone was over because we no longer had the one who could dry the tears of those who were hurt. Short of God on this earth, you know very well that you were our source of comfort and love. I told them that now it was time for even more understanding for each other, even more compassion and kindness with each other; now was the time to rise up and finally be the souls you have raised us to be. Now was the time to behave, do, act, and work in a way that would allow your name to be raised in praise. Now was the time to grow up. The "*farenet*"[43] time was over and gone—it was time to not only behave as we have been raised, but to be what we have been brought up to be. It was time to live up to the spirit you have embraced and anointed us with throughout all of our lives.

Isn't it interesting that one grows up when parents pass on? It happens so instantly when we find ourselves faced with the reality of assuming leadership, parenthood, and the positions of those who have raised us, upon their departure.

I said all these things because you know what, Almazesha? Well, I am afraid that our family will defragment. You were the glue that kept us all together, and now it is up to us to remain together

---

[43] A slang word with various meanings, here used to indicate "foolishness."

even though Ababi and you are no longer here with us physically to bring us all together around a meal. It is the flaring egos that I am afraid of. Some of us are so tired, I tell you, that any kind of emotional or subtle psychological aggravation is bound to send some of us far away. But wouldn't that be a pity.

Again, people are the way they are, and I suppose we cannot expect everyone to have the same kind of consciousness or ability to love unconditionally. In fact, I think we need to pray to be endowed with the patience, compassion, and largeness of heart to keep it all together.

Before I sat down that day, I told them I wanted to share with them the last joke (albeit a true story in this case) that I had shared with you. Some people were shaking their heads in disbelief that I would dare tell a joke in the midst of this day of mourning, but I felt it was okay. If you remember, there were so many comical incidents at so many other funerals we had. And how better to pay tribute to you, than to tell the last laugh we shared?

So, I told them a story that the priest from Freetown had told me one day, which one of the parishioners who was an ex-combatant had told him. I had called you to tell you about it. Do you remember how much we laughed? I could hardly breathe. Apparently, the Father worked with some ex-combatants, and after they were baptized and accepted the Lord in their lives, one of them told him about what happened one day as they raided a village.

So, these rebels would go looting, killing, and burning up villages. In one particular village, they entered the house. They found one couple, a husband and wife, hiding and shaking from fear. The rebel, the same one who was now baptized and fully converted to Christianity, told the Father that he had grabbed the woman by the hair and put her up against the wall, threatening to kill her, of course. And then he asked her as he shouted and pushed her around: "What what what is is your bloody name...what, what, is your f...<+?ing name?" With a shaky terrorized voice, she managed to say her name and replied: "Mariam."

The rebel was taken aback and then said, "Well, I know Mariam was the mother of Jesus, so you can go." He took her by the collar and pushed her out the door. Then he grabbed the husband and the same procedure took place: "What what what is your bloody name?" The man, all shaky and scared out of his mind, answered in a trembling voice: "My name is Jamal, but my friends call me Mariam!"

Gosh, the whole tent just broke out in laugher. I loved it. Then I sat down, and I felt we had had our first breath of air.

Do you know that I miss you every day?

Oh, today something happened. I took the train from the airport to come to Amsterdam Central Train station, and then I was to take a quick walk for about 1km. The weather was bad, so I got a taxi. It was suppose to be 7-8 Euro, but this crook charged me 20 Euros. After I dropped my bags at the hotel and confirmed the proper rate with the receptionist, I decided to walk back to the station to get his tag number and report him. You will be proud that I found him. He did not know why I was there, so I told him I might have forgotten some document in his car. That was all a cover for me to have enough time to write down his plates. Then together with the receptionist here, we called the central taxi and the police to report him.

I thought of you when I did that. Remember that taxi driver in Addis who had assaulted me and hit me with his car? Well, I also went out to find him, thanks to you sending me a car to find him. I felt avenged when the Federal Police arrested him. Can you believe that this guy had threatened to kill me? I am glad I found him and had him arrested. Now, to me, he remains a story—nothing more than that. If I had not found him, I would have always felt the thorn of being a victim.

I might have to stop writing now because my battery is low on the laptop and I forgot to bring an adaptor. I will write to you very soon.

I love you,
M

P.S. Did I tell you I saw you in my dream a few days ago? You had your green dress on and it was like you were twenty years younger. We were in the living room in Laïbet. You told us that you wanted to have a mattress on the floor to let your soul rest, and that you didn't want to lie in a bed. I cannot believe that I will not hold your hand again. I liked to hold your hand. I liked to see that our ring fingers looked identical. Can you believe that all I have of you is my ring finger? I even thought I wanted to get a tattoo like you. Not the big cross you have your forearm, but the little circle you did as a child on your hands. Okay, I go now. I hope to get some sleep. I love you always.

P.P.S. You know what is strange? You remember how I really didn't care about Ethiopian food? Well, you should see me now. I even asked Fofi to bring me some *kebay* (Ethiopian ghee). Back then, each time you wanted to give me some, I refused to take it, but now I want it. Isn't it bizarre? Tomorrow night I am going to look for an Ethiopian restaurant and eat there. I still don't know how to make *injera*. They never give you the proper recipe and it is a pain in the butt to try and figure it out. You know what I wish we did? I wish we had taken the time to learn how to make *injera* from you. I wish we had made a cookbook with all your recipes. Maybe I will try to do that with Koky this summer. Okay, now I am really going to bed. As usual, in person or in letter, I can never stop talking to you. I love you so much, and so forever. I am certain we will meet again very soon one day (not too soon though—first I have to raise my girls).

November 21, 2009

Emaye,

I am with Bene now in London. I finished my work in Amsterdam, and there was a layover in London, so I decided to spend some time with Bene and her family. She hasn't changed since you last saw her. She has two beautiful and sweet daughters, Violet and Alix. She has been so sweet with me. I told her about you. We didn't talk much about it, the same way we didn't talk much about her own recent loss. I know she knows, and she knows I know, so there was no need to talk. We are both confronted with a new reality about this whole life-and-death matter. My God, do you think we will manage to have the strength to go on? Will our lives be completely different from here on?

Everywhere I go, somehow you are on my mind. I want to tell my friends, but at the same time I don't want to open myself up. I would rather keep it inside. I try to avoid such conversations so I won't be unduly offended or hurt by thoughtless comments. Sometimes people just let their mouths run and say things that are insensitive.

Tomorrow I go home. I am spending the day with Bene, Violet, and Alix. John, her husband, is also a very nice person. You would have liked him, had you met him. He is a true *Jigna Ye Jigna Lej* (warrior, child of warriors).[44]

I love you, M

---

[44] In Amharic, *Jigna* is what we used to call the warriors of the land; nowadays, the term is also used to refer to someone with "the heart and spirit of a warrior."

November 28, 2009

Emaye,

Yesterday was two months since you left. I can't believe it's already two months—it seems like a long time. I wonder how it will be as the days and months and years start adding up. Do you think my memory will fade? I wonder if your memory will fade. There is an American singer who sings to someone he lost (his son? I am not sure). But in his lyrics he says, "Will you know my name when I see you in heaven?" And what about us? Will we know each other, Emaye, when we meet in Heaven?

Emaye, I want to believe that we will meet again. I want to know that we will be together again in heaven or somewhere in the sky. And so I wonder if you will still know my name? I know you will, because I will never forget you. You are so much part of me that forgetting you in any way would be forgetting my very self. What a silly question to ask. But you know, I don't think it is silly because there is no such thing as a silly question. All questions are valid. I mean, I could pass in a few months or years and then we would meet very early on, but what if I live another 50 years and I come and see you as an old grandmother—will you recognize me? I would be older than you when we meet, that would be very odd and funny. But I suppose that spirit is timeless, so it is our souls that meet, our eternal souls that meet in a place where we come for eternity, where everything is forever.

Something about the person's demeanor recalls the spirit of warriors long gone. *Jigna Ye Jigna Lej* means "Warrior, Child of Warriors" and implies the person comes from a long line of warriors or warrior-like people.

I saw you in my dream last night, as I do almost every night. Last night I saw that we were together in the living room, at Laïbet. I was sitting very close to you, as usual, and I took your hand. I think it was your left hand and I kissed it right where you have the *nikisat* (tattoo). I am not even sure it was a dream because it seemed so real. The touch of your hands, the smooth skin that bears the traces of the challenges, laughter, hard work, and tragedies you lived through. I miss you very much.

I miss holding hands with you, and most of all, I miss your smile. Last time we were together this past Easter, Matthias took a beautiful picture of you—one of the rare pictures that shows your true smile. I love it. I wish I had more of those pictures; still, I am grateful for the few that Matthias took. Your special smile is full of warmth, love, mischief, and humor, all at once. And then there is this very light perfume scent that engulfed me each time I entered your room. As I stepped into your room, poking my head around the door, I would find you sitting on your bed, reading or just resting, and I would land on your smile. You cannot imagine how good I felt just at that moment. There is no place in the world where I will be so comfortable or feel so safe, ever again. While Laïbet is a place that I have for long considered my country, your bedroom is what I consider my sanctuary forever. Each time I came to sleep in your room or stay with you for some time, I just had this sense of security and wellness. Nothing mattered. No matter what kind of stress was going on outside, no matter whether all hell broke loose, I just felt so good to be with you. That's what I miss now, and I wonder if I will ever find this same peace somewhere. I think at times that this is the peace I will find when I come to join you on the other side, maybe soon or maybe many years from now. I don't know. For the sake of my children and Matthias, I hope that I will still have many more years on Earth, but when my time comes, I will not fear to cross over because I know that on the other side, you will be there along with all of our loved ones who have crossed over.

You know, Rosi and Leoni go to an American School in Freetown so last Thursday, school was closed for Thanksgiving. We are not American so I did not cook a turkey—besides, where would I find a turkey in Freetown? But instead of the turkey party, we had a cheese, bread, and wine party with all the cheese I brought from Amsterdam. Matthias baked his famous German dark bread; you can't imagine how much he baked. There was bread enough to open a bakery. I cooked some light food and a couple of girlfriends brought additional salads and three quiches. We cooled the beer and the white wine and brought that bar furniture from downstairs to the living room, upstairs. There was so much commotion that day.

I thought of you that day. Do you remember I always called you when I had parties? I called for advice, but I also called because it was one more reason to chat with you and talk about the this-and-that of life. I love having parties. It is not necessarily for the party per se, but I love the process of the party.

You should see our place when there is a party in the air—there is so much preparation. Our caretaker Mousa is just like Gashe Tilahun. He is very nice but at times he can get loud and he can pick a fight quite easily with not much reason behind it. Otherwise, he is very hard working and he has a big heart. He is often misunderstood by most people around him because they just can't see his heart. When we have a party, however, he is the one I rely on the most. Yeshiye and I, we plan the menu and get things prepared a few days ahead. He is in charge of preparing the chairs, the garden, and the furniture in the living room. Then on the afternoon before the party, he rearranges the entire living room so that it fits the party. It is just like the times when you moved your dining room table to make it into a buffet. He also brings in some of the boys from the neighborhood. There are times we prepare the place for the evening party, and there are people in my living room that I don't even know. But it's all good, Emaye, it's just people from the neighborhood who come to help out.

You know what I am thinking? I know it's weird, but that dining room table in Laïbet has served so many purposes. It has seen and witnessed so much of our own history, and in a way, also the contemporary history of our country. It is a blessed and magic table. Ababi's coffin lay on it for the night of prayers and chanting, and again, the same table was used for you. This morning I was thinking of the time my own passing would come. I guess my coffin might not leave out of Laïbet, mostly likely because you are not there and I don't think we have the means nor the energy to do the mourning ceremony as you would do it. I thought about the end of my life and I was wondering where my body would be put to rest. It might not be in Debre Libanos, because it would be too far for Rosi and Leoni to visit me.

You know the night before you left us, I was at dinner at Nicolas and Stephanie's, the Brussels Airlines manager in Freetown. He had invited a number of us to have a full Belgian dinner with mussels and french fries with real Belgian mayonnaise. Anyway, at this dinner, I was talking with a friend, Ali from Australia/Germany, and for some reason we had a long conversation about Debre Libanos. I was telling him that in my family, we all know where our bodies will go at the end of our journey. We will all go to the family mausoleum. How strange that not even 12 hours later, I heard that you had gone, and just a few days later, I was on the plane to come and see you off. Life—it's such a strange thing, but this doesn't stop it from being beautiful, too. As you always said, it is when we know that we are not in control, that we are free to live and to love.

So, coming back to our party on Thursday night, it was great. You would have been happy to see how the guests were taken care of. I think we have all learned to entertain from you. When I say "we," I mean all of us, your children and grandchildren. You should see how my house buzzes when I announce a party.

You know what? Once the guests have been served, Yeshiye goes to the buffet and makes plates for all the drivers who have come with guests, the security guards, and all the others who have helped us with the event. She even sends plates of food out to some of the close neighbors, some whom we know and even those we don't know. There is a seamstress who has a shop down the street from our house. She is a bit far, sort of close to the main road. Well, her husband works in Ethiopia and one day we found out that she liked Ethiopian food; since that day, Yeshiye sends her plates of Ethiopian food, too! The food must be blessed because no matter what, there is always enough and even too much. Thank God for that.

Of course, Mousa gets preferential treatment in

Yeshiye's books. She really appreciates his hard work and also knows that he is not one to speak out or demand anything, so Yeshiye piles up a plate for him and gives him money to buy Stout beer. That's all he drinks; it's not far from our own *tela* (Ethiopian home-brewed dark beer).

The last guests on that night left a little before 3:00am. My feet felt like jello by that time, but I was happy about how everything went. During the party, I had conversations with myself, in my head, with you. I was going around the living room and veranda, making sure that everyone was well served, and through it all, it was as if I walked with you. So, I had this very girly conversation with you about the friends who had come over. I was introducing them to you, one by one, and I was happy to have you so close to me again. You would be so proud of me. I am sure you are anyway.

Emaye, you know, I let go of the cigarettes. Maybe that's why I get sleepy at parties, even when it's at our house. Past midnight, I start getting sleepy and then it's a struggle to stay up. Depending on which guests are still there, sometimes I just slip out and go upstairs and go to bed.

After the party on Thursday, we took the children to Franco Beach the following day. It is owned by an Italian Sierra Leonean couple, Franco and Florence, and we stayed two nights there. I feel at home when I go there because I know Aunty Florence well. We went there with a Dutch Vietnamese couple who have children in Rosi and Leoni's class. Again in the evening, over dinner, she told us her story, this Vietnamese/Dutch friend of ours. She was telling me about her grandmother and how her grandmother had raised her back home in Vietnam. She told us about the time she had to leave her grandmother, during the war, and flee to the Philippines. The family is planning on going back to Vietnam this summer to celebrate the grandmother's 80th birthday. I was happy for her, and at the same time I felt a pinch in my heart because we never celebrated your birthdays.

I would have loved to celebrate your birthday and your life and have you right there for us to be together in the celebration. It's an Ethiopian thing, this not having birthdays. People are so reserved. Are we afraid of showing our happiness too much, like someone is going to snatch it if we put it out there? But why? Why is it so? We miss so many chances to love and live, to laugh and reminisce. On the other hand, everyone is so busy hiding their age that birthday parties would be hard to celebrate.

I promise you I will celebrating my birthday until the last day of my life. In fact, and I know you will laugh when I say this, "Well, I am also going to tell my age, the way it is and not even take a day off!" Why can't we be happy for the years God has blessed us with?

Emaye, you know one day I was talking to Andiye, and he said that for him any woman older than 22 is just too old. I fell off my chair laughing when he said that. I can't believe that our culture is so against age. As if age is so bad. There is nothing bad with age—it is a beautiful thing. In every wrinkle marking our faces, in every gray hair we sport, there is such grace and beauty. I take both wrinkles and gray hair as a gift representing the blessings of being here in this world, the blessings of evolving through life and accumulating wisdom. Just because I am older, it does not mean my life is over! Or is it?

When I think of you and the age you might have, I always go back to the time I was born and you were 31 years old. That's how I know your age. So, I guess it makes you about 74 today.

Emaye, my dearest Emaye, did you think that was enough years for you to leave us? I don't think it was enough. I wish we could have been together to celebrate your 80th or even 90th. But I also know that you wanted to go, and I can understand that. For me, I would have loved to have you a little longer with us. It's just lonely without you.

Will we see each other again other than in my thoughts or in my dreams? For me, I feel that you have left physically but that in spirit you are still here. You know what's strange? Well, as much as I used to always be afraid to be alone or in the dark, since you left I have been completely brave. Not independently or of my own will, but rather because I know that you are now part of the spirit world and from wherever you are, you look over us and have become part of the angels who look over us.

You know, I even like the Virgin Mary a lot more. I didn't have any attachment to her because I could not relate to her; now, I relate to her as a mother and I feel so good to have her around. I think of you and your role as the amazing mother you have been to us all—and all of a sudden, I come to appreciate the Virgin Mary so much more.

Rosi has come down with fever today and I have to go take care of her, so I will write back tomorrow.

I love you always,
M

December 4, 2009

Emaye,

I saw you in my dreams last night. You were wearing one of your green dresses and walking down a moderate hill. For some reason I thought you must have been in Ababa Tiliku's house.

It's the second time I have seen you wearing a green dress. I asked Yeshiye whether you wore green a lot, and she told me it was your favorite color. I thought your favorite color was red? But now that I think about it, it looks like green was also among your favorites.

On my side, I am fine. I finished a section of my dissertation today. I also wrote about you in the section on my participants. I said how much I had learned from you and how all that I am is really a reflection of the time I spent with you.

The other day, I missed you a lot and since I could not call you, I called K. He was sweet and we spoke for a long time. I told him that Yeshiye was trying to get me to buy more cat food.

Emaye, you should see these two cats we have. They are so lazy! They don't even hunt lizards; they just sit and wait until we serve them food out of a can or some dried imported thing. Plus, one of them is a bit rude. He doesn't even say hello or come and stay with us. He just stays in his corner brooding and only comes near the kitchen when it is time to eat. You can understand why I refuse to buy him fancy food.

Today, my old friend Stephan came from Brussels; he

is moving to Freetown. Remember I used to tell you about some of his ideas for the HIV/AIDS project I was running. It's too bad that I never had a chance to invite him home to Laïbet. I always thought I would have a chance to do so one day, and I regret that he never met you. Anyway, I used to also tell him so much about you. He asked me how you were doing, and I told him you were fine. I just could not bring myself to tell him the truth. I didn't lie to him—I am sure you are fine, wherever you are. I just didn't tell him exactly where you were. It's better this way. I almost wanted to tell him that you had left, but I didn't. I am happy he is here. It's good to have old friends.

I have to go now; I am falling asleep. I love you always. Never forget that you have been, are, and always will be my most beloved teacher.

M

December 7, 2009

Emaye,

We spent the day at the beach yesterday. I drove out there with Rosi and Leoni; Matthias had already left earlier in the morning so that he could do a trek with some friends. I think you would have liked the beaches in Sierra Leone.

There is something different about Sierra Leone's beaches. The ocean is a lot gentler than anywhere else I have seen, and the sand is very fine and of nearly pure color. At River #2, which is the most common beach, the sand is very white. The water is warm—at times you don't even realize that you are in the water, because it is so warm. Other beaches have sand that is slightly different in color, and there is even one beach with black sand.

Don't worry about the girls being in the water. They can swim very well and they don't go in too far or without me or Matthias being with them. We try to be careful and are conscious that the waves can be dangerous even if you can swim.

I met a friend on the beach who just lost her father not even two weeks ago. I had not had the chance to visit her earlier, even though Matthias had told me about it last week. It's strange how before, I would always be shy to talk about a loss or give my condolences. Now, I just jump in and say all the things that come through my heart. I guess once we have lost someone dear, it makes us more able to express our own grief and also more able to reach out to others experiencing grief.

I talked for a while with my friend, and all that she told me is what I have gone through with you. Yes, some people think that losing a loved one who is considered "old" is not so bad. As if we can say that there is a cut off age, like if someone is 60 or 65, then we shouldn't be too sad. And of course if someone is 75 or 80 then, we should really not be sad. Don't people know that it's not about age, but about love?

At times it is painful to hear people's comments, so I was telling my friend that I have not shared your loss with many. I have kept it to myself. And you know, when people ask me how you are, I still reply that you are fine. My friend said that she wanted to change the structure of her speech and use the past tense to refer to her father, but I told her that she can always stay in the present, because for me even if you are not here physically, you are there for me in all other forms.

I dream of you almost every night. Last night again, I dreamt that I spent the night in your room. I was surprised to find you in your bed, sleeping in your usual curled position. You were facing the wall, with all its crosses, icons, and pictures of Jesus. When I spoke you turned to look at me, and for a moment I was a little scared. I thought that maybe this wasn't you. There was something different about you—you looked distant to me. Then I just jumped up and hugged you, and you smiled; I think you even laughed. I felt better then.

I could not sleep after that, so I spent about two hours just tossing and turning in my bed. For a moment I wanted to come to the office to work a bit, but I thought it best to force myself to rest.

In the morning, I was up before everyone. Leoni had

come to our bed and Matthias was still deeply asleep. I could not stop just gazing at them and thinking that this was a blessing, and even though we think such moments will be forever, these days will come to pass. I remember when I slept in your bed, with you on one side and Ababi on the other. Can you believe that those days are gone?

Matthias looks more and more like Ababi—it is the weirdest thing. When he cuts his hair short, I tell you, he is a spitting image. At times, I see that he is tired from work and my heart goes out to him. He doesn't deal with stress very well, and when there is stress it shows on his eyes and his face. His cheeks dip more and his eyes become melancholic. I find it funny that now I find myself behaving with Matthias like you used to behave with Ababi. I just want him to be happy and to be comfortable. I worry when he is not well, and when he is happy, my heart is in heaven.

Someday, these days we have with Rosi and Leoni coming to our bed, us making their lunch boxes, me picking them up from school, and us just planning some fun family time...well, one day this too will pass. I am so conscious of it that each moment is a moment not only of living but also of witnessing life and love as I live and experience my life.

We often forget to notice the blessings around us. I have been calling home a lot more these days, just to talk and chitchat. I am happy that I called you as much as I could, so I have no regrets. Except, well, I wish I had insisted that they pass you to me that Tuesday the 22nd of September when I called to have the girls speak to you.

There is still so much that I wish I could tell you, so much I want to ask you and talk about with you. I know we made the best of our time together, but I was hoping for more. It is a great lesson I have learned: Not to wait for tomorrow to say I love you or sit together to share and ask questions about the stories of our lives. At the end of the day, what really matters? Isn't it the quality of the relationships we have? What good is money and fame, if we don't have loved ones to share with? What good are all the achievements at work or in school or in life in general, if we don't have loved ones we can call and share the good news with? It's really all about relationship and working on ourselves so that we can show up as genuinely and authentically as possible. There is undeniable power in authenticity.

I think sometimes we are scared to be genuine, especially when it comes to love and relationships. Why are many of us so reluctant to tell our truth about love? Why can't we just say it? Why can't we just go on and hold the hand of the person we love? Is it fear of rejection? Or is there something else?

I have become more and more daring in telling people that I love them, be they family or friends. Sometimes it has brought me problems or been misunderstood—but overall, it's been good. I feel really good to tell someone I love that I love them.

On a different note, I have been thinking that this entire writing process has been a way for me to reflect on the time we had together. It has been a way for me to share our story with my daughters. I hope that they will then be able to share it with their children, and so forth. In fact, it is not just for my children; I hope that many can find themselves in our story.

You know, my passport is about to expire. I must go back home to have it renewed, as it seems there is no embassy near me that can renew it. As much as a part of me wants to renew it and hold on to it, a part of me is also ready to let go. I can't manage to come to terms with coming back to Addis and not being able to call you as soon as I land at Bole. Who will I call now? I know that everyone is still there, but for me, your absence is a major void. I almost don't want to go back. I am afraid it will confirm to me that you are really not there.

Will your room still have the scent of your perfume and the spirit I always knew? I sense I have lost my sanctuary. It doesn't matter now where I live, or what country I say I belong to—it's all the same. More and more, I have an urge to find a place that I can call home. Will there ever be a place that welcomes me and allows me to feel as you used to make me feel? I doubt it.

We grow up and stop being children when we lose our parents. That's how I feel now—I feel that I have finally become an adult. It's a strange feeling. Is this how you felt all your life? How did you manage to go on after losing your mother, and later on your father and all of those who stood around you like great trees stand framing around a *clairière* (clearing)?

Emaye, it is only now that I admire all you have done and accomplished. It is only now that I realize the magnitude of your contribution to our lives and the lives of so many. I dread the days that pass, because for each day that passes, you move further away in time and I am afraid that the memories will fade.

In about six months, I hope to finish writing you the

letters and the stories and make it all into a nice book. By September 27, 2010, I hope to come back home and feed all the men, women, and children who live outside the Debre Libanos Monastery. I will also do that at the Zenebework area, and prepare food for all those affected by Leprosy. We did that together many years ago, I am sure you remember. It was the most wonderful thing to do, and I just loved taking all the food we cooked at Laïbet to make a feast out in the Zenebework area. You know they still talk about it.

Well, yes, in September 2010 I will do this, God willing and I hope to also launch the book. And whatever comes as proceeds from this book, I will apply it to the children's project we run in Ethiopia. You know we now have over 10,000 boys and girls we support—we have a great design to do this and only spend about $3,000 per month for it. Anyway, these are my plans.

On the last day that I write for the manuscript, I will write you a letter that says the following:

Today is the last day I write our beautiful story. Emaye, it's almost been a year now since you have left. I have now completed the story I wanted to share with you. I hope that these stories will allow us to tell your story a thousand times over, to as many children as possible (young ones and grown-ups). You have been a beacon of hope for me. You have been a beacon of hope for the entire family. And when I say "family," I mean that in the same sense as you, in the greater sense. So many of us are so blessed to have known you and to have lived with you. I hope we can pass on what you have taught us through the generations.

You know what? Each time I visit a school to meet the

children we will support in your name, I will tell them your story in a very special way and I will start my talk in this way: "Lejoch, Lejoch. Endemin Wallachehu? Ande Teret Lengerachhu. Keltat Ande Ken, Ande Azawing Neberu, Kibert W/z Almaz Haile Mariam Yebalu Neber [Children, children. How are you today? Let me tell you a story. Once upon a time, there used to be one great sage, her name was Lady Almaz Haile-Mariam...]."

I love you always,

M

December 15, 2009

Emaye,

You have been so present for me these past days. I did not dream of you last night because I was up writing my dissertation, but I felt you in spirit around me. I had four cans of Diet Coke, two cans of Sprite, and three cans of beer... I heard you teasing me and saying: "Who are you fooling with the sodas?!"

Well, you know I don't drink coffee anymore. I have also completely stopped smoking. So, if I drink a beer once in a blue moon, I think it's acceptable ☺. Well, the truth is I am leaving for the Christmas holidays today with Rosi and Leoni, meeting Matthias in Schneppenbach and from there together with Oma an Opa we will go to spend two weeks in Egypt, one week on the Nile and another at some resort on the Red Sea. So, yes, I wanted to finish all my pending work so that I could be relaxed and enjoy my time with my little family and Oma and Opa. Anyway, so all the cans—no matter what they contained—were just motivation, a consumption to keep me going until I finished my first draft.

In the middle of the night I called Terriye in the US and spoke with her for an hour or more. It was good. I know that when the phone bill comes at the end of the month, it will possibly give me an instant heart attack, but I thought it was worth it. I so enjoyed talking to her. I could not stop. At first I talked to her with an upbeat energy and then when we hit the real truth of the matter, i.e. you, then it was hard. I could not speak anymore. I could not see anymore because the tears clouded my view.

Earlier in the day, I had called Koki to speak to her about that NGO I set up, and she told me that today was your 80th Day. I can't believe it's been so long. Have you been gone so long, Emaye? How will we manage when the days turn into months and the months turn into years? Etetila called me today, this morning in fact. It was a pleasant surprise. We keep our sorrows and tears tucked away deep in our hearts and try to be of good cheer to keep the spirit up. We all try to support each other.

As expected, I spoke to her with an upbeat spirit until we spoke of the truth of the matter, i.e. you, and then again I could not speak anymore. I cried again. I cried a lot. It was pain I felt in my gut. I told Etetila that I feel stateless, homeless. Your bedroom was the only place in the world where I felt at ease, and now that you are no longer there, I feel as though I have lost my sanctuary. Does it matter what nationality I am? Does it matter where I live? I don't think it matters, because no matter where I go, it will never be the same. I will never feel the comfort I felt with you.

Today Etetiye talked about the times you told her about your mother, Emama Berhane. She said that you used to tell stories of how your mother used to be. Well, Emaye, now I am also telling my story to my children about how my grandmother used to be. I can't believe I talk about you in the past tense. Does it mean it's all gone? I revive when I talk about you, especially when the person I am talking to does not yet know you have left. I also love talking about you with my close friends because I know they understand.

I have to go now, M

December 16, 2009

I have come to Oma and Opa's place in Schneppenbach, Germany again for the Christmas Holidays. Tomorrow we all go together to Egypt.

I will write to you once we get there.

I love you,
M

December 19, 2009

Emaye,

I am in Egypt, in Aswan—my first time in this country. I am thinking of you and especially about your comment, "Don't joke with a nation's lifeline," that you told us when years ago we came back from a party and told you how we teased an Egyptian friend about the fact that should the Ethiopians block the Nile, Egypt would be in trouble.

Well, I am in this country now and the people look like us. It is funny, however, because I hear them talk about how the Nile gets its source in Africa and they speak of the rest of us as Africans. I wish our people would hear that and realize that the world considers them Africans too.

Anyway, something happened today; actually, two things happened. I went to a perfume distillery and they also made glass containers, you know the pretty ones in crystal. We even saw a man make one right in front of us. I tell you, the store was full of these little bottles. I thought of buying you one, instantly, and then I sank into sadness because I remembered that you are with us in Spirit. The man who was explaining the essences and perfumes was a bit worried about me, because my face changed. I panicked. I could not breathe. How do you manage when you think of buying someone a gift and you know it would make that person happy, and then you realize they are no longer there? Then, I thought of buying a bottle for all the ladies in the house and giving it to them as a gift in your name, but it was too expensive. You know I have not changed—I am still chronically broke. But then Matthias bought me two bottles. I will give one to Enanaye in your name and I will keep one for me.

The other thing that happened is that we went to the Orthodox Church, and again, although I never really cared much for the Virgin Mary, I find that more and more I am drawn to her. I bought several icons. I bought one that reminds me of you, a small version of the large St. Mary icon you had in your room. Do you know which one I am talking about? It's the one you brought back from Jerusalem when you went there for surgery, in the very early 1970s. I remember coming to Bole to pick you up—gosh, I think almost the whole of Laïbet was at the airport that day to welcome you back.

Emaye, do I bug you when I write you letters? Am I disturbing you? I hope not, because writing you allows me to process your absence.

I am going to sleep now. Good night, Emaye.

I love you,
M

December 20, 2009

Emaye,

Tonight I spoke a long time with Oma about you and the life that you had. When I showed her the picture we took together (the one on the cover of this book), she thought it was Rosi. Isn't that funny?

It's good to be on this Nile River cruise. It avoids all the stress of the holiday. The only problem is that they have a buffet three times a day, and I have to tell you how much weight I have put on. I hope to lose the weight soon. This Middle Eastern cuisine is not good for me. I just love it so much that, appetite or not, I can't stop myself from indulging. Then of course, I regret every bite. You think I would learn my lesson, but come the next meal, I do the same thing all over again.

I danced with Rosi and Leoni for the first time. Rosiye is so shy, she reminds me of my own self; Leoni, on the other hand, is sweet but a bit more daring. Matthias took both of them and made them swirl on the dance floor. What a blessing to watch this—I wish you could have been there.

You know, Emaye, I was thinking of the summer you came to see us in Brussels, that time when you told me about boys, men, life, sex, and all. Well, did you know that soon after you left, I had my period? I was so happy that you had already explained it all to me. You will be happy to know that I took all your advice and did everything as you had told me. But there is one thing I wanted to tell you about.

You know, that same summer, after I had my period,

Enaniye took me to a doctor for a gynecology examination. Emaye, you never told me about that. Why didn't you tell me? I wish someone had at least prepared me for what to expect. I know that it is good to get check-ups and that this visit to the doctor was done with all good intentions, but Emaye, it was too much for me to handle.

I had no idea what to expect, and I was basically shocked out of my mind. The doctor was a woman and she was okay, but she could have been better. She did everything so mechanically, as if I was not even there. I felt like an object. Emaye, why is it that in our culture we never talk about the things that are so important? We always talk so much about everything, but when it comes to topics dealing with sexuality or anything near that topic, our mouths are sealed. I hate that. I know you think that I sometimes behave like a buffalo when I talk about these things, but it just makes me so angry that we hide and never discuss the things that are most essential in life. My God, someone could have told me what to expect that day. What would it have cost? Nothing other than saving me the shock and shame I felt. It all just happened, without a chance for me to ask questions, get explanations, or whatever.

I find it sad that in our culture we are led to go through matters of sexuality, both in terms of reproductive health and relationships with men, without acknowledging what takes place. We do it all, without being there—like it's happening to someone else. You know, after the checkup, on the way home, Enaniye did not talk to me in the car and I did not say a word either. Once we reached home, life continued as usual without ever mentioning again the kind of check-up it was.

Emaye, it is this silence that we continue to maintain that brings women to desperate situations. No one is willing to talk. For example, when you think that over 80% of women in our country have been subjected to excision, it is mad. It is even madder that no one ever really questions the practice—other than the organizations that have been established to fight against it. But it is not up to the organizations, foreign or local, to fight this: It is up to us to understand what is happening to our girls and to find ground to change the situation. The same applies to the fact that there are still a substantial number of rural girls abducted and given to marriage by force. Emaye, I am sure you know what happens to these girls. What do you say about this? Do you really think that there is nothing to do to stop the practice of abduction? Once when I was working in Addis, the time I was back there working with Médecins Sans Frontières, there was a story in the news that one rural girl shot and killed her abductor and then ran away to Addis. I could understand that she shot him; he basically kidnapped her and raped her to make sure that she would only marry him. Why in the world do we have to go through such violence? When I told some of the people I worked with that I could understand why she shot him, they seemed surprised. One man even said, "All he did was have sex with her—that's no reason to shoot someone!" Some men don't understand the meaning of rape. They think it is just sex. Actually, even some women don't understand and always blame the woman or girl for it. They always come up with excuses either related to culture or the woman's style of dress or that she had consented. It's very sad.

For me, even if people think I am like an elephant in a porcelain shop, I promise you that I will always speak out. Don't worry, I will never be rude, but I will always say what I have to say, especially regarding the topics that we so love to cover up. Sorry, I didn't mean to nag you. I just thought about this and wanted to take the time to tell you.

I have to go to bed now.

I love you,
M

December 22, 2009

Emaye,

Today is one day and 13 years ago that I last danced with you. Do you remember? We danced at my wedding and celebrated together the day of my marriage to Matthias.

I cannot believe it's only 13 years—it seems to be a lifetime, and at that time, little did I know that 13 years later, I would be without you in my life. I don't mean to cling, but I have to tell you that there is a huge hole in my heart that I cannot manage to fill. I feel a void in my life, a silence that no sound can enter, and an emptiness I had never before felt.

At least I comfort myself in knowing that I have called you and visited you as much as I could. Maybe I could have done more, but it is fair to say that we did well with each other.

I am on the Nile, Emaye, with Oma, Opa, Matthias, and the girls. It is good to be here. We are on a boat so there isn't much else we can do other than rest, relax, eat, sleep, and occasionally visit some historical places on the various stops the ship makes. What I love about being onboard this ship is that if you lose someone, you don't need a cell phone to call them—you can just check their room, the dining hall, the shops, or the terrace on the roof and you are bound to find them. I think you would have liked to be on this cruise.

There are many characters, and I laugh each time I see the old ladies dancing the night away. Last night I saw one dancing and she was just marvelous. I love how they just don't even care. Back home, I think if someone her age was found dancing in this way, they would have expedited her to the Holy Water Treatment Center. I smiled and laughed with you in my heart.

What I find interesting on this trip is all the different Egyptian dynasties that we have been seeing through their tombs, temples, and statues. How impermanent life is, and how little we know it! All the Queens and Kings of this land, as those of the lands of the world, built so much. Why? Maybe looking to being eternal, and they are eternal in this way. We still talk about them and we still tell of their legacies. Yet, at the end of the day, life is finite and the most we can make of it is to be kind to one another. Don't you think that this is a better legacy, one that is softer and sweeter to the heart?

We visited mausoleums and I thought of ours. I wonder if one day, many years from now, people will come to visit it and tell the story of those sleeping inside. I remember the bricklayer who so conscientiously laid the bricks and cement that sealed your tomb. Before he did that, we all put some flowers in, and finally, I put the flowers that Etiye Tsedalu had sent from Washington. I was happy to know that instead of the red bricks, your eternal bed would be facing the bush of flowers, even if only for a day or two before they too went to sleep.

I am not sure where I will be buried. It is not important for me, at least not anymore, because I know there is no space left where you are and I might have to go to the other mausoleum at Medhan Alem Church. It would be great to be cremated and then freed in a river somewhere—maybe even the Nile.

I keep thinking of the days when I was so caught up with my work, running up and down the city nonstop, and you always used to tell me: "My child, you should stop and rest once in a while; don't you know that even the Nile has stops along its path?" Well, I have learned to stop and rest, Emaye. I do that by writing, and by taking time to reflect and meditate.

It is sunset now. The wind is a bit fresh, but not so much that I need a sweater. It is that time I love, when the sun goes down gently and the day's activities slow down in cadence with an invisible, divine orchestra conductor.

Oma is sitting with me, reading a book, wearing the *Netela* she bought in Addis. She is just such a bubbly spirit. Opa is here too, and he is really like Ababi. He has a million questions, but only directed to Oma. The children are happy as they run between me, their father, and Oma and Opa. They've grown since you saw them last April. I am so glad we came to see you and I wish we had come again in the summer time, but it was not possible.

It's good to be here, on the Nile. I have time to dive into so many different spaces and times of our lives, both in the present and in the past. For now, I am soaking in all I can and taking in all the energy so that I can brand my spirit with the blessings we have.

The famous Nile, in the famous Egypt, the land of the Pharoahs—and we are not too far from home. Leoni and Rosi said that if we follow the Nile, we would end up in our country. They are conscious of their country and talk about it a lot. I, on the other hand, have a problem with it. What is a country really, if not those we love in it? And if they are not there, can one say that there is a country? I cannot imagine going back to Ethiopia and not being able to see you again.

You were the one I called each time I came and the last one I called before they told us to switch off our phones for take-off. Now, who do I call? I know that everyone is still there, but I just miss you and I am not sure when this feeling of emptiness will leave me. I doubt it ever will.

Emaye, I have never been so fat. Can you believe that I weigh close to 75kg—it's about 15KG more than my usual weight. And what scares me is that I don't even care. The challenge is that none of my clothes fit. Of course they don't fit, how could they? So, I have been wearing some pajama-looking yoga clothes. In the next weeks, I promise to make an effort and get back in shape. I put on all this weight since I came back to Freetown from Addis in September. The weight has just been adding on since. When I sit, I feel the folds of my tummy. Even when I was nine months pregnant I weighed much less than I do now. When I smile, my cheeks take up so much space on my face that my eyes disappear in some curvy, catty slit. I can't say that my eating habit has changed; what has changed definitely is how I feel inside. They say that stress, grief, and sadness can affect people in different ways. Some lose weight, some gain weight, some become quiet, and others do something completely different. For me, I think it turned out to be that I gain weight.

Love you,
M

December 23, 2009

Emaye,

I can't sleep. I have been up since about 3:00am. Rosi and Leoni decided to sleep with us today, so all four of us squeezed in the bed, but that's not why I couldn't sleep. It's Matthias who got up in the middle of the night and turned the light on for a minute or two; I woke up then and I have not been able to sleep. So, instead of tossing around and making unnecessary commotion that might wake up the children, I thought I best just get up and go to a corner in the room to write to you.

I have been meaning to tell you about all the gold you bought me. Well, you always thought that I lost it and you used to tell me that you would never buy me any jewelry because I would lose it. Well, Emaye, I did not lose it. It's a long story and I don't think I ever had a chance to tell you about it. But before I start telling you the story, you have to know that I loved each and every piece of jewelry you gave me, and even though I don't have them now, I will always have them in spirit.

Here is what happened. If you remember, back in the mid-1980s, after that entire episode where Enanaye had sent me to you for Holy Water Treatment, I returned back to Brussels and eventually to Washington, DC to continue my education. I was in my last year of high school and about to go to college. I started dating someone, a nice guy with parents from Ivory Coast and Morocco. His father was with the embassy. I was very conscious of all that you had told me about young men, so I did not jump into the relationship as many of my friends did. We dated for close to a year without ever getting intimate. Emaye, for the first 3-4 months, I didn't even kiss him. Well, let me be honest—this wasn't necessarily intentional, but because of a mixture of things. On one hand, I didn't want to rush into the relationship, and on the other, I simply did not know how to. Foolish reasons maybe, but this is the truth of why I didn't kiss this guy. I had never kissed anyone before, so how did you expect me to figure out how to do that?

I think this made our relationship more special. In any case, even though I was past eighteen, I did not feel pressured to jump into intimacy. In time, and in a very conscious way, we did get intimate. Everything was fine until I realized that I had missed my period. I bought one of the disposable pregnancy packets, which confirmed that I was in fact pregnant.

Emaye, I did not know what to do or who to turn to. Of course, I could have spoken to Etetila, but to say what? There was no way I could have brought the subject to Enanaye and Boubiye, can you imagine—I was sent for Holy Water Treatment because some guy had dropped me off and so much was assumed even though I had not done anything. Now, if I came and said that I was pregnant, I thought they would throw me out, so I kept it all to myself. I decided to get an abortion. But then again, I had no idea how or where to do that. So, as usual I started gathering information about it and started asking some women's clinics about it. You have no idea how expensive it can be. The most affordable service I found was with a nonprofit organization working with teenagers and reproductive health. They charged about $350 US dollars for a "termination of pregnancy" (that's how they call it) with full anesthesia and about $150 for one with only local anesthesia. You know I did not work at that time and I did not have any cash other than the $50 I received each month for pocket money.

By the time I found out all the information, I must have had about $30 on me and I had to come up with a total of $150 to have the procedure. I could have asked my boyfriend to pay for it, but you know I could not do that. You have raised us to manage our lives ourselves and independently, so I wanted to deal with this independently as well. The last thing I would do was ask a man for money. Hell, no. I would rather die.

I had to gather the money as quickly as possible because the clinic had informed me that they would only do the procedure for pregnancies that were less than eight weeks. Emaye, given the pressure, the only option I saw was to sell my jewelry.

I took all the pendants, bracelets, rings, earrings, and chains you had given me and went to various jewelry shops. I did not know how to go about it, and it felt odd to walk in and ask the clerks if they bought jewelry from people. I think some of the shops thought I was a thief because I had so much gold on me. Others might have thought I was a drug user or something like that. Of course I tried to do all this as discreetly as I could, but I think the stress I was going through was coming out in various ways.

Some people were around when I was in the process of selling the gold, and they teased me. They thought I was involved in drugs or some illicit thing. They had no idea what I was going through and I can't blame them for it, but their teasing was hurtful. I just took it and tried to go on with my day.

Finally I found a shop in Chevy Chase, Maryland, right by the apartment where we lived. They were willing to take the gold. I trusted them because it was a shop in a well-to-do neighborhood—but they were such crooks. They took it all and gave me $100 US Dollars. I was shocked at the price they gave me because I knew that what I had was worth so much more. But from a mixture of shame, stress, and pressure to get the money, I just walked away with the money. I had about $130 US dollars and I had to ask Etetila to give me the next month's pocket money in advance. All in all, that made it $180 US dollars.

On the weekend before I had the procedure, Fofi came to visit me from boarding school, and when she left, I remember I could not stop my tears. She too had no idea why I was crying. I did not tell her because I did not want to add stress to her life.

Then, the clinic called and said that on the day of the procedure I had to bring in a urine sample. The urine was no problem; my problem was finding a container to hold it. I looked around the apartment and there was just nothing proper. So, I went to the Giant, the one in Chevy Chase Plaza, and bought olives. I came back with the olives and put them on the dinner table. Etetila seemed puzzled about my olive consumption, since I had never really bought them or brought them home. We ate a few, and while she was in the kitchen preparing dinner, I threw most of them in the trash so I could have the container. I know that I could have just put them in something else, but I was not thinking straight that day.

Later, as we cleared the table after dinner, I stubbed my toe against a chair. It did not really hurt, but I remember that again, my tears just flowed out. Etetila was really puzzled and could not quite make out what the deal was with me.

I knew what was waiting for me the next day and I was both afraid of the procedure, of the unknown, and also extremely sad. Not to have anyone to talk to was very painful. I wanted to call you but could not muster the courage to do so. I felt so ashamed. After all that you had taught me, I thought I had miserably failed you. How I wish I had told someone, but that would not ever happen because I could not predict the reaction from all of you. You see, you could have been a great-grandmother many years ago. I am sorry, Emaye. I wish I had had the courage to tell you.

The next day, I left the apartment at the crack of dawn. They had told me to arrive at 7:00AM and I did not want to be late. I don't remember what excuse I gave Etetila, but I just left very early.

I was finished around noon. The procedure was horrible—to this day, I don't think I have ever gone through anything worse than that. The horrible thing was not only the fact that I was ending a pregnancy, but how it was done. The doctor, he was nasty looking and just nasty anyway. He was very fat and very pink in color; he looked like a giant pig. He had short, fat, sweaty fingers. He could not breathe very well, so he was breathing as if he had just come from running even though he was sitting. He was panting throughout the whole procedure. It felt very strange.

The nurse asked me to get on the table, and well, in came this doctor. He was so inconsiderate and of poor character. Without any greetings, any explanations, or any kind of reassurance about what was about to happen, just stuck some metal tool in me. From shock I just shut my legs with a snap, and I think I must have hit him with my knees because his glasses were dislodged. He looked up and glared at me. He fixed his glasses, and said in the meanest tone, "This can be quick and painless or long and painful—your choice." Can you believe this guy?

I did not say anything, and just took a deep breath and prayed to God that I could go through it as quickly as possible. The local anesthesia they injected me with was painful as well, because they had to inject it into the cervix. And then the termination of the pregnancy—I have no idea how they were doing that. All I heard were sounds that seemed to come from something not much different than a vacuum cleaner. Emaye, it was so bad that for the first time in my life, I was drenched in cold sweat. I smelled a pungent odor, then sadly realized that it was my own perspiration. I had taken a shower and used deodorant as we always do, but this smell was just very strong. When the procedure was finished, my entire body was trembling. I was soaked in sweat. I never knew that fear and pain could induce such pungent perspiration. My hair was plastered on my forehead from all the sweat. My eyeliner had smeared to the side of my eyes. This was it. I lay on the table with my heart pounding, not knowing if what I had just done was the right thing or not. You know how much I love children. I was just so worried to disappoint you and all those who had raised me.

They allowed me to remain there for about 30 minutes and then I drove home. They told me not to take a bath for some weeks, only showers. When I reached home, the apartment was empty. I just went to my room and collapsed on the bed, going to sleep for what seemed an eternity. For days and months, this whole thing affected me a lot. I guess what affected me most was the fact that I could not speak to anyone about it. I felt lonely. I didn't want to tell you either, because I thought it would be a letdown. I never told anyone about it.

Today I write this to you not only to tell you about the gold but to say that I wished we didn't make our standards so high. Or, I wish that even though we held high standards of manners and tradition, we could also acknowledge that part of being human is to make mistakes along the way. I wish you had taught us that that there is no shame in making mistakes. I am grateful that the procedure of the abortion did not kill me or damage my womb permanently. But as much as I am grateful for going safely through it, my heart goes out to those who are not as lucky as I was. So many young women go through such procedures through illegitimate ways and end up losing their lives or getting chronic complications. Did I tell you that back in the time I worked with the women in the red light district, I met so many who had had an abortion by so called traditional doctors? Emaye, it was horrible. I saw the tools they use. It's pretty bad, Emaye, really pretty bad. No matter how much society argues about the controversy of abortion, it's about time that our governments do something substantial to allow proper medical care.

I thought I was the only one who experienced this, especially within our family and community. But I learned later that many others have suffered the same fate. Emaye, would it not have been easier if we just came to you? What I find unfair is that for men, things are not so bad. How many male friends do I have who now tell me they have twenty-year-old children. "I had a baby when I was fifteen...I had her when I was eighteen...etc." is what they say when I ask them when they had the baby. Of course, it is always the girl who gets stuck with the baby and bears the burden of the societal reprimand. Society is often hard in its judgment of women and girls, especially our society in Ethiopia. The things we women do to be seen as proper, the things we go through in silence just to fit in or ensure that our name—or better yet, that the name of our family—is not dishonored.

I used to think that this was particular to our Ethiopian culture, but I have learned through the years that such behavior is prevalent in most cultures, and especially in those where religion, social recognition, family name, etc. hold value.

If I had come home telling you that I was pregnant, I know today that you would not have rebuked me. I know that now. But back then, I was not so sure. Maybe I know this today because I have had my own children and I know that if any one of them came to me with the news that she was expecting a baby, I would be happy and would certainly take them in and do all I could to make their experience a pleasant one. I don't regret the abortion anymore; I have had my time to let it go, and to also forgive myself for not knowing all my options at the time.

The greatest lesson I have learned from it is that no matter how much we think we know someone or how close we are, we should always assume that there might be sorrows, worries, and anxieties holding that person hostage. And maybe we need to learn to be gentler with each other, slower to judge or reprimand people around us. Maybe we need to relax a bit about life in general, because as much as life is a gift, it is also a gift that runs its course so quickly that we might lose opportunities to love and be loved if we get so preoccupied with the pettiness of ordinary issues and problems.

It's almost morning. I am going back to bed to try and get a bit of sleep. But before I go, Emaye, I have not seen you in my dreams in a long time. Does this mean your spirit has really left and moved on?

I love you always,
M

December 24, 2009

Emaye,

It is Christmas Eve here in Sharm Al-Sheik. The moon was fuzzy tonight, covered with clouds or should I say escorted by gentle clouds. She only showed half of her body, and as I walked out of the restaurant where we had dinner so many thoughts ran through my soul.

Emaye, this will be the first Christmas I don't call you to wish you *"Enkewan Adersesch* [Thank God—God allowed us to see this day]." We had a nice dinner tonight, at a seafood place. Opa, Oma, Rosi, Leoni, and Matthias all looked very good. I can't say the same for me—as I told you earlier, I have put on so much weight that I can't fit my clothes anymore. It's okay. I am sure that the people in the restaurant probably thought I was the girls' nanny. Well, okay, it wasn't so bad.

It is such a blessing to sit together and share this meal at Christmas. Times have changed. I remember Christmas at Laïbet. It was such a celebration: so many flowers, cakes, and sheep came to you as offerings, and the same amount you sent out to family, friends, and the community. It was about fellowship at that time. Now, Christmas has become more of a reason to engage in shopping therapy.

I saw so many kinds of people in the restaurant. There were new couples who were so obvious in the novelty of their love affair; there were old couples with the same harmony and suppleness as the relationship between an old hand and an old leather glove. There were families that sat in groups of four, five, and at times even eight and ten. Some families were beautiful, and you could see that they wanted to be together and were enjoying every moment of it. Others were not so endearing, reflecting a forced gathering.

Our table was quiet. The girls were tired because we had a long day. We arrived today from Luxor and it took time to find our way around this hotel. Emaye, this resort is so large—it's like a village. It's a huge place.

I am wondering about everyone else back home and all around the world. Where are they? What are they doing and how are they spending Christmas? I can't call or email, as there isn't much Internet and calling is unthinkable given the cost.

Love you,
M

December 27, 2009

Emaye,

Today is three months since you left. Tomorrow on the 28^{th,} it will be 33 years since we left Ethiopia for the first time.

I am still in Egypt. Did I tell you we went to visit the Monastery of St. Katherine? It is the oldest monastery in the world, built around the burning bush where Moses received the Ten Commandments. There were many tourists, so it was hard to find the peace and quiet to see the monastery, but nonetheless the inside was amazing. It was full of the world's oldest icons.

It's so interesting that since you left I have been drawn to the icons of the Virgin Mary. I just can't get enough of her—she represents you to me. She represents the ultimate Mother that I think I have lost.

We will stay here a few more days and then back to Germany.

I love you,
M

January 1, 2010

Emaye,

Well, we arrived back in Frankfurt last night. We had such a great time with Oma, Opa, and the girls. Rosi passed her diving test and is now a certified scuba diver (she will get her open water license later, when she is 15). Leoni also passed her license and did the junior course that they call "bubble maker."

I dove with both of them on their first dives together with the instructor. It was great to see them underwater. They were not allowed to go very deep, but even at 3-5 meters the colors you see underwater are so incredible, especially in the Red Sea. When Rosi went diving with Matthias, she saw a giant Napoleon fish—Emaye, the fish was bigger than the instructor, about two meters long. They are very gentle fish, so apparently the Napoleon looked at Rosi and the instructor with his huge eyeballs and went on his way. She had seen a smaller one a few days earlier (a little less than a meter). After seeing this underwater giant, Rosi was shaking and laughing because of the thrill. I know you think I am mad to take the girls diving, but you know, the earlier they learn such sports, the safer it is. I would rather they learn all this with me than later when I might not be around.

On the last night before our departure, Leoni was a bit ill, I think from a combination of exhaustion and food. She slept early, and slept in my bed. I did not sleep at all and for the short snooze I had, I dreamt I had gone to Laïbet. This time and for the first time in my dream, I dreamt that it was Laïbet without you. It was a very strange and lonely feeling, and it makes me cry even as I write this to you. There were a lot of other people there, people who on a normal day would not really have any authority in that compound. They were sitting in the living room and chatting. I could not see Solomon or Koky or any of the usual aunts, uncles, and cousins—it was all other people. I felt lonely even in my dream, and I had come to you to get help in taking care of Leoni. I wanted to sleep in your room, have her lay with you in your bed, and while she rested on your side, I was hoping that we could talk as we always do. Like that time in Vienna when we talked and talked in your room and everyone else had left the house. That time in Vienna was great—I will never forget the things we talked about. Who am I supposed to talk to now? I don't remember how the dream ended, only that I felt very lonely and abandoned.

You know, I wish you would somehow let me know where you are. I wish you would somehow let me know that you are still here. I feel odd at times, writing you these letters, but it is in these letters that I find comfort, at least for now.

I told Enanaye about the time I saw you in my dream, back in Freetown. And when I told you we were all very sad, you said, "No, it's your mother that is still deeply sad." So, Enaniye and I talked about it for a long time. You were right; she said that she is not managing to move forward. I can understand.

I have things to distract me and in times of distraction I am not sad, but there are moments when I hear a certain song, see a particular scene, or hear something and the thought of you not being with us anymore rushes back and engulfs me. Like last night, the man who picked us up from the airport, a neighbor of Opa and Oma running a taxi service, had the radio on in his van. As I entered, the song on the radio just threw me off. I thought of the time we traveled together from Brussels to Addis and we had to go through Frankfurt to transit. Do you remember? I feel terrible because as we got off the bus that led us from plane into the terminal, I rushed you. Not much, but I remember I still rushed you. This must be over twenty years ago. I am sorry I didn't let you get out of the bus at your own pace. I am sorry.

I really miss you very much. On that same trip, once we were on the plane, we were sitting in the first row in economy, and once in a while, I would go to the back, smoke my cigarette, and come back. You never said anything, even though now I know how smelly I must have been...and I thought back then that you couldn't smell the smoke if I sprayed perfume on. How foolish!

We celebrated the New Year at Oma and Opa's home. Oma is very much like you: She loves to have people around, and she likes to see people eating and enjoying themselves. Friends of hers, Max and Claudia, were there. Before leaving for Egypt, Oma agreed with them that we would do the Sylvester together—out here they refer to New Year's Eve as "Sylvester." They would cook a few things and Oma had some things in the freezer that she baked in the oven. Matthias went out to bring wine from Simon, the family with the vineyard not too far from Oma's. It was a good party. I did not make it to midnight, though, and went to bed by 10:00pm. I just could not make it. I was too tired. I can't believe that back in the day, we would stay up until the sun came up and the moon retired. Do you think I am getting old?

This morning I was arranging my purse and I found the glasses I was wearing for your funeral. They were broken. A few days ago, I was thinking that I should keep them for memory, and now they are broken. Maybe it's a sign that I should throw them away. Why should I keep them anyway? I don't want to have things that remind me of your funeral. So, I am going to throw them away.

What to expect on this New Year of 2010? It's the first time I will live without you. It's the first time I will not call you to say Merry Christmas or wish you a Happy Easter. It's the first of many years to come.

Mimi

January 2, 2010

Emaye,

Today I called Brussels to wish them a Happy New Year. I spoke to Boubiye and Enaniye; Essayas is there with all the children, Mahlett, Babychoo, Dodi, Samy, and Benoo. When I called, all the children had gone out to the movies along with Fofi. It was quiet in the house.

I had a long conversation with Boubiye. He is excited about our possible new posting in China because he knows China so well. You remember how often he used to travel there. Well, that was such a long time ago. He told me how China is a fantastic place, and how the Chinese are sharp, reserved, and mindful. He told me not to be turned off by the new wave of Chinese offensive on the world: there is a lot more to China than the new businessmen that seem to be all over the place. I suppose he is right—there is a lot more to China, as there is a lot more to any country, really.

My conversations with Enaniye have been different since you left. It makes me cry when I think about it. Why did it have to take so long for us to talk in this way? I feel we have wasted a lifetime. In a way, I always had you, so I did not want to make an effort in any other relationship. Now, Enaniye and I have a common sorrow, something in common that brings us closer. This thing we have, this thing that is now allowing us to relate better, is directly linked to your departure. So, as much as I am happy to have Enaniye in a whole different way, knowing that it is linked to your departure brings sadness to the picture. But I prefer to think about it as the love we had for you, and that brings me a better energy.

Do you remember a few days ago, I asked you to let me know that you are just away in flesh, that you are still around? Well, when I spoke to Enaniye, she said that she is not the same anymore. She feels that she doesn't have the same energy, that she's gotten old in a way. "I wish I just have time to finish this house," she said—you know, that is the house she is building in Kraineem. She spoke of you and said that you have been blessed with the "*tsdkan mot* [death of a saintly person]." She said she just hoped that she could finish up all that she is doing right now before she goes.

What struck me is that she said that you had *tsdkan mot* in such a calm and serene way. It cut something inside of me. I sensed a letting go, an acceptance that you are gone. If she is in a space where she is admitting your going, then, for some reason, it also took me to a place where I too could accept it, finally. Maybe this was the message that I was waiting for.

Mimi

January 3, 2010

Emaye,

Matthias brought out Christmas gifts that he had forgotten to deliver, mainly books and calendars. You know how each year he makes calendars with pictures from the past year. Well, we were all looking at the calendar and admiring the pictures when I saw the picture for the month of April—it was your picture, close up. It was your picture with such a beautiful smile and a happy spirit, your signature smile when you are most happy. It took me by surprise and just brought tears from I don't know where. I still cry silently when I look at that picture.

It's a blessing that we have those pictures. I am glad that we came to see you last April; at least we saw each other and Rosi and Leoni spent time with you.

If it weren't for the girls wanting to see their friends in Zambia, I would have stayed with you longer. But you know, the girls wanted to see their friends in Lusaka, so for the few days of break they had from school, I had to take them there and split the time we had between Addis and Lusaka.

I don't remember anymore how we said goodbye, but as usual I wanted to make it fast because I am never sure if I will see you again. And this time, well, my worst thoughts came true and without realizing, I had kissed you for the last time.

When I saw you at the funeral, you looked beautiful and asleep. There were too many people around and they had put the coffin a bit too high for me to lean in and kiss you, so all I could do was caress your right cheek with the back of my right hand. Your skin was soft as usual, and so smooth. You just looked so beautiful and at peace. And so you went as beautifully as you lived. Emaye, so, it seems this is it.

Soon it will be Christmas in Ethiopia, and I am dreading the day. I will call K[45] to wish him Merry Christmas. Etetila will be back in Ethiopia by then; she was in Washington for the Western Christmas. Other than Enaniye, it seems that all your children will be at Laïbet on Ethiopian Christmas, but on that day, I will be in Thailand. I am going away to finish writing my dissertation and finalize the book *Butterflies over Africa* (2009, Integral Publisher). I know you are wondering why I need to go so far to do that, but, well, I just want to go away. Fofi will be with me. It is also a chance for us to be together and spend time together, just the two of us.

Your departure this year has shaken us up. We are managing to live, of course, but I can't tell you how much we miss you. I think I am actually just afraid of what life might be without you. Isn't it silly to say this in a time where so many lose their parents to AIDS, war, accidents, etc. But you know, this deep sorrow I feel about losing you—this is my truth for now and I can't deny it. I am afraid of the loneliness in my soul because I will not have you to talk to anymore.

I can't bear to delete your number from my cell, so I am buying a new phone. I still remember our first number in Laïbet: 17890, and then they added a 1 in front and it became 11-78-90. For me, no matter where I was in the world, I knew that I could reach

---

[45] K is the nickname given to my uncle Solomon Makonnen.

you on that number and through the phone call, be home in a way. That always gave me a sense of safety and stability.

I cry for myself you know, because my sanctuary is gone. My safe haven in the world is gone. The peace, the security, and the safety I felt around you and especially when I came to your bedroom—all that is gone. I feel naked. I feel as though the roof of my house has been ripped away. Don't worry, though; I will manage to live. I will manage to go on. It's just that I miss you terribly.

At times I think that I have to get my act together and toughen up. How would I feel if I too passed and from heaven I could see that my Rosi and Leoni were not coping? I know it would make me frustrated. So, I know. And I don't want to frustrate you or worry you in your eternal sleep; I just have to write and tell you how I feel until it's all out.

You know, each time I write to you, my heart is heavy. Often I cry anew. Often I plunge into a sadness that I cannot explain in words, but afterwards, I feel relief and I feel enriched by all that you have done, all that you have been for me and for all of us.

Mimi

January 4, 2010

Emaye,

I have been up since about 5:00am today, still in Frankfurt. I could not sleep because it was too cold: The heater goes off at night and comes back on around 6:00am.

Last night I was trying to call Dana—you remember, my friend from Seattle? He came to see you in Addis back in 2006; you even have a picture of you together. Anyway, you know, he is very dear to me and we are connected in a strange way.

There is a 9-hour difference between where he is in Oregon (Portland) and here. I could not reach him last night, so I decided to call him this morning right when I woke up.

We had a nice conversation and made the rounds of updates of our lives. He wants to adopt an Ethiopian child and I have promised to help him. Anyway the reason that I talk about him is that he told me a story about a writer, from Burkina Faso who wrote a book that Dana was just now reading.

Dana told me the story of this man that allowed him to better understand my relationship with you. Well, of course my tears are never too far away, and off I went again engulfed in tears. What he said touched me. I explained to him that I feel I have fallen through the cracks. During the funeral and all of the mourning season, everyone seemed to be mourning from an acknowledged position, like being a child, a grandchild, a relative, an aunt, a friend, etc. But for me, Emaye, I wasn't just mourning as your grandchild—I mourn as someone who has lost a soulmate, a friend, and a teacher. It's not that I feel mine is a special mourning, but only that I feel lonely and unable to explain the depth of my sorrow. We all have different ways of expressing and living our grief, and it helps when others understand where we're coming from and how we are mourning.

When Dana said that to me this morning, I told him that I had put out a message to you to tell me that you are still around; I felt that what he had told me was yet another message or sign from you telling me that it's okay. So, of course, it made me cry—I am still crying as I type. Good thing I can type fast and well, because I can't see the screen properly as it is all blurry from tears. But I know I am typing okay.

I feel relieved.

Yesterday we visited Lydia, or "Milk Mama," as Matthias used to call her. She was the lady who used to bring milk for Matthias's family when he was growing up, and ever since I met her here in Schneppenbach many years ago, she has been very kind to me. We can't speak much together because you know my German is limited and only Oma understands when I speak. But through the gazes we exchange, there are many conversations that we have.

Anyway, we went to see her yesterday. Matthias had already left for Brussels with Rosi and Leoni, so it was just me, Oma, and Opa who went to see her. She lives just across the street from Oma. She had been ill for the past month—at least, that's what I knew.

When I saw her, she had the same smile and was very strong and independent as usual. But something in her had changed, and she seemed more fragile. Later on through the conversation, I learned that she had just had a heart bypass or transplant, I don't know which. She showed us the *schnit* (the incision). I thought of you and all the surgery you endured.

Throughout the conversation that she was having with Oma and Opa and two other visitors, I was choking up with tears. And of course I did not know where to hide. I pretended to sneeze at one point, at another point pretended to cough, and through and through pretended so much, to be able to suck up the tears. "*Ah, Yene wir haben uns so viel zu sagen* [Oh Yene we have so much to tell each other]," she said to me, "*zu viel zum besprechen* [so much to talk about]." There is a world of conversation in her eyes, and it was too much for me. I just could not hold her gaze. I had to look away.

She breaks my heart, and even though I can't speak the same language, there is something universal that links us—us people, human beings. It aches in my heart and at the same time it makes me feel good. As she told us about her bypass, I thought of Gashe Azmi who had so many heart surgeries and each time he came out smiling.

All of you, whom we have been blessed with, have taught us so much. You are all so anointed with the oil of compassion, and it breaks my heart. I see the strength, the courage in you but I also see the fragility, the innocence like a child. Now, here I am sitting alone in this big bed, typing letters to you that I trust reach you in one way or another.

In a couple of hours, I am leaving for Thailand. Fofi will be waiting for me at Frankfurt Airport; she might already be there now. I will continue to write from there.

I feel, however, that I have reached a point where I feel complete with what I had to say. God willing, if I feel very complete by Ethiopian Christmas, then that will be the day I send you my final letter. Of course, it is not my final conversation with you, because our conversations will continue for as long as I live. But for now, I think in this process, if I am ready I will end my conversation on Christmas day. If not, I will continue until Easter and end on the anniversary of the day we last kissed.

Mimi

January 7, 2010

Emaye,

Today is Christmas in Ethiopia. It's the first time I will not be visiting you or calling you to wish you *"Enkewan Adersesh Emaye, Melkam Gena* [Thank God—God allowed you to see this day, Merry Christmas]."

The girls have gone back to Freetown with Matthias, and I have stayed behind for about two weeks. I have gone on retreat to be silent for a while, to reflect the year that passed and welcome the New Year. I was thinking of calling home anyway, but it's not possible to call from where I am: I am in a secluded center and I think I would rather stay silent this year.

Fofi is with me, as she too wanted to go on retreat. We don't talk much, but when we do it's about past issues we want to resolve, present challenges we want to discuss, or future hopes we want to position. It is good to be quiet. It's good to be silent and be in a restricted mode of existence—it allows all the chatter to stop.

Did I ever tell you I shut down and retreat once or twice a year, if possible? Well, I have been doing this for a few years now and it's been a blessing. I think a lot of you, of what you have left us, and of how we will manage to keep it all together as you had it.

Of course, things are bound to change tremendously because you are not here anymore, but I think that each person of Laïbet is making an effort to live up to the legacy you have left. We have all become more tolerant, at least that's what I think. We have all become more accommodating to one another—I know I have.

The sorrow is still there, sitting inside the walls of my heart, and as much as it makes me sad, it is also a reminder of how much we love you and how much we miss you. I think of the good days as well, and often I laugh alone when I think of some of the stories. Do you remember that night in Brussels, when we were staying in the apart-hotel Wellington and it was summertime? You were sitting right by the window because it was so hot. It was late in the night, and all of us had gathered around you to listen to stories of your childhood—and then, as you looked out, your face seemed shocked and when we looked in the same direction, we all saw the man standing on the roof butt naked and pissing from the top of the roof onto the street. It was funny, and you were laughing so hard. We all laughed so hard. *"Tenam yelewom ende...ffhoh*! [Has he lost his mental health?!]" is what you said as you tried to come back to the story you were telling us. Those were the good days when we all laughed so easily.

I still laugh a lot. It's good to laugh. I mean, I don't just laugh like a fool but if the occasion presents itself and something funny happens, I usually can't help it. You know who is now very much like this: Rosi and Leoni. Especially Rosi—she just can't hold back a laugh.

I am so glad they got to know you, even if only a bit. They are so proud of you. They spent a few days in Brussels with Enaniye and Boubiye before leaving for Freetown. Fofi told me that as they entered the house and saw your picture, they were both choked up and tears filled their eyes. You know what breaks my heart is that they are so shy and so little that they cannot yet express their sorrow. I try my best to talk about you and tell them stories, so that they might speak about you and understand that even when someone is no longer here physically, that they are still with us in spirit and in our hearts.

The tough part about your going is that you take with you the last page of an era. I don't believe home will ever be the same for me. It is your largeness of heart that I miss, your tolerance and your generosity, and your ability to forgive and include everyone; it is how you make each person feel welcomed and how you remain strict while also full of love. It is that benchmark you establish for the order of the day. It is so much, Emaye, that I can't write it all down. There was something about you that will never, ever be replaced.

Me, I am still very lonely in my heart. Of course, I work and I do things here and there and I don't really speak about this lonely feeling to anyone, but it's there. Do you think it will ever go away? I don't think so. I know that you would tell me time will make things better, but I am not sure. I think of all the uncles, aunts, friends, parents, sisters, and brothers that you have buried, and how through and through you were always there for us. You never let the fact that you were mourning darken your face when we came to you; somehow you managed to still stand tall for us. You remained our rock, and now, what can we do when the rock is gone?

I suppose the rock within us has to emerge, but that will take a while for many of us.

Mimi

January 10, 2010

Emaye,

Did I tell you that I went away to Thailand? Yes, I did—I am here with Fofi, to finish my dissertation (*African Leadership: Perspective of 20 Senior African Leaders and Heads of State,* UMI/ProQuest, 2010). Now, the writing of this dissertation has such deep meaning to me not only because it is a collection of the thoughts of senior men and women in Africa about how to move the art of leadership forward, but also because in it I have your thoughts, the thoughts of Gashe Azmi, and of so many great people who have shaped my life and left a scent of their spirit lingering on my soul.

I woke up at around 5:30am to the sounds of the rooster testing his vocal chords, clearing his throat, or singing—I don't know which is more appropriate. For a while I thought I was in Laïbet. In my subconscious I tried to find the signs that I was really home again, but slowly I opened my eyes to realize that I was in my bungalow with Fofi sleeping next to me. I was slightly disappointed, like when I used to wake up from dreams that I thought were real, or when I would find lots of candy or magic things and hold them so tightly in my hand and then awake only to find my fist clenched on the illusion of the candy. I closed my eyes again and continued to listen to the rooster who sang for a few more minutes. And even though I was thousands of miles away from Laïbet, in my thoughts I went back there and I went back to your room and the times when I used to sleep over in Ababi's bed.

Just yesterday, I was telling Fofi how much I love the

early morning in Laïbet. It was magic for me to hear the sounds and scents of the morning, from Ababi's coughs to the sound of water sloshing in the bathroom and him making so much noise, to the sounds in the compound of hearing a mixture of roosters from afar and near, or the sounds of the rough morning voices of people like Gashe Tilahun or Ababa Belda. And then, little by little, the kitchen crew woke up, the kitchen woke up, and the voices from the compound became more and more like a beautiful and unpredictable cacophony. I just loved it.

The best was seeing you and Ababi all dressed up and the room completely cleaned and rearranged—and it would not even be 7:00am. When you opened your windows and the morning light shone through the bedroom with its rays dancing on the walls, that was the sign a new day was about to start.

Then breakfast used to come with coffee for you and café latte or cappuccino for Ababi, with some kind of eggs or gefelfel[46] covered up in injera. Isn't it interesting that at the time, many of us took those days for granted? Well, not really for granted, but while we were all grateful I think that none of us could really imagine what life would be without you and Ababi.

One thing for sure is that I have been transformed by your departure. I am very conscious of how life can pass so quickly, and that although we think we have years to come, in fact, those years we have pass like the blink of an eye. Can you believe that Rosi is now

---

[46] An Ethiopian dish in which the wot (stew) is mixed in with injera (Ethiopian bread), gefelfel is often eaten for breakfast or as a casual meal.

10 years old? Leoni is 8. Do you remember when I used to bring them to Laïbet and they would sleep on Ababi's bed while the rest of us sat and continued our conversations with you? It seems like yesterday. Now there are five beautiful great-grandchildren: along with Rosi and Leoni, there is Fana's Tariq and Noor in Vienna and baby Betty of Timmy.

Do you remember a few months ago that I wrote you about a comment my friend had made? He had asked me where I was in the process of mourning. Well, maybe he is right and maybe there is a process—for me, I have been missing you more and more each day. It has not gotten better. What is happening is that I am not really interested in coming back to Ethiopia again. Each time I think of coming back, I wonder where I will go and for what or whom would I come. I know everyone is still there, but still I think that I would have a hard time handling your not being there. I guess I am nowhere near the end of the "process of mourning," as my friend would say.

The rooster started singing again. I don't know if it is one or more roosters, but the sound is heartwarming for me. I wonder if roosters have the same language all over the world, because I swear that this one here sounds just like the ones we hear in Laïbet.

Yesterday, Fofi said that we have had a beautiful life and I was shocked a bit to hear her say that. I told that her we are still living and hope to continue living for some more time. And then we laughed. But she is right—we have had a beautiful life. What a blessing to grow up in Laïbet. What a blessing to be able to run around all day and come back home at night to wash up, eat dinner, and sleep cuddled between you and Ababi. What a blessing. Growing up there with you has made us who we are today. For my entire life, you have been my compass and my anchor, and today I find it difficult to assume that role for myself. Maybe that's what's so difficult.

Sometimes I think that I should stop being so sad, that it probably bothers your eternal rest. I think of what will happen when it's my turn to pass, and I would not want my children to be sad forever—I would want them to continue their lives and focus on the good times we had together. So, in light of that, yes, I am trying to be more cheerful, but I tell you it's not easy. Then I think of my many friends, especially in Rwanda, who have lost so many family members all at once because of genocide and I tell myself that I better just count my blessings that we had you for so long, that you lived such a great life, and that we were there to mourn you and have the most beautiful ceremony for you. I think of all the people who, for one reason or another, were not able to attend the funeral ceremonies of their loved ones and I think that we are lucky because most of us were there to bid you farewell and cry together. So, I think, it's time to reflect and move forward. I think that in my mind, but my heart is not budging.

At least I am writing you these letters, and that helps me to continue my conversations with you; it helps me meditate and somehow spiritually connect with you. When I write to you, I am in your space; I am at peace and I find my stability again. I will continue to write you forever until we meet again.

Talking about meeting again, did I ever tell you this story? About two years ago, a friend of mine passed away from a car accident and I was shocked and sad. I wrote Bob—you remember Bob my friend from

America who told the taxi driver to take him to Laïbet? Well, I wrote Bob about it and told him that I was very sad about the accident and the death of my friend. He wrote back tell me, "Don't worry, you will see him very soon." I replied, "...it's okay, I am not in a rush to see him again." As sad as I was, I had to laugh as I read the email. Sometimes we say things in trying to comfort people and we end up saying something else.

You know what I pray for? I pray to follow your path, to live like Ababi did, to always be aware of all the blessings I have been granted, to always be able to forgive, to be able to laugh through and through, and to be there for whoever needs me. I pray that Matthias and I can be there for Rosiye and Leoniye for as long as possible, and that in the time we have we can give them all the guidance, love, and direction to allow them to be ready for when we might not be there anymore. I think that's what is important—that we as parents give our children all they need to move forward from the day we are no longer there.

At times, I am so happy that I had the chance to talk to you so much, to ask you all those questions. I wish I had asked more, but I am happy with what I had. I thank God for it.

Emaye, the sun has risen and the day has started on this end. I am right in front of the Pacific Ocean, and it is calming to see the ocean so still. It is humbling and makes me think of how even though our lives are so short and our presence on this Earth so impermanent, some leave footprints through the beautiful things they do while they pass through this life. How many millions of years have the oceans been here? We live a maximum of 100 years at most, yet we have become so defiant to nature and the environment. We mislead ourselves in thinking that we are in control, but we are not at all.

In everything that you did, I saw a humanitarian heart that cared not only for people but for all living beings. I think of the perspectives you held and the width and distance of the horizon you could envision, and I remain in awe. If we could have a tenth of that, I think our lives would be different. This is how I feel this morning sitting in this bungalow, just a few meters from a calm ocean in a gentle breeze. When I look at how everything looks and works together, I can only surrender to life, allowing it to take me along with the flow and in all I do, come to realize that all things are impermanent except for love and compassion.

I have to start my day now. It's about 7:00am and I am going to wash up and continue working on editing the dissertation. I will be happy when it's all done. I so want it to be completed that at times I don't find motivation to work on it anymore. But I think of that story you used to tell us about the mother mouse who had so many babies and that after delivering so many baby mice with courage, she died delivering the very last baby mouse. So, I know that most of the work has been done for this dissertation and that the hard part is 90% done, and that I shouldn't die on this last leg of the process.

There is still so much I want to talk to you about. There is still such a need I have to just sit and listen to you, and just be there around you.

When we asked Rosi and Leoni to write something for the pamphlet that was prepared for you, they made a beautiful drawing each and wrote on it with curly, curvy, beautiful letters: "Almazesha, we will miss you always." This is so true for all of us, and it is especially true for me.

I will miss you always,
Mimi

January 15, 2010

Good morning Emaye,

I am just coming back from a massage. It feels so good. I think you would have enjoyed massage—it would have relaxed you. Anyway, during the massage my mind was time traveling back and forth, and for some reason I thought of the times in Brussels where I was slowly going into adolescence. What a time.

Things were changing so fast, and no one really told me what to expect. I had to play it all by ear. By the time we were about 13-14 years old, the girls in my class were officially going out with boys. They were not even having any discretion about it: During break time, you could see little couples lined up and stuck to the heaters in the bathroom. They were interlaced and kissed for the entire break. For the rest of us, it made it hard to use the restroom, since now, thanks to the "love in the air" season, we had both boys and girls in the girls' bathroom.

And as if that was not enough, the trend then evolved to skipping school all in all and spending time in the park next to the school or in the pub down the street. I went along a few times, and the conversation about dates, sex, boys, and so on took on a greater scale during these escapades. They used to go on and on about who did what with whom, or bragging about what they did with this or that boy. Eventually, when all the conversation was consumed, the lights were turned onto me to speak of whatever boyfriend I might have—but of course I did not have any boyfriend. You know that would be unheard of, the way we do things in our family. But the pressure remained. For a while, I told them that I was not dating anyone right at that moment. I could feel that they felt I didn't quite cut it for their companionship, so since I knew that my relationship with them would end, I decided to end it my way.

Guess what I did? Well, at the newspaper stand in front of our apartment they used to sell a series of books called S.A.S., I have no idea what it stands for. It was a raunchy kind of literature. So guess what your daughter did? She bought the book and learned whole passages by heart.

On Monday, when I went back to school, I could not wait until we skipped school again. The usual suspects came along.

> "I am so tired," I mumbled, like a fisherman
>   tossing out his line.
> "From what?" they asked, taking the bait.
> "This guy I am dating, he is just incredible." Now
>   I was starting to unfold the story.
> "What guy?"
> "He lives in Mons, at the barracks."
> "A soldier?"
> "Didn't look like one to me," I replied.
> "So what happened?"

As a good monk would recite parts of this or that teaching, I started to recite the passage I had learned by heart. I could see their eyes bulging out from both curiosity and disbelief as I continued on and on. Until, at one point, Anne, the greatest bully of all and one of the girls that we used to hang out with shouted: "*Il t'a QUOI?* [He did what to you?]" "*Il me laboura le dos,*" I replied with more cool than ice.

Now, they really had bulging eyes—and as for me, I

was not sure what I had actually implied! I suppose it might have been an important part of sex. Maybe even sex, itself...who knows? They nodded for me to continue, but alas, as I had learned the passage by heart, I had to start from the beginning again in order not to lose track. They seemed annoyed, but I insisted that I had to retell everything for the sake of clarity.

After I finished my long-winded recitation, I sat there without a smile, just a straight face. "That's why I am so tired," I told them, then added, "Please keep it to yourselves—I don't want anyone to know this." Of course, I knew that this was the best way to get them to broadcast everything I had just said to the entire school. Done deal, I thought to myself. Street credit established, and peace in my life at last.

The only trouble was that they started coming to ask for updates on this imaginary love affair I had described, and not only that, they also wanted my advice on their own love affairs. "Gosh, there is no end to this!" I thought. Well, that was the beginning of the rest of our lives. Even though today we don't speak about imaginary lovers and love affairs, I find that so much time is spent on trying to get a grip on our relationships and marriages. But you know what? Even to this day, I don't know how people spend so much time kissing. I still have not figured out how they manage to breathe. I certainly couldn't breathe in such circumstances—maybe it's my asthma?

I didn't really date anyone until I was well past eighteen. Well, I had some dates, but just to go to the movies and parties, nothing more. Nowadays, people would think it absurd and abnormal to wait so long, but for me, I found it was the best way. At least I was old enough to know exactly what I was getting into.

Okay, I will have more stories for you in a couple of days.

Remember that I love you, always,
Mimi

January 17, 2010

Emaye,

This morning I thought of you so much. I woke up thinking of you. I thought of you in the shower and thought of the days when you use to make the *tebel* (Holy water) for me. Do you remember? When I finished showering and started to dry myself, I suddenly started to weep and hid my face in the towel, as if I could find comfort in its folds. I have no idea why I wept so much. I guess it's because I miss you so much. Will this sorrow ever get out of the depth of my Being? It's the loneliness I have a hard time with, not being able to call you. Knowing I can't visit you anymore breaks my heart.

Whem Emama (Boubiye's mom) passed on, some people insisted on having an immediate burial. They couldn't even wait for him to fly back home, and they buried her without him. It was so unfair. It's unfair not to wait for a son or a daughter to come back to bid farewell to a parent who has passed on. I found the whole thing unfair then, and I find it even more unfair today, now that I know how much the process of saying goodbye one last time can help the bereaved. But people tend to get funny in times like this: One or two people usually ascend to some sort of commanding power and exercise their will over others in the name of "taking care of logistics." This can happen easily without contest, because often others are too torn to decipher what's happening.

I remember that neither Boubiye nor any of us for that matter were involved in packing her things up. I have no idea where all her belongings are. Do you remember that big belt she used to wear? Well, she would always joke with me and tell me that when she went, I could have her belt and wear or keep it for memory's sake. It's not important that I don't have it, though, because more than any material item for memory's sake, it's much more precious for me to keep the memories of the good times we shared, the stories and conversations we had. I cherish the life we shared together as the precious memories that will keep that loved one alive in my heart, in all our hearts. And no one can take that away.

Now in your case, I have no idea what is happening in Laïbet. I am afraid that things will be taken here and there by those who loved you and who want to keep something of you near them. I guess you would have let them take things, so who am I to say that it should all stay in Laïbet? I only wish that it could be done more transparently.

About two days after your ceremony at Debre Libanos, we were all in Laïbet and the tent was still full. I was cold so I grabbed your shawl and sat in the sun just outside the Tinishu Salon, right by where Solomon always sits—you know, the little corner in front of the coffee-grinding warehouse.

Out of nowhere, someone came and told me, "Oh, that's my shawl. She gave it to me before she died." I was shocked. I felt cold all over my body. I wanted to cry that you were hardly gone and now people were claiming this and that from you. What was going on? Now that you are no longer here, will I have to ask permission to wear your shawl or go around asking if it belongs to anyone? When did I ever ask permission in Laïbet? Whoever asks permission in their mother's house? But don't worry, I did not cry. I took it all in with a deep breath, and said, "Sorry, I did not know."

I took off the shawl, folded it, and handed it back to the person. Emaye, I was so hurt; it made me feel very sad and accentuated your loss. But you know what? Well, this will make you proud. I went the next day and ordered ten such shawls. There!

Can you believe that you were hardly gone and some people just appropriated things for themselves? I found it rude and insensitive.

I don't know why I am thinking of all these things today—I am so far away from home. Today I did a meditation, and through the mediation I went to your bedroom, which I always considered a sanctuary. I was so happy, so content. I felt so much at peace.

At times I want to keep your bedroom just as I last left it the last time and just in my heart. I don't want to come back there again; I am afraid of what I might find or not find. At other times, I want to come back and sit there in silence. At times I am afraid that since you are no longer there, maybe your scent is no longer there—the scent of your perfumes and the scent of the flowers in their vases.

I am trying to be strong and get through this mourning phase as best as I can, but the truth is that I am not managing. I know you would want me to get over it and continue my life but, Emaye, I am really not managing. I don't know why. I just can't get over it that you are no longer here. What is a ship without an anchor, but a vessel that floats aimlessly across the seas? That is how I feel: For now, my anchor is gone and although my little family is also my anchor, the anchor you were is of a different nature. It was about identity, roots, lineage, tradition, and so much more.

Let me not ramble on and stop here for today. It's beautiful outside—the weather is very mild to warm, the sun is shining, and the ocean is very clear. I will go for a swim. Mind you, not in the ocean; there is a nice pool at the hotel. I am still a bit scared to just get in the ocean like that. Isn't that strange, knowing that I have been scuba diving for years? Well, those are the contradictions I have learned to live with. I am afraid to get in the ocean to swim, but for diving I have no problem.

It's so good to write to you,
M

January 18, 2010

Emaye,

Today I heard tragic news. I spoke to Matthias in Freetown, and I also spoke to the girls about a birthday party they attended. There was a pool at the party, and apparently a small child who couldn't swim got into the pool and almost drowned. Rosi kept her afloat until an adult jumped in to take her out. This happened once in Lusaka, and we also almost lost a child. But the tragic news is that a friend of mine lost a child. I am not sure how it happened, but it seems to be another drowning accident. I am very shocked and can't even imagine how the parents are coping. I am completely in pieces about this tragic incident.

Why do such things happen, Emaye? Why? The parents are great people who are helpful to others, who lead a normal and good life. They are polite and good to people. I don't understand. I know we are not supposed to ask why, but I still am haunted with the why question. Where do we go for comfort? I am not saying that bad things can't happen to good people or that it should only happen to people who are rude and mean, but I can't make sense of what just happened.

Where is God in times like this? Where is He and why does He let such things happen?

You know, as sad as I am that you are no longer with us, physically, I feel blessed to have had you in my life for 43 years. How many people can say that they have had their grandmother for that long? It's rare. I am grateful for it.

I love you, M

January 22, 2010

Dear Emaye,

I am flying back to Freetown today, after two nights in Brussels. You know I am always a bit reluctant to spend too much time in Brussels because it brings back so many memories. This time, I chose to make a new beginning and I went with an open heart and spirit. I saw Boubiye and Enaniye, waiting for me and Fofi to arrive from Thailand. That was on Wednesday night, and we did not make it home until about 11:00pm or so.

For the first time in a long time, I was happy to be home. The next day, I woke up very early as usual, like around 5:45am and went down to make tea. Leoni called me around 6:00am and it was sweet to talk to her. She's been calling me regularly. Until she called, I was working in my room. I was dressed and had made my bed and cleaned my room, as you have always taught us. Enaniye picked up the phone in her room and came to my bedroom to pass me the phone.

I stayed with Enaniye for a couple of hours in the early part of the day. We spoke of you, of the times we had together and the time ahead when we will have to make do without you present. It was one of the first times I have spoken with Enaniye for so long. It felt good.

I have to go Emaye. I will write to you soon,
M

January 26, 2010

Emaye,

I am back in Freetown now; I flew in on Friday night. It took me a while to get out of the haze or fog of jet lag and travel.

Yesterday, an Ethiopian Airlines flight crashed as it took off from Beirut, Lebanon. So, far there are no survivors, and since you have left a terrible earthquake has tragically destroyed most of Haiti. Plus, you remember my friend I told you about two weeks ago, the one who lost her son? Well, I went to see her yesterday.

There is so much going on that is tragic, and I did not know what to tell my friend. There are no words to comfort a parent who has lost a child. I would not know what would comfort me in such a time. If all souls meet in Heaven, Emaye, I am sure you will see this angel of hers and I hope that somehow you can find your way to him and comfort him, wherever he is.

My friend told me that I have changed; I think I have changed, especially this year and since your departure. I feel older, not necessarily in terms of age, but in my heart and in my soul. There is a constant nostalgia of the days gone by and some kind of sorrow in my heart. The funny thing is that, at the same time, I find that I am a lot more engaged and conscious about life. I find that I celebrate life each day. Each day, I love Matthias more and I love my Rosi and Leoni more. But it does not stop at them—I think of all of us in the greater family, and I have a certain sense of love, forgiveness, and well-wishing going out to everyone. The same for my friends and even for people I see around on the street or that I know are in the world: I just wish them well. What is all this about? I don't know, and I am just assuming it's the process of an aging heart.

Boubiye has some kind of medical test today. He is in my thoughts and I have prayed, even if it is not an official prayer. I am constantly keeping him in my heart and thoughts. He was very sweet with me in Brussels; he came with me to the airport and we did the usual checking-in and then coffee and breakfast before my departure.

Emaye, life has passed so quickly. I know it's not over, but it has passed nonetheless, and so quickly. Now I understand how futile it is to take things so seriously. Now I understand why people say that if they had a second chance with life, they would spend more time with family, more time with their children, and more time with their loved ones. I am trying to do that.

Did I tell you that I decided to go back to the gym and exercise? Well, yes, I decided that, but the only time I found to go is very early in the morning. It's still dark outside, so I am waiting for it to get a bit light. I don't regret anything I did in my life, because it was all part of learning and becoming who I am today, but if there is one thing I would have changed, I think I would have been more conscious about my health a lot earlier on in life.

Emaye, I spoke to Solomon yesterday and it was nice to talk to him. I also spoke to Etetila, which was also nice. Enaniye had explained to me all the work that Etetila has been doing since you left in order to keep

Laïbet together. Actually, all eight of them have been working together and that makes me so happy. This is a great example for the rest of us, grandchildren and great-grandchildren.

I have to go now. Wish me luck in my new adventure with the gym—I hope I can make it a habit.

I love you always,
M

February 8, 2010

Emaye,

I did go to the gym finally. You know, it's not about the gym—it's about the habits that we build in our lives, the value we give to our health, and the commitment we sustain to be there, in the best possible shape, for our children and our loved ones.

Did I tell you that yesterday I saw my friend and she told me I changed? Yes, I think I have already told you this. But this morning I really felt that I have changed so much. I try to remember myself of a few years ago, and there is such a difference with who I am today. Of course, some things never change, so I guess what I am trying to say is that I feel I have deepened (if there is such a thing). I think I have ripened, maybe, if there is such a thing. It's not about maturity or more knowledge, but about the gentle wrinkles life has left on my heart. It's about the wrinkles that all the laughter and all the tears have bestowed on me, as if to mark their passage.

I love you so much, Emaye. I feel so blessed to have had you for so many years in my life. If I live to be 86 years old, then I will have lived half of that with you, and that is the best gift I could ever want as a grandchild.

All the beauty I see, I see because of you. It is through your eyes that I have seen most things in my life, and that has kept me in the light. I realize today that anytime I stepped out of the light and entered darkness—well, it was when I stopped looking through those eyes, and I stopped thinking with that heart you raised me to live with. Only then did I end up caught in the velcro of daily life on the dark side.

I don't regret the mistakes I have made. I am certain that everyone has their share of mistakes; we just don't entertain that in broad daylight. Mistakes are something that remains between us and our God. When I say I don't regret anything, I don't mean this in an arrogant way; I mean it in a way that rather recognizes the humanity in all of us, and I do it in recognition of my own humanity. Even though I aimed for the highest of standards in all aspects of my life, I have known the texture of the forces of darkness. In my heart, I have asked forgiveness for all those I may have hurt in the process, and again in my heart, I have also forgiven all of those who may have hurt me in one way or another.

It is such a relief to forgive. I did not know that, but I learned this year. I know it's a bit late to learn about that, but wouldn't you agree that the gift of forgiveness is just and only the grace of God? I know you always forgave everyone. It had always puzzled me how you would just forgive—even those who overtly wronged you. I suppose that life taught you that early on.

Emaye, when I think of your life, I just stay in amazement. I cannot imagine that you were younger than Rosi today when you married—just a year older than Leoni. You were just a child, a child made to grow up right away. What I just cannot believe is how you managed to raise your children and take care of your home in a way that was even more effective and more loving than what an adult could have done. You grew up with your children and they grew up with you.

Despite the fact that I know how blessed we are to have had you until now, and despite the fact that I am conscious of all the tragedies in the world and even among my own small circle of friends, I still miss you and at times, my tears still well up. I am trying to be strong and tough, but I am not always managing to keep it together.

It's strange how unexpected things just trigger me. Sometimes it's a song, or a phone call from someone I did not expect, or maybe a kind email or something I read—in any case, there are triggers and I know that once a trigger line is passed, I might as well just pull out the tissues to absorb the tears. I don't wipe them, because that smudges the eyeliner and I end up looking like a lonely raccoon.

For example, I spoke to Boubiye after his check up and I was really choked up again. He said he was driving back home with Enaniye, and he said "I love you" at the end and it just shot through my heart. Enaniye then added that he should also tell me that she too loves me, and that was enough to knot up my throat. I just miss you and I miss everyone too. I see how finite our days are and I realize that we are not here forever. I cry from gratefulness for having parents and grandparents and aunts and uncles and brothers and sisters and a whole family, as we have. I feel my heart just bulging with gratefulness, and I suppose the tears are a mixture of gratitude and nostalgia.

However much time I have left in this world, I hope I can remain conscious and aware of all the blessings. I pray that I bring happiness and joy wherever I go, as you did. I pray that I can share whatever blessings come my way with others, and with as many as possible.

I love you, I will write soon.
M

February 20, 2010

Emaye,

Today is Enaniye's and Boubiye's 45th wedding anniversary. I remember that you told me you were hardly thirty when they married. 45 years of marriage is quite something, but you and Ababi must have been married 56 years if I am correct in my calculations.

I have not written much to you these days, because I was just caught up with finishing my dissertation and also finishing that book I had started, reflecting on my work in Africa (*Butterflies Over Africa*, 2009, Integral Publishers).

I don't want to stop writing to you because when I write to you, I feel at peace. It's like we are talking.

Today has not been such a great day for me. I miss you a lot. I wish I could have talked to you today. Things just went all wrong, starting from our generator breaking down, to being stuck in a meeting with people who were unable to reach consensus, to an argument with Matthias....it's just not been good.

I miss you terribly. I wish I could call you or talk to you.

M

February 26, 2010

Emaye,

Today is a public holiday, the Muslim holiday for the birth of the Prophet Mohammed. I went to the gym very early in the morning as usual, and for some reason, all I could think of was you. All I could think of was the times we had together with Ababi and everyone at Laïbet. I cannot believe this time is over.

I now realize that everything has an end, as it has a beginning. As you started to build a home with Ababi and raise your children, you created a place for more people than the immediate family—you created a space where everyone was welcome, where everyone could have a meal and feel at home.

Sometimes I wonder if I have lost this privilege of having such a home. It was a privilege when we had it: a gift. Yes, I know that Laïbet is still there, but how empty it feels without you there.

Just yesterday, I was offered a short assignment to come to Ethiopia to facilitate and moderate a meeting. As much as I was happy about the opportunity to take this assignment, I couldn't help thinking how it would be to land back in Ethiopia and know that I will not be able to call you as soon as my plane lands.

I know I have to be grateful for all the years we had together. I know that there are so many people who are not even as fortunate as I was to have not only a grandmother, but one as wonderful as you. At the same time, Emaye, the sadness has not left my heart. At times when I am busy doing my work or running my daily routine, I can manage to remember you only in good spirit and with warm memories of the times we had. But there are also times when I am not so busy or when the burden of life becomes a bit too heavy; then I think of you, wishing and longing that I could reach you, call you, and talk to you to ease my loneliness.

Well, it's true—I feel very lonely, much more often than in the past. I know that I am blessed with Matthias and our two angels, but there is a hollowness I feel inside. I feel anchorless. Will I ever come home again to Ethiopia to live? Will I ever come and just be there as naturally as I used to when you were there? I doubt it. When you were there, I felt a sense of security, a sense of belonging, and a sense of knowing that I had a mother to whom I could go. Now, things are different; this mother is no longer there, at least not physically, and I miss her very much. It is not even good enough to tell you that I miss you. Much more than that, I feel a piece of me was broken off from my body and my soul. I feel that the page has turned, which of course it has. I know that the page has turned.

Emaye, I feel old in a way. I feel old in my heart, and I feel I have lost my right to the child in me.

Today is Etetila's birthday, so I will call her later to wish her a happy birthday. Did you know that Matthias and you have the same birthday on April 21st? I wish I had known your birthday when you were still with us; I would have been happy to celebrate it for you and with you.

It's such a pity that in our culture we don't celebrate birthdays. I am so envious of cultures where people celebrate their birthdays, and the older the person gets the more exciting the party is. Well, for me, if God gives me the years, you will see—I will celebrate each and every birthday I have.

It's not even been six months since you left, but it is almost a year since I last saw you. How I regret not coming to see you last August when you asked me to come. But I am in such a far away place, the ticket is crazy expensive to Addis, and on top of that, I just could not leave Matthias alone with the girls.

When I come to Ethiopia, in March if the assignment gets confirmed, I think I might come and visit you at the mausoleum. I want to come visit, but I am also reluctant—if I come visit you there, I will feel even more homeless. I prefer to think that you are with us in some special way, so I also don't want to come to the mausoleum. I have no idea what to do. I cannot move forward in my life.

When the time comes for me to go and leave this life's work, I hope that my Rosi and Leoni get on with their lives and don't dwell on my absence. So, I try to do that myself, regarding you, but I am not managing. It's hard. I just miss you, especially when times are tough and I need to talk to someone.

I have been going to sleep very early for weeks; I just prefer not to deal with the day. I go to the gym very early, leaving my house at 5:30am, and then I work all day. I am happy to be plunged into my work, because it helps me go along with life and not pay attention to too many of the issues I face right now.

I love you and I will write you soon,
M

March 21, 2010

Emaye,

This morning, Leoni ran to me and said, "It's Rosi's half birthday!" I like the concept of half birthdays, another reason to celebrate life and count the blessings.

The last time I heard your voice was the day after Rosi's birthday. It was Tuesday September 22, 2009, and my entire world has changed since.

You know what is strange? Well, when you asked me to come and see you as we spoke that day, I told you I was so far away and that I would have to come later in the year for Easter or during the summer. I just didn't realize that I should have jumped on the plane to come and say goodbye. I just didn't realize. I thought we had time to be together again and see each other as we usually did. I was stunned when I heard you had left, moved on from this world. I was just so stunned that I was not even sad right away. I mean, I was sad, but it was still very much at the surface. This recurrent and permanent hollowness and emptiness I have been feeling for months now had not yet emerged.

I was very composed when I heard. I even stayed two more days in Sierra Leone to complete my assignment. It is as if I wanted to clear my plate before turning to face my new life without you. Maybe it was better that way, better to be in shock for a while in order not to fall apart right away.

I find it hard not to be able to talk to you as we did before. I still have the urge to call you to ask for advice on some of my work issues or to tell you the latest joke I heard. I have missed you a lot these days. I know I didn't write you very often in the past weeks—I meant to write, but it didn't happen and I chose not to force it.

I went home, back to Addis, last week for that unexpected short assignment. I spent the first night in your room, and I was happy to see that nothing had changed and all things were as you left them. Nothing had changed at all—even the scent of the room is that light cologne scent that has been there for ages. It was good to see Solomon, Koky, and Essayas. Laïbet was the same in many ways, but without you there, it just feels lonely.

You know what was interesting? To me, it was as if you were still there, only I could not see you physically. I knocked on your door very gently and whispered the same words I always said when I came into your room: "*Emaye, ene negn* [Emaye, it's me]." My eyes landed on the right side of the room, scanning and searching in vain for the shape of your body sitting, resting, or sleeping. I couldn't find you. The bed was perfectly made, with not even a crease on the bed cover. I put my bags downs and came close to the bed, as if to kiss you, as I always did. But instead of finding you to kiss, I just stood there and tried to find you in spirit. I ran my hands over the bed and stood there quietly. Emaye, did you see me there? I felt as if you did.

I slept on Ababi's bed, as I always did. I left the little light on, as you always did. It did not take me any time to fall asleep, and the night passed very quickly. I slept very deeply, and in the morning, I woke up to the usual sounds of the breaking dawn at Laïbet.

Gashe Tilahun's voice broke the silence of the night. When I opened my eyes, I just stared forward. I was facing your way, and for a moment I pretended you had just gone to wash up and someone had come in to make your bed quickly. So, for a moment I just stayed like that, anticipating hearing your steps returning from the bathroom to the bedroom. But, of course, I heard nothing and I resigned myself to come out of this fantasy or denial or whatever you want to call it.

Do you remember that it was about this time last year when I came with Rosi and Leoni and we all slept in Ababi's bed? You were so worried that we would fall out of the bed. I am so glad the girls experienced spending the night with you. Sleeping over at Laïbet has always filled me with peace and also energy all at the same time. Emaye, can you believe that time has passed so fast and it is now almost a year since I last laid eyes on you?

Your picture, that one where you are wearing the reddish suit, is framed and set on your chair in the living room. I have the same picture in my study, taped on the wall opposite my desk, so each time I look up from my desk, I can look at you. There was also the picture you took with Ababi, you know, the one you took in the photo studio. It was part of the pictures that Enaniye insisted we take as a family when we came to visit around 1979. Both you and Ababi look beautiful and peaceful. I feel that the picture has changed since you passed on—it feels as though the picture has come alive and holds a story, the story of our lives. I looked at all these pictures and I wondered to myself whether you really existed or whether your/"our" story is one that existed only in my mind.

I spent the next two nights in the hotel where my assignment was and returned back to your room for the last night. The last night was a lot harder than the first. Koky spent the night with me and we spoke for a long while about how life is now—without you there. I think we all feel very lonely without you. It's like the big tree has been removed and we have no more shade to sit under. I personally feel so vulnerable. I feel as though I have no home to go back to. I know I have a house and my own little family, but you provided me with a place to return to anytime, a place where I could be a child again—a place where I was referred to as "*ye lej lej* [my child's child, meaning grandchild]."

Is it the fact that the chain seems broken that is hurting me? I am not sure; I just know that life is so different now. You know, the drive from Bole to Laïbet was strange because for the first time, I didn't call you to say I had landed safely and was on my way home. Well, in September I did not call you, but that was different—there was a crisis at hand which distracted me. Now, things were calm again and it was just an ordinary day like any other, which made it so obvious that things were very different now.

Leaving Addis was also strange. The plane took off and somehow I felt that it did not matter anymore how often or how soon I come back. Of course everyone else is still there, and I love and miss them equally. But something inside has turned off the urge to come back. Come back to whom? For what?

I had to overnight in Accra to connect to Freetown, and I took the chance to visit with Mr. Amoako. For the first time, I spoke with someone who knew you well and with whom I had to acknowledge your departure. It was strange. "I heard about Mom," he said, referring to you. "Yes, it's been hard on all of us," I replied. I was not sure I would keep my composure; I felt my throat knotting up. Then, thank God, he asked about Enaniye: "How is your mother?" "She is fine," I replied and then added, "She is having a hard time with Almazesha being gone." In the name of Enaniye, what I was really telling him was that I was having a hard time with you being gone. Anyway, I am still not managing to talk about you without my tears filling up.

Bye,
M

March 27, 2010

Emaye,

Today marks six months since you left.

Matthias and I arrived in Brussels with the girls.

We had lunch with Enaniye and Boubiye and Fofi. I feel that things have changed.

Last year about this time, I was packing to come and see you with the girls. Emaye, you would be proud to see them now. They have grown.

We are on our way now to travel to Canada to see Boubiye's son, Dominic, and his family.

I will write later,
M

April 3, 2010

Emaye,

I have been up since about 4:00am from jet lag.
There is a nine-hour time difference here in Port
Alberni, British Columbia, so we have been getting up
very early.

For the past days I have meant to write to you, but I
did not manage to take the time to write—maybe I
was even trying to avoid writing. Well, I think I was
possibly avoiding writing because I realized that at
this time last year we were together. At this time last
year, I had spent the night in your room with the
girls. Tomorrow will mark a year to the day since we
last looked into each other's eyes. How did a year go
by? And you know, at times, I still have the instinct
to pick up my cell to call you. There are days I wake
up after seeing you in my dreams and for a moment I
can't really tell whether it was a dream or whether it
was real, except the last two nights.

The last two nights I was conscious that as I slept I
was sunken in extreme sadness. I was dreaming of you
but I was also conscious that it was just a dream,
maybe a reflection of my subconscious thoughts.
They were strange dreams. The day before yesterday,
the dream was about something where you were on
trial and you were being acquitted by the people but
still held under accusation, in captivity. You were
very calm throughout the trial, and in fact, it was as if
you knew how things would unfold. The serenity you
had was absolute. I tried to help during the trial, but
later realized it was better to just witness it all and
stay still. At one level I knew I would lose you
through this trial, and that made me deeply sad. On

another level, I felt as though nothing could ever take you away from me and that our bond is timeless. Although it was hard, I realized that I had to surrender to what was happening. Inside my heart, I intuitively knew this was all about how things were meant to be. I had to learn to respect that and find my peace in this truth of destiny, or fatality of life, for lack of a better word. Isn't it strange how there is strength and peace in the process of surrender, yet at the same time, that doesn't necessarily take away the sting of sorrow.

Last night the dream was slightly different: It was just you and I in a discussion. We were somewhere in a valley, near a creek. You looked very young, wearing a *netela* with black *tilet*[47] but there was no funeral or loss I could sense. I guess you had the *netela* because it might have been time for mourning in general, similar to the times of the Red Terror[48] back in the late 1970s. We sat side by side. I had just come to see you as I usually do. You were not busy when I came; you were just sitting there in contemplation. I brought you the manuscript of this very book I am writing and you glanced through the pages. You held the manuscript with your left hand and fluttered the pages with pressure from your right thumb on the edges of the document. Once in a while, you stopped the fluttering to look more closely at one page or

---

[47] The *netela* is the traditional cotton shawl for women; *tilet* is the name given to the embroidered edges each *netela* has. There are thousands of designs and colors, and in times of mourning, women wear *netelas* with black *tilet*, usually with the *tilet* right on top of their heads.

[48] The Red Terror was a violent campaign that took place in Ethiopia under the rule of the Communist Regime to get rid of anti-revolutionary individuals and any kind of opposition.

another. You were reading without glasses. Then you looked up and told me that you would go through it more thoroughly.

I was hoping to continue writing until a time when I felt I had said it all to you. With this dream and with the awareness that the past few days mark the anniversary of the time I last kissed your hands, I am wondering if it is a sign to finally accept that it is time to stop writing.

I am not sure I want to stop writing—I am afraid that if I stop writing, I will lose this peculiar connection with you that the writing has allowed me. So far, I have been able to go on with my life and deal with your loss because now and again I come to this laptop to type away the stories, the thoughts, and the conversations that flow in my heart. I have an audience with you this way, and I don't feel so alone when I write you.

There are days when I am afraid of what life will be without you around. I am afraid that I have no one to take my fears, insecurities, and anxieties to. I am afraid that there will not be anyone to whom I can go to for council, guidance, and love. The trouble is that you provided so much light, not only in my life but in all of our lives. Now that you are not physically here with us, I have to adjust to continue receiving your light even though you are not present in the way that I would like.

So many things have happened since you left. One of the bigger changes is that I am now conscious of how important it is to get up and get going with life, as death takes away our loved ones. I say this because even though I am sad beyond words, I am thinking that had I been the one who left, I would want my children and my family not to mourn so long. I would want to know that my daughters could, despite my death, continue to live fully. I would want to know that, despite my departure, they continue to live well, with safety and security, and with the principles I have tried to impart to them. That's what I would want, so I am convinced that it is also what you would want. I think I am right and that you agree, but here's the thing: as much as I have this realization, the step between knowing something and actually doing it seems like a giant leap. I am still stuck in the "knowing" space and have not yet reached the space where I can do and "*be*" as I know.

Another new aspect of my life is that since you have gone, I have found peace with knowing that all life ends at some point in the physical world, but continues in spirit. What is born must die and what dies continues to live in spirit, in another field of existence. I was never really afraid to die, yet I had never really come to terms with it either. Now, I have come to terms with death. I never thought that I would see the day where I would have to live without you. Every day of my life for over four decades, you were present—how could I possibly conceive of my life without your presence?

The other day, I realized that the age difference between you and me is the same as the age difference between Rosi and me, but I am Rosi's mother and you are my grandmother. I see Rosi and Leoni now and I just sit in silence as I think of how you were my exact age when Fofi, Samson, and I emerged into this life. It blows my mind.

I also look at Rosi who is now ten and Leoni who is

now eight years old, and I can't imagine how you were only nine when you married. I can't imagine Rosi and Leoni in marriage right now. How could anyone think of giving girls of such age in marriage? I know that it happens in many parts of the world and that it still happens today, yet I can't imagine the impact this has on the life of the girl given away. At least we were lucky that you married Ababi, but how many are so lucky as to be matched with a caring husband? And with all this, how did you ever manage to do all the things you did in your life and build such a community around you?

It's Easter tomorrow; this year the Orthodox Easter is at the same time as the Catholic Easter. It's the first year I will not call you to wish you Happy Easter—I will just have to wish you Happy Easter in my heart and know that you will be in good hands celebrating Easter. I miss you.

I hear Dominic's babies waking up. Olivia is the oldest mouse, and she just came up from her room. I am going to play with her.

I will write you tomorrow.

I love you always,
M

April 9, 2010

Emaye,

I woke up in Whistler, BC this morning. We drove up last night from Dominic's place and will be here until the middle of next week, and then head back home to Freetown.

The mountains are spectacular. Snow is all over and of course I am freezing, but it's beautiful. Do you remember Kim, my friend from Freetown? Well, she is here and through her recommendation we booked a very cozy apartment built on the hills. It is like a duplex—but imagine a duplex with four levels. Rosi and Leoni are so happy there, jumping up and down the steps. Gavin and Olivia are not here yet; Dominic and Michelle, his wife, decided it was better for them to come with Michelle on Saturday. This way, we hope they can enjoy the stay without making it too stressful to get used to a new place.

When we checked in to the apartment and received all the explanations of the facilities, we were told that all calls are free, including local, domestic, and international. I didn't not believe it at first, because I don't know how that can be, but it seems true. For a moment I thought of calling you. As usual, it has not really sunk into my head, for real, that I can never call you again. Anyway, since there is a time difference of 9-10 hours with anyone I would call on my side of the world, I doubt that I will use this facility much. Maybe I will call Laïbet anyway and talk to Solomon or Koki. I will call Enaniye for sure and let her know how we are doing.

I didn't want to write about all this—in fact, I wanted

to tell you about my dream. I saw you in my dream last night and we spoke a bit. It was a ceremony, like a farewell for you. You were there as well, sitting on the high chair sharing in the various chanting, prayers, and praise songs. I have no idea where the place was, but it looked like some sort of official residence or large church structure. It was not a contemporary structure, however; it looked like an ancient Greek or Egyptian temple. There were so many priests draped in white *gabi* sitting or leaning on their sticks, listening to the chants at times, and at times chanting along. It seemed that the people, meaning us, were seated somewhere else, close but not too close. We could see the whole ceremony well. We could see you sitting in your chair as well. You looked very much at peace, taken by the chants. You were wearing the house robe you wore back in the 1970s when you went for surgery in Israel, that one with the brownish background and circles or bubble-looking designs all over. Your hair was also very different. I had never seen you with hair styled that way, except maybe in that one picture taken when you must have been fourteen or fifteen. It was parted at three quarters, and each part was pulled up toward the back; it looked like a split chignon. And then what I noticed was the perfectly round double pearls you wore as earrings. Even though the hair, the house robe, and the times did not belong to the same time (era), somehow it all made sense together.

I remember sitting crunched up by the gate of this church or residence and looking from afar at all the things that were going on. I was feeling torn up inside because I knew that you would depart at the end of this session and I did not feel ready for that. I did not feel ready for you to leave and for me to live without you. I also knew that all I could do was watch. I could not interrupt this ceremony—no one was allowed to interrupt it. It was like a blessing, an honor, to have this ceremony. It was a sacred send-off, and I knew from the look on your face you would not tolerate any interference.

At one point you had to move from your chair to another place within the same premises, and I took the occasion to jump up and follow you and ask you to at least introduce me to one of the priests so I could come and spend time with them when you would no longer be there. You were walking so fast, I had to almost run to catch up with you. I knew you heard me and then you turned and said, "*Koï, ande ehet aloo* [Wait a second, there is one nun]," and with these words you called on a nun. She was sitting along with many, many nuns, and as she heard your voice, she got up and rushed to us; the others followed as well. There were also clay figurines (pots, I thought at first) and they too morphed into women and rushed to us. In no time at all, I was surrounded by what seemed a legion of women, half were nuns and the other half seemed to be these clay pots turned into women. You looked at me, prompting me to speak up and explain to the women what I wanted. I looked at them and tried to say something but nothing came out. I was overwhelmed by their presence. I was overwhelmed by the love they had for you. I was overwhelmed by what you had done to serve them throughout your lifetime. I was overwhelmed by the fact that I knew this would be the last time I would speak to them in your presence, and that next time I would be there alone with them. I was just so overwhelmed by everything. I fell on my knees and became one with the ground. I tried to speak but nothing came out. All I felt was this sense of deep surrender and I wept, for what seemed an eternity. I wept in silence. I wept and wept and everything seemed to stop. I wept in my dream, and I woke up weeping.

Where does all this come from?

Yesterday as we drove up, Matthias was in one car with Rosi and Leoni and I drove with Dominic. It was a good opportunity to talk. We talked about work, about life, about our childhoods. In the process I was telling him so much about life in Laïbet. I was telling him about the times I spent with you, with Ababi, and with everyone at Laïbet. My biggest concern was that now that you are gone, I am afraid that everyone will be going their own way. Will we find the wisdom, patience, and tolerance to remain connected? I will do the best I can.

I keep thinking of our culture and how our culture stifles women. You know, Emaye, it's such a miracle for me to have Dominic and be able to see him with his little family. What a gift it is to have a brother and nieces and nephews. To think that his mother could have also opted to end the pregnancy, and if she had done that, I would not have a brother. Emaye, I regret my abortion, you know. I wish I had had the courage to come to you then.

Do you remember how around the late 1980s there were a number of babies born in our family? That is the time I would also have had the child I conceived. I watched from far as the new parents played with their newborns, and I kept my own story in my heart. Some of the new parents allowed me to play with their babies, and others kept quite a distance. It's okay. I have grown since. I have had a chance to have two of my own daughters, so although I regret this unborn child of mine, I also accept that it's just part of life.

I have to go now. Everyone is awake and is preparing for a day on the slopes—you know, I am not so bad now on skis. I know that if you were here, you would tease me and ask me, what would I have to lose if I just sat at home instead of risking breaking my neck at this age....Well, I just hope I still manage to fly back home without anything broken.

M

April 19, 2010

Emaye,

It seems that only the sparrows in the trees and I are up at this time, here in Brussels. The house is still very quiet and everyone is sleeping.

We had planned to travel on to Freetown last Thursday straight from Vancouver, but in Frankfurt we learned that our flight to Brussels had been canceled. It took me a while to find out exactly what had happened—most flights were being canceled due to the volcano eruption in Iceland. Just that day, close to 7,000 flights were canceled in Europe and most airports closed. We were lucky to be stranded in Frankfurt because we could just go home to Oma and Opa until we sorted out our way home. Eventually, we ended up taking the train to Brussels over the weekend, and hopefully this morning we will be taking our flight on to Freetown. We heard on the news that Zaventem Airport might open as of 8:00am today, but there is still no guarantee. In any case, I have told the girls that we will have to head to the airport early on and try our chances. If there is a flight, we will be going home. If not, well, we might stay in Brussels a few more days.

It's been good to be here for a couple of days. The girls were happy to be with Enaniye and Boubiye and Fofi; I was also happy to spend time here. I told Enaniye about the dream I had about you. Isn't it strange that I still could not describe the dream without tears falling? She asked me if the dream was about a farewell between you and me. I know deep inside that the dream may have been a farewell, but I could not say it or accept it, so I just told Enaniye that maybe the dream reflected the work you have done in your lifetime and how we might have to follow in your footsteps and continue your work. Maybe it's about finding a way to serve the larger community back home. Maybe the dream is about serving the destitute and the poor, the meek, and those who have given their lives to God.

Emaye, were you trying to say goodbye? I am not sure there could be a goodbye; or rather, I prefer to know that there is no goodbye. Since you left, I find that I am so much more religious. I long for more of our rituals, for tradition, and I have so many pictures of the Virgin Mary around my home. Given my lack of affection for her earlier, maybe as a reaction to how much everyone worshipped her and how much I could not relate to her, now you would be surprised to know that I even pray to her. I can relate to her—I find comfort in her. I can see how she can be and is the ultimate Mother of all.

We went to the shops near the Gare du Midi this afternoon to pick up a few things for Yeshiye. I was tempted to buy her a black sweater, something she could wear when she comes home this summer. I know she will be mourning you, and I wanted her to have a nice sweater suited for the moment. Then, I thought, don't buy a black sweater, so instead I bought her a beige one and also another taupe one. I think she will like both sweaters and they will look good on her. I am concerned about how she will manage to deal with your loss. She was so far away when it happened.

Did I tell you that I am hoping to bring Rosi and Leoni for some time in June? Yes, I want to come and stay at Laïbet with them. I want them to come and know that even though you are gone, you are still with us in spirit. Today, I was telling Enaniye about these plans and I also told her that once I visit this June, it will be a while until I come again. To my surprise, Enaniye said to me, "You said those same exact words to me in a dream." She was sad that I said that, but you know, Emaye, I just don't feel the same about coming home anymore. Despite the fact that everyone else is still there, something inside of me has lost the light. I have lost all interest. I feel so ordinary. I have lost the sense of being special to someone; I guess since you are not there anymore, I just don't feel it anymore. I remember that coming home was special when you were there. I could not wait for the plane to land to turn on my phone and call you. I could not wait to come and sit with you to tell you all the stories I had brought back. I wanted to unpack it all, slowly, seeing your reactions and your laughter as I told you the jokes and other funny things I had collected just for the pleasure of seeing you laugh.

Do I still have a country? Or was my sense of country and identity related to you? I think it's the latter, and I will have to make immense effort to remain connected.

Emaye, Emayiye, I miss you so much. Will my tears ever dry? Or is this forever? I feel old in my bones, like I have lived this life two times over. I feel that now I have to live for my daughters and all the children, for the next generation—it's not really about us anymore. I guess we have lived, played, and now it's time to "step up to the plate" as Fofi would say and take on our responsibilities to keep the story going, to keep the community going, and to keep the memories alive.

The strange thing is that I search for you everywhere: in pictures, in stories, in conversations. And no matter where I look, I only find your footprints and spiritual presence. If not for pictures, I think I would have a hard time believing that we had the life we had together. Did it even happen, I wonder sometimes?

Today, Enaniye said she wished she had shown you the pictures of the house she just built on the land you encouraged her to buy many years back. She had come to Addis with the picture, but when I asked if she had the chance to show you, she shook her head with regret. Well, I told her that I am sure you have seen the house in some other way. It's a beautiful house she built in Kraieneem—you would be very proud. How many have you built between Enaniye and you? You two should have been architects or real estate developers.

I will tell you more about my trip to Canada once I reach home. Now, I have to go get ready for the airport.

I love you,
M

May 2, 2010

Emaye,

I have meant to write to you since the last time I wrote; but I did not manage it. I keep on thinking about the last dream I had. Last night I worked until about 1:00am and I have now been up since 4:00am; I have not slept much. I had told our caretaker here in Freetown to turn off the generator when I went to bed last night, but then at 4:00am he called me, waking me up from the few hours of sleep I was trying to clock in. "Should I turn off the machine?" he asked. I don't know which part of the message he didn't understand when I called him before I went to bed asking him to turn the machine off. I guess he must have fallen back asleep, and I was so exhausted that I fell asleep right way. In any case, now I am up and I can't sleep. There is no light today, so I decided to come and write to you by candlelight.

Emaye, I keep thinking that the dream might have been your way to say goodbye and farewell—well, the dream was not too bad. It made me realize that you are in a better place now. It made me realize that you are honored where you are now, even more than you were among us. It made me realize that a soul like yours may not be among us very often, and that you may have possibly known that your life on this earth was just a mission and that you had to return to the place from which you came.

Each time I see Rosi and Leoni, now 10 and 8 years old, I can't believe that you were about their age when you started a family—a life that so many of us don't even start at thirty. Yesterday it was Saturday, and I worked all day in my little office. I am on this deadline for my dissertation, but as much as I tried to focus and work, Rosi and Leoni kept on coming in and out of my office asking for something or to sit or to take a nap. Rosi started to clean my office; she came in with two brooms and started moving things around. It disturbed me so much. But then, before getting all agitated, I thought I should just stop what I am doing and enjoy them. Rosi, who now thinks she is a big girl, fussed around the office sweeping and cleaning. Leoni, who can't help but follow the lead of Rosi and who also thinks she is a big girl, was sitting next to me with her journal, complaining that she could not focus and hence should not have to do her homework. And I was there thinking how incredible it is that around their age, you were made to take responsibility and start a family.

Of course, we benefited all from your starting out so young. And I, of all people, had the rare luxury of having such a young grandmother. Do you know how much you have touched my life? As I told you earlier, the age difference between you and me is the same age difference as that between me and Rosi. Although I can't say that I have the same level of patience and tolerance as you, I can understand how our relationship grew so close. Can you imagine if I was a grandmother right now? Of course I would be all over my grandchild.

I suppose I miss you so much because I miss our relationship. I miss your presence. I miss calling you and talking about work, business, life, politics, and whatever else—I just miss you and miss our conversations. I know that we will each have to go one day, and I am grateful for the years I had you next to me. But even though I am grateful and even though I recognize that all life ends at some point, I just can't come to accept that I will have to live without you for the rest of my life. Each day that passes, the day I last saw you gets further away. Each day, I rely more and more on pictures to recall and grasp what we lived together. And each day, I am a little afraid that I am losing you a little more.

When we were in Brussels just a few weeks ago, Enaniye made us some *shiro*.[49] It tasted so good, and then she told me what she had used to make it: the *shiro* was based on a *kulet*[50] made in Laïbet and prepared for *Doro Alicha*.[51] Enaniye told me that you had ordered that it be prepared for Enaniye to take to Brussels. As much as I enjoyed every bite, I have to admit that I was also trying to linger over each bite as if I could reach the moments and times when you were still with us.

Oh well, I find that I spend a lot of time just gazing and I catch myself lost in thought more often than not. I feel like I am waiting for someone who will not come home again. I know we will be together again someday—I know that. And until we meet again, I have to fulfill my own responsibilities, raise my children, do my work, and then maybe the time might come. I often pray that God gives me enough days to ensure that I see my children through; at the same time, I can't wait to be together again in eternity.

I am so happy to write to you. It has helped me live through my grief and not feel so abandoned. Through

---

[49] *Shiro* is an Ethiopian stew made with an onion base, chickpea powder, and spices.

[50] *Kulet* is the name given to the sautéed onion base that is the foundation of most Ethiopian dishes.

[51] *Doro Alicha* is a mild stew made of onions and chicken. It is a dish prepared for festivities and special occasions.

these letters, I have been able to work through many of the things that used to put lumps in my throat. I feel stronger now. I feel I can deal with what's ahead. I know that missing you will never stop, and that as life goes on, many more people might be added to the "I miss you" list until my turn comes.

I guess this might be one of the aspects of life that makes us grown-ups. When we no longer have our parents in our lives, it's like we are no longer children and we have to rise up to take up our role as "grown-ups" now, for the sake of the younger members of the family. Since you left, my heart has changed. I have changed. Enaniye says she feels twenty years older, and I am the same. I feel much older, much more aware of my responsibilities within my little family as well as within our community and possibly our country.

You were my country—without you, I don't feel connected to Ethiopia. I am always happy to visit, but I have lost the core attachment. There is no longer this urge I used to have to run to Laïbet to come and tell you what I had done or what I was about to do. Of course, everyone else is still there, I know. But, Emaye, there is a hole in my soul, like a big chunk has been cut out of me. I am not sad, you know. Don't worry, I am not sad; I just miss being with you and I feel extremely lonely. I find comfort in the Virgin Mary, and I have her icons all over the house and all over my office. It's funny how I didn't care too much about her before but now, my heart melts when I see her.

Be well, Emaye. I miss you, M

P.S. I have to finish doing the last revisions on my dissertation and submit it by Tuesday. Pray for me.

May 8, 2010

> When you were here, I had a ground to stand on.
> When you were here, I had a home to go to.
> I had someone who called to check if I ate that
>   day.
> Someone to ask me if I slept well or if my cold is
>   better.

Emaye, I miss you.

I don't know if most people miss their mother this much, and it doesn't really matter what most people do. I am okay in feeling how I feel.

There are days that I am really good, when I remember you with joy and happiness, and tell your jokes, and tell my friends the things we used to do together. But there are also days when just thinking of you fills my eyes with tears. Like today, for example, I just really miss you.

Yesterday, I went to the main office of the National Power Authority here in Freetown. A few days ago, their field workers came and cut our power line. I had tried to explain to them that I had been travelling and just returned, that I was in a meeting all day, and that I would pay first thing in the morning. But, Emaye, you should have seen the man or should I say "boy" that they sent. He was so rude—a true *neftam*.[52] I told him that I would pay for their transportation to come and cut our line if the bill was not paid the next day. But I guess the cost of a taxi was not good enough for him, so he and his mate talked to me like merchants

---

[52] Referring to someone with a runny nose, *neftam* is a local insult.

looking away from a poor buyer. They pissed me off so much that I told them they should go and cut whatever they want, but I also warned them that I would not remain dormant like a doormat for their rude behavior.

The next day, I sent my caretaker, Edward—you know, the one I hired after Mousa left. I told him to go and get me the number of the highest possible official in NPA because I had to report my case. He got me the number of the commercial director, and I spoke with the man on the phone and explained my case. I asked to come and see him, and he told me he was in the office each day at 7:00am. "Thank you, sir. I will see you tomorrow at 7:30am," I said. "It's 'Reverend,'" he replied. "Thank you, Reverend," I said. I wasn't sure if he was a real reverend or one of those who wear snake-leather shoes, like the one at that church up on Spur Road.

In any case, I went the next day and I was in his office at 7:30am. I had parked with hassles, albeit the hassles of the street boys who insist on directing traffic. Eventually I made it to his office and the minute I saw him, I calmed down. This was truly a man of God—anyone could see that by his demeanor. Anyway, for about an hour I explained to him how you raised us: how no matter what, respect, love, compassion, and empathy come first. I was so upset that I talked to him. Anyway, in the end he helped me settle my issue, and the same knucklehead who cut my line was sent back to reconnect us. Oh, the sweet savor of justice! I tell you, my tummy drank butter that day. You would have been proud.

I think of you this morning, because I would have so loved to call you to tell you about this. I feel very lonely without you. Even though I have my little family, my greater family, and my friends, I miss you nonetheless. Will this ever go away? I don't think so.

I have to go now.

I love you,
M

May 10, 2010

Emaye,

Emayiye, today I sent out the final version of my dissertation. For all the times you asked me how far along I was in the process, well Emaye, I think I am through now. I know that wherever you are you can hear me, "I am through Emaye. I finished!"

Words are not enough to tell you how much my world has changed since you left. How did you just slip by without me knowing? For all the dreams I used to have and called you to interpret, this time I failed to interpret the message. I had dreamed of your departure—I just never thought that this time would be for real. I thought I was just having a nightmare about the day you would not be with us anymore, because the dream was not a nightmare at all. It was just you, Gashe Mulugeta, and I having a conversation. Little did I know that he had come to pick you up and take you to the land where all our forefathers await us.

I have gone on with life now. Each day, I do my routine of dressing the kids, serving breakfast, seeing them off, doing my work, and then eventually picking them up from school like you used to pick us up. And then we have our *mekeses* (snack) and do homework. By the time we complete the homework, it's night time and we shower, prepare clothes for the next day, prepare school bags, and I serve dinner. But as I go through my routine, in the background of my soul there is a hole—some sort of hollow space that emerged the day you left. It wasn't entirely clear to me when I heard the news that you had passed, but in the days and months following, this hollow space took on more and more definition. It is unavoidable for me, and I know it well and find refuge in it, mostly, and sorrow.

Just now, I was wondering if it is the contrast between the joys we've had and the sorrow that we feel that brings the wrinkles on our face—the traces of life. How different when you compare the faces of grown-ups or the bereaved with the faces of new babes who only know freedom and carefree living.

I spoke with Enaniye today, and she is still missing you very much. She says your loss has aged her by at least twenty years, and I can understand. I suppose you and she were not really like daughter and mother, but more like sisters. Me, well—I wonder when the day will come that I will not swell with tears when I think of you.

Did I tell you I am planning to go to Laïbet this June? I will be going with Rosi and Leoni. I want them to realize what happened and know that you might not be there in person to welcome them. Maybe they can realize that although you have left us in this gross realm of existence, you will always remain with us in spirit. I know it's not enough—how can you kiss a spirit, let alone hug or share a meal together? I feel so old. I feel that our life together is so far away, something like a fairy tale. There are times I wonder whether you really existed or not, whether I am imagining the years we spent together. I wonder. I stand there gazing and learn to snap out of my daydreams, and then I land back on earth and look at your picture that I stuck on the wall facing my desk. At times, I light a candle, and as long as the candle burns the flame brings me close to you.

You know, I have been so good since you left. You have no idea—I have been so so darn good. It's like I am more accountable to you and the way you have raised us all. It's like everything I do must be up to the standards that you established for me and all of us.

Most of all, I miss talking to you. Your number is still on my cell, and at times I am tempted to make it ring but then, I don't. I just let it be. It would kill me if it rang and someone else answered.

How lucky I am for the years I spent with you. My grandchild, if I ever have one, will not have as much time with me as I have had with you. By the time I have a first grandchild, it's very likely that I would be in my late sixties or seventies, but then, what a pity that I will not be able to know this child as an adult— as you have known me.

Well, let me not exasperate you with complaints. Here's something new: Emaye, I have decided that I will join the political party you established. We will have to change the name; it cannot be called All Amhara People Party. I know that you fought against this name and that you were forced to use it by the powers that be. If I ever get involved, we will have to call it One Ethiopia or Unity or the Liberal Democrat Party.

I love you, always,
M

May 17, 2010

Emaye,

I had already turned off my laptop to go to sleep, and then I took time to unwind on the balcony, the one off of my bedroom. The girls are sleeping with me tonight and have been for a week now, since Matthias is traveling. I watched them sleep, then went out on the balcony to just unwind before going to bed. I like to sit there and look out at the city. Freetown is very pretty; its hills and shoreline can be seen from many places and often from unexpected vantage points. For me, sitting on this balcony in the night is a great way to just contemplate what happened in the day, what happens tomorrow, and what happened/happens through time. My thoughts just go on a wild ride on this balcony, mixing events, times, people, and scents and senses of times long gone. I am exhausted, but as I sat there I thought of you, and in parallel I thought of how my life unfolded. Many things were unpredictable, but one thing that I realize happened much in line with what you have said: the story of men, in general, in my life.

You know, right after grad school, I thought that I had to be dating Ethiopian men. I don't know why I thought that. I didn't know many who were not related to us, so the likelihood of me finding an Ethiopian man to date was very low. But I guess once you have an idea in your head, it has a way of manifesting. Gosh, Emaye, it was a roller coaster trip. These guys, they're a trip.

You remember how you told me that I married someone who can bear with me, and that if I had married an Ethiopian man he would have sent me back to you, possibly even before the *Meles* on Tuesday. Well, you were right on the money there. I think back on the few relationships I had, or rather the few dates I had, and it was one disaster after another. Something just did not add up. I think it can't be the men; it must be me. Maybe I am just too much of a radical or free spirit; maybe I am too much outside the system—but whatever it is, it did not work out. Far from that: It just was like a war zone.

The main problem was that these guys don't express themselves. I don't get it. They hardly ever say "I love you," much less utter a compliment. In fact, they can't even say how much they enjoy or do not enjoy a woman's company. Incredible! I have never, ever seen such things. Well, there are a few men I thought were okay, but either they were related to me or they were already with someone else. All the ones I found to be available, were just very difficult characters.

Once I was dating this guy whom everyone was insisting I marry. Good God, well, that would have been a short marriage. I am sure we would have been divorced within a year or less. He was just such an arrogant, self-worshiping, egoistic fool. He thought he was the next best thing since peanut butter and jelly sandwiches. And he might have been to a certain extent, save for his utter inability to say something nice or to say something genuine.

The entire few months that we dated, he was just pretending to be Mr. Tough Intellectual Guy. Things did not go down well. At the beginning, I guess because he may have also been told that he should marry me, he was sending me cards and flowers, making calls, and the whole shebang. He was calling me a lot, and then he visited often as well. He did not live in the same country, so this started out as a long-distance relationship from the get go. This behavior lasted for a few months. Then, one time he came to visit, he invited me for dinner, insisting that we go to a piano bar somewhere out in the suburbs of Washington, DC. Of course, I could see him coming and knew very well what he was heading for. I didn't say anything and went along with it.

Eventually we drove back to town, and although I am geographically challenged, I knew that he was not driving me back to my apartment but driving to his hotel. So, on the way, I asked him to stop at a drug store and buy condoms. Emaye, you have no idea—it is as if I had said the most sinful thing. He looked so shocked. I don't know why, because it was obvious that the evening was going to end that way. He parked the car at the 7/11 and looked at me with a face I will never forget. The color on his face had disappeared—would you understand if I tell you he became pale? He said, "*Anchi...Atafrim*? [You...are you not ashamed of yourself?]" I did not understand why I should be. I told him that my health was important to me and until we both got tested and decided on a commitment, nothing was happening with me without protection. He was caught in a contradiction: On the one hand, I think he could not deny what he was aiming for that night; and on the other hand, he wanted to pretend that he had nothing in mind. But then, here's the catch—he had already done so much to prepare for the evening launch that at this point it would be his loss if he continued to pretend that he had nothing in mind. It was almost funny to see hypocrisy in action.

Well, finally the whole ordeal ended with him sighing in surrender, and he opened the car door and stepped out into the store. That's when I called him and told him to get the Life Style ones and not the Trojan, because the other ones are better. He almost fell down when I said that and came right back in to sit down. "*Anchi Balege* [You mannerless/rude person]," he said to me. I was shocked. "How does recommending the better product make me a *Balege*?" I asked. He had no answer.

So, this is how this relationship started. It was certainly short lived. He visited me several times after that, then a few months later he called to say he was coming for Christmas. I was happy. I think that in the process, I had started to fall for him in a way. I think I just convinced myself that it would be best for everyone (me, him, and our families) if we could tie the knot. Oh, but that wasn't going to be the case. When he called to tell me that he was coming for Christmas, I told him that I looked forward to it and couldn't wait. That's when he said, "I am not just coming for you; I have to see my sisters." Okay, I decided, fine. Just on the spot, I knew this was not going to go anywhere. I think because he knew I was starting to like him, he had drawn back. He didn't send cards anymore, and there were no more flowers or anything like that. I could see that I was starting to wait for his calls and I had started to literally be happy when he emerged, spending the rest of my time waiting for him. I hate when that happens—I just can't stand it. You know, once you fall for someone, it's hard to get back your senses. It's important to regain consciousness as soon as possible. So, I decided the relationship had to end; I wasn't going to be with a man who was not straightforward or wanted to play mind games.

But before I ended it, I thought I needed to take him

on a ride. And that's what I did. He finally showed up at Christmas and I played my role of the potential excited fiancée being visited by the one and only eligible bachelor in our little Ethiopian community. He didn't notice any changes. I played along. On the second or third time we met, we went for dinner. I drove. I had picked him up from his holy sisters and our dinner went on without incidents. Then, before I dropped him off, I felt the time was right to break off the relationship.

He was about to get out of the car when I called him back. "I have something I need to share with you," I said. He nodded, indicating that he was listening. I looked down at my feet, played with the steering wheel, and finally lit a cigarette and told him: "There's someone else." Again, the same shocked face, like the one he had when I asked him to stop and buy condoms. I did not give him time to reply or ask questions. He just looked shocked, as if no one could compare to him. Can you believe this guy? I wish I could have the same kind of utter confidence. Where do these fools get this belief that they are the best thing on this Earth? He could not see how there could be someone else, and he seemed insulted.

"She is really beautiful," I continued. Well, well—you thought you had seen a shocked face before, you hadn't ever seen one until you saw his face then. "What did you say?" he asked. So, I repeated: "SHE IS REALLY BEAUTIFUL." Stuttering a bit, he asked, "What do you mean, *she*?" "We met at work. I am in love with her and I can't live without her," I replied. There was a deadening silence in the car and he seemed lost for arguments.

Emaye, that's when all hell broke loose. There was

such confusion on his part—I have never seen someone with such a confused look. He was smiling, then not. He wanted to ask questions but no words came out of his mouth; it was as if there was a perverted pleasure in wanting to know more. At one point, he started laughing nervously. Meanwhile I smoked my cigarette with the desolate look of someone caught in a love triangle. As soon as I stubbed out the cigarette, I started the car again and told him that I had to go now and I would call him later. Yeah, right. I never called again nor did I take his calls.

Eventually, he returned to his duty station abroad. I was not done with him, though—there was still the final stroke to be imparted. So, I called him one day, when I knew it was the middle of the night for him (it was a weekday). "Did I wake you?" I asked. "No, no," he denied even though I knew from the sound of his voice that I had woken him from deep sleep. "Good, I am glad you were up," I said. "I wanted to tell you that I am going back home soon. I promise to go up country and find a very nice girl who I will personally train to cook your favorite food, fetch your shoes when you come from work, make parties for your friends, be quiet when you watch TV, and possibly be good in bed too." He seemed a bit confused once more about what I had said. So, I clarified: "I mean, I will find you a good wife, one who will suit your needs. As for me, it's not going to work, so please don't ever call me again. I will call you once I have found the girl and trained her to cater to you. Goodnight, you can go back to sleep now. Sweet dreams." That's how it ended.

He tried to contact me again, but I did not answer. I believe he thinks I am crazy or possibly a lunatic, but

I don't care. I just can't stand men who behave like such hypocrite pigs. Can you even imagine my life, if I had married this fellow? Got out of that one, I tell you. I don't regret anything in this relationship; in fact, it taught me a lot.

In relationships, most of the time there is the one who is the player and the one who is played—rare are the relationships where there is equitable exchange. For me, I decided through this relationship that if there was going to be play, not only was I not going to be the one played, but I would make sure that I invented the game. How many times do we have to cry ourselves to sleep or wait for these fools to call us? How many times do we have to fit ourselves to all sorts of images, sizes, and behaviors just to please these fools, just hoping that they find us somewhat attractive? We, ourselves, are the ones who have to know that we are attractive as we are, as God created us. It is not for a man to tell me whether I am beautiful or not. It is not for a man to tell me whether the sun shines or not—it's up to me to make those realities happen.

I have been in too many relationships where I had to go the extra mile to make it work while they just sat back and enjoyed. From this one guy on, I changed completely. I said "no" to such jerks, and if anyone was going to be jerked around, it wasn't going to be me. Okay, I know you think that what I did was not graceful. I know it wasn't, and on a good day, I would not do that. But he upset me so much that I couldn't just let it go—I had to get in a few points for my sanity. Now, I tell you this story as a story; I am not even upset by it anymore. I have seen him many times after that weddings or receptions, and we are cordial. I feel great that I wasn't one of his victims.

Maybe it's not fair to build such a bad image of men. Of course, not all men are like this just as not all women are angels. I think the moral of the story for me is that we have to be conscious about how we touch the lives of others around us. People who are consciously hurtful to others are selfish, I think. They are mean and it is beholden on us to defend our rights as much as we can. It is up to us to reclaim our humanity and our dignity. How can someone tell me that I am "*Balege*" because I asked him to buy condoms? What's that about? How can he pretend to be shocked when I tell him what brand to buy? It's this whole thing they have about marrying a virgin—for what, exactly? For their own egos, or is it because they can better manipulate a virgin?

I don't believe in this virgin business. I am not advocating for girls to be irresponsible, but I am advocating for a conscious "*prise de conscience* [awareness and consciousness]" for all that our feminine self entails and for us each to be respected for that. Right now, I feel that there is a serious bias in our communities: The burden is on women to please men. Men, on the other hand, don't have to even bother with being there for their women. It's not okay. If we have to be virgins, then both the man and the woman should be a virgin.

I know what you would have said: "*Ena min yehun new yemintiyew*? [And so, what are you suggesting be done?]" Well, I am not suggesting anything; I am just saying that women have to stand up for their rights and not allow men to jerk them around. I know you would laugh—don't laugh, this is serious.

I love you always,
Mimi

June 17, 2010

Emaye,

Good morning. Yesterday at breakfast I sat with Rosi and Leoni and for some reason, I decided to tell them that when we go to Ethiopia, next week, we will be staying in your room. I told them that even though they might not see you there anymore, they have to know you are always there with us. I told them you would be there in spirit and that you would be happy we are back in your bedroom sleeping on Ababi's bed. There was silence for a while, and then Rosi said, "*Mais c'est possible que quelqu'un pleure* [But it's possible that someone might cry]." Again silence, and Leoni's tears started rolling. Leoni has always been so deep; she can understand things that you would not expect her to understand at her age, only 8 years old. She wept almost in silence, but I could see that her tears were coming from another time—as if she knew you as an adult, as if she sensed your absence as much as any other adult who had grown to love you so much. Rosi is also very deep. The difference with Rosi is that she just keeps her emotions inside, whether joy or sorrow, being almost too shy to show them. You can imagine that with me and my tears at the tip of my nose, I also started crying.

I told the girls that it's good to cry—it's good to let it out because it allows us to heal and deal with the sorrow we feel. What I find crazy is that even though it's now been over eight months since you left, we are still each holding the grief right under our skin. It is the legacy you left and the fact that we will no longer have the chance to sit with you, ever again, that makes us so vulnerable; at least, for me, that's what it is.

I mean, does grief ever go away? When I think of you, my sadness is almost selfish. I am deeply sad because I miss you so much—I just miss you terribly. I thought that in time I would get over it, but it hasn't seemed to happen.

You remember that I told you when a friend of mine asked me where I was in the process of grief, and I was so stunned that he referred to it as a process? I realize now that he was right—there is certainly a process, and it seems to take mighty long for me. I carry a void inside my heart, one that had never existed before because it was the place you occupied in my life and in my heart. At the same time, because of this void, I find that I have transformed into a different person—not older in time or calendar years as we know them, but older in terms of eternity. I have leaped into another being, and each thing I do has a mark of you. Since you have left, you can't believe how proper I have been; it's almost as if I feel even more responsible to uphold what you raised me to be. There is a sense of discipline or responsibility (I can't find the right word) that has emerged and that aligns with how you conducted your own life and how you interacted with everyone.

One thing that I see in myself now is a new capacity to forgive. I was always amazed at how much you could forgive others, even in the worst cases. Do you remember when the manager you had hired for Abul Buna used the time that you were in prison to ask the merchants in Mercato for loans, by saying that the factory needed money and that it would all be paid back once you were released? And then, of course, he ran away with the money to the United States. It must have been at least $200,000 US, if not more. I asked you to let me find him and bring him to justice, and to this day, I remember what you said: "*Meches min ye derreg; messlot new. Gize yastemirwal. Egziabere mech yassalfal sayastemir* [Well, what can we do? He thought that, but time will teach him. God doesn't let things pass without teaching us what we need to learn.]" I was shocked by your answer then, but today I realize how the way you lived leaving everything to God while you continued to work hard—this was one of your key capacities and traits of wisdom. Of course, time will show us; of course, God sees it all and whatever happens that we may not understand will be explained in time as we gain the maturity to listen to the whispers of Spirit.

Forgiveness is important, but it's hard. I can't lie, most of my life if people wronged me, I preferred to get even or, better yet, to make my revenge—today, however, I can't say that anymore. I am not so much into revenge or evening the score, because it doesn't matter in the end. Our revenge or gift might be our capacity to reflect on what such situations have to teach us. Talking about forgiveness: A few days ago, I was in email contact with an old girlfriend, and to make a long story short, it seems that this friendship has ended. I might have hurt her in ways I did not mean to. The full story is too long to explain, but coming back to forgiveness, a major part of forgiveness is allowing a dialogue to bring clarity, understanding, and ground to move forward. It seems that when we are hurt, we confuse forgiveness with shutting people out—when you shut someone out, it doesn't mean you have forgiven them. At least in this case, I think this is what's happening; my girlfriend was not really willing to listen or give me a chance to explain things to her. She may have forgiven me or she may not—I don't know. Okay, I know that as much as grief is a process, possibly forgiveness also has a process. Maybe she was not ready to listen to my side of the story; maybe she is not interested. Whatever it may be, on my part I will try to understand her side and I just wish her well.

I think we learn forgiveness faster when we experience being on the other side of the equation and needing to be forgiven. It's so easy to sit behind our walls, refusing to see or hear the side of the one who might need to be forgiven. But, alas, when we find ourselves on the other side of the wall being shut out—then and often only then do we understand the humanity of forgiveness. We can only forgive when we can identify with the offender and are able to see that, given the circumstances, we too could have behaved or done what the so-called offender has done. I was a person with such a well organized archive of offenses and I never, ever forgave anyone; I have now learned to let go and forgive. I feel so much lighter. It's such a sense of freedom not to carry the load of baggage. And you know, at the end of the day, life is so short—what good is it to hold on to emotions that don't add to the quality of our lives? Is there ever a human being who can claim he or she has no fault?

When I am able to recognize my own faults or even recognize in the wrongdoings of others that, given the situation, I might have also compromised myself, then I am able to humble myself. A friend of mine once said: "Poverty compromises values." He may have been talking about financial poverty, but you know, this poverty can be at all levels. It can be poverty of the heart, poverty of emotions, lack of balance in our lives, and so on that might lead us to compromise our values.

I have to go now. I will come back tomorrow or later.

Did you I tell you we are finally leaving Freetown?
Yes, we are relocating to Beijing. It will be tough, as
usual, to settle somewhere new. But I have learned
the ropes of this moving business, so this time I
should be okay. In a few days, we will have a farewell
party, the last party we have here. I hope it will be
good.

I have to go now,
M

June 21, 2010

Emaye,

Tonight I am heading back home to Laïbet. First I will stop in Accra for about a week and then continue on to Addis. It's been hectic this past couple of weeks—just last Friday we had our farewell party here in Freetown. It was nice. You would have been happy about the way we organized it: Nothing short of what you have taught us. I must have had about twenty or so guys organized to take care of the drinks, food, and service, including a few guys to clean up as the party went on. You know what you would have been happy about? Well, guess what—I even had someone to just make sure that the bathroom was in order, meaning that he had to step in after each person went in to make sure that it was flushed, freshened, and sorted for the next person. What I missed the most was talking to you—do you remember how we talked each time I had some event at home? Well, on this Friday afternoon as we all rushed about preparing for the evening party, I thought of you. I even took out my cell to call you and then once again, I was stunned. I had forgotten that I could not call you.

Isn't it funny how I still don't understand that you are not here with us in person. The great thing is that I have been talking to you more than ever, because you are in my thoughts always. Each time I do something, I think of you. Hey, guess what? We caught three thieves at the party—the guards caught one and I busted two. It was just like back at Laïbet when people sometimes were busted red-handed. Well, the first thief was someone I knew who ran off with someone else's purse, but as he ran outside our gate, the purse opened and the money flew out. Complete drama. The security guards now had some reason to get all worked up and excited. Kawuta, my driver, called me on my cell. "Missis, you have to come," he said. "We have a situation." He came to get me from the party and I walked down to the gate with him, only to find the poor man busted with the purse. He was a cleaner whom I knew and wanted to invite. He is so young. He was in shock—he had about fifteen guys around him including security guards, a few bodyguards that had come with the guests, and a number of drivers who were standing about. Of course, there were also the passers-by who stopped just for the action. And so, as I walked down escorted by Kawuta and the other guys, I thought of you and the times that you would be summoned by the Shola neighborhood to come and provide your mediation.

My security guards were ready to call the police on this poor guy; one of them even whipped out his handcuffs and wanted to immobilize the guy. I understood something this evening—yes, there are thieves Emaye, but do they always mean bad? Are they always conscious of their actions, or is it that they are so desperate that they just rob people and run for their lives? I am not defending thieves, but I am seeing that they might act out of ignorance or desperation. At least, I know this was the case with this particular young man. I had to interfere and walk him away from the crowd. I took him to a corner of the garden and asked him why he did it. Why would he behave in this way, in this home of mine that I opened to him? He claimed that he just found the bag and he ran out of panic. I don't know. I can't really say whether he was being truthful or lying. In any case, I did not want to have the burden of a possibly innocent person on my conscious, so I negotiated hard with the security guys, the drivers, and the police to leave him alone. I think they would have all been very happy to beat him up. It's a strange feeling to witness this urge that people have for mob justice. The woman whose bag it was also got involved at some point. She was happy to find all her money and IDs; her camera and phone were missing, but it was too late to find them as the bag had already been passed from one man to the other. Anyway, I told the guy to go home. I told the guards to get back to their posts, and I told the drivers to get back to their respective cars. I went back to the party.

That's when I started moving around the cool boxes, and to my surprise, one of the backpacks the waiters had left under the table next to the cool boxes fell and I heard the sound of a bottle. It was suspicious. I proceeded to open the backpack, only to find it stuffed with the most expensive wine bottles and liquor. I immediately frisked the other backpack and felt the same shape. I didn't say anything; I just took the bags and locked them up in Yeshiye's bedroom. The party continued. I told you that I had about 5-6 waiters, and I had no idea whose bags these were. I didn't want to create a scene, so I said nothing. They continued to serve. Finally, a few hours later at about 2:00am when the number of guests was dwindling, I told the guys to take a break and just sit down for food and drinks. I gave each of them some money for their service, knowing very well that two of them were thieves. Mind you, at the beginning of the evening I had briefed them in terms of what I expected from them and also made sure that they ate and drank before the party started. This is what you have taught us, and we continue to do it. After this post-party break, they had to tidy up a bit and finally go home. This was the *curva*.[53]

One of the guys came and asked me if I had seen a green backpack—of course I had. In fact, I had a green one and a red one. But instead of answering him directly, I said, "Green or red?" Then this foolish boy said, "Mine is green—the red is for him" and pointed to his friend. "Good," I said, "come with me to the back." His friend was apprehensive and even wanted to deny that the bag was his, but finally relented and followed me to the kitchen. From the kitchen, I headed to the hallway and on to Yeshiye's room. "Get in here," I told them. One of the guys refused, but then the security who had escorted them just repeated what I said with a stronger voice. The boys entered the room and the bags were on the floor. "*Dis na you da bag you de ax fo*? [Is this the bag you asked for?]" I asked. They were stuck. "*Openam* [Open it]," I said to them, and they reluctantly did. The bottles were sitting in there, almost shy to be unveiled in such a manner. The one guy said he didn't know how the bottles got in his bag; the other went further and claimed that, in fact, his phone was stolen. Crazy. Can you imagine, Emaye? We had some back and forth about them stealing or not, and why and why not, etc. Finally, I took my bottles out and told them to get back to the party. I felt bad for them. They were young. They thought they knew better; they thought they were smarter, that they could manage to hussle their way out of being busted. I would have loved to call you to tell you all this in person, but knowing where you are, I am sure you saw it all in spirit. Can you imagine how Ababi would have

---

[53] *Curva* means "curve," maybe from Italian. I often heard this word on the street when people threatened each other that they would take revenge one day.

gotten a kick over me catching two—even three—thieves in one night?

It was all fun anyway. After the party, there were about ten of us left out of about 200 guests at the peak of the party, so we decided to go out. It was already very late, I think about 3:30am or so. Madness. Anyway, we went out and I had such a blast. There are days like this when all things fall in place, when the right crowd gathers and the right music plays. It was a good moment. It was just about 6:00am when I finally hit my bed. I know what you are thinking—I know you think I was being irresponsible to do that, but you know it was fun.

My locks have grown, you know, so when I was out at the club, a girl stopped me and started talking to me about reggae. She started singing to me and I sang back to her. Maybe that is madness, to be singing in the bathroom at 5:00am with a stranger. I started giggling as I sang, or better yet, shouted the reggae lyrics with her. I giggled because I thought of you and wondered how hard you would laugh if you saw me doing what I did. *"Belesh belesh shint bet tizefgni jemer?* [And now, you even sing in the bathroom?]" Yes, well, I did.

Gosh, I miss telling you all this in person though I am happy to be able to write it to you. Anyway, long story short, the farewell went well and now I am flying to Accra with Rosi and Leoni on a new airline called ASKY (African Sky). It seems to be a branch of Ethiopian Airlines, but I am not certain. This evening, as I walked across the tarmac to reach the plane, I remembered that the last time I came to Addis for vacation with the girls was in April last year. We had come to see you—now, not even a year later, we are coming back but you have left for another place. As the plane's lights flickered and the wheels of our hand luggage squeaked along, I looked at Rosi and Leoni walking in front of me and my heart melted. It melted because, Emaye, you were blessed to see five great-grandchildren, your children's children's children. I will be lucky to see even my children's children, let alone the great-grands.

Well, it's true. "*Atschnikiyachew* [Don't stress them out]"—yes, I hear you and I am not doing that. It's just that I think they should know and be prepared. In fact, talking about being prepared, Yeshiye will be reaching home on Wednesday. I wrote an email to Etetila to tell her to be ready for Yeshiye, not just picking her up but also knowing that she has not been there since you left. The Laïbet crew better be ready for the mourning of Yeshiye; she's been holding it in for almost nine months now. I could see in the last few weeks that she's been losing weight. She's been slightly depressed inside. I could see it, but it might not have been apparent to others.

We met a most beautiful being in Freetown called Yordanos; she is from Eritrea and grew up in Addis. Emaye, this girl is so nice you can't believe it. If she had met you just for a moment, I am sure the two of you would have resonated so much. In any case, Yordanos is so sweet that she took Yeshiye shopping and then took her home to her house and did her hair for her. "*Min beehon fuwah belish new kezi yemitihegiw* [No matter what, you will only go from here looking glamorous]," she used to say. She's been so sweet. Today, she came to our place with all four of her children to say goodbye to us. She might be staying longer in Freetown, so we will not see her again for a long time. Of course, there were tears. How can you say goodbye without tears? And this one, Emaye, this Yourdanos, she is worse than me—she can laugh in a heartbeat and can cry just as fast.

For me, I think I found another sister in this world.

Emaye, I am almost landing in Accra. I will write to you tomorrow. Did I tell you that I will be going to Mr. Amoako's office on Wednesday to present my book? Well, yes, I am going. What an honor, hey? This is the man who has inspired me so much, and now I am going to him with the fruits of my inspiration. I am so happy. I have brought a copy for you, too. I will leave it in your room by your bedside. Emaye, I think you left us too early. I had so much more to tell you. I wanted to be with you forever.

I love you,
M

June 27, 2010

Emaye,

It's now 2:10am here in Addis, and I am sitting at the foot of your bed. Rosi and Leoni are deep asleep on Ababi's bed and I can hear Tiliku Wosha barking randomly outside. The house is so quiet: Only the ticking of the clock that hangs by your bedside and the sound of Rosi and Leoni breathing and slightly snoring interrupt the silence of the night. Before going to bed, I thought I would write to you once more and maybe for the last time. Maybe it's not the last time, but I feel this is a good moment to finalize my letters to you. Of course, my conversations with you will continue in my heart for as long as I live. For now, however, I think it's time to complete this conversation we started almost a year ago.

We arrived from Accra tonight, where I stayed for about five days. As you have always said, *Wodaj kezemed belay new* (some friends can be more than blood family), I was lucky to have such *Wodajoch* (beloved friends) in Accra. I have told you about them many times before: my friends Samson and Rahel Terrefe. We stayed with them during our time in Accra and it was nothing short of staying with brothers and sisters. They have been so generous with us. On Thursday night, Rahel organized a dinner with all the ladies of Accra. You would have been so proud—there were at least 10-12 of us, all ladies. You know what the most beautiful part was? Well, we were all from both Ethiopia and Eritrea.

It's amazing how despite the fact that our respective governments have banned such relationships, the people are still together. You had always said it—we are one people and we are brothers and sisters. I cannot wait for the day when the borders between our countries are open and we can freely come and go.

For the first time in many years, our arrival at Bole airport in Addis was hassle-free. There was always so much stress with customs and passport control, but today they were pleasant. For once, I felt that maybe there is a chance that we, Ethiopians, can come back with a full spirit of coming HOME. I am very torn about this country. On one side, I love it and I can't wait for the day that I will live here once again, together with my family and without feeling harassed. On the other hand, while I see the potential our country can have, the unbelievable lack of freedom robs my hopes. Things are just so complicated and the worst part for me, Emaye, is that it is hard to know what people really think. We tend to say one thing and actually mean and think something completely different. Maybe it's me who didn't really get the flow of things here, but I don't think so, because many of my friends have the same frustration. In a way, I have to confess that this situation pulls me toward getting involved in the public sector. But I just don't think I can handle all the innuendos, all the between-the-lines meanings of things, and especially I worry that my lack of trust in the system will stifle me. So, I suppose for now, I will stay out until things are more "user-friendly," as they say.

When we arrived at Laïbet, the first thing was to call Gashe Tilahun to make sure that Tiliku Wosha was either far away or restrained. That dog—I know that he only listens to you and to Gashe Tilahun, and he is getting so big. What in the world does he eat? Gashe

Tilahun has not changed a bit. He is still as tall, as strong, and as in charge of the compound. What a blessing to have someone like him as part of our family. Etetila, Koki and K were still up when we arrived. The girls were a bit at a loss when we came into the living room: Unlike the last time we arrived, they only found your picture framed and set on your chair. I thought they would break down, but they were silent. I know they are sad not to find you here. I did my best to prepare them for this. I have told them you are always with us in Spirit and are now an angel in heaven—an angel they can always call on.

For me, I didn't get a chance to talk to you as I came in. I didn't want to even look at your picture too much; it's still hard for me to know that you have left for now. I will have to wait until I meet you in heaven. I am sure that when I come to heaven, the angels at the gate might put me on probation for a while—no, I am joking. I am sure they will let me in.

Did I tell you that about two weeks ago, while I was still in Freetown, I saw you in my dreams? This time you were dancing, and you looked so great. I have actually never seen you dancing, except for my wedding. Do you remember that we danced together? Gosh, what a party that was. All of you insisted that I invite the whole community—insane. I am glad I stood my ground and limited it to only those people I knew personally. You were so upset with me that I only gave you twenty invitation cards, and I still laugh when I think that you xeroxed the invites and still brought in a busload of people. That was funny. In fact, you know it is from you that I have learned to do whatever I feel in my heart regardless of the rules and regulations—might as well go for what you want! This is how we can make things happen, especially innovative things or fun things. God, I know that there is always a risk associated with that, especially with those who set the rules and directives. But at the end of the day, I think that those same people who set rules and regulations might appreciate people who stand their ground and demand change or adjustments.

I lit the candle that was at your bedside and the one that was on your vanity, and I turned on that little bedside lamp that you always left lit through the night. I am happy to see that all your things are still as you left them. Nothing has moved. Even your make-up case is still there next to the sink in the bathroom. Everything is just as you left it, and what a gift that is for all of us as we come to visit Laïbet.

When I went to wash up, I opened the little window in the bathroom. I looked out, and all the memories of the times before we left for Brussels came gushing in. We did so much mischief from this little window! We jumped out of it to hide from the tutors who came to make us study, we stood on the bidet to look out at the neighbors' house, and we even used to hide in the bathroom to trick Ababi and get in there while he was bathing. He would find us and bust us out quickly, and we ran out giggling. So many memories.

Before I sat to write, I went to your other vanity, the one to the left of the big bed where all your perfumes are lined up. I tried to find the one you wore regularly and sprayed it all over me. Maybe I overdid it, but it was my way of soaking in your scent.

Emaye, I am not sad anymore about your departure; I just still miss you immensely. It's about a year and two months since I brought the girls to see you, and not even a year since you left. Each day that passes is painful to me because the day I last kissed you and the day I last talked to you are getting further away. I will never kiss your hand again, nor will I sit at the foot of your bed and tell you the one thousand and one stories I often had for you. Nor will I listen to your voice and hear the stories of the days gone by or hear about your new projects. No, this will not happen anymore—but the good news is that all of it is still in my heart, and now even though I don't see you in person, I can be with you at all times and forever.

I have you in my heart. I have you in my spirit and in my soul, and more than ever before I can sense that I am enacting a lot more of what you taught me. I just wish I could have the chance to talk to you. I just miss talking to you so much; there isn't really anyone I can talk to as I was able to talk to you.

I find that I am often silent and lost in my thoughts. I go places in my imagination where I sit on the veranda with you or Ababi and listen to us talk. It's daydreaming, maybe, or it's just my way of remaining connected to my roots—these roots that have anchored me in Laïbet.

Emaye, I have brought you a copy of the book I completed: *Butterflies Over Africa* (Integral Publisher, 2009). I have not written anything in it yet—I will do that tomorrow morning. The cover is a picture that Matthias took when he hiked in the Semen Mountains in April 2009. Remember, I stayed with you and the girls while he was up there with his friend Bernd and then they both came to see you?

The girls brought princess dresses for Baby Betty. Emaye, wasn't it a blessing that you saw five of your great-grandchildren? I will be lucky if I even see one or two grandchildren. I hope that the stories in this book will give these great-grandchildren and all the rest to come one aspect of the story of Laïbet. I hope that more of us write about our perspectives and the lives we spent with you.

Tomorrow is Maheltt's graduation from the Lycee Francais; she completed her baccalaureat and graduated with distinctions. Can you believe that the little baby we welcomed to the world back at the Filoha Hospital is now graduating from Lycee? Time flies. I personally cannot believe it, because I remember her birth very clearly. The whole of Laïbet was at the lobby of the hospital—what a welcome she received. As soon as I heard she was born, I rushed back home and told Ababi. "The baby is born," I told him. He was in the bedroom putting on cologne and getting ready to go somewhere. "Whose baby?" he asked. "Essayas and Geni's, have you not heard?" I said, and then I asked him, "What should we call her?" and he replied, "Salasebesh." Those were the good old days. More good days are still to come, I hope. Talking about names, Fofi told me that Enaniye and Boubiye had wanted to call me "Akebe" because that's where they found out they were expecting. Akebe is a nice name—I think it would have suited me, don't you?

Rosi has asked me to get her the same shawl you had made for her. I am going to order that tomorrow, and I will also order one for Leoni. We love the shawls, and when we wear them we feel we are being wrapped in your arms. You were actually wearing the white shawl over your shoulder as you sat on the balcony with your glasses and the gown from Israel, the day I saw that dream I failed to interpret.

Oh, I forgot to tell you: In Accra, I made a presentation at ACET, that's the organization that Mr. Amoako started for economic transformation. He asked me to read his favorite line, and it was a passage that talked about what you use to tell me: "Change happens a moment at a time." He gave such a warm introduction about the book, but also about our family. You know that he had so much love and respect for you, and to this day, he speaks about you in those same loving and respectful ways. It was hard for me to read the passage because he knew that you had passed on, and of course, I knew he knew and it took me to a place in my heart that was quite emotional.

Emaye, it's been almost an hour since I started writing. It's about 3:15am now and I better go to bed because tomorrow is a long day. We have a big party planned for Maheltt, a graduation at the Sheraton with about 25 of us. I think this might be one of the largest tables made up of only family. I am glad I am here with the girls in time to participate in the graduation. Tomorrow we take a whole group to get their hair done and get prettied up. Well, I won't do my hair as it is in dreadlocks, but maybe I will get a manicure or something like that, or just sit out at the coffeeshop and read a book or catch up on the calls I have to make.

Rosi and Leoni are sleeping so peacefully, Emaye. How happy I am that I am sitting here, talking and writing to you and watching them sleep in this sacred space where so many of us—even all of us—find a sanctuary. Of all the places in the world, your room is the one and only place where my soul feels completely free and at rest. I love you for that, and for making this space for us.

I just realized that today is the 27th and it's exactly nine months to the day since you parted from us. Before I head to bed and sleep in the middle between Rosi and Leoni, I wanted to write you my last few words. Before that, though, a quick thought: I just remembered that Fofi and I used to sleep in the middle of you and Ababi in this very bed. Now it seems that I am in the middle again, but your great-granddaughters will be on my sides this time around. Don't worry about them falling off the bed; I will make sure I keep an eye on them.

As I told you back on December 7, 2009, on the last day that I write toward this manuscript, I will write you a letter that says the following. And as promised, here is my last letter to you:

I thought it would take me about a year to write, but it's only been nine months. I thought I would complete all the stories, but I realize I have only just begun.

Today is the last day I write our beautiful story. Emaye, it may not have been a year of writing to you as I had expected, but it's a little over half a year. I now realize that the stories I wanted to share with you may never be completed, simply because my love for you will never be completed. It is what keeps me going and it is what I hope to pass on to my daughters and also to all those with whom my path will cross—that they too may share the spirit I was privileged to grow under. It's almost been a year since you left. I have completed part of the story I wanted to share with you; the other part I will tell you throughout my life in gentle whispers from my heart, as you used to whisper to me when I was a baby. I hope that these stories will allow us to tell your story a thousand times over to as many children as possible (young ones and grownups). You have been a beacon of hope for me, and for the entire family—and when I say family, I mean that in the same sense as you, in the greater sense. So many of us are so blessed to have known you and lived with you. I hope we can pass on what you have taught us through the generations.

You know what? Each time I get a chance to tell your story, I will tell them your story in a very special way and I will start my talk in this way: "Lejoch, Lejoch. Endemin Wallachehu? Ande Teret Lengerachhu. Keltat Ande Ken, Ande Azawing Neberu, Kibert W/z Almaz Haile Mariam Yebalu Neber [Children, children. How are you? Let me tell you a story. Once upon a time, there was a sage, she was called Lady Almaz Haile Mariam]…"

Would it be repeating myself if I tell you again how much I so dearly love you, and how much more I so deeply miss you? From all the people who have touched my life, you are the one who most affected me and who has allowed me to become the person I am today. There are so many things I want to say to express my gratitude and my gratefulness for being born under the shade of the wonderful eternal tree that you have been for us all. I feel so indebted to live up to your expectations, and my only hope is that when the time comes for me to join you in heaven, well, I just hope that when we meet you will tell me: "Gobez yene lej metashilegn? [Well done, my child—have you come to me now?]"

I love you always,
M

July 1, 2010

Emaye,

Tomorrow is our last day in Addis, Emaye. Our week here has been filled with so much family time—I wish you could have seen how much Rosi and Leoni melted into Laïbet. They were not as shy as usual; they spent so much time playing with Essayas's children Beniam and Samy, and also hanging out with Koki, Etetila and Kidist, "K", and me. They just sat with us in the Tinishu Salon and listened to our conversations, just as we used to do when we were small. Nothing gets past these children. They notice everything and absorb so much of what we talk about.

Mahlett's graduation at the Sheraton was fabulous. Emaye, you should see how big these kids are—born not even a few years ago, and today you can see them so tall and elegant, almost trying to pass for grown adults. My eyes filled with tears when I saw Mahlett come down the steps towards the ballroom. Emaye, she looked so beautiful. I felt the same intense emotion that took over my entire body when I stood in that hospital lobby and heard that she was born. I remember running back home to tell Ababi. This all seems like yesterday, and yet it's been about seventeen or eighteen years. Can you believe that?

I finally saw Terriye and Gashe Getachew this afternoon. Terriye looks so good; she is doing so much better. And Gashe seemed so complete and full of energy. Of course, seeing Terriye brought up all the tears because it's the first time I've seen her since you left. Do you remember that last time I saw her was when I was here about two years ago during the rainy season? We hugged for a long time and through this long hug, I think we sort of shared our grief in silence. I tried hard to distract myself so as not to start crying afresh. I stayed with them for a couple of hours and we talked and talked, and talked, and talked. We laughed a lot—the usual jokes. We spoke of you and spoke of our lives. It's strange that so many people are still talking about how you have touched their lives. Even Ato Solomon can't stop talking about you: He can't find the words to express how much of a mother you were for him, especially when he lost his wife.

It's again very late and I wasn't going to write to you because I am so tired. But as I came and sat on your bed and pulled back the covers to slip into bed, I looked around the room, listened to the silence of the night, and for some reason, I thought I had to open up my computer to say what I had to say to you.

Tonight, Rosi, Leoni, Samy, and Benu all played in your room for hours. Later on right before going to bed, I saw your nail polish by your bedside. I told Rosi and Leoni that these were the last polishes you used, and then the three of us sat in a circle and polished our nails.

I am sitting in your bed and looking ahead to the vanity facing the bed. I am looking at the candle I have lit on the vanity and wondering how many times you must have looked at it from this same angle.

I can't help but think about the time we first returned to Addis after our exile. Do you remember? It was sometime in the summer in the late 1970s. Was it 1978 or was it 1979? I can't remember anymore. Emaye, I was so happy to come back to you. I was so happy to just go home, to return to the place where I spoke the same language and people looked like me—most of all, to a place where I could be once more *Ye Woizero Almaz Ye Lej Lej* (Mme. Almaz's child's child). I love the way we refer to grandchildren. It is even more soothing to hear the words "Child's Child" because it shows the link, the lineage, and the love.

That first trip back home was a dream to me. Fofi and I were put on an Air France flight from Brussels, through Djibouti, to Addis. We flew alone with tags hanging around our necks, and I felt such a sense of independence. I am sure Fofi felt the same. We sat alone on the flight, ordered our own drinks, chose our own meals, and went through the flights like all other adult passengers.

Once in Addis, we disembarked down the steps from the aircraft. The sun, the air, and the spirit of Ethiopia engulfed us—homecoming in full swing. It felt great. We were coming home finally, and I would for the first time come back to the Laïbet I left. I felt like a grown person, even though I must have been just about twelve or thirteen years old, maximum. Once we reached the arrival lounge, the flight attendant took us by the hand and handed us over to a row of uncles waiting for us. Gashe Gemeda was at the Bole as well, waiting for us outside.

Emaye, it is hard to explain the emotions that emerged when I saw how many of my uncles, aunts, and relatives were there to receive us. For the first time since being in Brussels, I felt this sense of relief of being in a place that I could call home.

Of course, I was well aware that the Communist Derg Government was in full force during this time. Did you know that the customs officers turned our suitcases inside and out without the slightest discretion? The good thing was that our suitcases were packed decently, so there was no underwear or such flying out as they stirred the contents of the suitcases. I remember how you always used to tell us to be proper, whether it was in the way we dressed, the way we packed, or the way we interacted with others. No matter what we did, we had to be proper—packing was no exception.

I cringed when I could witness out of the corner of my eye, other passenger suitcases at the customs tables being literally gutted out—all their stuff being flung out and then stuffed back again in such a rush that the suitcases hardly ever closed again. I knew the customs officers were doing their work, but I can't help thinking that they took a bit of perverse pleasure in making incoming and outgoing passengers squirm. Of course, let's not forget the passengers who had things to dissemble about, be it hard currency or documents that might be perceived to be anti-revolution. Anyway, Fofi and I got through customs. They gave us a bit of a hard time for the cameras we had, though, the ones stolen by some airport pickpockets. We did not pay much attention to our things because we were busy kissing and hugging everyone.

There is something so very special about coming home from a pseudo-exile. All things were bright and all things stood out. The scent of the air was different, the people looked like us, and we understood their language. Finally, we were not foreigners anymore—we were home.

In the parking lot, the same fleet of old cars was

waiting for us: Fiatuwa, Braziluwa, and Volswa. Each car had maintained the scent we knew so well. I just wanted to sit inside and breathe in the familiar scent. Volswa, which at the time was still very much only Ababi's car, smelled like his cologne. She was clean as clean could be, and no matter her power, she always kept steady on the road. Fiatuwa, the one you bought for Essayas, she had this leathery scent inside. She was very roomy and that is the car in which we rode back to Laïbet. Wouldn't you agree that Braziluwa would have been called brave if she were a person? Not much attention was ever given to her, but throughout the years she always stood present to service our family. Of course, who says "car" says "driver," and it was only natural to see a number of people from Laïbet who worked as drivers or who were just part of the community waiting for us by the car. Emaye, I have no words to tell you how happy I felt that day. I was finally home. I wanted to sit on the ground and just feel the asphalt or run my fingers through the dust, the loam, whatever I could find on the ground. I understand now the people who kiss the ground when they come home from exile. It's an overwhelming feeling of relief and release.

I could not wait to drive back to Laïbet. I wanted to run to you and Ababi, to come and kiss you and tell you all the stories I had collected. But as you know, I spent the better half of the first few hours just crying from joy, and then went to bed. You know, entering the living room at Laïbet with all the carpets and the perfectly arranged furniture, flowers, pictures, tables, just everything there—it was so comforting to me. I was happy to find you the same way I had left you. I was happy the house was still as I remembered it; nothing had changed. Even now, Emaye, things are as you left them, and each time I enter the living room,

I enter fully conscious of the life we had together.

As much as my emotions were out of control when I came back the first time, back in the late 1970s, I can tell you that the same emotions emerged when I came back this time with Rosi and Leoni. I miss kissing your hand. I miss seeing your smile. I miss the "us," Emaye.

I miss you so much,
Mimi

PART VII: REFLECTIONS

Now that she is gone, I remain with the imprints of her spirit

Only when Almazesha left us did I realize my entire sense of identity was so closely tied to her existence—my sense of country, duty, and responsibility all came from her. Of course, my immediate family played a great role in that as well, but in essence what Almazesha instilled in me is what defines me.

When people asked me where I was from, I would so proudly say, "I am Ethiopian"; that pride is not necessarily related to the country itself, but to the loving life and situation I enjoyed in Laïbet. It would have been more accurate for me to say, "I am from Laïbet." Laïbet is a country in my heart, a place that cannot be defined as a house. It's a community—an overgrown compound that grew with us. Laïbet has a life of its own: that's what I am learning now.

When we had Almazesha and Ababi, Laïbet represented for me—and I can even say, for all of my family—a place we could always come back to. It was home. It still is home, and it's my refuge.

Many years ago, I was working for Cogema Inc., the U.S. subsidiary of a French multinational. One day, a senior cadre from Paris relocated to our office in Bethesda. His name was Monsieur Gaye, and he was very kind and generous. He was very French, if there is such a thing. I remember that when he spoke to his wife or anyone in his family, he always ended the call by telling them how much he loved them. He never closed his office door and he spoke freely, so we would all hear: "*Je t'aime mon amour, oui, je t'aime et je t'embrasse. Porte te toi bien bisoux, allez, oui, je t'aime et j'appelerai demain.* [I love you my love, yes, I love you and I send you kisses. Be well, and many kisses to you. Okay, yes, I love you and I will call you tomorrow.]" Anyway, to make a long story short, he told me the story of a friend of his who had just lost a parent. He said to me that this friend said, "*Tant qu'on a des parents, on peut rester enfant* [As long as we have parents, we can remain a child]." I never forgot this.

Then on another occasion, on a beautiful early spring evening, he invited me for a drink at one of the restaurants right by Mazza Gallerie in Chevy Chase, Maryland. I ordered a cookies-and-cream ice cream smoothie with extra fudge and a bottom of Kahlua or some other chocolate liqueur. I think he had ordered a margarita, and I was in heaven with my decadent cocktail. The weather was warm, there was a light breeze, and in front of me I had this amazing concoction of my favorite ice cream flavor. It was so thick that the straw was no good—I had to use my spoon. As I plunged myself in this indulgence, I asked him if he could say, at this stage of his life and career, that he had found happiness. I was happy with my ice cream and did not think of this question as one to start a long conversation. Here is what he said to me: "*La vie nous offre des petits trésors tout au long de notre chemin, et moi, je collectionne ces petits trésors et a la fin, je vois que j'ai un collier magnifique avec toutes les bonnes choses, les bons moments, les moments forts, etc.* [Life offers us small treasures all along our path, and I—I collect these small treasures and at the end, I see that I have a magnificent necklace with all the good things, the good moments, the strong moments, etc.]" I also never forgot this. Today I know that what M. Gaye said to me was very close to the truth I would learn through the years.

I can see today that I, too, have collected many gems and little treasures that life has offered me. I have kept these gems in my heart and in my soul, and at times when the occasion merits, I can share them. I think the sharing of our treasures multiplies them and their value—giving and sharing are almost selfish acts for me. Giving and seeing someone happy makes me even happier than the person receiving, even more than receiving something myself. There is something about giving that is great—it fills me with life and revamps my soul with great energy. I love to give, especially when I know I have found something that suits the person or something that will make the person very happy. This joy of giving is something we have all learned from Almazesha. She was very mischievous with it, too, so that we had no idea how many lives she had touched and how many men, women, and children from all walks of life she had supported, helped, and brought smiles to—until the day of the funeral ceremony. There was no end to the number of people who came to pay their respects and share what she had done for them. She would always give in such a thoughtful, heart-full, generous way, and most of all in a way that was always discrete. It makes me wonder at times whether her giving was not led by whispers from Spirit.

When we are quiet we can hear Spirit. I know when I hear that voice inside, the one that comes from the abyss of my soul; unless I act on the voice I hear, I remain for days with an unsettled heart. It's a relief to follow that voice. This being that we call Spirit, I think for some it is God, and for others it is the voice of the ancestors, those who loved us and passed on. To me, it is both the voice of God and the voice of those who have loved me and have moved on to the next world.

At times I think that things were easier when everyone was around and alive, especially when I get off track and get outside the light. Now, I feel a sense of obligation to stay on track, even though it is sometimes fun to get off track and let my hair down for a day or two. I feel I have to remain in the light because I don't want to disappoint or let down the Spirit of Almazesha, Ababi, and so many others who have gone. I often think of Gashe Azmi, who was like a second grandfather for my sisters and me.

But when we get beyond the grief and reach a place where we can celebrate the lives and the Spirits of the ones we loved, then I think there is a renewed energy that comes to lift us up. I think that we end up growing wings, in a way. I know I have so changed and transformed that I see the world differently. I almost feel as though I have embodied my loved ones; I have been enriched by taking on their Spirit, as we all have. It's like they anoint us with the love, in a way that will make the love last forever and then some.

The only thing is, I still very much miss them. I still

very much wish I could just have a telephone call with them or hear their voices again. It happens often in my dreams, and each day that I have dreamt such a dream, I spend the day lit and filled with inspiration.

I have learned one lesson in all this: to live each day as if it is the last. I have learned to live each moment as if it is the last; I have overcome my shyness and I tell my friends and family how much I love them. They think I am silly, but I don't really care. At least I have said it to them, and should we never see each other again, well, I will rest in peace knowing that I have done all that I could when I could.

I have learned to say I'm sorry and apologize for the hurt I may have brought onto others; at the same time, I have learned to forgive whatever hurt is brought onto me. It's peaceful this way.

At times we get so wrapped up in our lives—it all gets polarized on ourselves. Yet, if we open up and think of others, we can understand that no matter what the life situation, we all carry our respective problems, issues, and personal challenges as well as our respective hopes, wishes, and dreams. I have learned from Almazesha and my family in general to recognize this reality, the reality that each of us comes with comparable ups and downs, challenges and opportunities. This awareness allows us to have more compassion toward one another and to create a kind field of existence, one where empathy can lead our actions.

From here onward

"I stand on the back of those who have come before me," says a Yoruba proverb. This is absolute truth.

I stand on the back of Almazesha and Ababi.
I stand on the back of all the people of Laïbet,
our family, friends, and relatives who have shaped
me in who I am today.
I stand on the back of my parents, Enaniye and
Boubiye.
I stand on the back of Emama and Emiye from
Harrar;
I stand on the back of Gashe Azmi and his shining
legacy of love and compassion;
Yes, I stand on the back of my people
And the entire legion of souls of men and women
who have come before me;
Yes, I stand on the back of my people, as our
children, grandchildren,
And generations to come will also stand on our
backs.
Yes, and in this truth I find my peace.
I find the silence that defines and shapes me and
anoints me with timeless oil.
I am an African.
I stand on the back of all the African men and
women
Who have given us this land we call ours.
Ubuntu.
I am because we are.
I wear the colors of my forefathers and ancestors.
I carry the dreams I have inherited.
I see these dreams in your eyes
And know that you, too, are part of me.

We are truly the make-up of our past
And today we hold, in our hands, the choice—
The choice to envision and manifest the tomorrow
*   we wish,*
The choice to carry forth the flame we have
*   received*
In the course of our lives, and then, when the end
*   comes along*
We are to pass on this flame to those who come after
*   us.*
We are to share the dreams that have been shared
*   with us.*
Ubuntu.
They are because we've been,
And so goes the cycle of life.
It never stops;
It always goes on.
And we bear the responsibility of telling the stories
So that they know
And understand where they come from
And why it's essential we carry forth the flame.
                —"Ubuntu: I am because We are"
                    (Yene Assegid, 2010)

Some things are timeless: The gems of what we inherit come in stories. Through the stories we learn about love, and about compassion. We can understand the importance of courage and the need to have a big heart. The big heart drives our vision, allows us to forgive, and keeps us on track. It is this big heart I hope and intend to honor throughout my life, from here to the end.

My life so far has been a blessing—I have seen enough of everything and this allows me not to fret about anything at all. I can understand clearly how finite life is and how each day is precious. There is not a moment to waste! Why waste a moment when each moment can be an opportunity to make miracles happen in many small ways and put smiles on the faces of those around us?

Emayiye has left me with the imprints of her soul. But it is not only her—it is also Gashe Azmi, Ababa Bitstate, Ababi, Emama, Emiye, and so many more. How many can I name? It is not possible to list them all; it would be like trying to count the stars that light up the sky at night. There are so many such souls who touched, touch, and still continue to touch our hearts. We just have to be grateful for the collective that has come before us—not limited to members of our families and friends, but including all people of the world who have done their share in their lifetime to make this world a better place.

It does not take great projects or loads of money to make miracles happen. A miracle happens simply with a smile to a stranger, an encouraging word to someone in distress, or a forgiving eye to those who fall off track. These are the miracles, and they add up to create the most beautiful field of connectedness. It flows because it's natural—it's easy because it's just simply good.

Do I have to wait for old friends to call me, or can I just pick up the phone or drop an email to tell them they were in my thoughts? Spirit whispers to us to take such small actions, but our mind often discards the message as nonsense. It is not nonsense—we all need one another, not for material things but just for a sense of warmth, a sense that we belong and that we are loved. It takes effort to be unkind, because unkindness is not natural to human beings. It's much easier to soften our judgmental gaze; once we try it one time, it's a feeling that we can never part with. It is simply very clear that this is the way to go.

I believe in Spirit

I believe in Spirit
Spirit that lives within
The One that is eternal
Dwelling in our hearts
Allowing us also, in a way, to be eternal
Me and you for eternity
Through Spirit, I know
We shall together remain
Always and forever
I speak to Spirit often
In dreams, in thoughts,
and in so many different ways.
I hear Spirit's whispers of love
Conversations long gone
Slowly pouring down like honey over me
Comforting me always
Holding me steady when all things fall apart
Embracing me gently
When my heart weeps for you
Random thoughts flooding in
At times hijacking my mind
Yes, it's like that with Spirit
At times it's a scent
Or maybe a song,
At times an old joke
Making me laugh again, as we used to laugh back then
Sometimes I see you smile
I see the sun's rays reflecting in your eyes
At times it's the silence
Sometimes it's an old friend crossing paths with me
... But no matter what it is

I know it's the work of Spirit honoring our lives.
It's Spirit allowing me to celebrate the "us"
There is so much more to say,
But instead of words, I'd rather sit here
And gaze into your eyes
Words might spoil the message of my heart
For now my beloved, let me just tell you that
Through Spirit your memories live
Forever with me
And it makes me happy
Until we meet again
Remember I love you

–"I believe in Spirit"
(Yene Assegid, 2010)

EPILOGUE

Addis Ababa–June 26, 2011. It's not 6:00am yet. I woke up to the sound of the *Kidasse* (Mass) coming from the *Selasse Bete-Kristian* (Trinity Church), the one next to the Palace at Arat Kilo. The sound of the chants came very clearly into my room, as if to transport me to a time centuries ago. I remained in my bed with my eyes closed, just listening to the chants of the *Kidasse*. Although I have never understood the lyrics because it is in the Geez language, the sounds are soothing and reassuring. We have listened to the same chants in good times and hard times, in times of peace and times of war—it has been the one constant through the years. The priests, monks, and deacons worship through these chants, almost pleading, it seems, with God the merciful.

As I remained lying in my bed, thoughts and memories of our lives gracefully floated through my mind. The rainy season has started in Ethiopia, the time when the air holds a cold wetness and the mist takes its time before lifting off the city. It's a good time to be here—a time to slow down, to cocoon and tell stories. And as my dear friend Rahel Azmi would say, "It's time to stay warm wrapped up in a Gabi with a nice cup of *Atmit*" (a very warm, grain-based Ethiopian drink). I can hear the chirping and humming of birds starting up their day. I feel good, especially after the great celebration we shared yesterday.

Rosi, Leoni, and I checked into the Hilton around this time yesterday, after a very long flight from Beijing. We arrived just in time for Debbiye's wedding. The eldest daughter of my maternal uncle Daniel, the pastor, Debbiye married her childhood friend Ermias.

The wheel of our lives has continued to turn—the veranda of Laïbet saw a new bride. If it could, I am sure the veranda would have had tears of joy yesterday as Debbiye stepped out from the living room onto the veranda arm in arm with her groom. She has run up and down this veranda from the time she was a baby until now. As much as we wept and mourned the last time we gathered as a family on this veranda, on the occasion of Almazesha's loss, yesterday, we wept again for joy and gratefulness as we celebrated a new union there. When Ermias came into Laïbet, with all his groomsmen, singing songs of praise, Debbiye waited inside amidst all of us who came from all over the world to share that moment with her. I am not sure there are words to express the depth of gratefulness we all felt in this moment—gratefulness for love, for life, and for all that a family circle can be. I stood by the door of the living room and witnessed as Ermias with his entourage stepped into the living room. As he crossed the threshold, their lives became one and we welcomed our new son and brother. It was beautiful.

I looked behind me at the corner right behind the door, where the phone used to be back in the day; the corner table was still there but instead of the phone there was a black-and-white portrait of Almazesha and Ababi. I know this picture well, taken sometime in the early 1980s. As I smiled at the picture, it seemed to be alive and conscious. I looked at it for a while, and through the picture I felt their presence in that moment of life celebration. It was as if they offered their presence from afar, loving and celebrating with us.

Is it conceivable that we learn to love deeper, when we have experienced loss? Is it conceivable that loss, pain, and grief—once healed—offer us a path to forgive more, to love more, and to be more present in our lives? Maybe so...I know it is true for me. I love more, now that my grief is healed. My tears of loss have dried and given way to laughter, almost a conscious laughter if there can be such a thing.

Since the time of Almazesha's passing, a little less than two years ago, we have lost many more loved ones, sometimes to illness and others just completely unexpectedly. The worst losses seem to be the unexpected ones, because the shock makes it so hard to grieve. We have all wept and mourned through these years, and as we all came together again on the day of celebration for Debbiye and Ermias, I felt for the first time the texture of the loving ground that holds us together. Despite the challenges, despite our times of grieving, coming together engulfed us all with such a sense of gratefulness. We will be together in hard times and good times, for tears of joy or tears of sadness—and the beauty of it all is that we can show up just the way we are in the moment and know we will be accepted, just the way we are. Isn't that what it is all about, after all. Almazesha taught us so.

Forget Not the Sparrows blog and more:

www.forgetnotthesparrows.com
www.anafricanstory.com

Also by Yene Assegid:

Butterflies Over Africa:
Perspectives in Transforming the Continent
(available from Amazon and Barnes & Noble)
www.butterfliesoverafrica.com

By Way of Love:
Tapping into the Power of Your Warrior Heart
(forthcoming from Shola Stories)
www.bywayoflove.com

Author's biography:

Yene Assegid's career began in economic development and social welfare in Africa, for the improvement of the lives of children and women, who are the most materially underprivileged. The harsh and tragic reality she witnessed through her grassroots work led her beyond issues such as HIV/AIDS, child welfare, or poverty to what she believes is the core cause of these issues: current collective mindsets, inertia, lack of ownership, and lack of accountability both in the existing quality of leadership and in development policy formulation. She is the founder of everyONE, a non-profit organization based in Ethiopia (www.everyonesworld.org) supporting communities affected by HIV through self-development and empowerment initiatives. Yene lives in Beijing, China with her family, and spends her time writing, researching, teaching, and coaching in the field of leadership, transformation, and change, with corporate and civil society clients in several countries. Her next book, *By Way of Love*, is based on the lessons on "Warrior-ship" she received from her Grandmother and offers Leadership wisdom and insights to transform lives. Yene holds an MBA as well as a PhD in Humanities with a focus on Transformation and Change in Human Systems.